Practicing Enlightenment

Hume and the Formation
of a Literary Career

192.4 C462p

Jerome Christensen

Practicing Enlightenment
Hume and the Formation of a Literary Career

The University of Wisconsin Press

Published 1987

The University of Wisconsin Press
114 North Murray Street
Madison, Wisconsin 53715

The University of Wisconsin Press, Ltd.
1 Gower Street
London WC1E 6HA, England

Printed in the United States of America

For LC CIP information see the colophon

ISBN 0-299-10750-7 cloth
ISBN 0-299-10754-X paper

Publication of this book was made possible in part by a grant from the Andrew W. Mellon Foundation.

An earlier version of chapter 1, "Hume's Social Composition," appeared in *Representations*, © 1985 by The Regents of the University of California. Reprinted from *Representations*, Vol. Fall, No. 12, Fall 1985, pp. 44–65, by permission of the Regents.

Cover illustration: detail from *Boys Peeping at Nature* by William Hogarth, courtesy of the Print Collection, Lewis Walpole Library, Yale University.

FOR MY PARENTS

Nice customs curtsey to great kings
William Hazlitt

Contents

Acknowledgments

I would like to thank the following colleagues and friends whose thoughtful commentary on portions of this manuscript has been of great assistance: Sharon Cameron, Jonathan Crewe, William Epstein, Frances Ferguson, Avrom Fleishman, Neil Hertz, Michael McKeon, and Ronald Paulson. My thanks also to the editors of *Representations* for allowing me to reprint a revised version of "Hume's Social Composition," which appeared in the Fall 1985 issue of that journal, as the first chapter of this book. Finally, I would like to acknowledge my deep debt to Ernest Campbell Mossner's magisterial biography of David Hume without which this study would have been unwritten, indeed, unthought.

Abbreviations of Works Cited

Dialogues   David Hume. *Dialogues Concerning Natural Religion*. Ed. Norman Kemp Smith. Indianapolis: Bobbs-Merrill, 1980.

ECHU   David Hume. *Enquiries Concerning the Human Understanding and Concerning the Principles of Morals*. Ed. L. A. Selby-Bigge. 2d ed. Oxford: Clarendon, 1962.

ECPM   David Hume. *An Enquiry Concerning the Principles of Morals*. Ed. J. B. Schneewind. Indianapolis: Hackett, 1983.

G&G   Third volume of *The Philosophical Works of David Hume*. Ed. T. H. Green and T. H. Grose. 4 vols. London, 1874–75; reprinted, Aalen: Scientia Verlag, 1964.

HL   *The Letters of David Hume*. Ed. J.Y.T. Greig. 2 vols. Oxford: Clarendon, 1932.

Mossner   Ernest Campbell Mossner. *The Life of David Hume*. 2d ed. Oxford: Clarendon, 1980.

NHL   *New Letters of David Hume*. Ed. R. Klibansky and E. C. Mossner. Oxford: Clarendon, 1954.

Ritchie   Thomas Edward Ritchie. *An Account of the Life and Writings of David Hume, Esq*. London: Cadell & Davies, 1807.

ST   David Hume. *Of the Standard of Taste and Other Essays*. Ed. John W. Lenz. Indianapolis: Bobbs-Merrill, 1965.

T   David Hume. *A Treatise of Human Nature*. Ed. L. A. Selby-Bigge, 2d ed. Rev. P. H. Nidditch. Oxford: Clarendon, 1978.

Practicing Enlightenment

Hume and the Formation
of a Literary Career

Introduction

Joyce suddenly asked some such question as, "How could the idealist Hume write a history?" Beckett replied, "A history of representations."

Richard Ellman, *James Joyce*

Such then should be the regularity of all our actions, that in the economy of life, as in a connected discourse, all things may agree and correspond.

Cicero, *Offices*

The theatrical dream of being all things to all men received its theoretical justification in the moral and political philosophy of eighteenth-century Britain. That theory received its most elegant and incisive statement in David Hume's *A Treatise of Human Nature,* which comprises an epistemology based on a deontologized system of representation, an ethics reducible to sympathetic exchange, and a social anthropology anchored in convention. That statement in turn received its fullest embodiment in Hume's career. At different times Hume was a student of the law, a clerk to a Bristol merchant, a writer of philosophical treatises, a tutor, a military adjutant, a librarian, a composer of *belles lettres,* a historian, an embassy secretary, and a Parisian *saloniere.* He intermittently resided at his family estate of Ninewells, in Edinburgh, in Reims, in London, and in Paris. That the personal identity which underwent those changes was anything but fictitious we can safely doubt. Our doubt is warranted by Hume's skeptical *tour de force* in the penultimate chapter of book 1 of the *Treatise.* We can *safely* doubt because of our assurance that Hume's social identity was continuous. From the first and at all times Hume was, as he affirms in his autobiography, a man of letters (*HL,* 1:3).

For Hume "man of letters" offered a social identity of great resilience and power because it was at every point congruent with the marvelously adaptive idea of society that Hume composed in his works. As man of letters Hume was at once a social actor, filling a specific role that could (at the cost only of a certain sensuous immediacy) comprise numerous particular occupations and what Edward Said has called a "textual attitude"[1]—in Hume's case an elastic representational practice laboring to

1. Edward W. Said, *Orientalism* (New York: Vintage, 1979), pp. 92–93.

3

perfect an imitation of a social reality that was conceived of as discursive through and through. I will endeavor to show not only that Hume "intended and effected the production of a body of writing systematically in accord with the postulates on which he intentionally based it,"[2] but also that he projected that body of writing in a symbolic practice, a career, that exploited, facilitated, and epitomized the operations of the commercial society which it persuasively represented. Because he lacked any ascriptive ties that would inhibit his exemplary mobility and because he acted within a theater of representations of his own design, the man of letters could hope for a success that would surpass that of the king, who sought to be one thing to all men; the courtier, who sought to be all things to one man; and even Garrick, whose protean changes were restricted to the stage at Drury Lane.

Hume's hope for success cannot be separated from a wish to dominate—effortlessly, invisibly, and *naturally*, without intrigue, scepter, or histrionics. The exercise of this wish cannot be extricated from his advocacy of that science of man that contributes most efficiently to the workings of the market economy. I take as a premise of this study (as it is of Hume's own work) that both the nature (or structure) of wishes (or desire) and the conditions of their exercise are discursively constituted. In *Anti-Oedipus*, a "schizoanalysis" of the capitalist deformation of desire, Gilles Deleuze and Felix Guattari forcefully argue that the "deliberate creation of lack as a function of the market economy is the art of a dominant class."[3] As man of letters, it is Hume's office to create that lack in others and in himself. It is the singularity of the Enlightenment man of letters that his lack of anything in particular is the condition of his art of the general, of his ability to *form* by affiliation a class that could reasonably hope to dominate not by virtue of a God-given right or a historically sanctioned prerogative but by means of a refined and refining prose.

The chapters that follow will not attempt a full-dress reconstruction of the past, a narrative of the way things actually went in some real world. Rather, I aim to give an intelligible account of the discursive constitution and transactions of a historical *figure*, the Enlightenment man of letters. In a loose sense the orientation of this essay is biographical—loose because the biography is anchored neither in the heroic ego nor in the instrumental body. This biographical practice might be called either "nonmimetic" or, better, Johnsonian, after Johnson's explanation to Boswell

2. J.G.A. Pocock, *Virtue, Commerce, and History* (Cambridge: Cambridge Univ. Press, 1985), p. 25.
3. Gilles Deleuze and Felix Guattari, *Anti-Oedipus: Capitalism and Schizophrenia*, trans. Robert Hurley, Mark Seem, and Helen R. Lane (New York: Viking, 1977), p. 28.

that he esteems "biography, as giving us what comes near to ourselves, what we can turn to use."[4] Nearness is not a matter of narcissistic reflection, but of something near to hand, of a life-writing that stimulates work. Here the biographical enterprise takes off from the premises that Hume's life can usefully be worked out in terms of his writing (both according to the way "living" is represented in his texts and according to the way those texts were deployed) and that both life and writing execute a strategy. At the most general level that strategy serves the interest of the discourse in reproducing itself. More specifically, the career of the man of letters deploys a strategy for achieving immunity or exemption from the forces of decay and death. The this-worldly name for that exemption in the second half of the eighteenth century is "independence." Its otherworldly corollary is "fame." Those goals are no doubt idealisms, and a suspicious desublimation is practiced here. As far as I can tell, at their deepest reach my suspicions are bound up with an unregenerate romanticism, which rejects the hygiene of enlightenment as a program of paralysis; and I conceive of this essay as preliminary to a study of Byronic, strong romanticism which will work those prejudices into an argument. My suspicions have a more respectable pedigree out of Gramsci's theoretical profile of the traditional intellectual, which analyzes the "ideological and political consequences" of European intellectuals' faith in their "uninterrupted historical continuity" and their utopian confidence in their ability to maintain autonomy and independence from the ruling class in what Hume still called the "republic of letters." Gramsci's oddly Ciceronian characterization of intellectuals as "'officers' of the ruling class [responsible] for the exercise of the subordinate functions of social hegemony and political government" fits my version of the man of letters. Two goals of this study will be to describe the composition of the grounds for "spontaneous consent" and to show how that composition gives way to coercion in "moments of crisis in command and direction."[5] My suspicions also owe

4. *Boswell's Journal of "A Tour to the Hebrides,"* ed. Frederick A. Pottle and Charles H. Bennett (New York: Literary Guild, 1936), p. 55.

5. Antonio Gramsci, "The Formation of Intellectuals," in *The Modern Prince and Other Writings*, trans. Louis Marks (1957; rpt. New York: International Publishers, 1980), pp. 120, 124. Although the claim by John Herman Randall, Jr., that "Hume wrote for two purposes: to make money, and to gain a literary reputation" is no doubt true, its truth, as I will have occasion to repeat below, is a very limited one; see Randall, *The Career of Philosophy from the Middle Ages to the Enlightenment*, 3 vols. (New York: Columbia Univ. Press, 1962), 1:631. Even without reference to Gramscian notions of hegemony, it ought to be clear that making money and securing a reputation are not aims that can be easily harmonized for a man of letters in the eighteenth century; because they do not belong to the same order of ambition, those aims have little to say about the specific shape Hume's career took. My characteriza-

something to the armed skepticism of Michel Foucault and to the example of Stephen Greenblatt, who has been so effective in exposing what Foucault has nicknamed the "techniques of the self" put into play by Renaissance literature.[6] The eighteenth-century man of letters is, however, neither courtier nor client and is not yet a professional. Hume's fidelity to the beautiful idealisms of the ancients, his dream of a greatness beyond reproach, his skepticism regarding the matching of causes with effects, and his confidence in the force of his rhetoric diverted him from the path of a prudent attention to the incidental protocols of everyday ambition.

The career of the man of letters begins with a radical abstraction of self. Investigating that technical accomplishment tells more about the constitution of this figure than would a "thicker" story summoning up the particular circumstances on which that abstraction operated. No matter how we itch to rub the gloss off, the language of the general remains as proper to the man of letters' role as Pope's Augustan diction is to Homer's epic. Johnson again: "Minute enquiries into the force of words are less necessary in translating Homer than other poets, because his positions are general, and his representations natural, with very little dependence on local or temporary customs, on those changeable scenes of artificial life, which, by mingling original with accidental notions, and crowding the mind with images which time effaces, produces ambiguity in diction, and obscurity in books."[7] "Minute enquiries into the force of words" will not be avoided here—indeed, they will be the very life of this analysis—but

---

tion of Hume does, however, come close to falling under the "fig leaf" school of Enlightenment critiques identified by Charles Camic, who attacks Lucien Goldmann, Karl Mannheim, and Roy Pascal for their shared presupposition that the "intellectuals of the Enlightenment were 'the philosophical exponents of bourgeois capitalism.'" At a certain level of generality such approaches do sound foolish enough, and Camic's answer—specific attention to the social basis of the Scottish Enlightenment and the thinkers that formed it— is tactically shrewd. But no one can avoid the pitfalls of generalization, and even Camic has to exempt Hume from his exemption of Scottish enlighteners as capitalistic collaborators. See Camic, *Experience and Enlightenment: Socialization for Cultural Change in Eighteenth-Century Scotland* (Chicago: Univ. of Chicago Press, 1983), pp. 78–79. There is no truth at stake here; persuasiveness depends on what one means by such words as "philosophical," "exponent," "bourgeois," and "capitalism." More importantly, however, it depends on how carefully (or cleverly) one generalizes whatever meanings one can establish—a strategic issue well understood by Hume, whether we regard him as an exponent of capitalism, enlightenment, or David Hume himself.

6. See Stephen Greenblatt, *Renaissance Self-Fashioning* (Chicago: Univ. of Chicago Press, 1980). Foucault uses the phrase in the second volume of his *History of Sexuality: The Use of Pleasure*, trans. Robert Hurley (New York: Pantheon, 1985), p. 11.

7. "Pope," *Lives of the English Poets*, 2 vols. (1906; rpt. London: Oxford Univ. Press, 1967), 2:241–42.

words will be engaged on their own terms; this inquiry does not presume a referent that would either be denied by or be unrecognizable to the word users. My biographical strategy is to describe Hume's own, to give it credit for the scope of its ambition, the magnitude of its achievement, and, finally, to explore the way Hume's own words coalesce into a context by which his practice can be judged.

From the time it first came into currency during the Renaissance, "man of letters" was used loosely, sometimes to denominate a man who earned his living solely from his writing; sometimes to identify a man who had attained a certain eminence by his writings; sometimes a man who, steeped in the classics and the moderns, had turned his hand to the occasional essay or poem; and sometimes even to denote a man who did not write at all but who fraternized with those who did. Although generally honorific, it was never entirely free of the stigma of commerce, for the condition of possibility for the man of letters, and the basis for all his subsequent claims of independence, is the existence of the printing press and the publishing business.[8] In his *adagium* "Festina Lente" Erasmus, who is entitled to be called the first man of letters, binds the possibility of his career to the opportunities for publication, republication, and dissemination of books made available by the Aldine Press. The career of the Renaissance man of letters cannot, of course, be separated from the humanist project of reclaiming the classics; it was self-consciously based on ancient, particularly Ciceronian, precedent. Yet printing was crucial. Cicero called himself "orator," a title which did not apply to the authors of Aldus's books. If orator was already a mediation of a variety of disciplines and occupations, the man of letters accomplished a remediation of oratory by exploiting the new technology of printing, which allowed for a universality and a permanence only dreamed of by Cicero. Moreover, the humanist did not merely retrieve classical texts in order to preserve them; he corrected them in order to extirpate corruptions and recover the original; and in the texts so restored the interposition of the corrector remained in the graphic difference made by print.

The press made possible the man of letters, but it also determined

8. In her landmark work *The Printing Press as an Agent of Change* (1979; rpt., 2 vols. in 1, Cambridge: Cambridge Univ. Press, 1982), Elizabeth Eisenstein notes that that "Febvre and Martin suggest [in their *The Coming of the Book*], it is a 'neologism' to use the term 'man of letters' before the advent of printing" (p. 153). And Rémy G. Saisselin remarks in his *Literary Enterprise in Eighteenth-Century France* (Detroit: Wayne State Univ. Press, 1979) that Jean-Jacques Garnier, author of *L'Homme de lettres* (1764), "found the origin of the man of letters in the modern sense in the sixteenth century, with the invention and development of printing" (p. 136).

his equivocal stature. Publication increasingly made possible authorial independence from court and church (and here the career of Pope, as of Erasmus before him, is a benchmark); yet publication depended on an eager, intelligent, and affluent public, which bought, stored, and occasionally read books. The rubric "man of letters" had to include readers—not all, of course (the various retrenchments from universalism constitute one of the most interesting features of this phenomenon), but enough that the pretense of Ciceronian republicanism could be sustained, despite the eclipse it suffered in the seventeenth century prior to its resuscitation by Bayle.

The emergence of romanticism coincided with a perceived split between the imperatives of modern commerce and the subjunctives of classical humanism. For Coleridge "man of letters" came close to being a term of opprobrium. In the *Biographia Literaria*, for example, he offers the "simple advice," "Be not merely a man of letters." Elsewhere I have argued that for Coleridge "man of letters" should be taken literally: he imagines a man of type capable of being indefinitely reset.[9] There is good contextual support for that interpretation. Coleridge quotes J.G.E. Herder's dour vision: "With the greatest possible solicitude avoid authorship. Too early or immoderately employed, it makes the head *waste* and the heart empty; even were there not other worse consequences. A person, who reads only to print in all probability reads amiss; and he, who sends away through the pen and the press every thought, the moment it occurs to him, will in a short time have sent all away, and will become a mere journeyman of the printing-office, a *compositor.*"[10] Later Marx would doubt the possibility of an *Iliad* coexisting with the printing press and bid farewell to "the song and saga and the muse [which] necessarily come to

9. Christensen, *Coleridge's Blessed Machine of Language* (Ithaca: Cornell Univ. Press, 1981), pp. 163–67, and "The Impropriety of Coleridge's Literary Life," in *Romanticism and Language*, ed. Arden Reed (Ithaca: Cornell Univ. Press, 1984), pp. 156–67.

10. Samuel Taylor Coleridge, *Biographia Literaria*, ed. James Engell and W. Jackson Bate, 2 vols., vol. 7 of *The Collected Works of Samuel Taylor Coleridge*, gen. ed. Kathleen Coburn (Princeton: Princeton Univ. Press, 1983), 1:229, 231. The *topos* of the mechanization of the author—which characteristically seems to emerge at points where the wish for paternal benevolence, in the form of patronage, or paternal discipline, in the form of ancient authority, acquires an irrational force—also appears in Oliver Goldsmith's *An Enquiry into the Present State of Polite Learning in Europe*, where he complains that a "long habit of writing for bread . . . turns the ambition of every author at last into avarice. He finds that money procures all those advantages, that respect, and that ease which he vainly expected from fame. Thus the man who, under the protection of the great, might have done honour to humanity, when only patronised by the bookseller becomes a thing little superior to the fellow who works at the press." *The Works of Oliver Goldsmith*, ed. Peter Cunningham, 10 vols. (New York: Putnam's, 1908), 6:73.

an end with the printer's bar."[11] Herder's dirge anticipates Marx's elegy; for Herder it is not Homer who has become extinct, but the author himself—he has become a laborer who mechanically arranges the letters that spell out the lexicon of his existence. Becoming a *mere* man of letters was a fearful possibility of oppressive literalism; one's *biographia literaria* could be imagined as a life in, or rather of, the text.

For Coleridge that fate of literalism was adumbrated by the associationist philosophy of Locke, Hume, and Hartley, which atomized experience into a welter of sense impressions and imagined the mind as the receptacle where impressions (in Hartley designated by the letters A, B, C, D, etc.) were received, recorded as corresponding ideas (a, b, c, d, etc.), and bundled into aggregates (*abba*, *bccb*, etc.) of order and significance which by various recombinations mechanically directed behavior. Coleridge claimed to have proved that associationism, despite or because of the literalistic precision which characterized it in all of its parts, from its tendentious notation to its brittle hermeneutics, could account for nothing but a delirious "streaminess of association." But even Coleridge's most systematic attempts at refuting the associationists invariably eddied into reflections that attested to the irrepressible resurgence of automatism and that demonstrated how such associations could uncannily mimic the procedures of sober reason. For Coleridge, the man of letters' fate simulated man's estate: the dread of being lettered by the texts one professes to author is the nightmare of the languaged mind. Neither Herder nor Coleridge could seriously imagine himself as an ally of an Aldus; the man of letters had come to regard himself as a wage slave to anonymous capitalists. No longer figured as an instrument for spreading light, the press came to be seen as an imposing machine which churned out ephemeral commodities, exacted soul-destroying labor, and chained genius to the caprices of a debased reading public.[12] Coleridge echoed Herder's lament from a perspective earned by years of such labor. A perceptive watchman over the darkling plain of social change, who had observed the introduction of both the Stanhope steel press and the more powerful steam press, Coleridge was acutely aware of the industrialization of the book trade and

11. Marx, *Grundrisse*, trans. Martin Nicolaus (New York: Vintage, 1973), p. 111.

12. For Coleridge authorship could have no true professional status. When pursued for bread and board it was necessarily corrupted by the taint of trade. His two therapeutic substitutes for the man of letters, the individual poet and the corporate clerisy, are specifically imagined as figures securely quarantined from the pollution of commerce. Coleridge associated the deplorable commercialization of literature with the rise of the reviews. For a sympathetic discussion of the nineteenth-century professional man of letters that begins with that phenomenon, see John Gross, *The Rise and Fall of the Man of Letters: A Study of the Idiosyncratic and the Humane in Modern Literature* (New York: Collier, 1969).

the dissolution of the Ciceronian ethos of the "gentleman," which had gilded the humanist notion of the man of letters.[13] What Herder, writing in 1790 after the fall of the Bastille, suspected, Coleridge, writing during the consummation of the Napoleonic empire, confirmed: the Enlightenment was over, the philosophes and the republic of letters for which they stood were discredited.

Between Bayle and the French Revolution, just before the full manifestation of industrial capitalism, Hume could still believe that the republic of letters might be instituted and maintained by the cooperative labor of men of letters. "Our connection with each other," he wrote to an anonymous disputant, "as men of letters is greater than our difference as adhering to different sects or systems. Let us revive the happy times, when Atticus and Cassius the Epicureans, Cicero the Academic, and Brutus the Stoic, could, all of them, live in unreserved friendship together, and were insensible to all those distinctions, except so far as they furnished agreeable matter to discourse and conversation" (HL, 1:172–73). For Hume and his fellow men of letters the general term that subsumed "discourse" and "conversation" was "correspondence." "Man of letters," as I shall use it here, names a career conducted in the second half of the eighteenth century as an enterprise of ramifying correspondences. I want to load up the word *correspondence* as much as possible; none of the definitions canvassed by the *OED* can be left out of the reckoning. In the empiricist epistemology knowledge depends on the correspondence or analogy between sense impressions and mental ideas. Causation is a correspondence between ideas inferred from their customary succession and from principles of succession (*ECHU*, pp. 54–55). And though Hume discredits the supposed logical connection between the minute organization of all members of the natural world and a designing God, "the correspondence of . . . parts," which is thought to distinguish natural phenomena, is never doubted (*Dialogues*, p. 154). Morally, the empiricist ethic of sympathy presupposed a continual and natural correspondence or exchange of ideas between one person and another. Socially, letters facilitated sympathetic transactions over great distances; correspondence by post joined minds from remote parts of the world—an open communication between intellectual and social equals. The word applied to both sexual and social intercourse and was deftly employed to perform the chiasmic balance of keeping the sexual social and giving the social the edge of the sexual. Correspondence as a credible basis for knowledge, as an incentive for progress, and as an instrument for exchange of informa-

13. For Coleridge's nostalgic version of Cicero's gentlemanliness, see the second of "Satyrane's Letters" in *Biographia Literaria*, 2:176.

tion and goods formed the basis for an economic theory grounded in the unalterable correspondence of supply with demand.

As the last generalist or the first ideologist, the man of letters positioned himself on the margins of professional discourse. No doubt he provided certain specific "services for [his] fellow citizens and the state," but these services were not specialized in the sense of being codified so as to lead to a "carefully regulated vocational training" or a "recognized hierarchy of promotion."[14] David Hume was the exemplary British man of letters during the second half of the eighteenth century. Not only was he the most challenging and thoroughgoing moral philosopher who had emerged in the British Isles since Hobbes; he was also a man of multifarious talents, which he successfully applied to diverse literary genres and worldly occupations. Moreover, unlike Samuel Johnson, his only rival, Hume practiced that true cosmopolitanism without which even the greatest erudition and versatility cannot escape the character of eccentricity or fanaticism.[15] Hume's career was devoted to making as many correspondences as possible—and not simply to their increase, but to their refinement. Correspondence was a principle of association and of derivation. It made possible both a horizontal exchange across the boundaries of the mind, the self, and the state and a vertical integration of particulars— discrete ideas and occupations—within a more general, regulative discourse. To correspond was the man of letters' passion; to correspond was his labor. And it was in part because for him passion and labor *were* coincident that the man of letters could make the claims for disinterested independence and the position of greatest generality in the system he describes. He discovers a system of correspondences in which all necessarily, *naturally* participate; he demonstrates that only he corresponds to

14. These are two indices for eighteenth-century professionalism proposed by Geoffrey Holmes, *Augustan England: Professions, State, and Society, 1680–1730* (London: Allen & Unwin, 1982), pp. 13 and 7. Yet being a man of letters does qualify as a profession if we adhere to the "general dimensions" of the "ideal-type of profession" summarized by Magli Larson: "The cognitive dimension is centered on the body of knowledge and techniques which the professionals apply in their work, and on the training necessary to master such knowledge and skills; the normative dimension covers the service orientation of professionals, and their distinctive ethics, which justify the privilege of self-regulation granted them by society; the evaluative dimension implicitly compares professions' singular characteristics of autonomy and prestige." *The Rise of Professionalism* (Berkeley and Los Angeles: Univ. of California Press, 1977), p. ix. Each of those dimensions applies to the eighteenth-century man of letters. The lesson seems to be that the more generally we describe the professional the more the description fits the man of letters, who seeks to occupy precisely that place where the particular gives way to the general, interest to disinterest.

15. On the general topic of cosmopolitanism in the second half of the eighteenth century and on Hume as an exemplar of the cosmopolitan ethos, see Thomas J. Schlereth, *The Cosmopolitan Ideal in Enlightenment Thought* (Notre Dame: Univ. of Notre Dame Press, 1977).

that system in all its dimensions. Historically, the eighteenth-century man of letters was descended from classical and Renaissance progenitors. Equipped with an epistemology and a social theory which abstracted that derivation into another variety of inference, the eighteenth-century man of letters could, however, claim a freedom from genealogy congruent with the freedom from historical entailment he assigned to market society. The man of letters invented an economics emancipated from history and politics and assigned himself the position of exemplary economic man whose own history was a career designed to correspond in all its refinements with the economic mechanism.

Not something that was caused or produced in the past, that had a beginning, middle, and end, the career of letters was a practice, or, to put it in the terms that Northrop Frye used to characterize the artistic formations of the "age of sensibility," a "process." Like the poems and novels Frye described, and like the society whose economy his career reflects, the man of letters' practice was "maintained at at a continuous present by various devices of repetition." [16] Throughout we will examine the "various devices of repetition" that Hume used to maintain a "continuous present." One important device was the deployment of a version of the deconstructionist's "always already." Humean retrospect reassures us that there never was anything but a fictional point of origin for the formation of society, which is precisely that which is always forming and reforming itself—nor is there a point of termination for the indefinite reproduction and refinement of social conventions: creation and destruction are cancelled under the dispensation of an ongoing maintenance. In Chapter 1 we will look at the way this view of social formation is given narrative expression by Hume and at the way that narrative reflects on his own stance. Another device is the management of the metaphor and method of correspondence. The extension of correspondence across the whole field of human activity—the constitution of the human as a site of correspondences—presupposes that anything that matters is something that is capable of being repeated or reproduced and valuable only once it has been reproduced. Hume is unambiguous: "A noble emulation is the source of every excellence" (*ST*, p. 93). Hume's practice deconstructs the moment of production by exploiting the liability to reproduction which is its aboriginal dynamic.

That project encounters two especially salient sources of tension. The first inheres in the ostensible strain between the notion of a "continuous present" and "devices of repetition." Repetition presupposes inter-

---

16. Northrop Frye, "Towards Defining an Age of Sensibility," in *Fables of Identity: Studies in Poetic Mythology* (New York: Harcourt, Brace, 1963), p. 133.

ruption, which is both the condition of and a menace to correspondence. When things are going smoothly, interruptions function as articulations of the social formation, differences that prevent stasis by enabling elaboration and refinement. Logically—even, some might say, historically—interruption as articulation is jeopardized by interruption as discontinuity, a radical difference that could disrupt the orderly operation of the mechanism. Yet the relation of articulation and discontinuity need not be a simple opposition. Indeed, from the vantage that the man of letters tries to adopt, discontinuity is no real threat, only an imagined one (imagined as logic and history are imagined), an idea that can be trapped by correspondence, assigned a discursive place in relation to articulation as articulation stands to an undivided whole. Represented as an idea of interruption or suspension, discontinuity can be subjected to the economics of the imagination and defused of any subversive potential. According to the Humean faith, people generally believe that no matter what happens things will go on pretty much as they have. And people's belief should be proof against violent change or revolutionary innovation: a change is real only when it is generally believed to have occurred, and by virtue of that belief all change becomes regular, customary, normal. The great adaptability of a continuous present that is able to recuperate any difference and exploit it as a means of indefinite elaboration, a resilience epitomized by the career of the man of letters, reflects what Max Horkheimer and Theodor Adorno have called the "totalitarianism" of the Enlightenment or what Jean Baudrillard has described as the hegemony of the capitalist code.[17] I am less concerned to challenge the theoretical legitimacy of this globally recuperative regime than to test it locally in its practice, to examine the ways in which the continuous present of Hume's career, which sets about to impersonate the Enlightenment, exploits devices of repetition to engage or evade imagined difference and real discontinuity.

The tension in the notion of "devices of repetition" involves the implicit acknowledgment that process occurs only by dint of some kind of intervention, an adjustment or correction. It is Hume's policy to describe this intervention as merely technical—in contrast to the "violent method" he associates with the arbitrary exercise of power by the monarch and with political action in general. By transforming violent method into mild technique Hume endeavors to make all devices of repetition systematic. Yet it is hard to conceive of a machine, even one so superbly fashioned that it systematically integrates engine and engineer, without

17. Max Horkheimer and Theodor W. Adorno, *Dialectic of Enlightenment*, trans. John Cumming (New York: Seabury, 1972), p. 24, and Jean Baudrillard, *The Mirror of Production*, trans. Mark Poster (St. Louis: Telos, 1975).

at some point along the line imagining an overseer somehow outside of the system he manages. This participant/observer or, better, participant/ manager paradox is a familiar Humean problem: a mechanistic model of a mind composed solely of atomistic representations, however accurate it may be as a description of mental processes, cannot account for self-consciousness, the various organizations of and decisions about representations, without positing the contradiction of a self-watching representation.[18] Hume was alert to the problem. On occasion he treated the contradiction of something that was both completely inside the system and yet supervising it as a logical difficulty that required solution; but in general he exploited it as just another articulation, a productive inconsistency. The plain fact was that this ostensibly irreducible contradiction did not have catastrophic consequences either for the mind that tried to think it or for the society that lived it. Moreover, its very perdurability inscribed a place for someone who was not only capable of thinking that contradiction but of figuring it in his practice, someone who could assume the socially unique (albeit psychologically common) position of being both inside and outside. Sustaining that place entailed the rhetorical labor of representing its necessity again and again, thereby making the contradiction customary and transforming it from threat into stimulus. The famous set piece that concludes book 1 of the *Treatise* dramatizes the truth of Gilles Deleuze and Felix Guattari's Humean aphorism that "no one has died from contradictions." Hume shares their insight that "it is *in order to function* that a social machine must *not function well*. . . . The death of a social machine has never been heralded by a disharmony or a dysfunction; on the contrary, social machines make a habit of feeding on the contradictions they give rise to, on the crises they provoke, on the anxieties they *engender*, and on the infernal operations they regenerate."[19] In Hume, rhetoric is both the sign of logical contradiction or inconsistency and the device for putting inconsistency to work. It is because of the inexorable failure of rationality either to work on its own terms or to account satisfactorily for the behavior of humans in society that rhetoric becomes inevitable, not merely as the expression of the failure of rationality but as the remedy for its lapse. The person whose structural function is to apply that remedy and to exemplify its virtue is the man of letters, the rhetorician of enlightenment, whose office it was "to maintain the ordinary correspondence of life."[20]

18. On this paradox, see Daniel Dennett, *Brainstorms* (Montgomery, Vt.: Bradford Books, 1978), pp. 101–2.

19. Deleuze and Guattari, *Anti-Oedipus*, p. 151.

20. Edmund Burke, *A Philosophical Enquiry into the Origin of Our Ideas of the Sublime and the Beautiful*, ed. J. T. Boulton (Notre Dame: Univ. of Notre Dame Press, 1958), p. 11.

I want to make as strong a case as possible for the recuperative power of the Humean model of the social formation and for the capacity of Humean practice forcefully to represent that model. I shall argue that it was natural for Hume to plan a career that would succeed by its plastic imitation of the general mechanism that Hume identified as operative within society at large. I shall show that by tactically employing the techniques of abstraction, curtailment, adjustment, and diversification the man of letters could reasonably aspire to the selfsame immunity from rupture theoretically enjoyed by society itself. Then I will show how the enterprise failed. I cannot dictate anyone's judgment of what that failure means. It is possible to see it as entailing a thoroughgoing critique of the hegemony that Hume represents; such is the response I would prefer. Or it is possible to see the failure as inevitable, whether according to some ideological construct, some theory that explains all surprises in terms of an even more general discourse, or according to common sense. The appeal to common sense strikes me as the more powerful one. It would go something like this: "Well, sure. But things don't always work out as you plan." That is no doubt true. But it is a historically conditioned truth, and one specifically associated with the name of Hume, whose project as moral philosopher was above all to reinscribe the disturbing within the customary. That things don't work out as you plan may be one of those home truths that goes without saying, but, as I will argue (following Pierre Bourdieu), the difference between what goes without saying and what must be said, between doxa and orthodoxy, is a line that was being deliberately and forcefully drawn in the eighteenth century. In the face of drastic social change that affected the habitual life of all classes, it became necessary to ideologize the customary, to theorize about practical knowledge. The reterritorialization of what makes up practical and what theoretical knowledge, the institution of the customary, was and is being *imposed* by some people on other people. To say what it is that goes without saying is a means of domination. That saying was the enterprise of the man of letters, Hume *primus inter pares*.

The approach I have adopted in this essay is broadly historicist insofar as I attempt to describe the mutually implicated formations of the career and the society in the language of their composition. Hume would have to read relatively little written after 1789 in order to rebut me. Yet I am dealing with a discourse that is deliberately universalizing, thoroughly secular, and strenuously ahistorical; and my argument will be conducted at a level of generality correspondent as much as possible (and there are limits) with that of the texts under consideration, in which the particular is always heavily marked as illustration or exception. This policy will contribute to a certain rarification of context that, I imagine, might discomfit the true historicist, and especially the Marxist. Although Marxist terminology will make its appearance, its use will be strictly tactical. I am of the opinion—shared by critics as diverse as Deleuze, Guattari, Adorno, Horkheimer, Foucault, and Baudrillard—that Marxism in its various guises clings to the insupportable belief that people or societies or modes of production *are* killed by contradictions. In particular, I agree with Baudrillard that in Marx the functional place of contradiction in the elaboration of political economy has not been fully realized. Baudrillard argues persuasively that by insisting on a definition of man as a producer Marx remains entrapped within that "mirror of production" which permits the indefinite reflection on itself that is the capitalist mode of reproduction. From Hume on, reproduction was inscribed as the "always already" within any productive act or mode.

This inadvertent complicity between Marxism and political economy may occur as a consequence of the shared convention that economics is the context of final resort. I will have much to say about economics in what follows, and though early on and intermittently thereafter economics will refer to a specialized discourse concerned with questions of wealth, production, consumption, and exchange, that usage will gradually be superseded by the employment of economy not as a particular context but as a way of talking about the relationships among, indeed the interchangeability of, contexts. In this latter and general usage *economy* will have the sense of a territory or system in which everything corresponds, in which social theory, epistemology, and economics can be mapped without distortion or remainder one on top of another, like the transparent diagrams of different parts of the human organism inserted in encyclopedias. What interests me is that which cannot be diagrammed but which is both unignorable and urgent. As the encyclopedia is the best emblem of the economy, so Robert Darnton's study of the publishing of the *Encyclopédie* provides the most concise illustration of this resistant difference. The *Encyclopédie* was filled with plates, many of them reproductions of machinery and workshops, and all of those luminously abstract—cleansed of dirt and sweat, of labor. In many of those beautiful and expensive books there were, however, dark smudges, the deliberate impressions of the inky thumbs of the printers whose labor made the books possible but who were abstracted from the books they made.[21] Now it would be possible to refer those acts of vandalism, those unlettered signatures, to an incipient class consciousness and perform a Marxist analysis

---

21. Robert Darnton, *The Business of Enlightenment: A Publishing History of the "Encyclopédie,"* *1775–1800* (Cambridge: Harvard Univ. Press, 1979), pp. 228–30. Darnton reconstructs a fascinating brief life of one of the workers whose thumbprint appears in a specific quarto.

of the relations of production in the eighteenth-century printing shop. But that would in effect be to *reproduce* the *Encyclopédie*, only this time with the smudges mechanically imprinted on the pages, thereby recovering them for an enlightenment discourse at the cost of what made them singular: that they could not be reprinted and were unassimilable by the economics and the economy which mutually implicate production and reproduction, which define man as he or she who simulates herself.

As far as I know, there were no thumbprints on the pages of the *Treatise* or on *The History of England,* although there were similar tactics practiced by compositors to make felt their absence from the books they helped to form: on occasion they willfully reversed Hume's intended meaning by substituting negatives for positives or the names of Whigs for Tories; once they maliciously retained references he had instructed to be deleted. My concern here, however, will only incidentally be with workers as such, all but invisible creatures in the discourse of Hume. Less invisible and equally, threateningly marginal are two other species of being: the women that Hume conversed with in the salons of Paris and Jean-Jacques Rousseau, who in a notorious episode (omitted from Hume's autobiography) contested Hume's claims to good faith. I shall try to register the ways in which French women and Rousseau resisted the correspondence imposed on them.

A brief synopsis of the argument chapter by chapter might be helpful.

In the first chapter I develop the model of the career and show its relation to Hume's theory of society. I put into play certain terms that will be used repeatedly later: *induction, composition, incapacitation,* and *imitation* are most important. I argue that Hume fashions a model of society that works according to mechanical principles but that crucially requires the assistance of someone who can persuasively represent it to the human beings who are to compose it. Connections are drawn between Hume's ideological aims and other projects underway in Great Britain during the second half of the eighteenth century.

In Chapter 2 I compare two autobiographical texts from late and early in Hume's career. First, I look at the brief "My Own Life," which Hume composed as a summary statement at the end of his life to prefix all subsequent collections of his work. An analysis of the dexterity with which Hume attempts to assure his continued fame and exert posthumous control over his canon leads to a consideration of the early letter to Dr. Arbuthnot, in which Hume, struggling with an uneasiness that has all the marks of nervous breakdown, devises a remedy for his illness that is simultaneously a technique for writing. Hume cures himself by surrendering the dream of perfect health as he empowers his writing by giving up the ambition of revolutionary success. Hume discovers that rhetoric can (romantically) be imagined to triumph over death and disease insofar as the body can be abstracted into discourse. The remainder of the book will be a development of the implications of the versatile style of mitigation and remediation that Hume devises here.

Hume's style, like Hume's moral philosophy, presupposes the enslavement of reason to passion, but, as I try to demonstrate in Chapter 3, it also involves the mastery of passion by representation. In a reading of the second book of Hume's *Treatise*, "Of the Passions," I analyze the strategy behind Hume's characterization of the passions in general and of sympathy in particular, as well as explore the tactics by which Hume persuasively enforces that characterization.

Any style or manner of composition involves both an agonistic competition with another and an idea of an audience to which it is addressed. In Chapter 4, I argue that Hume understood the modernity of his style as a deliberate supersession of the oratorical posture that powerfully informed classical notions of rhetoric and as a substitution of the female reader of polite letters for the monarchical auditor as arbiter of its success. An important corollary of this modernity is the elevation of the role of ambassador, gallant *saloniere*, and belletrist to a position of carefully mitigated but unmistakable authority. I conclude the chapter with a reading of a letter to Hume from one of his most devoted female readers, which attempts to show how, within the conventions available to her, one woman writes back to Hume, resisting her complete subordination to his project of compelling and self-interested mediation.

Chapter 5, "The Commerce of Letters," is the longest chapter and the place where I display as fully as possible the literal implications of Hume's metaphorical project. That is, I try to show how Hume describes a certain general course of things, which is the economy operant in all varieties of human endeavor, and then I argue that that general course is a reflection of the literary career as Hume represents it in his practice. Much of the chapter is devoted to readings of Hume's essays in economics, with the aim of showing that Hume privileges the role of the merchant as middleman within the economy he describes, and of showing that the privilege is meant to rebound on the essayist as mediator between parties, discourses, and epochs. This privilege depends on a theory of representation and on a concept of credit. It also depends on occluding the difference between the ideal type of the middleman and the emergent historical figure of the capitalist undertaker—obscurity that works to the benefit of the essayist in that he can take profit from his cognitive superiority over the merchant (he is the possessor of an intelligence the trader does not have) and in that he can hide from himself as well as from others the crucial difference that capital (as opposed to mere intelligence or mere technical facility) makes in raising one economic agent to superiority over another. I have no interest in showing that Hume was ever anything other than a metaphorical middleman, because it was in Hume's interest to convince himself that being metaphorical was sufficient, that he could capitalize himself by representation alone. I maintain that Hume fashioned an argument of extraordinary subtlety and power, which, by means of its indefinite self-adjustments and recuperations, can account for everything except for its own failure successfully to impose its analogical web on reality. The last third of the chapter criticizes this idealization by fitting Hume into the context of the book trade in the late eighteenth century and then fitting the book trade into the context of political control. The moral is that there are real capitalists and metaphorical ones. And in the crunch the real will win out, especially if the state lends a hand.

The last two chapters develop a narrative that conducts Hume from his arrival in the Parisian salons as the celebrated "infidel" to the final playing out of the disastrous relationship with J. J. Rousseau, whom Hume conducted to England from France. Chapter 6 tests Hume's experiences in the salon against the ideal model of correspondence and conversation which the salons were supposed to exemplify. I analyze the way the salons in general and Hume in particular aimed resolutely to manage the disruptive potential of difference—political, social, and especially gender difference. Close readings of letters between Hume and various men and women advance the argument that such management occurred at the price of considerable distortion, which appears in a language constantly struggling to adhere to destabilized conventions, and that it was successfully contested by at least one woman, the Comtesse de Bouffleurs, who briefly forced Hume to return to the body he had abstracted himself from at the outset of his career.

In the final chapter I present a reading of the text that is systematically omitted from all collections of Hume's work (in fidelity to his intentions). The text is the *Exposé Succinct de la contestation, qui s'est élévée entre M. Hume et M. Rousseau; avec les pièces justificatives*, Hume's publication of the letters exchanged between him and Rousseau, soldered together by Hume's narrative and resting on Hume's notes. Hume published the text in order to preempt Rousseau's threatened slander, which was to have taken the form of a charge that Hume had conspired to defame Rousseau's character. Rousseau never published the charges against which Hume defended. In that sense Hume's tactic was successful. But in a more grave sense Hume lost all claims to a good character forever, since his preemption of Rousseau—against all the principles by which Hume had defined the moral privilege of the man of letters and according to which he had conducted his career—performed the defamation that Rousseau feared, thus substantiating the worst suspicions regarding the good offices of enlightenment. By examining both the text and context of this last instance of Hume's practice, I will trace the logic by which Hume's self-defense led to the surrender of all those representations of which his self had been composed. I will show how Rousseau's victory and Hume's shame are ineluctably bonded.

1
Hume's Social Composition

What more agreeable personage can one form for himself than that of a
country gentleman living decently and frugally upon his fortune and composing all the differences within the sphere of his activity, giving the law to
a whole neighbourhood and they gratefully submitting to it?

The Professor of Law at Edinburgh
to his students (1726)[1]

I want to get started with Hume by examining what it means to get
started *in* Hume. This will involve beginning in the middle of things,
since, as we shall see, it is the working paradox of Hume's stories of
beginnings, his histories, that we can detect no origin that categorically
separates the way things are going on now from some past when things
were completely different. Hume's narratives do not advance from first
things to last; the action they both imitate and enact is the induction that
gives rise to, refines, and regulates all social formations. By beginning
with particular narratives in Hume's writings I intend to perform my own
imitation: to show how they work individually and how in association they
represent a general idea of formation. That maneuver completed, I shall
conclude this chapter by indicating what is at stake in Hume's indirect
procedure both for the social world represented and for the writer who
represents it.

I

Let us begin with a capsule narrative from the essay "Of the Rise and
Progress of the Arts and Sciences":

> We may conclude, that there is no subject in which we must pro-
> ceed with more caution than in tracing the history of the arts and

1. Quoted in T. C. Smout, *A History of the Scottish People: 1560–1830* (1969; rpt. London:
Fontana, 1985), p. 263.

sciences, lest we assign causes which never existed, and reduce what is merely contingent to stable and universal principles. Those who cultivate the sciences in any state are always few in number; the passion which governs them limited; their taste and judgment delicate and easily perverted; and their application disturbed with the smallest accident. Chance, therefore, or secret and unknown causes, must have a great influence on the rise and progress of all the refined arts.

The key word here, that which establishes the temperament of the analysis, is "caution." "Caution" dictates the initial distinction between the perceptibly contingent and the fancied universal and leads the investigator to a differentiation of differences. But his careful catalog of differences of scale, elusive and variable delicacies, perversions, and accidents conducts Hume to the brink of "chance" or "secret and unknown causes," where the inquirer teeters at the limit of intelligibility, that edge where the historical understanding verges on breakdown. The paragraph ends. And then a new one begins:

> But there is a reason which induces me not to ascribe the matter altogether to chance. Though the persons who cultivate the sciences with such astonishing success as to attract the admiration of posterity, be always few in all nations and all ages, it is impossible but a share of the same spirit and genius must be antecedently diffused throughout the people among whom they arise, in order to produce, form, and cultivate, from their earliest infancy, the taste and judgment of those eminent writers. The mass cannot be altogether insipid from which such refined spirits are extracted. *There is a God within us*, says Ovid, *who breathes that divine fire by which we are animated.* Poets in all ages have advanced this claim to inspiration. There is not, however, any thing supernatural in the case. Their fire is not kindled from heaven. It only runs along the earth, is caught from one breast to another, and burns brightest where the materials are best prepared and most happily disposed. The question, therefore, concerning the rise and progress of the arts and sciences is not altogether a question concerning the taste, genius, and spirit of a few, but concerning those of a whole people, and may therefore be accounted for, in some measure, by general causes and principles. (*ST*, pp. 74–75)

Serenity is restored. As potential discontinuity submits to the sway of general causes and principles, so is the inquirer rescued from the threat of unintelligibility. The narrator dramatizes the story he tells.

The movement of caution is, like the practice of art, a process of refinement: the analysis of increasingly delicate differences advances to the verge of chance, a boundary where caution and caprice meet. Clear thinking has refined itself to the point of its imagined extinction. It is, however, the imagination of breakdown that permits the passage from the particular to the whole, from chance to general principle, from one paragraph to another. For it is in the imminence of collapse, when the understanding does not know where to turn, that "a reason" appears that is capable of inducing the wavering, weakened mind. A reason, not *the* reason, and least of all, not reason itself. Indeed, not just a reason but almost any reason: for in the imagined breakdown of the understanding, any reason will have enough of a charge to attract a thought attenuated to the point of annihilation. But if any reason would do, this reason is nonetheless a singularly appropriate one; for it is not only a charged body, a mass, but the idea of mass which induces the cautious mind and corrects its excessive refinement of causes.[2]

The idea of annihilation supplies the essential opening for induction, which retrospectively discovers a necessary connection between an effect and a cause. Induction is the mechanics that connects effects to causes; and what Hume typically calls "separation" or "interruption," or what I have called, somewhat dramatically, "breakdown," is necessary to its operation. Breakdown, then, is a *functional* discontinuity which halts the indefinite unraveling of a bundle of particulars; it appears as the distinct idea of a rupture which permits the correction of erratic differences by and into a more general organization, a newly manifest, that is, no longer secret, cause. In a sense the cause has always been there, though occulted, but the plot of discovery is crucial, for it demonstrates that the

2. Cf. Newton: "I wish we could derive the rest of the phenomena of Nature by the same kind of reasoning from mechanical principles, for I am induced by many reasons to suspect that they may all depend upon certain forces by which the particles of bodies, by some causes hitherto unknown, are either mutually impelled towards one another, and cohere in regular figures, or are repeled and recede from one another." Preface to *Principia* (1686), quoted in Peter Jones, *Hume's Sentiments: Their Ciceronian and French Context* (Edinburgh: Edinburgh Univ. Press, 1982), p. 13. Useful accounts of Hume's supersession of the Newtonian model are offered by Richard Kuhn and John P. Wright. Kuhn argues that the "republic of letters" in which Hume had his being represented a higher, more moral nature than the physical world that Newton claims to have mastered. Kuhn, "Hume's Republic and the Universe of Newton," in *Eighteenth-Century Studies Presented to Arthur M. Wilson*, ed. Peter Gay (Hanover, N.H.: Univ. Press of New England, 1972), esp. pp. 76–77. After considering the dispute with John Stewart which arose in 1754 over Hume's characterization of Newton, Wright determines that the disagreement resulted from Hume's fundamental and enabling denial of the Newtonian *a priori* assumption of an "active power" in the physical (and by extension psychological) universe. Wright, *The Sceptical Realism of David Hume* (Minneapolis: Univ. of Minnesota Press, 1983), pp. 162–65.

causal is causative not by virtue of its logical priority but because of its *explanatory* power, its ability to supply a good reason; the imagination has been redirected through the induction of a highly charged reason, a massive and clear idea.

"A reason" functions within Hume's investigative passage in the same way that the "whole people" operates within the world at large. "A reason" or "a whole people" is an idea of mass which induces ostensibly aleatory, potentially anarchic particulars across a surface of propensities that mobilize and contain energy. The articulated territory described by this induction is in both form and function a composition—a specifically social composition.[3] I have adopted the term *composition*, which does not appear in this section of "Rise and Progress," from a passage in the *Treatise* that describes a similar process: "Thus bridges are built; harbours open'd; ramparts rais'd; canals form'd; fleets equip'd; and armies disciplin'd; every where, by the care of government, which tho' compos'd of men subject to all human infirmities, becomes by one of the finest and most subtle inventions imaginable, a composition, that is, in some measure exempted from all these infirmities" (*T,* p. 539).

Composition was, as Goethe later complained, a favorite and loaded word for Enlightenment thinkers.[4] It had the virtue of evoking a structured whole to which could be ascribed the kind of physical power Newton attributed to mass, but which was not itself a substance: everything occurs on the surface. The idea of mass, the mass of idea. Here is Hume abstracting the epistemology he will develop in the *Treatise:* "And therefore it must be our several particular perceptions, that compose the mind. I say, *compose* the mind, not *belong* to it. The mind is not a substance, in which the perceptions inhere" (*T,* p. 658). Mind, a material space which inducts the perceptions that compose it, is a mental composition, just as government is a political composition, and just as a whole people is a social composition; the same mechanics applies to each, for "why should the case be so different between the public and an individual, as to make us establish different maxims of conduct for each?" (G&G, p. 361).[5] We

3. For a more general discussion of this process of social formation see Gilles Deleuze and Felix Guattari, *Anti-Oedipus: Capitalism and Schizophrenia,* trans. Robert Hurley, Mark Seem, and Helen R. Lane (New York: Viking, 1977), pp. 1–50.

4. "The French use the expression *composition,* in speaking of the productions of nature. I can certainly put together the individual parts of a machine made of separate pieces, and, upon such a subject, speak of a composition; but not when I have in my mind the individual parts of an organic whole, which produce themselves with life, and are pervaded with soul." Johann Peter Eckermann, *Words of Goethe,* Oxenford trans. (New York: Classic Publishing, 1933), p. 376.

5. Cf. also Hume's comment in "Of Refinement in the Arts" that "human happiness . . . seems to consist in three ingredients . . . ; yet no one ingredient can be entirely wanting

need not do so because the *"general rule* reaches beyond those instances, from which it arose" (*T*, p. 499). Among the string of analogical compositions Hume investigates, society has precedence as name for the composition of greatest generality.

If that claim appears less than indubitable, it is because of a competing claim for generality implicitly advanced by the writer who represents doubly the social composition: both by depicting it as a process of composition and by imitating it in the process of his composition. The experience of reading Hume's passage seems to correspond with his act of writing. We read as though together with the author we were subject to chance or accident, hanging on the verge of breakdown, and rescued by a reason. The "as though" is, of course, crucial: we do not really fear an actual unraveling into the stochastic; the "as though" conditions our reading and is itself determined by a trust in a reason that underwrites the process of reading. We trust, that is, that although we may be reading a writing to the moment, that writing is nonetheless already a composition. Hume's impressive passage induces a belief in the social composition by representing its idea with "force and vividness," a rhetorical strategy that is especially effective by virtue of an indirection in its deployment. "I will venture to affirm, that, perhaps the chief benefit, which results from philosophy, arises in an indirect manner, and proceeds more from its secret, insensible influence, than from its immediate application" (G&G, 222–24).

The movement across the well-disposed mass of the social composition delineates the path of the artistic career. The career, as I would define it, is the path into which contingent particulars of individual genius are induced by the antecedent mass of an under-standing reason which graphs the aleatory particulars of talent and taste as intelligible functions of the social surface. All perversions and accidents of individual artists are "in some measure" contained by the general principle of the social composition which describes an intelligible course. This model of the career does not negate the quirks of individual psychology; it merely generalizes those differences, correcting their singularity by displaying how they correspond to all other individualities. Chief among those correspondences is the supervisory practice of the essayistic man of letters, whose career adjusts the particular with the general, the influence of the writer with the induction of society, in a systematically mutual reinforcement. And because it both induces and is induced, Hume's writing is the practice that most perfectly conforms with the general course of things.

---

without destroying, in some measure, the relish of the whole composition" (*ST*, p. 49), and his observation in the *Treatise* that it "is still true that every distinct perception, which enters into the composition of the mind, is a distinct existence" (*T*, p. 259).

"To induce," then, is the verb for power in Hume. It governs invention, composition, and all formations of belief. It is the predicate that directs the principles of resemblance, contiguity, and causation to purposive activity. It is not so much a trope as tropism itself, the gravity that turns mere contingency toward reason, indefinite desire toward any proximate, if incomplete satisfaction. Taking the passage from "Of the Rise and Progress" as our guide, we could conclude that idiosyncratic differences precede a practice which composes them into a social order. "But," as Didier Deleule argues in his brilliant reading of Hume, "this is not to say that order is substituted for disorder . . .; it would be preferable to say, in effect, that society . . . does not exceed in its function the limitation of disorder. . . . [Society] limits the effects [of disorder] by inflection, by correction."[6] Instead of supposing a relation of precedence which entails substitution (negation and replacement), we need to imagine a concurrence of events which entails continual composition or, in Deleule's terms, remediation, correction. Precedence is both there and not there; one idea succeeds another, but nothing really changes.

The strategic usefulness of Hume's ambiguity about precedence, the productive tension between function and origin, and the crucial place of induction in the formation of society are most evident in the long, syncopated philosophical narrative in book 3 of the *Treatise*, "Of the Origin of Justice and Property," where Hume takes as his ostensible subject how society got started.

It is clear *why* society was formed. "Of all the animals, with which this globe is peopled, there is none towards whom nature seems, at first sight, to have exercis'd more cruelty than towards man, in the numberless wants and necessities, with which she has loaded him, and in the slender means, which she affords to the relieving these necessities. In other creatures these two particulars generally compensate each other. . . . In man alone, this unnatural conjunction of infirmity, and of necessity, may be observ'd in its greatest perfection." Perfect in his fashion, "man alone" is a site of disequilibrium in a world of balance, a singular and "unnatural conjunction of infirmity and of necessity."[7] Natural man is naturally unnatural man. "'Tis by society alone he is able to supply his defects, and raise himself up to an equality with his fellow-creatures, and even acquire

6. Didier Deleule, *Hume et la naissance du liberalisme economique* (Paris: Editions Aubier Montaigne, 1979), p. 48. Of all the commentaries on Hume, it is Deleule's to which I am most indebted, especially for his insight into the general importance of remediation and correction in Hume's economy.

7. Cf. Deleule, who observes that "the secret of the [economic] action is in the divergence [*écart*] which separates the immensity of needs/desires and the natural parsimony" (*Hume et la naissance*, p. 56).

a superiority above them. By society all his infirmities are compensated." Society represents a distinct and decisive advantage because the three inconveniences of man alone—insufficient force, lack of expertise in any particular art, and vulnerability to "misery and ruin"—are overmatched by three social remedies: the "conjunction of forces," the "partition of employments," and "mutual succour" (*T,* p. 485).

The reason *for* society is to supply those remedies. "But in order to *form* society, 'tis requisite not only that it be advantageous, but also that men be sensible of its advantages; and 'tis impossible, in their wild uncultivated state, that by study and reflexion alone, they should ever be able to attain this knowledge" (*T,* p. 486; emphasis added). Subject to the same Humean epistemology as everyone else, natural unnatural man could not be sensible of what he had not yet experienced. In order to respect that deficiency and yet to bridge the gap that separates the savage from society, Hume goes on to reconstruct imaginatively a domestic economy that would remedy the weaknesses of natural unnatural man by simple genealogical extension based solely on the "natural appetite betwixt the sexes" (*T,* p. 486). But it won't work. Society will always stand slightly beyond the family group, the very naturalness of which is its flaw: there is too intimate a connection between the family unit and the individual; society depends on remote connections having the force of close ones, on the cultivation of a willing tendency in the individual to adjust to an oblique and deferred satisfaction of his needs.[8]

Because the natural society of the family cannot extricate natural unnatural man from his predicament, the "remedy, then, is not deriv'd from nature, but from *artifice;* or more properly speaking, nature provides a remedy, in the judgment and the understanding, for what is irregular and incommodious in the affections. . . . This can be done after no other

---

8. If we were to speculate on why Hume does not *want* the family to work as a model for the formation of society, we might conjecture that it is because in the genealogical format that Hume imagines the father is too powerful. Not only is he the source for all the filiations that tie the group together, but he also rules that group by command rather than by the social arrangement of contracts based on the milder performative of the promise. Although in his relatively sparse commentary on the family Hume never directly challenges the dominance of the father, nonetheless his social anthropology circumscribes the power of the father either to ordain or maintain society and indirectly contributes to the mitigation of the patriarchy that was occurring on a variety of fronts in the eighteenth century. Even Hume's insistence on the crucial social significance of female chastity (pp. 570–73), though it incontestably figures women as a species of property, has the corollary of figuring the potentially commanding male, whose word is law and whose law is an act of phallic violence, as a property owner whose passions are mediated by the conventions of society and are enacted only within the diminutive marketplace that Lawrence Stone has called the "companionate marriage."

manner, than by a convention enter'd into by all the members of the society." This convention, which establishes a man's property as "some object related to him . . . is not natural, but moral, and founded on justice. . . . The origin of justice explains that of property. The same artifice gives rise to both" (*T*, pp. 489–91). It is in the artificial establishment of justice and property that society is formed. This artifice bridges the gap between the solitary man and society: on one side are partial, propertyless savages, variable passions, and changeable objects; on the other are all men, morality, and fixed property relations.

If human convention is the only way to explain the origin of society, it nonetheless remains difficult to understand how this convention arose without men having any previous knowledge or experience of it.[9] To attribute the formation of society to artifice only returns us to the same query one step back: how did the artifice arise that caused this transition from nature to society? Who was the artificer? Not God, surely. For Hume the cause of the transformation must be embedded in the formation; the transition from nature must be owed to a dynamism that is itself natural. That dynamism is to be found in the perfect disequilibrium that distinguishes natural man and enforces on him a savage solitude. The imbalance is owed to "this avidity . . . of acquiring goods and possessions for ourselves and our nearest friends, [which] is insatiable, perpetual, universal, and directly destructive of society. . . . So that upon the whole, we are to esteem the difficulties in the establishment of society, to be greater or less, according to those we encounter in regulating and restraining this passion" (*T*, pp. 491–92).

Now it cannot be that, though resistlessly impelled by a consuming passion, man *sees* that it would be to the advantage of his avidity to socialize. Avidity is not one passion among others. It is identical with and constitutive of the original existence of man himself. Man alone is no

9. As Hume observes in his essay "Of the Origin of Government," "Though this progress of human affairs may appear certain and inevitable, and though the support which allegiance brings to justice be founded on obvious principles of human nature, it cannot be expected that men should beforehand be able to discover them or foresee their operation" (G&G, 3:115). Barry Stroud seems to acknowledge this difficulty in his commentary on this section of the *Treatise* when he remarks that "the set of rules or institutions will be 'artificial' in being *somehow* deliberately decided on or adopted," but Stroud effaces the ambiguity by concluding that "the convention or agreement is therefore arrived at because each man *sees* that it is to his advantage to abide by it as long as others do. *Once* men recognize that just actions tend to preserve the stability of society they will get sentiments of approbation from those acts." Stroud, *Hume* (London: Routledge & Kegan Paul, 1977), pp. 202, 203; emphasis added. As the "sees" begs the question of how one can view something that is not yet existent and of which one can therefore form no impression (*recognize* that one has never cognized), so the "once" merely reproduces the presupposition involved in Hume's own narrative slippage.

more capable of getting perspective on his avidity than he is of independent reflection. Indeed, he is incapable of reflection because he is possessed by avidity. If man cannot see his own avidity in order to turn it to his advantage, the crucial turn that avidity takes toward advantage must come from the passion itself.

> There is no passion, therefore, capable of controlling the interested affection, but the very affection itself, by an alteration of its direction. Now this alteration must necessarily take place upon the least reflection; since 'tis evident, that the passion is much better satisfy'd by its restraint, than by its liberty, and that by preserving society, we make much greater advances in the acquiring possessions, than by running into the solitary and forlorn condition, which must follow upon violence and an universal license. . . . For whether the passion of self-interest be esteemed vicious or virtuous, 'tis all a case; since itself alone restrains it; so that if it be virtuous, men become social by their virtue; if vicious, their vice has the same effect. (*T*, p. 492)

This is a passage of signal importance in Hume. Not only does the notion of a self-restraining passion allow Hume to conceive of a way out of savagery into society that is determined by a mechanism intrinsic to the nature of man, but the same mechanism is also one on which Hume can rely in every context. It operates in economics and history; and it may be said to characterize Hume's style itself, which John Richetti aptly describes as being a "literary manner" of "built-in self-regulation."[10]

Observe that Hume does not find the mechanism of self-restraint immediately but invents it cautiously; the statement of self-restraint is explicitly made only in the concluding sentence of the passage above, and that statement is an adjustment of an inference which it does not quite match up with. Restraint is, first of all, a turn or alteration of direction, which "must *necessarily* take place upon the least reflection." But whose reflection? It cannot be the savage's. I would suggest that it is Hume's (and by extension his companionable reader's) "least reflection" which governs or produces the necessity for an alteration of direction in avidity—since if everything rests on avidity and if we can explain the

---

10. John Richetti, *Philosophical Writing* (Cambridge: Harvard Univ. Press, 1983) p. 199. One might extend the context beyond the environment of Hume's writings proper and maintain that this invention was *mutatis mutandis* the emblematic statement of what Foucault characterizes as the discourse of "generalized punishment" in the eighteenth century, a regime that efficiently punished malefactors by setting "the force that drove the criminal to the crime against itself." Michel Foucault, *Discipline and Punish*, trans. Alan Sheridan (New York: Vintage, 1979) p. 106.

formation of society, as surely we can and must, then the least reflection tells us that avidity must restrain itself by altering its direction. This reading reproduces the intervention in the represented by the represented by the representer we tracked in "Of the Rise and Progress." Here the discovery of the necessity for an alteration of the direction of avidity doubles as the imposition of that new direction; an effect on affect has apparently been accomplished by a reflection that does not evidently subsist on the same discursive or epistemic level as the passions.[11] Hume has no interest in what may have "actually" happened to some hypothetical savage in some fabulous past. What matters is that Hume—and, through Hume, the reader—can see the advantage in such a reorientation; seeing that advantage has all that has ever been necessary for its occurrence; seeing is believing.

All in all, a subtle maneuver—perhaps oversubtle. At least, the volatile complex of desire and reflection quickly congeals into the static and tendentious concept of "self-interest." "Self-interest" presents none of the problems for Hume that avidity does because, as the hyphen graphically indicates, a reflexive change of direction is already built into the term. That is, self-interest is not a synonym for avidity but a derivation of avidity that does everything Hume wants that other, elementary passion to do but which it cannot perform without some intervention. It is not hard to accept that an individual whose distinctive passion is self-interest could devise and commit himself to the artifice of justice; on the contrary, it is hard to imagine how that could even be a problem, how an individual impelled by self-interest could ever be conceived of apart from conventions of justice and promise. The slippage from avidity to self-interest is something of a cheat, and a potentially costly one. Self-interest perfects avidity but at the cost of transforming a dynamic disequilibrium into a stately balance, discharging force for the sake of attaining a rather uninteresting coherence.

Uninteresting and transitory. In tacit acknowledgment of the incapacity of a self-restraining passion to do the work he wants, Hume resorts to yet another narrative:

11. In *The Passions and the Interests: Political Arguments for Capitalism before Its Triumph* (Princeton: Princeton Univ. Press, 1977), Albert O. Hirschman uses this passage to exemplify the strategy of designating a passion that will "*countervail itself*," a strategy which he sees as the most successful way of dealing with the threat passions presented to social harmony and economic efficiency (the other two, older alternatives were repressing or harnessing the passions). He comments, "One might of course quibble that to avow the need for some reason or reflection, however 'least,' means to introduce an alien element . . . into an arena in which only passion is supposed to fight with passion" (p. 25). My claim is that such quibbling is the mode of attention required to get at what Hume is *doing* in this passage.

After men have found by experience, that their selfishness and confin'd generosity, acting at their liberty, *totally incapacitate them for society;* and at the same time have observ'd, that society is necessary to the satisfaction of those very passions, they are naturally *induc'd* to lay themselves under the restraint of such rules, as may render their commerce more safe and commodious. To the *imposition* then, and observance of these rules, both in general, and in every particular instance, they are at first *mov'd*[12] only by a regard to interest; and this motive, on the first formation of society, is sufficiently strong and forcible. (*T,* pp. 498–99; emphasis added)

That looks rather slipshod, especially after all the preceding refinements: the same inconsistencies reappear, evidently to be rehearsed rather than resolved. The signal difference, however, is that for the first time Hume explicitly grounds his story of origins in the power of induction. Induction is the essential power: without its natural operation the experience of men, buffeted and confused in a state of nature, could have no purpose, neither motivation nor end. Its timely force is felt at exactly that moment when men discover that they are totally incapacitated by their passions for the society which alone can supply the means for the satisfaction of those passions. The restraints of conventions under which men are naturally induced to lay themselves will remedy incapacity but *not* by capacitating man, by empowering him; rather, these restraints will do so by imposing the general rule of induction, which requires that the particular be redirected into the general, the individual into the social whole.[13] The capacity of men to satisfy themselves is never acquired. Passions will be satisfied in some measure, certainly, but only through the process of induction. Men will be accustomed to their incapacity, which, under the sway of induction, will never appear as total because the disequilibrating gap between wants and satisfactions, though necessary, is never actually absolute, is, on the contrary, constantly being narrowed and refined, a process which is the *dynamis* of *continuing* social formation and of the labor of each individual part within the social composition. Hume can tolerate

12. Substituted for "induc'd" in the original edition.
13. "*All the elements of morality (sympathies) are given naturally, but are impotent by themselves to constitute a moral world.* The partialities, the particuliar interests cannot be totalized naturally, since they are excluded. A whole can only be invented, as the only possible invention is that of a whole. This implication makes manifest the moral problem. Justice is not a principle of nature, it is a *rule*, a law of construction the role of which is to organize in a whole the elements, the principles of nature themselves." Gilles Deleuze, *Empirisme et subjectivité: Essai sur la nature humaine selon Hume* (Paris: Presses Universitaires de France, 1953), p. 28.

inconsistencies in his argument because he has found a narrative mechanics which puts inconsistency to work as the functional incapacitation of particulars that makes induction both possible and irresistible. Breakdown will always and can only be a syncopated interruption which continually reinscribes the incapacity of any individual subject, monarch, or state as the difference necessary for the remedial induction of the social composition.

We may, however, ask whether a necessary difference is really a difference. After all, a professed fiction lies at the heart of Hume's natural history. Man's experience of his total incapacitation for society, Hume avers, occurs in a state of nature before society was formed; yet at the same time it is true that man's "very first state and situation may justly be esteem'd social. This, however, hinders not but that philosophers may, if they please, extend their reasoning to the suppos'd *state of nature;* provided they allow it to be a mere philosophical fiction, which never had, and never cou'd have, any reality" (*T,* p. 493). Bold Hume, to assail so openly the premise that seems to underwrite his historical procedure. But in some sense the stroke is enjoined by Hume's commitment to induction.

Inducing has two equally effective and practically inseparable variants: induction and inducement, both of which are constituents of the social composition. A whole people will, by mechanical induction, obeying the laws of Newtonian physics, forcefully draw partialities and individualities and forcefully distribute them in oblique channels across its strategically disposed mass in a social composition. And we can understand how men who have had no experience of the advantages of society can come to assent with others in a convention. The association of a particularly lively or striking idea with a present impression forms a belief, which is "nothing but an idea, that is different from a fiction, not in the nature, or the order of its parts, but in the *manner* of its being conceiv'd" (*T,* p. 628). When conceived in a manner more lively, more striking, the idea of society is an inducement to belief. If induction describes the mechanical properties of the convention of men, inducement describes the rhetorical properties, the artifices by which, facing a fearful, ignorant, or stubborn resistance, "we may induce the imagination to advance a step farther" (*T,* p. 257). Individuals are drawn into society because it is an eloquent machine. Induction and inducement canvass the only qualities that turn disorder and chance into greater wholes: force and vivacity.

Such a construction can apply, however, only to the way society is *now* being formed out of partial human nature; it cannot convince of the manner in which society *was* formed out of nature. Any explanation that depends on the tropism of induction and inducement presupposes the existence of the social composition prior to the individual elements that will form and always are forming it. That is why, for Hume, we can understand the passage from nature to society historically only if we understand nature as a "philosophical fiction." We can understand the origin of society, its history, only if we rid ourselves of the idea that there was any time before society, that society has any history except for that which is going on right now.[14]

If it is true that society is there from the very beginning, why posit something more primordial? One answer is that if the hypothesis of the state of nature makes possible a certain kind of philosophical narrative, of the "theory of the origin of society" genre, the blunt admission of the fictionality of that hypothesis asserts the unphilosophical or literary status of such narratives. When theory proclaims itself as not merely conjectural but otiose, a curious relation between theory and practice is established. Theory, which in the best of cases is for the empiricist an inference that follows evidence, is here cast as entirely superfluous to a practice (the formation of society) which is going on now and will go on anyway regardless of the way it is formulated or how we theorize about it. An antihistorical history, Hume's theory of the origin of justice is also an antitheoretical theory, which applies its force to the displacement of theories that do grant some privilege to the theoretical, such as contract theories of the origin of society. Hume's "theory" of the origin of society, like his passages of uninhibited skepticism, has no consequences.[15] It is incapacitated by its conjectural character, by its inconsistencies, by its admission that the concept of nature which it presupposes is a fiction, and by its conviction that none of that really matters since things will go on pretty much as they always have anyway. In other words, Hume's theory of the origin of society enacts the incapacitation for society which is its subject. The theoretical weakness of Hume's account is its practical strength, or rather, its strength as a practice which reflects the general practice of a social composition which, though composed of theories subject to all logical "infirmities, becomes by one of the finest and most subtle inventions imaginable, a composition, that is, in some measure *exempted* from all these infirmities." The typical story that Hume tells ends with the attain-

14. As John B. Stewart argues, "The account of how the rudiments of justice and governance are realized is unhistorical—not in the sense that this process never takes place, but because it takes place always." *The Moral and Political Philosophy of David Hume* (New York: Columbia Univ. Press, 1963), p. 161.

15. For contemporary versions of this claim see Stanley Fish, *Is There a Text in This Class? The Authority of Interpretive Communities* (Cambridge: Harvard Univ. Press, 1980), pp. 370–71, and Steven Knapp and Walter Benn Michaels, "Against Theory," *Critical Inquiry* 8 (Summer 1982): 736–42.

ment not of satisfaction but of exemption—for society, for government, for the way the world goes. Both his narrative practice and his career—of which that practice is a synechdochic part—are designed to attain that exemption for himself, an exemption conferred by the reader, who is induced to such a belief whether he trusts the teller or the tale.

II

If avidity possesses man it is because man does not possess what he wants—from the beginning and forever. Avidity is a relation to an already existent object constituted by an ineradicable distance; it is not a productive desire that seeks to realize its object, to bring something about.[16] To place avidity in nature, singled out as the categorically human natural passion, is to make man alone incapable of merely surviving, or, to put it in economic terms, it is the move replacing the motive of subsistence with that of gain which Karl Polanyi has argued is the inaugural move of "the great transformation" engineered by classical liberal economics.[17] This move asserts a particular definition of man that reinforces a particular economic theory by generalizing it from the beginning until now. We might say that it is the linchpin in a particular ideology, except that Hume's formulation calls for a stronger statement, since the object to which the avid self relates is itself an idea. The social theory intersects with the epistemology in its endeavor to represent how we can be partially satisfied by the idea of the thing rather than by the thing itself, by property rather than by objects.[18] Hume's story is at once the invention of ideology and its justification as only a generalization of the way we come to believe anyhow. If ideological, the *Treatise* is an ideology of ideology, removed from any truth claims except the claim that the truth will take care of itself, and it is therefore remarkably resistant to any "science" that would dismantle its mechanism. This conceptualization might be compared with Fredric Jameson's deployment of the term *ideology* "in Althusser's sense as a representational structure which allows the individual subject to conceive or imagine his or her lived relationship to transpersonal realities such as the social structure or the collective logic of His-

16. For comment on the distinction between "relation to" rather than "realization of" see P'all S. Ardal, *Passion and Value in Hume's "Treatise"* (Edinburgh: Edinburgh Univ. Press, 1966), p. 19.

17. Karl Polanyi, *The Great Transformation* (New York: Rinehart, 1944), p. 41.

18. As Stroud says, "Property and possessions are the *raison d'être* of the institution of justice. In fact, without the 'artifice' of justice there would be no such thing as property at all. Simply to have something in one's hand or pocket is not necessarily to own it" (*Hume*, p. 201).

tory."[19] In Jameson's and Althusser's terms Hume can be regarded as producing an ideology of ideology inasmuch as he not only devises a representational structure but represents the very capacity of representational structures adequately to perform the kind of mediative work that is their ideological function.[20]

Hume was not alone in this project. For example, a similar kind of second-order representation is dramatized in the second act of Oliver Goldsmith's *She Stoops to Conquer*, when Mr. Hardcastle, the prospective father of the bride, in the course of educating his servants on the conduct proper to their attendance on polite dinners, admonishes: "You must not be so talkative, Diggory. You must be all attention to the guests. You must hear us talk, and not think of talking; you must see us drink, and not think of drinking; you must see us eat, and not think of eating." To bring the rustics up to the standards of modern society, Hardcastle imposes a representational structure that ideologizes the relation between the servants and the social reality in which they perform by transforming talking, drinking, and eating into ideas that keep the servants in their places. The code "socializes" them, by transforming natural avidity for satisfaction into reflections. What makes this an ideology of ideology is that in this instance Hardcastle avows the rationale of the theater itself, which is similarly a place where people come not simply to be an audience but to learn how to be an audience, to see actors talk, drink, and eat without thinking of doing the same.

The theater is the determinant model in the eighteenth century for the capacity of ideology to do its work, for ideas to satisfy. Endorsements of theatricality, like the practice of empiricist moral philosophy, invariably do the second-order work (which must come first) of providing an ideology of ideology. This practice is characteristically manifested as a thematic contest between theater and narrative. Hardcastle's theatrical training of his servants in *She Stoops to Conquer* is ironic because it is

19. Fredric Jameson, *The Political Unconscious: Narrative as a Socially Symbolic Act* (Ithaca: Cornell Univ. Press, 1981), p. 30.

20. Such a reflexive formulation is, I believe, the best antidote to the kind of forced artifice evident in a dichotomy like the one advanced by David Miller: "'Philosophy' refers to the epistemological and meta-ethical premises which Hume brought to the study of society and politics; 'ideology' to the set of empirical and moral assumptions which came to him immediately from his social and political environment." *Philosophy and Ideology in Hume's Political Thought* (Oxford: Oxford Univ. Press, 1981), p. 13. A much more useful formulation is supplied by Donald Livingston: "It is one of Hume's great discoveries," he observes, "that rules 'are able to impose on the very senses' (*T*, 374) and that we have no direct access to the world through either sense or memory that is not mediated by an interpretation of the imagination." *Hume's Philosophy of Common Life* (Chicago: Univ. of Chicago Press, 1984), p. 240.

Hardcastle—former soldier in the wars, chief of the local militia, exponent of republican and country virtues—who personifies the "value" of narrative in the play. At his introduction to Hastings and Marlowe, Hardcastle is set off by their metaphorical usage of "battle," "campaign," and "ammunition" into a recounting of his actual campaign with the duke of Marlborough. But Hardcastle is continually interrupted by the disdainful young men; he never does get to tell his story. We are meant to feel spared; no doubt the story would have been boring. Indeed, characterizing story-telling as boring, as an antisocial practice which aborts social exchange by monopolizing someone's attention, is precisely the point of the scene. What is at stake in this code is suggested by the association of narrative with a historical past and specifically with a military expedition. The story that Hardcastle tries to tell is about a violent application of force that disrupted the social conventions customarily governing polite societies. His narrative of that action is another instance of such a forcible disruption; and although it is a ludicrously weaker act than Marlborough's, the narrative keeps alive the possibility of another historical event, similarly violent, that cannot be anticipated or defended against by the self-regulation of the social composition.

In their adoption of military language as metaphors to heighten the excitement of courtship, Hastings and Marlow personify the claims of the theater to be able to retrieve the past and display it on the stage of the continuous present, to reduce military violence to a discursive code that can be transposed into a social setting where in its reiteration it no longer disrupts, but instead enlivens the ideational commerce between the sexes in the same way as does the fashionable finery they wear. The ability of Marlow and Hastings to interrupt Hardcastle's narrative represents the wish, shared by Goldsmith and Hume, that the code of theater can overpower the eventful, the unconventional, the socially disruptive. Although the youths' success in the second act depends on a case of mistaken identity, which allows them brazenly to express the contempt they feel, mistaken identity is merely a sign, especially for Marlow, of an incomplete synthesis of personality with role. As a consequence of the ungainliness of his pose, he provokes the antagonism it is in his interest to quell. His education by Kate—which parallels in another register the education of Diggory by Hardcastle (Marlowe is at first tongue-tied with ladies and glib with barmaids because he cannot see a woman without thinking of wenching)—leads to such a synthesis and gently consummates the mild hegemony of the theater.[21]

21. On the relations between theater and narrative in the eighteenth century, see Ronald Paulson, "Life as Journey and as Theater: Two Eighteenth-Century Narrative Structures," *New Literary History* 8 (Autumn 1976): 43–58.

On the occasion of his defense of William Wilkie's long narrative poem *The Epigoniad,* Hume was explicit in his depreciation of narrative: "The story of a poem," he asserts, "whatever may be imagined, is the least essential part of it; the force of the versification, the vivacity of the images, the justness of the descriptions, the natural play of the passions, are the chief circumstances which distinguish the great poet from the prosaic novelist, and give him so high a rank among the heroes in literature.[22] Although Hume does acknowledge that *The Epigoniad* might be an unfortunate title, it is clear from this remark that it is just because Wilkie's poem *is* an epigoniad that he approves of it. "We are not," Hume writes of Homer and the Greek tragedians, "interested in the fortunes and sentiments of such rough heroes" (*ST,* p. 22). As the poem remedies the vulgar addiction to action by supplying tasteful embellishments, so it prepares for replacing the ancient heroes of warfare with late-blooming "heroes in literature," whose force is a matter of versification rather than arms, the indirect function of a code of representation rather than of direct application. Part of the complexity of the section "On the origin of justice and property" in the *Treatise* is owed to a practice that both exploits the power of narrative by telling stories of the origin of society and negates it by cavalierly introducing inconsistencies.[23] Or at least Hume's procedure looks cavalier, until the crucial narrative lapse of the transition from nature to society cannily returns as a strategic impasse both in narrative and of narrative, an impasse which permits the interposition of a reflecting device that at once turns nature into society and narrative into theater, and gives us the perspective to see that we have been in society and the theater all along—persuades us that there is nothing much to tell.[24]

22. "Letter from Mr. Hume to the Authors of the Critical Respecting Mr. Wilkie's *Epigoniad,* 2d edit.," Ritchie, p. 432.

23. For another example of the conflict between theater and narrative in Hume, see the essay "Of Tragedy," where tragedy is praised for the way "the whole impulse of those [melancholy] passions is converted into pleasure," and which concludes with the disdainful comment, "What so disagreeable as the dismal, gloomy, disastrous stories, with which melancholy people entertain their companions? The uneasy passion being there raised alone, unaccompanied with any spirit, genius, or eloquence, conveys a pure uneasiness, and is attended with nothing that can soften it into pleasure or satisfaction" (*ST,* pp. 32, 37). When Hume endorses conversation he emphasizes its dialogic and, implicitly, its dramatic propriety in contrast with a kind of monopolistic aggression: "In conversation, the lively spirit of dialogue is *agreeable,* even to those who desire not to have any share in the discourse [the theatrical spectators]: Hence the teller of long stories, or the pompous declaimer, is very little approved of. But most men desire likewise their turn in the conversation, and regard, with a very evil eye, that loquacity, which deprives them of a right they are naturally so jealous of" (*ECPM,* p. 69).

24. Although our views of Hume's style and of his historiographic aims differ, I have profited from John Sitter's stimulating discussion in "The Flight from History in Mid-

There are specific political and economic referents for Hume's ideological project. Take Karl Polanyi's model of the transformation of the motive of subsistence into the motive of gain, for example. Samuel Johnson's comment that the "improvements of the Scotch are for immediate profit, they do not yet think it worthwhile to plant what will not produce something to be eaten or sold in a very little time,"[25] provides an idea of the Scottish context in which Hume's project of transformation might translate into specific economic policy and suggests the way "reflection" operates in such a transformation: the Scots need to stop committing their resources to the ends of immediate consumption (i.e., living hand-to-mouth, putting objects in their pockets or stomachs) and begin to "think it worthwhile"[26] to delay, to plan, to capitalize (i.e., to turn physical objects, foodstuffs, into property); the Scots must learn to see food and not think of eating.[27] Moreover, Johnson's prescription for the Scots is owed to a carefully maintained, theatrical distance which allows him to reflect.

We should be wary of conceding too much to this kind of proprietary empiricism, however. Johnson's picture of Scottish agriculture is not very accurate, especially as regards the Lowlands. Specific acts of legislation from the late seventeenth century and sporadic instances of careful investment and management had already contributed to a transformation of lowland Scottish agriculture. Moreover, agriculture was not representative of Scottish commerce and industry as a whole, which had already undergone considerable growth by the time of Johnson's visit.[28] There was no pure subsistence economy in the Scottish Lowlands: there had always been markets in Scotland and therefore also something of a market

---

Century Poetry," in *Literary Loneliness in Mid-Eighteenth-Century England* (Ithaca: Cornell Univ. Press, 1982), pp. 77–103.

25. Johnson to Mrs. Thrale, Sept. 6, 1773, quoted in Peter Mathias, *The Transformation of England: Essays in the Economic and Social History of England in the Eighteenth Century* (New York: Columbia Univ. Press, 1979), p. 301.

26. "Worthwhile" neatly encapsulates the transformation of the idea of profit Johnson wants to induce: the creation of surplus value requires the identification of value, "worth," and time "while."

27. The Scots could expect as the immediate effects of their "education" conditions similar to those experienced by the commercialized country workers in England in the eighteenth century: "As more country workers lost common rights and became proletarianized, fewer had wood for firing, a cow for milk, or hens for eggs. Fewer brewed and baked for themselves: even country folk were buying bread in shops." Roy Porter, *English Society in the Eighteenth Century* (Harmondsworth: Penguin Books, 1982), p. 106.

28. For a survey of economic development in Scotland during the eighteenth century see Anand C. Chitnis, *The Scottish Enlightenment: A Social History* (Totawa, N.J.: Rowman & Littlefield, 1976), pp. 11–21. See also the section "The Prelude to the Take-Off, 1690–1780" in Smout, *History*, pp. 223–30.

economy. Conversely, the advance of capitalism did not altogether extirpate the motive of subsistence.[29] To reify a transformation of subsistence into gain is, regardless of one's attitude toward it, to have already been induced to accept Hume's ideology of ideology and acknowledge the authority of a discourse of the general, to have, in a crucial way, granted to Hume the exemption he seeks.

When Hume's ideological project is referred to the Highlands the picture changes, for then it becomes clear that it is not merely the difference between one stage and another that is overdetermined but the categories themselves. Though ostensibly polar, subsistence and gain, like Hume's nature and society, are both firmly situated within the general horizon of political economy. That region is ruled by the law of scarcity, which makes subsistence necessary for natural man (he has to scratch to eat) and at the same time makes subsistence and natural man impossible (one man's subsistence will always be another man's gain). But the initial perception of scarcity, quite apart from the "secondary" perception of advantage, presupposes a *measurement* of human demands against nature's supply. That is, it presupposes a man who, if he should somehow fail to see the advantage in the self-interested circulation of property, might be a bad economist (a mercantilist perhaps), but would be *homo economicus* all the same. Hume's version of man presupposes political economy just as his version of society presupposes capitalism. It is part of Hume's design to exclude any contrary vision, such as that of the primitive who "in his symbolic exchanges . . . *does not gauge himself in relation to Nature*. He is not aware of Necessity, a Law that takes effect only with the objectification of Nature. The Law takes its definitive form in capitalist political economy; moreover, it is only the philosophical expression of Scarcity. Scarcity, which itself arises in the market economy, is not a *given* dimension of the economy. Rather it is what *produces* and *reproduces* economic

29. For a general critique of Polanyi on these lines see Fernand Braudel, *The Wheels of Commerce*, vol. 2 of *Civilization and Capitalism: Fifteenth–Eighteenth Century*, trans. Sian Reynolds (New York: Harper & Row, 1982), pp. 225–28. Braudel also notes that "Quesnay was hostile to the demand for 'luxury of decoration,' and favored 'subsistence consumption,' that is an increase in everyday demand for the 'productive class'" (p. 177). The universality of the market is also affirmed by Marcel Mauss, who comments that "the market is a human phenomenon which we believe to be familiar to every known society. Markets are found before the development of merchants, and before their most important innovation, currency as we know it." *The Gift: Forms and Functions of Exchange in Archaic Societies*, trans. Ian Cunnison (New York: Norton, 1967), p. 2. As we will see in Chapter 5, stories of the time when markets began are not peculiar to socialist myths of the fall but are also found in liberal myths of the rise, which attribute market creation to the canny heroism of the enterprising merchant.

exchange."[30] For there to be scarcity there must be a relation to an objec-
tified nature; in other words, there must already be property. For there to
be scarcity there must be a gauger, someone to mirror and measure, to
excise value and inscribe the dramatic diastole of production and consumption on the indefinite narrative of symbolic exchange.[31] In the Scottish
context out of which Hume wrote and which he continually sought to
redefine, the excluded or repressed alternative to political economy was
the primitive society of the Highland clan. Hume's embrace of epigoniads
of various sorts was a contribution to the deliberate transformation of the
Highlands from a society that was dominated by "strategy rather than
economy"[32] into a modern market economy. Among the array of techniques, ranging from the nuanced to the brutal, developed to complete
the extinction of the clans, conspicuously effective was the Humean denial that there ever could be a society dominated by strategy (called "reason" in the *Treatise*), the claim that all societies are dominated by economy, whether its members know it or not. The chieftains' discovery of
economy and the expiration of the clans were twin consequences of the
careful gauging by ministers and men of letters of the cash value of goods
and services that had previously been deployed symbolically. Clan chief-
tans were induced to recognize themselves as merely subsistence farmers
in a suddenly scarce economy *in order* that they would be driven to gain.
In the prosecution of such a strategy "subsistence" is a fiction of the same
impressive tactical utility as "nature" is in Hume's text. And in both cases
the campaign is worth conducting not because of some necessity for self-
defense against either Highlanders or natural savages but because a positive profit accrues to the gauger. In the name of the Law of Economy,
one strategy, the mastery of inducement, drives out another, the mastery
of obligation. Retrospect makes it hard not to believe that the "best reason *always* permits a winning game."[33]

Despite its clear fictionality, then, subsistence remains an important
concept for Hume, and not merely as a ruse. Something like subsistence
persists as a goal in the transformed version of man that Hume represents.

30. Jean Baudrillard, *The Mirror of Production*, trans. Mark Poster (St. Louis: Telos, 1975),
p. 59.

31. Cf. Henry MacKenzie's ironic rendering of this economic fact in chapter 19 of *The
Man of Feeling*, where the pimp/gauger, emblem for the pure middleman, outmaneuvers
Harley with the baronet and acquires the lease to the crown lands that would have allowed
the faded aristocrat and natural man to renew his depleted patrimony.

32. R. H. Campbell, *Scotland since 1707: The Rise of an Industrial Society* (New York: Barnes
& Noble, 1965), p. 7.

33. Michel Serres, *Hermes: Literature, Science, Philosophy*, ed. and trans. Josue V. Harari
and David F. Bell (Baltimore: Johns Hopkins Univ. Press, 1982), p. 21.

It emerges as the "exemption" that, Hume gauges, society "in some measure" attains from the infirmities of which it is composed. "Exemption" and a string of synonyms like "competence" and "independence" that stretches to the far (and curved) horizon of "credit" ramify throughout Hume's work—not only to characterize the society which composes but also the philosopher or, as he comes to call himself, the man of letters, who actively represents that composition and abets the induction of the social mechanism by adding vividness to force, thereby inducing belief. But exemption from what? It is one of the peculiarities of Hume's moral philosophy that its recuperative capacity is so great as all but to render the philosophy itself superfluous (a strategic maneuver that I shall return to in the next chapter): the concept of infirmity, like that of nature, seems to take on the spectral translucency of fiction. It is Hume's success rather than his failure which accounts for the incredulity with which we greet an admonition like this:

> Property must be stable, and must be fix'd by general rules. Tho' in one instance the public be a sufferer, this momentary ill is amply compensated by the steady prosecution of the rule, and by the peace and order, which it establishes in society. And even every individual person must find himself a gainer, on ballancing the account; since, without justice, society must immediately dissolve, and every one must fall into that savage; and solitary condition, which is infinitely worse than the worst situation that can possibly be suppos'd in society. (*T*, p. 497)

Hume's "ought" is so well supervised by his "is" that this vision of potential anarchy seems a crude bogeyman trotted out not to prevent rebellious deviance but simply as another instrument in the stylistic repertoire that Hume has developed to induce belief in an incapacitation which itself seems vaguely fictive, so convincingly has it been annexed to an increase of satisfactions. The invocation of catastrophe seems a reassuring indulgence.[34]

Exemption could, however, be interpreted not as a refuge but as a privilege that enfranchises an action generally not permitted. In order to develop that implication we have only to return to the passage on the formation of society and observe the connection between the power of society to induce men to lay themselves under restraint and the "impo-

---

34. In a strong sense the concept of total loss is necessary to convince men who have been constituted by avidity that everyone will be a gainer. There is a curious way in which the fictionalization of nature makes society, which was proposed as the supplier of *increased* satisfaction, responsible for *any* gain at all. Nature as fiction is nature as cipher: within that empty concept all satisfactions are hallucinatory. Enter Rousseau.

sition" of rules. This stuttering shift from a mechanism of self-restraint to the glancing acknowledgment of an external application of restraint springs from an equivocalness in the concept of incapacitation. In order for induction or inducement to work their influence, men must be incapacitated *for* society. I have argued that this is a teleological formulation, the purpose of incapacitation being to furnish a deficiency which society can supplement, an interruption across which induction can work. But it is hard to see how men's "selfishness and confined generosity, acting at their liberty" could incapacitate them unless such liberty were an actual fact in a state of nature that, however, we know is a fiction. If to *have been* incapacitated is not the same as *being* weak,[35] the narrative must record an imposition of the deficiency that makes induction possible. If the proposition of induction presupposes the substitution of a model of social reproduction (and philosophical representation) for a model that allots productive power to man alone or to men and women combined into families, thus naturalizing power into a Newtonian force that is as common and irresistible as sense itself, then the conjunction of induction with imposition reinscribes the necessity of the application of power by somebody on some bodies at some particular place and time.[36] If it is true that "that which Hume calls a general rule is an institution,"[37] the exemption that the social composition achieves and that the writer endeavors to attain by fashioning a career that reflects the social dynamics he represents is the privilege of exercising power, imposing rule as if it were a natural necessity.

Joyce Appleby has demonstrated that the "idea of man as a consuming animal with boundless appetites, capable of driving the economy to new levels of prosperity, arrived with the economic literature of the 1690's." She is especially acute in her explanation of the lag between this liberal consensus and an economic policy that, acting on that belief, would relinquish mercantilist measures for insuring a favorable balance of trade abroad and compelling the labor of the poor at home. "The acceptance of the idea of economic rationality," she writes,

35. Cf. David Hartley, who, in the *Observations on Man, His Frame, His Duty, and His Expectations*, 2 vols. (1749; rpt. New York: Garland, 1971), 2:138–39, makes the case for the miraculous intervention of God in human history according to the aboriginal, infantile weakness of man.

36. One might say that Hume's natural history implies the adoption of a "new etymological narrative"; in a reversal of the "classical mode" he etymologizes power as *potestas*, not *potentia*. On etymology and power see Nancy Streuver, "Fables of Power," *Representations*, Fall 1983, pp. 108–27, esp. p. 119.

37. Deleuze, *Empirisme*, p. 36.

was the key step in the triumph of modern liberalism, because the natural economic laws depended upon natural modes of behavior. Before the laws could be accepted, the description of human nature supporting them had to be credible. Historically, however, before economic rationality became a learned pattern of response, explicit control was necessary to secure working-class discipline. . . . The spendthrift with a feast or famine mentality had to be transformed into the shrewd saver, and the saver had to become an orderly, but compulsive, investor and consumer. Market thinking could be relied upon only after the variety of forces influencing personal preferences in the use of time and wealth had been ruthlessly narrowed to one—the likelihood of gain.

Appleby is certainly correct that this "radical reductionism was the essence of [Adam] Smith's economic rationality."[38] But before Smith, Hume. Hume's contribution is crucial because of the way in which explicit control is made implicit, part of the definition of man's avidity itself, enabling the continual, gentle management of that avidity by the inductive force of the social composition and those who vividly represent it. All is never implicit, however. An imposition must occur; man must be reduced into an incapacitated figure who, intoxicated by greed rather than grapes, will labor in the vineyard of ideology. "With the generalization of political economy," which is Hume's policy and his career, "it becomes more and more evident that its first principle is not in the exploitation of labor as a productive force . . . but in the imposition of a form, of a general code of rational abstraction, in which capitalist production is only a particular case."[39] That imposition, the last vestige of direct power, is, however occluded, remarked on again and again in Hume. In this imposition of a code that makes economic rationality natural are marked the claims both for exemption from the machine that identifies the supervisor and, as we shall see in Chapter 5, for a kind of control over the code that identifies the aspiring monopolist of a new hegemony.

Michel Foucault has distinguished between two kinds of power: "the juridical, . . . liberal, conception of political power (found in the *philosophes* of the eighteenth century)" and a "non-economic analysis of power." The former is an economic theory because in it (as in Marxist conceptions)

---

38. Joyce Appleby, "Ideology and Theory: The Tension between Political and Economic Liberalism in Seventeenth-Century England," *American Historical Review* 81 (June 1976): 509 and 514–15.

39. Baudrillard, *The Mirror of Production*, p. 129.

power is taken to be a right, which one is able to possess like a commodity, and which one can in consequence transfer or alienate, either wholly or partially, through a legal act or through some act that establishes a right, such as takes place through cession or contract. Power is that concrete power which every individual holds, and whose partial or total cession enables political power or sovereignty to be established. This theoretical construction is essentially based on the idea that the constitution of political power obeys the model of a legal transaction involving a contractual type of exchange.

The latter, which must be advanced against that conception, is

> in the first place the assertion that power is neither given, nor exchanged, nor recovered, but rather exercised, and that it only exists in action. Again, we have at our disposal another assertion to the effect that power is not primarily the maintenance and reproduction of economic relations, but is above all a relation of force.[40]

The salience of Hume's natural history inheres in its articulation of both theories, or, rather, in its representation of the necessity that the contractual exchange of property rights, motivated by self-interest, not spring from the barren fiction of nature but be imposed within the composition that regulates those exchanges by induction and inducement. Hume's text would be both the representation that supplements the mechanical induction of the social composition and the act that makes such supplementation necessary, an imposition of incapacity that makes the career of the man of letters essential to the convention of men but exempt from the infirmity of power that afflicts them.

40. Michel Foucault, "Two Lectures," in *Power/Knowledge: Selected Interviews and Other Writings, 1972–1977*, ed. Colin Gordon, trans. Gordon et al. (New York: Pantheon, 1980), pp. 88–89.

2
Pen in Hand

But where is the reward of virtue? And what recompense has Nature provided for such important sacrifices as those of life and fortune, which we
must often make?

"The Stoic"

While I, miserable Wretch that I am, have put my chief Confidence in thee;
& relinquishing the Sword, the Gown, the Cassock, & the Toilette, have
trusted to thee alone for my Fortune & my Fame.

HL, 1:52

I

Chronologically, "My Own Life" is Hume's last essay. It is also, in a more
general sense, his final composition, the one that pulls everything together, both narratively and practically: Hume's various employments are
induced across a whole life, which is written in order that it can prefix the
collected works. The risk in such a maneuver is admitted straight off: "It
is difficult for a man to speak long of himself without vanity; therefore, I
shall be short. It may be thought an instance of vanity that I pretend at
all to write my life; but this Narrative shall contain little more than the
History of my Writings; as, indeed, almost all my life has been spent in
literary pursuits and occupations" (*HL*, 1:1).[1] Against the appearance of
vanity, the generic affliction of autobiography, Hume will construct a series of defenses. The first is to be "short." But though Hume seems to
promise a brief history of his writings, he also allows himself a "little
more"—a narrative design which imitates the life itself, "almost all" of
which has been "spent in literary pursuits and occupations."[2] Hume's

1. All quotations from the autobiography are taken from the reprint in *HL*, 1:1–7.
2. Leaving aside the question of evaluation, Roy Pascal is not quite accurate when he
asserts that "Hume's *Life*, important historically as one of the first extended accounts by a
writer of his literary progress, fails to reach greatness because of Hume's unwillingness to
tell us of anything but the facts directly relevant to his publications; from it one could

characterization of his life ingeniously cancels the implication of partiality: a narrative of writings with "a little more" will be a full and adequate account of a life that has "almost all" been devoted to writing. The brevity of the autobiography can be understood in terms of this legitimating symmetry. It too is a little more added to a life, almost all of which has been "spent in literary pursuits and occupations," in order to represent that little more within writing, thus spending (or investing) everything in literature.

Hume's strategy of abbreviation is most salient at the beginning of the last paragraph of "My Own Life": "To conclude historically with my own character. I am, or rather was (for that is the style I must now use in speaking of myself, which emboldens me the more to speak my sentiments); I was, I say. . . ." Hume here adopts a posthumous style: posthumous because the historical perspective, so lightly taken, which allows the writer to characterize "Hume," the author of those works whose relations he narrates, is a position beyond the grave. Death is written here—a death that is, paradoxically, an empowerment. Hume can be more open about his sentiments not because he has chosen to be more sincere but because those sentiments have become characters, representative objects rather than passions. Those characters are now in a determinate relation to an "I" that is the little more that survives, like a posthumous narrator, the death of whatever it was that was possessed by those sentiments and that might have been damaged by expressing them. By being posthumously characterized, the sentiments of the writer are included within his writings and adequated with the narrative of those writings.

The best characterization of the posthumous "I," then, is the style which it "must use"—as if only that death which necessarily comes to all had forced the "I" to know itself as a well-formed sequence of properties. Yet that style and that necessity indisputably fulfill the plan of life Hume adopted from the outset:

> My studious disposition, my sobriety, and my industry, gave my
> family a notion that the law was a proper profession for me; but I
> found an unsurmountable aversion to every thing but the pursuits
> of philosophy and general learning; and while they fancied I was
> poring upon Voet and Vinnius, Cicero and Virgil were the authors
> which I was secretly devouring.

---

scarcely guess at the content of his Essays." *Design and Truth in Autobiography* (Cambridge: Harvard Univ. Press, 1960), p. 15. Hume tells us a little more than the bare facts, and the relation between the "little more" and the facts is of considerable importance in assessing the conduct of the *Essays*.

My very slender fortune, however, being unsuitable to this plan of life, and my health being a little broken by my ardent application, I was tempted, or rather forced, to make a very feeble trial for entering into a more active scene of life.

Hume's autobiography attempts to engineer the adjustment by which a plan of life comes to absorb natural necessity to its ends. Hume's life, all of it, until the writing of the autobiography, has been a detour compounded of necessity and design. Driven by necessity he blended his life in letters with a variety of occupations—tutor, aide-de-camp, librarian, undersecretary—so that it could sooner or later acquire the strength to stand independently, a strength that is paradoxically announced by the final breakdown of health that has negated all other necessities. Because practical activity is represented as merely instrumental, Hume's plan of life comes to look very much like a death wish. The wish for death seems to be part and parcel of the "ruling passion" for a permanent "literary fame" that has sustained him through all vicissitudes. But, having said that, we have to acknowledge a rhetorical versatility that permits death itself to be troped as merely the last interruption, and one that seals off a "life" and a fame exempt from all infirmities. A self-imposed death anticipates the inevitable, biological death; the necessitous is preempted and composed by Humean artifice.[3] The "I" that writes (as opposed to the "I" that is characterized) would be so impartial that the death of its subject self would be of no great import. Hume's is a stoical autobiography, then, which, utterly without vanity, narrates a life that accomplishes its own death—a project that differs from suicide in that unlike the stoic, who finds in suicide a point of devastation "where his drive for control becomes totally and unsurpassably self-referential in a final triumph over

---

3. Barry Lydgate comments on the difference between the textual practice of Montaigne and the practice of those authors of whom Montaigne says (in Lydgate's paraphrase) that "the only trustworthy perspective . . . is the unified perspective of death": "Nothing so drastic as a real death is necessary to render the *Essais* trustworthy. In a compositional method that respects the integrity of what is already printed, each successive printing represents a literary death in the context of biological life, a new definition point that allows the author both to be and to know. Self-description becomes self-understanding, which, described in its turn, can lead to greater self-knowledge, and so on indefinitely." Lydgate, "Mortgaging One's Work to the World: Publication and the Structure of Montaigne's *Essais*," *PMLA* 96 (March 1981): 221. Similar in that they each represent death, Montaigne and Hume are considerably different in how and why they represent it. There is only one autobiographical essay in the canon of Hume, for whom self-description becomes self-control rather than self-knowledge. Death is represented only once—not because it is singular but because its representation identifies it as only another correspondent of that technical incapacitation that occurs continually.

the world outside,"[4] the historical "I" of Hume enjoys the profit of existing beyond its natural terminus—in the paragraph that follows the shift
to the past tense and in the corpus that the autobiography constitutes and
supervises.

If stoical, there is also something oddly romantic about a gesture that
treats death as merely a facilitating interruption, as a good career move.
And if part of the forcefulness of this gesture derives from its authoritative
uniqueness (one can only write one's death *once*, if it is actually going to
count as death), there is something odd in the similarity between Hume's
last text and his first. In the unpublished and fragmentary "Essay on
Chivalry" Hume initiates his attack on romance with the comment:

> 'Tis observable of the human mind, that when it is smit with any
> idea of merit or perfection beyond what its faculties can attain, and
> in the pursuit of which it uses not reason and experience for its
> guide, it knows no mean, but as it gives the rein, and even adds the
> spur, to every florid conceit or fancy, runs in a moment quite wide
> of nature. Thus we find, when, without discretion, it indulges its
> devote terrors, that working in such fairy-ground, it quickly buries
> itself in its own whimsies and chimeras, and raises up to itself a new
> set of passions, affections, desires, objects, and, in short, a perfectly
> new world of its own, inhabited by different beings, and regulated
> by different laws from this of ours.[5]

Hume's critique of romance (and of philosophy, with which he identifies
it) attributes to the fantasist a delusional plot of self-dissolution, burial,
and resurrection that is not only a thin encoding of the Christian myth
(see Hume's association of life in fairyland with "religious exercise") but
is also the template for the procedure by which Hume attempts to solidify
his canon and assure himself of literary fame in "My Own Life." There
he reckons on a "speedy dissolution" that enables him to be "detached
from Life," buries himself in the chimera of the past tense in order to
raise himself up in the perfectly new world of literary fame, which is
"inhabited by different beings, and regulated by different laws from this
of ours." Now, I do not expose the romance in Hume's final stoical gesture
in order to destroy its pretense. On the contrary, I want to recover the full
force of its pretense, to mystify a Humean rhetoric that is too often considered to be naturalistic, and to question the status of a canon that is too

4. Gordon Braden, *Renaissance Tragedy and the Senecan Tradition: Anger's Privilege* (New Haven: Yale Univ. Press, 1985), p. 24.

5. "David Hume's 'An Historical Essay on Chivalry and Modern Honour'" ed. Ernest
Campbell Mossner, *Modern Philology* 45 (August 1947): 57.

often taken for granted. What is astonishing about Hume's gesture is not its romantic basis but that it *worked*, that the wishfulness that constitutes romance proved to have a power over the cultural reality that Hume's books and Hume's reputation inhabit. Hume's wish fulfilled itself in the fame which is indubitably his.[6] It may be that its romantic basis takes a little of the "lustre" off Hume's reputation, or it may be that the historical fact of Hume's success has the retrospective effect of either mooting or naturalizing a rhetoric that in its own terms seems so delusional. In any case, it is clear that because of its romantic basis and because it does not stake its success on truth claims, Hume's work cannot be confuted by argument. Hume's work can be effectively opposed only if it is regarded not as a series of propositions but as a literary practice aimed at attaining a reputation exempt from contingency. Authentic opposition to Hume will require a willingness to defame.

The intensity of Hume's effort to dictate to futurity is apparent even without reference to "On Chivalry." If the autobiography does everything it can to adequate itself with itself and neutralize the prematurity that is a structural flaw in all self-writing, which can never actually bring its representation of completion into line with the empirical moment of death, Hume's nervousness about his success manifests itself as the production of another text. Subsequent to the autobiography Hume wrote a last will and testament in which he stipulated that henceforth all collected editions of his work would begin with "My Own Life." The last is made first. Prefixed by a postscript, the canon will tolerate no further adjustments; there can be no doubt about which texts belong to Hume and in what order they fall. This is a strong but a curious move. The tactical positioning of the autobiography indicates a wavering of faith in the mechanical inductive force of the composition which it represents; the natural history of Hume's writings, which had emerged as the merest exercise of inference, comes to appear as *willed*. Regulation gives way to prescription. The "I" that wills is neither the character of Hume nor the posthumous writer who represents that character; this "I" would elude all incapacitation by speaking with the power of law.

The deployment of "My Own Life" as the prefix to and authoriza-

---

6. Albeit ironically. Hume sought literary fame and has for the most part achieved a lesser philosophical fame. Hume sought to achieve what Joseph Harrison has called, in an unpublished essay on William Blake, "canonical self-inscription," but, as Hume consistently attests, the canon he had in mind was not the history of the great dead philosophers. Rather, he sought to create a canon that would have the classical, particularly Ciceronian virtues of comprehensiveness and independence. Hume's canon would stand on its own as the work of an independent man of letters. Hume did fail in the sense that he could not foresee or prevent the appropriation of his work by post-Kantian professional philosophy.

tion of the collected works of David Hume displays a prematurity of a different kind from that so skillfully put to use by the posthumous style. It is a prematurity which cannot readily be associated with any particular manner, which may not be a "style" at all. That may seem an occult notion unless we recognize that Hume supplies some precedent for it when in "My Own Life" he juxtaposes a narrative of genealogy with a narrative of composition. Hume figures three of his books as children: the *Treatise*, which "fell *deadborn* from the press," and the two volumes of the *History of the Stuarts*, which are described as brothers. The pathos of paternity is augmented by the appreciation of an informed reader that this is Hume's sole formal acknowledgment of the *Treatise*. For Hume to own the *Treatise* in this fashion is both to terminate it and make it peculiarly difficult to narrate its connection with the subsequent works that Hume is intent on collecting.

I do not mean to say that the epitaph on the *Treatise* is the end of it either in Hume's career or in the autobiography. On the contrary, Hume candidly describes the use to which he put the *Treatise* after its demise. "I had always entertained a Notion," he writes, "that my want of Success, in publishing the Treatise of human Nature, had proceeded more from the manner than the matter; and that I had been guilty of a very usual Indiscretion, in going to the Press too early. I therefore cast the first part of that work anew in the Enquiry concerning human Understanding, which was published while I was at Turin." Again, "I there [at his brother's house] composed . . . my Enquiry concerning the Principles of Morals, which is another part of my Treatise, that I cast anew." The extension of the genealogical metaphor by means of the suggestive reference to the publication of the *Treatise* as an "indiscretion" invites us to fill in the outlines of the event: Hume's first and premature "cast" into the press spawned a deadborn child, always a possibility in "the barren and perilous Adventure of Bookmaking" (*HL*, 2:287). The second and third times he was more experienced, and more discreet. He revised and published, cast anew parts of the *Treatise* with sufficient prudence to insure healthy issue. The *Treatise* occupies the place of nature—a savage child, disorderly in its manner, dies, marking a breakdown that is both a natural end and the end of nature. What follows is the socialization of the *Treatise*, accomplished by a refinement into parts, which permits augmentation of force, partition of employments, and mutual succor—accomplished, that is, by a manner of labor vindicated by the eventual success of Hume's career as a man of letters.

So much is intelligible about the fate of the *Treatise* in the terms that the *Treatise* supplies. But what is curious is the way the natural metaphor applied to the *Treatise* disturbs the passage to success. For Hume to have

further offspring the child has to die. Moreover, by the logic of this metaphor, Hume's "casting anew," the artifice by which the essays are prepared for publication, is a remolding and a throwing forth of the parts of
a dead child. Hume's manner is indiscreet. Why metaphorically animate
an object whose only purpose is to be dead? His narrative of the passage
that makes all his living works post-*Treatise* conveys the necessity of a
violence done to nature, an imposition that impartially slices through the
metaphorical body. Which is the fiction: that the *Treatise* was a natural
child or that it died naturally?

The representation of tactics of authorization as the imposition of
law and of a cut (on the body of a child, the body of the book) might
stretch our faith in the adequation of style and necessity. Hume's exclu-
sions ought to snap it. If "My Own Life" does not claim to be a full-scale
autobiography, jammed with the particulars of Hume's life and opinions,
it does announce itself and is deployed as the "History of my Writings."
Conjecture does not have to carry us very far to find a biographical event
the exclusion of which Hume's modest demurral might be designed to
justify. The most notable section of Hume's career omitted from his narrative is its most notorious episode, Hume's friendship and violent break
with Jean-Jacques Rousseau, which was performed before all of Europe
in 1766. There is no distinctive interruption which evinces the omission.
Instead, the absence of the Rousseau episode is marked in the "little
more" that Hume adds to the history of his writings, the last paragraph,
where Hume shifts to the past tense as he concludes historically with a
romantic summation of his own character:

> In a word, though most men any wise eminent, have found reason
> to complain of Calumny, I never was touched, or even attacked by
> her baleful Tooth: And though I wantonly exposed myself to the
> Rage of both civil and religious Factions, they seemed to be dis-
> armed in my behalf of their wonted Fury: My Friends never had
> occasion to vindicate any one circumstance of my Character and
> Conduct: Not but the zealots, we may well suppose, shou'd have
> been glad to invent and propagate any Story to my Disadvantage,
> but they coud never find any which, they thought, woud wear the
> Face of Probability.

Yes and no. If by zealots we mean the religious fanatics who did not even
murmur at the publication of the *Treatise*, yes; but if we take into account
a wholly singular zealot, Rousseau, then the answer is no. For Rousseau
was the great calumniator of Hume's character in his later years, and it
was against Rousseau that Hume's friends rose together to vindicate his
conduct. What is peculiar about this omission is not its existence—Hume

admits to selectivity—but the way this instance of shortening lengthens the text, abetting rather than preventing vanity. The text enacts an odd countereconomy whereby the little less produces a little more: a paragraph of negative constructions and denials ("never soured," "not unacceptable," "I never was touched") which concludes, "I cannot say there is no vanity in making this funeral oration of myself, but I hope it is not a misplaced one; and this is a matter of fact which is easily cleared and ascertained." Negatives are redeemed by a skeptical assurance in common sense: "I cannot say there is no vanity" because no "I" can "say" without vanity. All may be vanity, but there are better and worse examples; vanity, like every other passion, is "in some measure"; the question is to what use that passion is put. In one sense the hope that this vanity is not "misplaced" is as confident as its confession: the burden of proof is placed on the reader, who *as* reader, comprised by Hume's composition, proves the fact of Hume's literary fame and is induced to assent to Hume's decorum. But in another sense the hope expresses an uncertainty about how things are placed, a doubt about whether everything *has* been composed in the most effective manner. Not unnaturally. For there is another matter of fact that is not mentioned in Hume's autobiography, though it belongs in any history of his writings, another text written by Hume that is not gathered into the works collected under the authorizing prefix of "My Own Life": *Exposé Succinct de la contestation, qui s'est élévée entre M. Hume et M. Rousseau; avec les pièces justicatives*. That fact must be cleared and ascertained (a task to which I shall turn in Chapter 7) before one can judge, finally, whether Hume's life attains the composure it designs, whether his vanity is misplaced.

II

From the perspective of the writer, before the adoption of a "historical style," before publication, before the career, the *Treatise* does not look like a book; Hume does not conceive of it as a child. Instead it appears as "loose bits of Paper; here a hint of a passion, there a Phenomenon in the mind accounted for, in another the alteration of these accounts; sometimes a remark upon an Author I have been reading, And none of them worth to any Body & I believe scarce to myself" (*HL*, 1:9). Such at least is the first comment we have on what was to become the *Treatise*. Hume's letter to Michael Ramsay precedes by some seven years his famous letter to Dr. Arbuthnot (*HL*, 1:12–18), which also characterizes the *Treatise*: "I believe . . . that little more is requir'd to make a man succeed in this Study than to throw off all Prejudices either for his own Opinions or for those of others. At least this is all I have to depend on for the Truth of my Reasonings, which I have multiply'd to such a degree, that within these three years, I find I have scribled many a Quire of Paper, in which there is nothing contain'd but my own Inventions." Seven years from "loose bits of Paper" to "many a Quire." It is as if no history has happened, as if we have traversed an inchoate state of uncomposed, disorderly impressions and ideas. *Almost* no history that is, for one discovery has occurred: "I found that the moral Philosophy transmitted to us by Antiquity, labor'd under the same Inconvenience that has been found in their natural Philosophy, of being entirely Hypothetical, & depending more upon Invention than Experience" (*HL,* 1:16). Hume has learned the necessity of trusting to experience instead of to hypotheses. Where did that discovery come from and where besides to an indefinite multiplication of inventions does it lead? Hume's letter to Dr. Arbuthnot attempts to answer those questions. Not a history of his writings, it is the clinical account of a disease.[7]

Hume describes his youthful inclination to "Books & Letters," his conviction, early developed, that "nothing yet [had been] establisht in either of [the] two Sciences" of philosophy and polite letters, and his search for "some new Medium, by which Truth might be establisht." He relates that,

> after much Study, & Reflection on this, at last, when I was about 18 Years of Age, there seem'd to be open'd up to me a new Scene of Thought, which transported me beyond Measure, & made me, with an Ardor natural to young men, throw up every other Pleasure or Business to apply entirely to it. The Law which was the Business I design'd to follow, appear'd nauseous to me, & I cou'd think of no other way of pushing my Fortune in the World, but that of a Scholar & Philosopher. I was infinitely happy in this Course of Life for some Months; till at last, about the beginning of Septr 1729, all my Ardor seem'd in a moment to be extinguisht, & I cou'd no longer raise my Mind to that pitch, which formerly gave me such excessive Pleasure.

7. Unless otherwise identified, subsequent quotations of Hume in this chapter are taken from the letter to Arbuthnot (misidentified as George Cheyne by Greig) in *HL* 1:12–18. The most influential treatment of this letter in the context of tracing the origins of Hume's thought is Norman Kemp Smith's in his *Philosophy of David Hume: A Critical Study of Its Origins and Central Doctrines* (London: Macmillan, 1941), pp. 14–17. For two recent discussions of this letter see John Sitter, *Literary Loneliness in Mid-Eighteenth-Century England* (Ithaca: Cornell Univ. Press, 1982), pp. 31–37, and John A. Dussinger, "David Hume's Denial of Personal Identity: The Making of a Skeptic," *American Imago* 37 (1980):334–50.

There followed a "Coldness," which he attributed to a "Laziness of Temper," and which afflicted him for nine months.

> There was another particular, which contributed more than any thing, to waste my Spirits & bring on me this Distemper, which was, that having read many Books of Morality, such as Cicero, Seneca & Plutarch, & being smit with their beautiful Representations of Virtue & Philosophy, I undertook the Improvement of my Temper & Will, along with my Reason & Understanding. I was continually fortifying myself with Reflections against Death, & Poverty, & Shame, & Pain, & all the Calamities of Life. These no doubt are exceeding useful, when join'd with an active Life; because the Occasion being presented along with the Reflection, works it into the Soul, & makes it take a deep impression, but in solitude they serve to little other Purpose, than to waste the Spirits, the Force of the Mind meeting with no Resistance, but wasting itself in the Air, like our Arm when it misses its Aim. This however I did not learn but by Experience, & till I had already ruin'd my Health, tho' I was not sensible of it.

The Hume glimpsed in this account, a youth of infinite happiness, ardor, and excessive pleasure, who exercises without restraint the force of his mind, is one that we shall not encounter again in his subsequent writings. By definition, since all of those characteristics are associated with an enthusiastic philosophizing which not only antedates all the texts that comprise the Hume we can come to know but which obstructed the production of those texts. Solitary and fervent, the young Hume's reading produced reflections that left no impression on him, or at least did not impel him to make any impressions on others—those others who, as members of society, would supply the "resistance" necessary to turn a moral imagination to moral use or who, as readers, would confirm the reality of the philosopher's grandiose conceptions.[8] Solitude is a state of reading (or "learning" or "study"), and reading means vulnerability to being "smit with . . . beautiful Representations of Virtue & Philosophy."

8. On the general importance of resistance in Enlightenment strategy Max Horkheimer and Theodor W. Adorno comment: "Every spiritual resistance [enlightenment] encounters serves merely to increase its strength. Which means that enlightenment still recognizes itself even in myths. Whatever myths the resistance may appeal to, by virtue of the very fact that they become arguments in the process of opposition, they acknowledge the principle of dissolvent rationality for which they reproach the Enlightenment." *The Dialectic of Enlightenment,* trans. John Cumming (New York: Seabury, 1972), p. 6. See also Hubert L. Dreyfus's and Paul Rabinow's commentary on Foucault's *Discipline and Punish* in *Michel Foucault: Beyond Structuralism and Hermeneutics,* 2d ed. (Chicago: Univ. of Chicago Press, 1983), p. 143.

Such representations have a considerable power: they encourage one to attempt improvement and fortification. But though they arouse the idea of power they do not transfer power. Self-fortification occurs on the grounds of an illusory self-sufficiency. The cloistered reader imagines a strength that overcomes everything instantly and thus tests itself against nothing actually.[9]

The stimulus of the classical moralists was pornographic, or at least appears so by its effect on the young philosopher, who, struck (smit) by the ancients, became enamored of (smit with) their example and, aroused to a conviction of a kind of phallic omnipotence, smote the air with his arm in an onanistic waste of spirit. Solitary reading of the classical moralists catapulted Hume into a blockage compounded of autoerotic power fantasies and feelings of waste. Moral writing has had vicious consequences.[10] Importantly, for the young Hume acting morally is identified with writing moral philosophy, representing unto others as one has been represented to: utility is inextricably bound up with exchange. Or, not quite as one has been represented to, for as we shall see, although this reading experience became for Hume a touchstone for the power available to a deeply attractive kind of representation, it was a mode whose attractions he had to resist. Hume would not smite.

The question why he *had* to resist comes to the same as what was unsatisfying about onanistic reflection, what was vicious about waste.[11]

9. Cf. Hume's later discussion of a similar state in "The Stoic," where he admonishes: "Your indolence itself becomes a fatigue; your pleasure itself creates disgust. The mind, unexercised, finds every delight insipid and loathsome; and ere yet the body, full of noxious humors, feels the torment of its multiplied diseases, your nobler part is sensible of the invading poison, and seeks in vain to relieve its anxiety by new pleasures, which still augment the fatal malady" (*ST,* p. 110).

10. What I have called the pornographic stimulation of the classical might less sensationally be described as its romantic power. See Hume's characterization of it in the passage from the essay "On Chivalry," discussed above: "Philosophy, . . . tho' it cannot produce a different world in which we may wander, makes us act in this as if we were different Beings from the rest of mankind; at least makes us frame to ourselves, tho' we cannot execute them, Rules of conduct different from these which are set to us by Nature" (p. 57). The same impulse gives rise in the author and the reader to the taste for an extravagantly strenuous philosophy and "that Monster of Romantick Chivalry." As we shall see in Chapter 4, Hume's practice as an essayist was aimed at reforming both philosophical writing and the chivalric mode by mitigating their power to smite.

11. This is not an idle question. For a later attack on the presuppositions of political economy which bases its critique on the symbolic, communal efficaciousness of waste, see Wordsworth's "The Old Cumberland Beggar." Or, nearer to hand, cf. Boswell's account of Johnson's rejection of mechanicism: "'If,' said he, 'a man says he would rather be the machine, I cannot argue with him. He is a different being from me.' I said a man, as a machine, might have agreeable sensations; he might have music. 'No,' said he, 'he could not have music, at least no power of producing music, for he who can produce music may let it alone.

For Hume, as for the ancients summoned to testify by Foucault, "sexual austerity" should not be understood "as an expression of, or commentary on, deep and essential prohibitions, but as the elaboration and stylization of an activity in the exercise of its power and the practice of its liberty."[12] For Hume in particular, neither reflection nor waste can ever be pure: reflection is always annexed to an "occasion," and waste is always subjected to an economy. Or, to put it another way, ideas are not without impressions. Experience teaches us that one must resist being smitten by making us "sensible" that reflection and waste are the fluxions of disease:

> Some Scurvy Sports broke out on my Fingers, the first Winter I fell ill, about which I consulted a very knowing Physician, who gave me some Medicines . . . & at the same time gave me a Warning against the Vapors, which . . . I fancy'd myself so far remov'd from . . . that I despis'd his Warning. At last about April 1730, when I was 19 Years of Age, a Symptom, which I had notic'd a little from the beginning, encreas'd considerably, so that tho' it was no Uneasyness, the Novelty of it made me ask Advice. It was what they call a Ptyalism or Watryness in the mouth. Upon my mentioning it to my Physician, he laught at me, & told me I was now a Brother, for that I had fairly got the Disease of the Learned.

Hume became sensible of the wastefulness of his reflection when he discovered that it had ruined his health, when he discovered, that is, that it was not pure waste but disease. Reading and reflection produce a kind of writing in the sensible impression of a "Symptom." Waste has, then, a kind of value, for the symptoms that mark the ruin of health make Hume a legible text to the right kind of reader, a practitioner. The arm may miss its aim, but that action does not go unrecorded; it is documented by "scurvy spots" at the ends of the fingers. The voice that goes unused in the silent passion does not fall into utterlessness, but writes its silence into a "Watryness in the mouth." These symptoms, which Hume noticed but could not understand, forced him out of the study, and inserted him into a discourse: he sought the advice of a specialist, who informed him that he was become, although solitary, a "Brother."[13] Although the illness

He who can play upon a fiddle may break it.'" *Boswell's Journal of "A Tour to the Hebrides,"* ed. Frederick A. Pottle and Charles H. Bennett (New York: Literary Guild, 1936), p. 85.

12. Michel Foucault, *The Use of Pleasure,* vol. 2 of *The History of Sexuality,* trans. Robert Hurley (New York: Pantheon, 1985), pp. 136–37.

13. It was a French rather than an English doctor, Samuel A.A.D. Tissot, who, in 1768, systematically discoursed upon the modern variant of the disease of the learned, *De la santé des gens de lettres.* Discussing symptoms, he mentions that the "diseases of men of letters have two principal sources: the hard work of the mind and the continuous repose of the body; to make an exact tableau of these one need but trace in detail the nefarious effects of

had ruined Hume's health, no one, as the expert must tell us, has a disease alone: disease may threaten one's survival, but disease also inducts us into a community of sufferers, affiliated by the same symptoms. The appearance of the symptom is, as it were, a natural resistance to being smitten by the beautiful representations of the classical moralists—resistance as a form of automatic writing, of compulsive discursiveness, and of forced affiliation.[14]

The account of the "Disease of the Learned" to Arbuthnot is the pattern for the analysis of inductive affiliation within the *Treatise* as it is the condition of possibility for the composition of the *Treatise* itself. Hume's filiative reading of the ancients ends badly; his failure is experienced as symptoms of a disease that make it vital for Hume to seek the advice of a professional man. Hume did not arbitrarily decide to affiliate himself, to become a brother and a patient. Affiliation is as natural as disease and the desire for a cure.

To say that affiliation is there from the beginning is not to deny a graduation of the kind of connections Hume makes. Hume first consulted a professional man of medicine who could prescribe a drug, diet, or regi-

---

these two causes." Tissot distinguishes between ordinary readers and his subjects according to the criterion of wasteful effects and effects that are diseased, to be sure, but symptomatic of a nobler pursuit: "The inconveniences of frivolous books are a waste of time and tired eyesight; but those who by the power and liaison of ideas lift the soul beyond itself and force it to meditate wear out the spirit and exhaust the body, and the greater and longer this pleasure the more fatal the results." Quoted in Rémy G. Saisselin, *The Literary Enterprise in Eighteenth-Century France* (Detroit: Wayne State Univ. Press, 1979), p. 141.

14. Edward Said has written of "the transition from a failed idea or possibility of filiation to a kind of compensatory order that . . . provides men and women with a new form of relationship, . . . affiliation." Said calls it "the deliberately explicit goal" of writers like Eliot, Lukacs, or Freud, "of using that new order to reinstate vestiges of the kind of authority associated in the past with filiative order." He remarks on the difference that "if a filial relationship was held together by natural bonds and natural forms of authority—involving obedience, fear, love, respect, and instinctual conflict—the new affiliative relationship changes these bonds into what seem to be transpersonal forms—such as guild consciousness, consensus, collegiality, professional respect, class, and the hegemony of a dominant culture. The filiative scheme belongs to the realms of nature and of 'life,' whereas affiliation belongs exclusively to culture and society." Said, *The World, the Text, and the Critic* (Cambridge: Harvard Univ. Press, 1983), pp. 19–20. Said's basic distinction seems right enough, but the attempt to tie it to late-nineteenth-century thinkers is mistaken. Cf., for example, the telling change of spelling that the young David made in his name, from Home to Hume—an allegory of deliberate affiliation. Anglicizing is useful only to a second son, who, because he will not come into the estate, must think about becoming useful. That Hume will not inherit his father's estate is perfectly just. That he must affiliate with others in order to make his fortune is perfectly necessary. Hume is the Home that must leave home—not because he is prodigal but because in moral submission to the authority of the hierarchical system of law into which he is born he must be prudent. Hume retains the family name but adjusts it in order to facilitate the affiliations which are his lot in life, the means to his livelihood.

men that would cure a disease that he understood as merely organic, albeit particular to the "Learned." He records his diligent observance of the prescription he received and his moderate improvement: he succeeded in "abating the Symptoms for a little time." A summation in direct address follows: "Thus I have given you a full account of the Condition of my Body, & without staying to ask Pardon, as I ought to do, for so tedious a Story, shall explain to you how my Mind stood all this time, which on every Occasion, especially in this Distemper, have a very near Connexion together." This prelude to a catalog of another group of symptoms evinces Hume's revised appraisal of his disease as a more complicated phenomenon, an "Occasion" which mutually implicated mind and body. Consequently, Hume has sought out Dr. Arbuthnot, a man who is not only a "skillful Physician" but also "a man of Letters, of Wit, of Good Sense, & of great Humanity." Arbuthnot looks like a specialist to one who is afflicted with a general malady. It takes a physician who is a man of letters, one for whom every bodily occasion is the opportunity for mental reflection, to cure the disease of the learned.

The condition of Hume's mind, excited and unsettled by sporadic bursts of insight and power, is the condition of the incipient *Treatise:*

> Having now Time & Leizure to cool my inflam'd Imaginations, I began to consider seriously, how I shou'd proceed in my Philosophical Enquiries. I found that the moral Philosophy transmitted to us by Antiquity, labor'd under the same Inconvenience that has been found in their natural Philosophy, of being entirely Hypothetical, & depending more upon Invention than Experience. Every one consulted his Fancy in erecting Schemes of Virtue & of Happiness, without regarding human Nature, upon which every moral Conclusion must depend. This therefore I resolved to make my principal Study, & the Source from which I wou'd derive every Truth in Criticism as well as Morality. I believe 'tis a certain Fact that most of the Philosophers who have gone before us, have been overthrown by the Greatness of their Genius & that little more is requir'd to make a man succeed in this Study than to throw off all Prejudices either for his own Opinions or for those of others. At least this is all I have to depend on for the Truth of my reasonings, which I have multiply'd to such a degree, that within these three Years, I find I have scribled many a Quire of Paper, in which there is nothing contained but my own Inventions.

This is the first substantive characterization in Hume's writings of what will be the enabling empiricist perspective of the *Treatise*, that which will distinguish it from all previous philosophical texts. The passage also dramatically identifies the experience from which Hume derived his method of trusting only to experience. Hume contrasts his method with those "Philosophers who have gone before us, [who] have been overthrown by the Greatness of their Genius." But if we ask who those unfortunate philosophers are, the only answer suggested by Hume is "the moral Philosophy transmitted to us by Antiquity." It is as if Locke, Descartes, Malebranches, and Hutcheson—all those modern philosophers on whom Hume depended and against whom he wrote—never existed. In what possible sense could such a misprision be justified? In what possible sense could it be fair to say that those philosophers from antiquity who *transmitted* to us moral philosophy were *overthrown* by their genius?

Hume's conclusions are entailed by the appearance of those symptoms, which convinced him that the transmission of the moral philosophy of Seneca, Plutarch, and Cicero was an overthrow of genius, insofar as reading those authors provoked spasmodic identification and onanistic reflection. Ancient moral philosophy was of such force that it overpowered all moral consequences, ending only in a reader who smote the empty air. The group of "philosophers who have gone before" must thus be expanded to include not only the classical moralists but also David Hume, who is made a genius by their genius and is overthrown in their overthrow. Hume can disregard all intermediate philosophers because his reading of the ancients has been entirely unmediated; and the experience of failed filiation grounds a philosophy which can rest neither on hypothesis nor authority but on experience, since experience, becoming *sensible* of the waste of spirits consequent upon the exaltation of genius, is all that makes it possible for Hume to write any philosophy at all. Hume becomes the representative modern philosopher by becoming the only modern philosopher who has experienced the overthrow of the ancients—an overthrow which is figured on his body as it will be inscribed on the pages of the *Treatise*. Hume's overthrow is his disease. But that disease which cuts him off from the halcyon days of solitary, omnipotent reflection is also the defense against overthrow by his own genius because it is in the disease and out of the disease that he recognizes a production: he "finds" he has scribbled many a quire, just as he finds he has scurvy spots on his hands. Despite the blockage of writing there are pages and pages of script. The interdiction on invention coincides with a multiplicity of inventions.

But, Hume writes, that is not the same as health. He complains that all the writing he has done to this point has not

> been done to any Purpose. . . . My Disease was a cruel Incumbrance on Me. I found that I was not able to follow out any Train of Thought, by one continued Stretch of View, but by repeated Interruptions, & by refreshing my Eye from Time to Time upon other Objects. Yet with this Inconvenience I have collected the rude Ma-

terials for many volumes; but in reducing these to Words, when one must bring the Idea he comprehended in gross, nearer to him, so as to contemplate its minutest Parts & keep it steddily, in his Eye, so as to copy these Parts in Order, this I found impracticable for me, nor were my Spirits equal to so severe an Employment. Here lay my greatest Calamity—I had no Hopes of delivering my Opinions with such Elegance & Neatness, as to draw to me the Attention of the World, & I wou'd rather live & dye in Obscurity than Produce them maim'd & imperfect.

Improvement refines wants. Hume began with an account of a disease generated by an incapacity to write, then described his discovery of a writing symptomatic of the disease. Now he complains of the inhibitions on reducing those assorted scribblings into words and words into a neat and elegant whole. He identifies a perfected book as both the cure for the disorder of the collected materials and the more than metaphoric cure for the disease of the learned. Hume, then, suffers from the complaint of not being able to compose a unified book. He cannot write the book because he is oppressed by the fantastic hope that on its publication his enormous need for attention would be fully satisfied by the responsive attention of the world. Hume imagines an economy of ideal correspondence: my full attention produces a unified book which is exchanged for your full attention. An economy and an emblem of narcissistic satisfaction: the book to be delivered by the labor of writing will be a Humunculus reflecting in all its parts its author, whose perfection must by ratified in the reflexive admiration of its readers. Any lapse or disorder in the book, any mutilation, would jar that delicate nexus of condign fascination; the writer would discover his own flaws in the averted eyes of disgusted readers. Rather than suffer that failed filiation, rather than deliver his child into the world maimed and imperfect, he would abort the project and live and die in obscurity.

Wanting a cure, the one grim consolation lies in a conviction of singularity: "Such a miserable Disappointment I scarce ever remember to have heard of. The small Distance betwixt me & perfect Health makes me the more uneasy in my present Situation. Tis a Weakness rather than a Lowness of Spirits which troubles me, & there seems to be as great a Difference betwixt my Distemper & common Vapors, as betwixt Vapors & Madness." If this unheard-of predicament suggests the perfect disequilibrium between infirmity and necessity which providentially singles man out among the creatures, then it may be appropriate to ask whether the desire for perfect health is actually healthy. After all, it is the idea of the beautiful book that produces, as if by association, thoughts of death.

It is necessary to ascertain exactly where Hume is in the composition of the *Treatise*. This is not the sort of empirical question that can be settled by comparison of the manuscript materials left over from 1734 with the published work, since it is the status of that published work as a composition that is in question. Instead we need to inquire into the relation between what the *Treatise* is and Hume's ideas of what the *Treatise* might be. We may begin by distinguishing between the composition and the writing of the *Treatise*, for although Hume's complaint testifies to his failure to finish the *Treatise* as a book, it is fair to say that the *Treatise* has been written. It has been written as those symptoms that appeared to mark the extrication of Hume from the thrall of the ancients and the overthrow of their authority—an overthrow documented by the marks on his hands and the notations on his paper that make Hume a writer despite himself. The assertion that "little more is requir'd to make a man succeed in this study than to throw off all Prejudices for his own Opinions or for this of others" implicitly identifies a completion. It also executes a transformation: the "little more," as in "My Own Life," indicates a surplus of vanity, here attached to a notion of success. That "little more" of organizing, connecting, embodying the scattered impressions that lies between the writing of the text and the success of the book is the exact analogue to the "small distance" between Hume and that "perfect health" which he requires to compose.

The irony of Hume's conception of success is that the result he imagines looks very much like the state of stunned admiration he had escaped. He wants to turn the *Treatise* into a beautiful representation which will fix on him the attention of an audience smitten with its neatness and elegance: in the transformation of notes and quires into a book, the text "itself" seems to vanish or, rather, it becomes a completely adequate representation of a perfect self, perfectly appreciated. When I call this narcissistic, I mean roughly what Hume does in his observation that "authors have this privilege in common with lovers, and founded on the same reason, that they are both besotted with a blind fondness of their object" (*HL*, 1:27). By "narcissistic" I intend to indicate the intransitive character of this relationship, which may be a transaction of sorts, but can only be imagined as the first and last transaction in a system that is no real economy because it is not dynamic: to succeed in this fashion is to be completely and permanently esteemed and thus relieved of the necessity of ever writing another book. It is the dream of a savage, or of a genius who prepares his own overthrow by making himself vulnerable to the merest violence: a muttered comment, an averted glance, the very passage of time, or any movement in space would be enough to mar this elegant representation, to maim this imagined body.[15]

---

15. As Hume's reference to Cicero suggests, the dream of the savage or the genius is

Yet if this notion of narcissistic satisfaction is associated with the request for a cure from Dr. Arbuthnot, the fact that the letter was not posted implies that Hume has at least temporarily abandoned the fantasy of perfect health. He writes of his "despair of ever recovering." The scene on which he now enters is completely different from that which he came upon as a youth. But more significant than his despair of a cure are the *remedial* measures he takes to

> keep myself from being Melancholy on so dismal a Prospect. . . .
> Being sensible that all my Philosophy wou'd never make me contented in my present Situation, I began to rouze up myself; & being encourag'd by Instances of Recovery from worse degrees of this Distemper, as well as by the Assurances of my Physicians, I began to think of something more effectual, than I had hitherto try'd. I found, that as there are two things very bad for this Distemper, Study & Idleness, so there are two things very good, Business & Diversion; & that my whole Time was spent betwixt the bad, with little or no Share of the Good. For this reason I resolved to seek out a more active life, & tho' I cou'd not quit my Pretensions in Learning, but with my last Breath, to lay them aside for some time, in order the more effectually to resume them.

Rather than follow through on his appeal to a physician, preferred among his kind because he is a man of many parts, Hume determines to partition himself, to put down his study and indolence and to take up business and diversion. This is, as the cliché would have it, to make a virtue of necessity. For in taking up business (Hume mentions his imminent removal to Bristol, where he will clerk for a trader) Hume chooses to encumber himself with an occupation as he has been encumbered by his disease: both occupation and disease have the same immediate result, to divert him from his composition of the *Treatise*—but the differences that make business and diversion virtues are that, though driven by disease to this course, Hume controls the choice of a particular activity, and

---

scarcely distinguishable from the dream of oratory—applause without delay or diminution. Hume fantasizes in "Of Eloquence" that "whenever the true genius arises, *he* draws to him the attention of every one, and immediately appears superior to his rival" (*ST*, p. 69). Here is Goldsmith in a similar vein: "Of all kinds of success, that of an orator is the most pleasing. Upon other occasions, the applause we deserve is conferred in our absence, and we are insensible of the pleasure we have given; but in eloquence, the victory and the triumph are inseparable. We read our own glory in the face of every spectator; the audience is moved, the antagonist is defeated, and the whole circle bursts into unsolicited applause." *The Bee*, no. 7, in *The Works of Oliver Goldsmith*, ed. Peter Cunningham, 10 vols. (New York: Putnam's), 6:269. See Chapter 4 below for a discussion of Hume's rejection of the oratorical model.

can, moreover, improvise a way to represent necessity as a *course* of action in a narrative of regular cycles of diversion and resumption.

That ability is empirically derived; one finding is prepared for by another: "I found that I was not able to follow out any Train of Thought, by one continued Stretch of View, but by *repeated* Interruptions, & by refreshing my Eye from Time to Time upon other Objects" (emphasis added). The first interruption is the natural effect of the disease—a moment of inadvertence disturbing the deliberate application of the mind. But at some point the interruptions are "found" to be "repeated," a point where the affiliative ambiguity of "found"—which hovers between the innocent "discover" and the knowing "invent," and which is congruent with the moment of reflection that turns savage avidity into social self-interest—effects an almost imperceptible transition between the natural and the artificial, where, that is, the symptom of the disease becomes a remedy for the disease, where a necessitous disruption of a train of thought becomes a technique for continuing the train. Finding repeated interruption is practically indistinguishable from representing interruption. Interruption thus becomes part of the process of composition, so that what had been suffered by a patient can be imposed by an author as a home remedy.[16]

Hume has revised his understanding of the symptom: it has changed from being an effect of the disease into a metaphor for the disease, an interruption that articulates a train of thought. It now appears as what it always was, not something that disrupts what can no longer be called writing but something that facilitates the mechanical composition of greater wholes out of individual ideas. The metaphorization of symptom

16. A stoic trait—at least according to Gordon Braden, who declares that "stoicism's central strength is its calculus of adaptation to unchangeable realities" (*Renaissance Tragedy and the Senecan Tradition*, p. 17). Compare Freud's discussion of symptoms as "transcriptions" of "a number of emotionally cathected processes, wishes and desires. . . . These mental processes," he comments, "being held back in a state of unconsciousness, strive to obtain an expression that shall be appropriate to their emotional importance—to obtain discharge; and in the case of hysteria they find such an expression (by means of the process of 'conversion') in somatic phenomena, that is, in hysterical symptoms. By systematically turning these symptoms back (with the help of a special technique) in emotionally cathected ideas—ideas that will now have become conscious—it is possible to obtain the most accurate knowledge of the nature and origin of these formerly unconscious psychical structures." Sigmund Freud, *Three Essays on the Theory of Human Sexuality*, trans. James Strachey (New York: Basic Books, 1962), p. 30. Patient and analyst, Hume develops the symptoms and in the course of this letter develops the technique to turn those symptoms back into conscious ideas. The knowledge that he obtains, however, is not of the origin of psychic structures but of the process of conversion and reconversion ("turning . . . back") that identifies the special technique common to hysteric and sympathetic doctor. The *locus classicus* of Hume's application of the principle of conversion in aesthetics is the essay "Of Tragedy."

coincides with an emphasis on a globalizing tendency under the rubric of thought or idea, which establishes a series of correspondences subject to indefinite extrapolation, as for example, in "My Own Life," where Hume reiterates "symptom" with the casualness appropriate to a dead metaphor, even employing it (although perhaps a bit nervously) as a trope on which to pin his hopes for fame, when he speaks of seeing "many Symptoms of my literary Reputation's breaking out at last with additional Lustre." Hence if Hume finds the specific kind of diversion of refreshing the eye does not work when the time comes to reduce "the rude Materials" into "Words [what could these materials have been before they were words, what kind of writing is being openly repressed in such a reconstruction?], when he must bring the idea he comprehended in gross, nearer to him, so as to contemplate its minutest Parts, & keep it steddily in his Eye, so as to copy these Parts in Order," he nonetheless is provided with an analogical logic that prepares him to cope with the greater problem: he opts for a greater diversion, not refreshment of the eye but revival of the whole man by the interruption of study with a life in business. Because he is practicing the same technique of repeating interruption to fulfill his ambition of eventual order, there is no essential difference between the kind of diversion he employs in his study and that which he engages in Bristol. Both are the same kind of composition, a composition in which the production of material, of writing, has either been finished or eclipsed, a composition which is a history of writing rather than writing itself, a composition in which whatever one finds can by careful, improvisatory representation be put to some kind of advantage. The bundles of notes and quires of paper are the closest one can get to pure waste that is precisely *not* economic. It is because such mere writing has no use, stands in no relation to anyone, produces no advantage, and therefore cannot be exchanged that Hume gets sick.[17] Nothing if not psychosomatic, Hume's disease is an incapacitating self-imposition which appears as a symptom, a metaphor for writing. Although it is a "wasteful" interruption, the symptom, unlike the "rude Materials," enables his induction into a discourse of correspondences, an indefinite exchange motivated by the vivid idea of eventual advantage. By metaphorizing interruption Hume turns the necessitous into a remedial technique and technique into a way of life. He represents life not as a single idea or as a neat and elegant body but as a process of continual adjustment, a career, and establishes the grounds for the eventual transformation of an existential moment of crisis

17. On the concept of waste and its pertinence to a critique of both Marxism and political economy, see Jean Baudrillard's *The Mirror of Production*, trans. Mark Poster (St. Louis: Telos, 1975), pp. 143–145 and passim.

into the functional articulation of a formula: "Human happiness, according to the most received notions, seems to consist in three ingredients: action, pleasure, and indolence: and though these ingredients ought to be mixed in different proportions, according to the particular disposition of the person; yet no one ingredient can be entirely wanting, without destroying, in some measure, the relish of the whole composition" (*ST,* p. 49). Formulas invite definitions, and the Humean man of letters might be faithfully defined by inverting Julia Kristeva's characterization of modern poetry, which she describes as an "artistic practice [which] is the laboratory of a minimal signifying structure, its maximum dissolution, and the eternal return of both." [18] Hume's *discursive* practice is the laboratory of a *maximal* signifying structure, its *minimum* dissolution, and the *regular* return of both. Although the propriety of the definition is clear from Hume's letter, its implications can be clarified only by an exploration of the career which it distills.

In the event, Hume does not post his letter to Arbuthnot. He no longer needs a specialist or a professional because he has learned to read himself—a reading which writes itself. The letter has done its work as representation and instance of the technique by which Hume can remediate the disease of the learned; the wish for a cure, for a complete embodiment and total success, has been adjusted to take advantage of the dynamic singularity intrinsic to "the small Distance betwixt me & perfect Health"—a gap which Hume will generalize as the dynamic articulation of a variety of contexts, indeed of contextualization itself and of the context he has become. [19] If Hume henceforth will be characterized by a "certain moral complacency," [20] the complacency, not unearned, is a professional virtue. No longer a mere philosopher or writer, he is now by virtue of necessity a man of letters.

18. Julia Kristeva, "The Ethics of Linguistics," in *Desire and Language: A Semiotic Approach to Literature and Art,* ed. Leon S. Roudiez, trans. Thomas Gora, Alice Jardine, and Leon S. Roudiez (New York: Columbia Univ. Press, 1980), p. 25.

19. Cf. this account with Charles Camic's prescription of the conditions for the emergence of cultural change from "experiences from which individuals can infer orientations that differ from preestablished attitudes and assumptions." Camic's conditions (considerably condensed) are (1) the "cognitive capacity actually to draw from [experiences] whatever principles they imply," (2) commitment to the principles, and (3) generalization of "their orientations to fields outside of the setting in which they were constructed." *Experience and Enlightenment: Socialization for Cultural Change in Eighteenth-Century Scotland* (Chicago: Univ. of Chicago Press, 1983), pp. 107–8.

20. John Dunn, "From Applied Theology to Social Analysis," in *Wealth and Virtue: The Shaping of Political Economy in the Scottish Enlightenment,* ed. Istvan Hont and Michael Ignatieff (Cambridge: Cambridge Univ. Press, 1983), p. 133.

3
The Practice of Passion

Here then is the only expedient, from which we can hope for success in our philosophical researches, . . . to march up directly to the capital or center of these sciences, to human nature itself; which being once masters of, we may every where else hope for an easy victory.

Treatise, Introduction

Hume's letter to Arbuthnot conforms to his natural history of society: the wish for total success corresponds to the savage's futile pursuit of complete satisfaction, while Hume's accommodation to an articulated practice of remedial indirection parallels the social reorientation of the passions of natural man. There is no clear analogue in the *Treatise*, however, for the production of "rude Material," the multiplication of as yet unworded inventions on quires of paper. I cannot display this primordial writing, but I hope to show the way the history of Hume's writings makes such a material hypothesis necessary and at the same time strains to disable it.

So far we have cooperated with Hume. Cooperation has meant temporarily forgetting that the letter to Dr. Arbuthnot was written after a course of action had already been settled upon. Cooperation has also meant provisionally accepting the homology between symptoms of a disease and disorderly notes. That entailed acquiescing to the charm of a metaphor that was retrospectively imposed to induce belief in the symptomatic resemblance between two entirely disparate phenomena. As I have argued in Chapter 2, it might be suspected that Hume encourages the belief in his writer's block *in order to* transform writing into composition—for in fact there is no evidence of any block on writing, only on publishing. But such uncooperative suspicions do not make it any easier to imagine what a simple, unfiliated and unaffiliated text would be like. How could we attach to "rude Material" any idea that would not deprive it of its "original existence"?

The term "original existence," the Humean version of an irreducible simple, appears in the analysis of the passions in book 2 of the *Treatise*. In order to test what we can say about simples—simple texts or simple passions—in Hume it will be necessary to detour through that territory. "A passion is," Hume asserts, "an original existence, or, if you will, modification of existence, and contains not any representative quality, which renders it a copy of any existence or modification. When I am angry, I am actually possesst with the passion, and in that emotion have no more a reference to any other object, than when I am thirsty, or sick, or more than five foot high" (*T,* p. 415) This general claim of passional integrity echoes the assertion that inaugurates Hume's account of the indirect passions early in book 2: "The passions of PRIDE and HUMILITY being simple and uniform impressions, 'tis impossible we can ever, by a multitude of words, give a just definition of them, or indeed of any of the passions. The utmost we can pretend to is a description of them, by an enumeration of such circumstances, as attend them: But as these words, *pride* and *humility,* are of general use, and the impressions they represent the most common of any, every one, of himself, will be able to form a just idea of them, without any danger of mistake" (*T,* p. 277). Say what he will about these simples, Hume cannot produce an exact definition. But by the same token, whatever he says can do no harm to a reader who rests on the assurance of his own unarticulated experience. Saying cannot violate the authority of what goes without saying. Strictly speaking, however, Hume concedes to his reader not the authority of his private experience of pride but his ability to form a "just idea" of the passion; and if this is so, authority returns to Hume, as one whose idea of pride, regardless of its definitional status, can be relied on to be just. Hume is the writer who trusts to everyone's experience—an investment which returns to him an increase in the authority of his own experience as justly representative.

When Hume turns to examine those "simple and uniform impressions" and to enumerate the circumstances that "attend" them, he begins with the obvious fact "that pride and humility, tho' directly contrary, have yet the same OBJECT. This object is self. . . . Here the view always fixes when we are actuated by either of these passions" (*T,* p. 277). Already the claim that passion is without "reference to any other object" has lost some of its force. Moreover, that reference to self describes a representational space disposed before a subject, a seeing "I." "Pride and humility," Hume continues, "being once rais'd, immediately turn our attention to ourself, and regard that as their ultimate and final object" (p. 278). Hume's pronomial contortions split the duties of the passions between solicitation of an "I" that is a subject and reference to a self that is an object. What was simple has become double.

Hume's equivocalness expresses his parsimony. He wants to explain the causes that produce the pride and humility that produce the object of the self, but he also wants to rule out the possibility that "each distinct cause is adapted to the passion by a distinct set of principles." The result would be a "monstrous heap of principles" that would "overload our hypotheses" (*T*, p. 282). Parsimony dictates the search for a single principle adaptive to each new causal phenomenon—identified as the idea of a cause divided between a quality that produces "a separate pain or pleasure" and a subject "on which the qualities are placed, [which is] related to self" (pp. 285–86). After noting that that supposition of a dual cause aligns with the established duality of the passion, divided between a uniform impression and a necessary connection to an object, Hume ejaculates, "true system breaks in upon me with an irresistible evidence. That cause, which excites the passion, is related to the object, which nature has attributed to the passion; the sensation, which the cause separately produces, is related to the sensation of the passion: From this double relation of ideas and impressions the passion is deriv'd" (p. 286). Division of the cause permits a double relation; this doubleness both reduces a monstrous variety and stabilizes what had been equivocal. System appears.

Systematization changes things. Hume can no longer say: "Here then is a passion plac'd betwixt two ideas, of which the one produces it, and the other is produc'd by it. The first idea, therefore, represents the *cause*, the second the *object* of the passion" (*T*, p. 278). There is no place in the diagram of the system where production occurs. The passion of pride cannot be the producer of its object, the idea of self, since that object must already be present to the mind in order for the necessary relation between it and the subject of the cause to transpire. By the same token the cause cannot be said to produce the effect. If Hume can say that the "quality, which operates on the passion, produces separately an impression resembling it" (p. 289), it does not seem possible for him to claim that the quality *causes* pride; the passion itself must somehow be there for there to be a resemblance. The diagram makes pride intelligible while finessing or perhaps abolishing the supposed necessity of a causal explanation. What "produces" pride (which has a place *in* the diagram but is also the only legitimate caption that we might place *under* the diagram) in Hume's text is the systematic *representation* of the passion. System seems to imitate or reflect, but system also constitutes.

Granted, Hume's system has problems; he will have to reformulate it repeatedly. But that is just the point. Problem follows problem in Hume's text—systematically unfolding a discourse that is always intelligible, if never definitive. System does not eliminate inconsistencies; it redistributes them, exploiting equivocal references as opportunities for further elaboration. In this instance we cannot point to any simple quality or impression that is pride or that causes it, but we can point to a schema which maps all the possible places where pride could appear. System is a way of anticipating the passion by representing it to oneself, much as the miser, Hume will argue (*T,* p. 314), enjoys his riches by his anticipation of the goods that they have power to obtain. The success of the systematization of pride is in the capacity of a set of representations justly to take the place of whatever we might feel.

That every passion is an articulable system expresses the irreducible sociality that disciplines every human feeling or wish.

> We can form no wish, which has not a reference to society. A perfect solitude is, perhaps, the greatest punishment we can suffer. Every pleasure languishes when enjoy'd a-part from company, and every pain becomes more cruel and intolerable. Whatever other passions we may be actuated by; pride, ambition, avarice, curiosity, revenge, or lust; the soul or animating principle of them all is sympathy; nor wou'd they have any force, were we to abstract entirely from the thoughts and sentiments of others. Let all the powers and elements of nature conspire to serve and obey one man: Let the sun rise and set at his command: The sea and rivers roll as he pleases, and the earth furnish spontaneously whatever may be useful or agreeable to him: He will still be miserable, till you give him some one person at least, with whom he may share his happiness, and whose esteem and friendship he may enjoy. (*T,* p. 363)

Hume, as we know, writes from experience. This image of the solitary as a lonely god—which evokes the Longinian sublime and anticipates Johnson's mad astronomer, Godwin's Falkland, and the spoiled deity of Byron's *Cain*—also recalls the Hume who reported to Dr. Arbuthnot his enchantment by the classical moralists. Invested with godlike powers, the solitary man, like the zealous Hume of that letter, could not fail to be overthrown by the greatness of his genius. Yet Hume's own experience founds a general syntax that, like the natural history of society in book 3, is used to preempt experience. Let us imagine a wish that seems not to refer to society, say the wish to be godlike; for Hume, to state the wish is to imagine the condition, which is to refer to the need for the social that would emerge as the flaw and as the remedy for the flaw in that self-sufficiency. Keep in mind that this is the wish of a man who, already in society, experiences the state of self-consummating commands only in his imagination. Hume offers the double consolation for the imaginary quality of that condition that if realized it would both make him miserable and refer him back to the social world *in which he is anyway.* The typical Humean moral is that getting what we want makes us miserable. Wishing, however, does not make us miserable, because every wish is embedded in a miniature narrative that gives it a harmlessly romantic character. The wish languidly expresses the uneasiness inherent in social life in order to reinscribe the individual within society, still unsatisfied but resigned to his uneasiness as a better lot than misery, which he need not experience because he has only been wishing. There is no "danger of any mistake" in forming a just idea of solitary pleasure.

Yet if the moral is that getting what we want would make us miserable, that moral cannot be formed without reference to something quite different from any of the Humean passions, whether wishing, being proud or humble, loving or hating. Hume's statement acknowledges a slippage between wishing and commanding that cannot quite be entirely effaced by its neat self-restraint. By painting the aspiration to command as a fantasy of omnipotence Hume displays his zeal to extirpate any belief in a form of action that realizes rather than refers wants, of any form of productivity that could be regarded as the power of the subject rather than simply a name for one of those relations that constitute subjectivity. That distortion marks the wishfulness of Hume's generalization about wishes—as though by characterizing commanding thus, he could by divine decree exile it from the republic of passions and actions that is regulated by the science of man.

This notion of command is a parodic heightening of the sign of aristocratic style and status which the bourgeois philosopher hopes to curtail by socialization and supersede by a more efficient form of imposition. For the bourgeois the ability to command can be imagined only as the addendum of a wish. Hume deploys this caricature of commanding much as he does the philosophical fiction of nature—bundling awkward and dangerous notions under the catchall rubric of the fictive in order that they can at once be recognized and disabled. Hume's notion of command reflects what Fredric Jameson calls the "commodification of labor power . . .[which made it] possible for the first time to separate the unique quality and concrete content of a particular activity from its abstract organization or end, and to study the latter in isolation."[1] Command is imagined as a labor that may create a world that is nothing more than the far end of abstraction. Similarly, command has been commodified for the bourgeois reader of Hume's text, who can easily experience it through his or her expression of a wish that makes possible possession but that defrauds possession of any concrete content. One knows command through the fulfillment of a wish and as wish fulfillment.

I have said that the place of "wish" in Hume's statement that "we

1. Fredric Jameson, *The Political Unconscious* (Ithaca: Cornell Univ. Press, 1981), p. 66.

can form no wish which has not a reference to society" could be filled by any passion or by "passion" itself. What makes such substitution possible is the conviction that the "animating principle" of all passions is sympathy. Sympathy gives life to the diagram; it makes Hume's social machine run. Sympathy is the "propensity" we have "to receive by communication [others'] inclinations and sentiments, however different from, or even contrary to our own" (*T,* p. 316). This propensity is shared by everyone as the disposition to communicate with anyone. To animate his diagram Hume adds only a ductility of conveyance and a liability to conversion: "'Tis indeed evident, that when we sympathize with the passions and sentiments of others, these movements appear at first in *our* mind as mere ideas, and are conceiv'd to belong to another person, as we conceive any other matter of fact. 'Tis also evident, that the ideas of the affections of others are converted into the very impressions they represent, and that the passions arise in conformity to the images we form of them" (p. 319).[2] Passions arise from images formed through simple conversion.

Hume would seem to have left ample room for mistake. How do we know that the passion which by virtue of our idea of it we conceive to belong to another person is in fact the passion that that person actually feels?[3] Hume's preferred answer, that we know it as well as we know any other "matter of fact," by the sort of probabilistic inferences we make every day, is not very satisfactory. For unlike most material facts, the passions that we perceive could be the effect of dissimulation. How do we know that the ideas of passions are authentic and not feigned as they are in the theater? The simple and, I think, decisive answer is that it does not make any difference one way or another. The case of the theater does not threaten Hume's model of sympathy because that model is fully theatrical; the "mind is a kind of theatre" (*T,* p. 253), and the theater is that place designed to enable the free exchange of simulated feelings. Hume never shows any interest in the way an actor forms his ideas or any concern for the actual presence or absence of the feelings represented. If he had attended to the problem, the ready and agreeable solution would have been that the actor, who is subject to the same mechanical operations of the spirit as everyone else, forms his ideas and his passions ac-

2. For Hume's practical application of this principle see the discussion of the tragic pleasure in "Of Tragedy." Ralph Cohen focuses on this aspect of Hume's tragic theory in "The Transformation of Passion: A Study of Hume's Theories of Tragedy," *Philological Quarterly* 41, no. 2 (1962): 450–64.

3. This problem impinges on the general issue of the reliability of evidence and the probability of signs. The fullest treatment of the subject is Douglas Lane Patey's *Probability and Literary form: Philosophic Theory and Literary Practice in the Augustan Age* (Cambridge: Cambridge Univ. Press, 1984), esp. pp. 35–74.

cording to the same process of sympathy by which he then communicates them to his audience.[4]

The theatrical metaphor does a lot of work for Hume. For example, our sense that the ideas of the affections "belong to another person" is clearly a conception of property. The conversion of that property, that idea, into my own impression looks like lawless exploitation of the "looseness and easy transition" of external goods. Sympathy is theft. Or would be theft were it not that every feeling occurs in a "kind of theatre." The sympathy by which we come to feel is legitimated and governed by theatrical convention, which, like the more general convention of society, allows for the expression of man's native avidity but forces it to reflect on itself. The theater, like sympathy at large, works as an implicit guarantor of property rights because appropriation conventionalized is not the theft of property but its transfer. Post-Cartesian representation of the passions contributed both to the stability of their possession and to the facility of their transfer in an exchange with another passion owner. That exchange occurs across the footlights: the audience receives the communicated passions of the actors, and the actors receive their *emotional* reward (or punishment) by sympathy with the audiences's response to *them*.[5] So is it in

4. On the return in the eighteenth century to an acting style based on mimicry, which presumes that "the actor does *not* in any significant degree take on the identity of the character he is imitating," see Jonas Barish, *The Antitheatrical Prejudice* (Berkeley and Los Angeles; Univ. of California Press, 1981), pp. 277–78. Mimicry still obtains when the basis is not behavior but an idea, as in the instructions of Aaron Hill, who trained actors according to the principles that, first, "imagination must conceive a *strong idea* of the passion" and that "that idea cannot *strongly* be conceived, without impressing its own form upon the muscles of the *face*," which cannot be done "without communicating, instantly, the same impression, to the muscles of the *body*," so that "the muscles of the body . . . must, in their natural, and not to be avoided consequence, by impelling or retarding the flow of animal spirits, transmit their own conceiv'd sensation, to the sound of the *voice*, and to the disposition of the *gesture*." "*An Essay on the Art of Acting*," *The Works of Aaron Hill*, 4 vols. (London: 1755), 3:356. David Garrick, the prototype of the actor who exercises a sympathetic imagination, extended mimicry, but it is doubtful that he transcended it. For a useful discussion of the transformations of acting theory and practice in the first half of the eighteenth century which insists on the radical innovation of Garrick, see George Winchester Stone, Jr., and George M. Kahrl, *David Garrick: A Critical Biography* (Carbondale: Southern Illinois Univ. Press, 1979), pp. 30–39. For an excellent discussion of the relationship between theatricality and sympathy, see David Marshall, "Adam Smith and the Theatricality of Moral Sentiments," *Critical Inquiry*, June 1984, pp. 592–613.

5. "A man, who enters the theatre, is immediately struck with the view of so great a multitude, participating of one common amusement; and experiences, from their very aspect, a superior sensibility or disposition of being affected with every sentiment which he shares with his fellow-creatures.

"He observes the actors to be animated by the appearance of a full audience, and raised

the theater of the world. There is no danger of mistake: every reading of another's feeling is an idea naturally converted into an impression, represented, returned; every interpretation is a reliable communication.

First mentioned in the section "Of the Love of Fame," sympathy does not receive Hume's direct attention again until section 5 of part 2, "Of Our Esteem for the Rich and Powerful." As Hume has shown in his earlier meditation on the nature of power, "riches and power" are indissolubly connected. There Hume picks his way through an argument that ties power to its exercise with the proviso that exercise is "either actual or probable, and that we consider a person as endow'd with any ability when we find from past experience, that 'tis probable, or at least possible, he may exert it" (*T,* p. 313). "Actual" exercise turns into probable exercise which, in turn, eases to the mere possibility of exercise. "Power" has become something to be possessed rather than to be deployed. Hence if men are convinced that there is no external inhibition on their exercise of power, "their imagination easily anticipates the satisfaction, and conveys the *same* joy as if they were persuaded of its real and actual existence." There is no need to exercise the power at all.

> A miser receives delight from his money; that is, from the *power* it affords him of procuring all the pleasures and conveniences of life, tho' he knows he has enjoy'd his riches for forty years without ever enjoying them; and consequently cannot conclude, by any species of reasoning, that the real existence of these pleasures is nearer, than if he were entirely depriv'd of all his possessions. But tho' he cannot form any such conclusion in a way of reasoning concerning the nearer approach of the pleasure, 'tis certain he *imagines* it to approach nearer, whenever all external obstacles are removed, along with the more powerful motives of interest and danger, which oppose it. (*T,* p. 314)

The figure of the miser seals the connection between riches and power. If the "very essence of riches consists in the power of procuring the pleasures and conveniences of life," and power means probability of exercise, and probability causes anticipation, and this "anticipation of pleasure is, in itself, a very considerable pleasure," then representation alone, without any reference to a reality but referring only to "itself" in the "double relation of impressions and ideas" has the capacity to "produce" all the satisfaction anyone could want. The gap between the representation,

---

to a degree of enthusiasm, which they cannot command in any solitary or calm moment" (*ECPM*, p. 44).

funded by the idea of wealth, and whatever reality to which it might be supposed to refer need never be crossed. Hume's lily of the field, the miser neither sows nor spins. Wealthy by definition, he does not labor to acquire riches. Passion can be satisfied by the imagination: "infinite riches in a little room."

The miser is a figure of capable imagination. In other contexts, such as a celebration of "the Delicacy of Taste and Passion," his self-sufficiency might be regarded as an unattainable goal of exquisite (and inexpensive) enjoyment (*ST,* p. 26). But in the *Treatise,* as in the essays on economics, his extraordinarily satisfying self-involvement is worrisome.[6] Given that Hume successfully explains why the miser does not exercise his power (spend his money), he has made it that much more difficult to understand why anyone should disburse gold when he could hoard it and still reap its advantages. From a perspective that we might call "mercantilist," the miser, who gets the most for least, is the most economic of all men; from a more liberal and enlightened perspective the miser is potentially the most diseconomic of all men: his refusal to circulate money stops the animating flow of exchange. We can, of course, easily imagine some restrictions on the miser's self-sufficiency. The model works only in the absence of any external inhibitions—a condition that will scarcely ever be found in reality. Moreover, although we would all like to be misers, the precondition of such pleasure is a fund of riches that most must labor to attain. In that respect, the miser is not only the supreme rhetorician who successfully persuades himself of his own satisfaction but a rhetorical ornament who induces our labor. Although diseconomic at the micro level of the circulation of capital, for Hume the miser is economic at a more general level because he excites the desire and mobilizes the activity of those who would like to have a correspondent security and power. He also serves who sits and counts.

Yet if the miser is not the man on the street, he nonetheless presents a serious challenge to the economy he sustains.[7] External inhibitions are by definition contingent; they entail no principle of self-restraint affecting

6. Cf. Hume's treatment of "hoarding" within the context of his hydraulics of international trade in "Of the Balance of Trade," G&G, pp. 340–41 (discussed in Chap. 5, below).

7. Classically. See, for example, Defoe's expressed preference for thieves, who are guilty only of "a wrong transferring of Riches" over misers, who "lock up the Tools of the Industrious." *Taxes no charge* (1690), pp. 15, 27, quoted in Joyce Oldham Appleby, *Economic Thought and Ideology in Seventeenth-Century England* (Princeton: Princeton Univ. Press, 1978), p. 210. Johnson's view, which Boswell paints as paradoxical, emphasizes the indubitable "influence" and authority of the miser on the opinions of others, which says much for a "practice of life" that is "philosophically" "contemptible." *Boswell's Journal of "A Tour to the Hebrides,"* ed. Frederick A. Pottle and Charles H. Bennett (New York: Literary Guild, 1936), p. 85.

the miser's self-fulfilling avidity. Indeed, cannot his anticipation be taken one step further? Why should imagination fly to possible goods and traverse the circuitous path of double relations when it can rest at home? If, as Hume repeatedly avers, the mind is naturally indolent, why should the miser put his imagination to work? Is it not likely that the miser will come to esteem his representations themselves, fall in love with his gold? The miser would seem to be that singular figure whose wishes need have no reference to society. As a creature the miser is afflicted with regressive desire; as a figure he afflicts Hume's arguments with regressive implications. For the miser in book 2 tropes the transported reader of the classical moralists that Hume had represented in the letter to Arbuthnot. He lives in a world of his own regulation. The crisis of a moral life that has no moral consequences is recapitulated by the problem of an economist who is diseconomic. Reader and miser are both smitten and exalted by representation. Hence we already know why the miser cannot be a figure of adequacy. Like the narcissist, like Hume, reader of Cicero, Seneca, and Plutarch, he will be overthrown by the greatness of his genius; he will get sick. There must be a disease of the hoarder as there is a disease of the learned. The miser slides naturally into misery.

Hume defers addressing the side effects of miserliness. Of immediate concern is the use to which that figure can be put by those who would like to be misers but lack the wherewithal. Sympathy is their remedy. This is because "riches and power alone, even tho' unemploy'd, naturally cause esteem and respect; and consequently these passions arise not from the idea of any beautiful or agreeable objects. 'Tis true; money implies a kind of representation of such objects, by the power it affords of obtaining them; and for that reason may still be esteem'd proper to convey those agreeable images, which may give rise to the passion. But as this prospect is very distant, 'tis more natural for us to take a contiguous object, *viz.* the satisfaction, which this power affords the person, who is possesst of it" (*T*, p. 359). The idea of money makes it possible for those without money of their own to form an idea of the satisfaction it brings and thereby to obtain sympathetically the same satisfaction as wealth affords the rich man. Not only, then, are goods unnecessary to the rich; money is unnecessary to everyone else for whom the rich man is the cynosure. Sympathy is wealth. Our ability to represent a possible satisfaction is the acquisition of satisfaction, since pleasure arises from the imagination's felicitous affection for reference. Sympathy remedies the diseconomic potential of the miser for the rest of society because it revises particular riches into a more general practice of representation. Contingency, which is squeezed out of the ideal instance of the miser, can, in the generalization of sympathy, be both recognized and regulated; society internalizes external inhibitions and accidents as the necessary and natural articulations of its continuous elaboration. In other words, the fixation and fetishism which are the mistakes endangering the *solitary* miser are protected against by the natural transition of persons who appear before us on the stage of society.

As a sympathetic observer, I stand in the same relation to the rich man's real wealth as the rich man stands toward whatever real goods his wealth might empower him to acquire. The capacity to represent to myself the satisfaction of a rich man is a power of satisfying myself equivalent to his. Riches are representations and representations are riches. The chiasmus emblematizes the specular apparatus Hume installs: "In general we may remark, that the minds of men are mirrors to one another, not only because they reflect each others emotions, but also because those rays of passions, sentiments and opinions may be often reverberated, and may decay away by insensible degrees. Thus the pleasure, which a rich man receives from his possessions, being thrown upon the beholder, causes a pleasure and esteem; which sentiments again, being perceiv'd and sympathiz'd with, encrease the pleasure of the possessor; and, being once more reflected, become a new foundation for pleasure and esteem in the beholder" (*T*, p. 365). There is nothing particular being reflected in these mirrors, these two minds beholding in reverberant esteem. The specularity involves no labor—sympathy does the work of work—nor does it anticipate any realizable good: it is a pure transaction of mutual profit. Hume's image represents the imaging of representation itself as a self-contained, animated system. It can stand for that ideal of effortless consummation which Hume vouchsafes to Arbuthnot: a mutuality of attention attendant upon neat and elegant representation. Yet if the apparatus which Hume represents here goes far in forcing the readjustment of our earlier characterization of that aim as savage narcissicism, it nonetheless suggests why Hume had to reject that aim as a possible model for his career. For, as Hume indicates, the reverberation of esteem is subject to "decay," an entropy opposed to the consummate tropism of sympathy. To be caught within the apparatus of reflection, no matter how indirectly satisfying it is, is to be subjected to a decay; and Hume's implicit rejection of the goal of a fixed dyad of attention for his writing is remarked on here by his distance from the mirroring apparatus he represents—a distance attained by his representation of the apparatus in his text as a theater of impressions.

"The mind is a kind of theatre, where several perceptions successively make their appearance; pass, re-pass, glide away, and mingle in an infinite variety of postures and situations" (*T*, p. 253). Gilles Deleuze is one among many who has rejected the metaphor of the theater as a contaminant in book 1. "We ought not," he writes, "respect the comparison of the theater," and he cites Hume's monitory addendum, which warns us not to be misled by the comparison, "for the successive perceptions only . . . constitute the mind; nor have we the most distant notion of the place, where these scenes are represented, or of the materials, of which it is compos'd."[8] John Richetti, who observes that "the analogy contains a hint of human steadiness, a spectator somehow apart from all that flux, moved and delighted in a precise manner by its various patterns," also notes "the logical contradiction," but persuasively argues that even the "retraction admits the possibility of imagining a scene and understanding the dramatic materials used in this theater. The image is a glimpse of a certain organization of experience that negates, at least in part, the severe naturalism of Hume's theory." Unlike Deleuze, who is attracted to the fluxional aspect of Hume's atomistic version of the mind and who is troubled less by the flaw in logic than by the organizing impulse it betrays, Richetti endorses Hume's disclosure here as representative of a literary posture that ironizes the scientific pretense that he indulges elsewhere in the *Treatise*. "In Hume as he asks to be read," Richetti comments, "writing is the ultimate and sure relation, providing almost in spite of his intentions as a thinker a perspective tending to stabilize or at least to ground in dependable rhetorical relationships the unruly perceptual relationships his thought so intensely explores."[9] Richetti's admirable sensitivity to Humean nuance, to the intention that is unintended, does not, however, solve anything; rather it merely substitutes another "clarifying image" for the one that Hume has equivocally advanced: Hume's "bundle of impressions" becomes Hume's "theater" becomes Richetti's "writing"—a complicitous enterprise of stabilizing a rhetorical relationship which enacts the instability it professes to correct. Writing, as Richetti understands it, cannot be the ultimate and sure relation, since that writing is itself staged within the theater or the composition that is the *Treatise*.

The claim to know how Hume asks to be read accepts Hume's invitation to "suppose we cou'd see clearly into the breast of another, and observe that succession of perceptions, which constitutes his mind or thinking principle" (*T,* p. 260). One can "see" into the breast of another in order to determine an ultimate and final relation only by virtue of a sympathy that presupposes that one is simultaneously being seen. Ri-

8. Gilles Deleuze, *Empirisme et subjectivité: Essai sur la nature humaine selon Hume* (Paris: Presses Universitaires de France, 1953), p. 3.
9. John J. Richetti, *Philosophical Writing* (Cambridge: Harvard Univ. Press, 1983), p. 222.

chetti's claim for the dependability of Hume's rhetoric and his mastery over his writing suggests a complication of that reflection—Hume can see his being seen—but no break with it. To posit some form of direct, stable relation topples one into indirection; writing always comes back to a version of spectatorship. To imagine a Hume who asks us to read him in a certain way means accepting the view of passion and property that Hume enforces and to find oneself trapped within the apparatus of the sympathetically reverberant mirrors that Hume represents in book 2.

To read Hume as he does *not* ask to be read is to notice the asymmetry that emerges in such passages as the mirror image and the theater conceit. Obviously, someone or something must stand outside of the mirroring apparatus in order to describe its operation; just as clearly, there must be someone observing the relations between spectators and actors in the theater in order to register the affiliation of their passions; and there must be an "I" in the mind to observe or attend to the "production" of the object self from the passion of pride.[10] But such points are not particularly telling; the reader can always match up with and correspond to that notional observer, whether characterized as philosopher or writer, by imaginatively assuming his place within the designated terrain. But if that terrain (and its indefinite extensions) is not to be considered as a simple imitation of some paradigmatic reality, it must have been designed. The apparatus of mirroring must have been constructed and installed, and by a designer who, unlike the god of Cleanthes in the *Dialogues Concerning Natural Religion*, is *not* entailed as just another inference, a god or writer who would finally be a feature of the system he supposedly produced, and who would look just like us. The asymmetry of Hume's relation to his text and the mind, society, or theater it represents inheres in the necessity of postulating a designer who allows us no direct relation with him, who is separated from his construction by a cut that is the condition of its composition and the undependable technique of his mastery; that cut insures that all stable relations are merely rhetorical means of persuading us that we are in harmony with him, can see into his breast.

I say "merely rhetorical" because the mereness of rhetoric as a form of influence hangs on the vulnerability of that tropism to the entropy of "decay." Unless we deny that decay is possible, that a reality more severe than any naturalism that Hume represents is in force, is going on right now, even though it cannot be represented, someone offstage has to take responsibility for imposing new metaphors, new compositions that will

10. See Daniel C. Dennett on Hume's "notorious non-solution to the problem of self-reflexive representations" in *Brainstorms: Philosophical Essays on Mind and Psychology* (Montgomery, Vt.: Bradford Books, 1978), pp. 101–2.

remedy the inevitable wearing away of the persuasiveness of any particular performance. Someone has to protect us from reality. Richetti is doubtless right in rejecting the naive reading of the *Treatise* which discovers "'expressions of metaphysical agony'" in such spectacular passages as the section on personal identity in book 1; but to replace the existential with ironic literary mastery is to domesticate a project that stakes its power not in shadow conflict with a staged disorder but against the real, which is simply everything that would undo Hume's project and which therefore makes it necessary for it to be done and done again: "An evil may be real, tho' its cause has no relation to us: It may be real, without being peculiar: it may be real without shewing itself to others: It may be real, without being constant: And it may be real, without falling under the general rules" (*T,* p. 294).[11] What Hume says of the real can be said of the composer of the narrative of Hume's writings. "Hume" is the name for that practice which is always out ahead of our reading of the *Treatise* as its composer but which is at any point always able to convince us that in us he has met his match in sensibility and ironic subtlety.

At stake here is the problem of Hume's humanism, never more trenchantly put than by Theodor Adorno:

> Hume, whose work bears witness in every sentence to his real humanism, yet who dismisses the self as a prejudice, expresses in this contradiction the nature of psychology as such. In this he even has truth on his side, for that which posits itself as "I" is indeed mere prejudice, an ideological hypostasization of the abstract centres of domination, criticism of which demands the removal of the ideology of "personality." But its removal also makes the residue all the easier to dominate.[12]

The dark irony for Adorno, which is part of the dialectic of enlightenment, is that this move beyond humanism, in the name and style of humanism, against that which dominates the human, makes what is left after the demolition a "residue all the easier to dominate." One cannot just recover the self that with whatever imprudence has been disposed of—or if one can, one can do so only within the precincts of the theatrical metaphor and according to a rhetorical staging, which may render the "I" as literary but at the same time exposes the literary as something more than "moral qualification," as a newly minted ideological hypostatization

11. Even this admission of a reality that is unrepresentable (it is something that does not show itself to others) defends against such a reality by persuasively defining it as an evil.

12. Theodor Adorno, *Minima Moralia: Reflections from Damaged Life*, trans. E.F.N. Jephcott (London: Verso, 1978), p. 64. Although we differ in our interpretations, I am indebted to John Richetti's suggestion of the pertinence of Adorno (*Philosophical Writing*, p. 236).

of the center of domination that is all the more powerful by virtue of its appropriation of a discourse humanistic in every sentence.

Hume's ideal is "the system from which all and everything follows." [13] The literary is not a qualification of Hume's system, too narrowly defined as a mechanistic, associationist epistemology, but is an elaboration of it, that which follows from the purposive contradictions, from every inconsistency, of the mechanical model. We have to think in stages and recognize in Hume an embedded and quite particular system (association) in which everything follows, a more general system (mechanics) from which everything (the literary) follows, and the most general system, which contains the mechanistic model and whatever might follow from it. Any level that can be directly examined cannot be the final level of the system but merely a stage from which something else can follow, though (and here is where I differ with Adorno's characterization of Hume) not in a dialectical manner which generates contradictions and suffers or inflicts ironies, but in a narrative sequence which merely affects irony to charm the ironic. What follows the breakdown of the mechanism is a literary control. That adjustment is made possible by a prevenient Hume who disposes the system but who cannot be directly examined or represented. If we consider the *Treatise* as a text defecated of any substantial "I," we can understand it as a residue—nuanced, articulated, inconsistent, full of opportunities for sympathy—all the easier to dominate.

The most convenient way to illustrate this Humean usage is to look at how he stages eight "Experiments to Confirm this System" in the extraordinary section 2, part 2 of book 2, which more than anywhere else in the *Treatise* justifies calling Hume a "physicist of emotions." [14] Each "experiment" is a marvel of Humean dexterity, beginning with a hypothesis which is then narratively tested against an "experience" that makes "evident" its soundness. By the fourth experiment the schema has been established. The reader could, Hume concedes, pursue his solitary way; "reason alone may convince us, without any farther experiment." "But," Hume adds, "to leave as little room for doubt as possible, let us renew our experiments." It is as if a kind of absolutist ambition to smother all doubt, to drive out any possibility of reason alone impells Hume to a virtuosic display of his mastery:

13. An ideal attributed to the Enlightenment in general by Max Horkheimer and Theodor W. Adorno, *Dialectic of Enlightenment*, trans. John Cumming (New York: Seabury, 1972), p. 7.

14. Jerome Neu, *Emotion, Thought, Therapy: A Study of Hume and Spinoza and the Relationship of Philosophical Theories of the Emotions to Psychological Theories of Therapy* (Berkeley and Los Angeles: Univ. of California Press, 1977), p. 1.

That I may be sure I am not mistaken in this experiment, I remove first one relation; then another; and find, that each removal destroys the passion, and leaves the object perfectly indifferent. But I am not content with this. I make a still farther trial; and instead of removing the relation, I only change it for one of a different kind. I suppose the virtue to belong to my companion, not to myself; and observe what follows from this alteration. I immediately perceive the affections to wheel about, and leaving pride, where there is only one relation, *viz.* of impressions, fall to the side of love, where they are attracted by a double relation of impressions and ideas. By repeating . . . [and] changing anew . . . I bring . . . ; and by a new repetition, I again place. . . . Being fully convinc'd . . . , I try the effects of the other; and by changing . . . , convert. . . . The effect still answers expectation. . . . To continue . . . I change anew . . . , and suppose. . . . What follows? What is usual. A subsequent change. . . . This . . . I convert . . . by a new change . . . ; and find, after all, that I have compleated the round, and have by these changes brought back the passion to that very situation in which I first found it. (*T,* pp. 336–37)

Even without the ellipses the passage is a parody of Hume's procedure in the *Treatise.* Springing from the reasonable, it plunges us into a whirl of changes which, like the narrative revisions in the natural history of society, only return us again and again to where we began. The nakedness of the pretense to be conducting an actual experiment, performed before our eyes, is ostentatious. If an experiment is a way to anticipate real experience of the passions by controlled representation, this rendition belies any possibility of reference to experience by a manipulation of representations that in its velocity (which my ellipses only accentuate) outstrips any possibility of referential orientation. In a passage on the passions we do not know what to feel.[15] But we notice that one point of orientation remains constant amidst the whirl—the "I" which remains unmoved through all the vicissitudes of passion. And the recognition of that constancy, whenever it occurs, coincides with the discovery of the literariness of all this: that Hume is not so much conducting an experiment as displaying the *rhetoric* of experimentalism. That discovery is the

15. Compare the more famous staging of this in the section "Of Personal Identity": "Where am I, or what? From what causes do I derive my existence, and to what condition shall I return? Whose favour shall I court, and whose anger must I dread? . . . I am confounded with all these questions, and begin to fancy myself in the most deplorable condition imaginable, environed with the deepest darkness, and utterly deprived of the use of every member and faculty" (*T,* pp. 253–54).

occasion of a move much like the one Thomas Weiskel has assigned to the negative or reader's sublime; we convert humility into pride by sympathizing with the control over the properties not of the passions but of language.[16] *I* acquire control by troping *authorial* control as the secret referent, the meaning of the experience. The place I return to is "I," which I imagine as the equivalent to Hume. Or so the story might run.

Submission to control feels like the acquisition of control. At our best we do not produce a reading but reproduce in our imagination a being written, an idea that is always the property of David Hume. This kind of reading inevitably works to the advantage of Hume. Not only does it certify his mastery as writer, but it does so in a natural—that is Humean—fashion, because it appears to rely only on our propensity to associate. Hume's text makes it practically impossible to produce a reading that is not in some guise or another a reproduction, that does not ratify his philosophy or reify his writing, that does not come back to the same old prejudices. This is what Horkheimer and Adorno call the "totalitarianism" of the Enlightenment: "Its untruth does not consist in what its romantic enemies have always reproached it for: analytical method, return to elements, dissolution through reflective thought, but instead in the fact that for enlightenment the process is always decided from the start. When in mathematical procedure the unknown becomes the unknown quantity of the equation, this marks it as well-known even before any value is inserted."[17] Process is already product. Writing is already a composition. Moral qualification is the systematic insertion of value into an equation designed to admit a multiplicity of adjustments.

"Hume" is a considerably less global abstraction than "Enlightenment." But focus on Hume is justified at least in part by his endeavor to compose a career that would convincingly impersonate the Enlightenment, that would take advantage of the machine.[18] There is, however, sufficient reason even in Horkheimer and Adorno's concept of the insertion of value. Mathematical procedure as imagined by the Enlightenment is a machine for propagating the well-known under the guise of discovering the unknown; although everything is virtually decided from the outset, elaboration of the system requires both the idea of the unknown and the insertion of value, if only to give the appearance of something being learned, changed, or settled. The notion of "decay" in the specular

16. Thomas Weiskel, *The Romantic Sublime: Studies in the Structure and Psychology of Transcendence* (Baltimore: Johns Hopkins Univ. Press, 1976), pp. 23–29.

17. Horkheimer and Adorno, *Dialectic of Enlightenment*, p. 24.

18. Cf. Horkheimer and Adorno: "Thinking objectifies itself to become an automatic, self-activating process; an impersonation of the machine that it produces itself so that ultimately the machine can replace it" (*Dialectic of Enlightenment*, p. 25).

apparatus of sympathy, like the appearance of "chance or secret causes" in Hume's investigation of the rise of the arts, describes just such an idea of the unknown. That it is subject to decay would seem to be a real weakness in the apparatus; but it is the presupposition of Hume's composition that decay, like chance, is a quantity, has "some measure." Its appearance (which cannot be perceived by any participant in the sympathetic transaction) is the opportunity for the remedial insertion of value by a supervisory figure who turns the "unknown," which may be regarded as a potential threat to the system, into its functional articulation. From the point of view of the supervisor the decay of reflection marks his cognitive advantage, technical opportunity, and social privilege.[19] Although supervision is built into the system of representation that Hume describes, not everyone can be a supervisor of that system for reasons that divide between the structural and the economic. Structurally, the process of preemption requires a position that is advantageous in relation to all others. Economically, the position of supervisor, like all other desirable attributes, is restricted by the principle of scarcity, which makes nature impossible and which motivates the deflection of desire from goods to riches to representations.

But representations are themselves scarce. The term that supervenes over that scarcity is "fame." Though nominally the subject of its own section, fame as such receives little attention; it is squeezed in between the analysis of sympathy and an analytical narrative of the case of "men of good families, but narrow circumstances [who] leave their friends and country" (*T*, p. 322). In what he says about fame Hume seems most interested in developing it as a reciprocal relation between the praised and the praiser: "We receive a much greater satisfaction from the approbation of those whom we ourselves esteem and approve of, than of those whom we hate and despise" (p. 321). In this light fame is hardly distinguishable from the kind of general esteem that arouses pride. But Hume indicates that love of fame is more discriminating than pride: "The praises of others never give us much pleasure, unless they concur with our own opinion, and extol us for those qualities, in which we chiefly excel. A mere soldier little values the character of eloquence: A gownman of courage: A bishop of humor: Or a merchant of learning." Approbation in general becomes reputation in particular by its connection with qualities which are ascribed

19. For another version of how a corruption, theoretically destructive or unknown, is quantified and put to use for the benefit of all according to the technique of a few, see Hume's discussion of "unphilosophical probability" in the *Treatise* (pp. 144–46), where he employs the metaphor of the printing press in order both to acknowledge the inevitability of decay and to render that decay functional to the continual reproduction of texts. The passage is discussed in Chapter 5 below.

to an individual according to the type of his profession. Characters are scarce, and it is the concern of each man to acquire that which should properly belong to him. A happy distribution depends, of course, on the indifference of individuals to characters which are not apportioned to their position; such reputations might be valueless or damaging: for example, a reputation for humor might very well do the bishop active harm.

When in the next paragraph Hume takes up the case of "men of good families, but narrow circumstances [who] leave their friends and countries," however, he shifts his attention from the strength of ascriptive ties, probable signs. "We shall be unknown, say they, where we go. No body will suspect from what family we are sprung. We shall be remov'd from all our friends and acquaintance, and our poverty and meanness will by that means sit more easy upon us" (*T,* p. 322). This passage is the equivalent in Hume of the Cartesian reduction—here, however, social rather than epistemological, in which the exile, all but posthumous in the death of every natural connection, discards all character and declasses himself in order to protect himself from contempt.[20] By concealing "his birth from those among whom he lives," hiding his "pretensions to a better fortune," and taking up "mechanical employments," the exile adjusts that character *given* to him by his family in order to *devise* a character which he can present to strangers and which, if successfully contrived, "must contribute very much to his ease and satisfaction." Hume writes from experience. His own journey from Ninewells, first to Bristol, and then to provincial Reims, parallels this tale, with the important exception that Hume left a family which was not itself narrowly circumstanced, although one in which *he* as second son was provided only with slender means. Hume does not say what usually follows upon exile and ignominy. But it would seem that if the scarcity of wealth narrows circumstance, the general scarcity of characters presents an opportunity to the straitened. "The wily solitary is already *homo oeconomicus*"; radical alienation means radical socialization.[21] Because there is no longer a character proper to him the exile can be at ease with any and all reputations: courage, eloquence, learning, and humor. The more the better. His wealth is an array of representations of the self. Though he pursues "mechanical employments," he is not a

---

20. My use of "Cartesian" is not intended to imply that Descartes is exempt from social causes. For a sociological consideration of the basis of the Cartesian reduction see Albert William Levi's chapter on Descartes in his *Philosophy as Social Expression* (Chicago: Univ. of Chicago Press, 1974), pp. 163–230.

21. The quotation is from Horkheimer and Adorno, *Dialectic of Enlightenment,* p. 61; the formula is the converse of their proposition that "radical socialization means radiacl alienation" (p. 62).

mechanical, however much he is disguised; "mechanical employments" is a generalized and generalizing activity of tactical indirection adopted in place of that lot which nature supplied him, as it has supplied courage or cowardice to the soldier, prudence or folly to the merchant. Out of scarcity the exile can mechanically compose a man of many parts; he can manage his relations with strangers by presenting a character that is proper to each, a stimulus to sympathy—eloquence to bishops, learning to gownmen. The exile is prepared to compose the kind of life that will make possible an autobiography like Hume's "My Own Life." By his composition of himself into a social man of articulate characters, the exile can hope to amass disparate reputations into the symbolic capital of universal fame, to return from his foreign adventure as a man of letters, that figure who has all the properties so scarcely distributed among his fellow men. If not all things to all men, the man of letters is more things to more men than is anyone else. The exile is the one figure in the *Treatise*, excepting the miser, who does not find solitude miserable, but instead finds it a source of ease and satisfaction. Like the miser, he is a figure of exemption, in part accomplished by a strategic position and a tactical facility that permit him to "raise what speculations [he pleases] upon others" and in part owed to a scarcity of representations that enables him to imagine his satisfaction.[22]

Hume's advance in book 2 involves a gradual abandonment of the systematic rigor of his model of the passions and an adjustment to circumstances which sociably enacts for his reader the accommodations that all of us have to make in order to preserve some kind of balance. That such adjustments need to be made and are being made all the time goes without saying. But there is a difference between saying what goes without saying and merely leaving it unsaid. The advance to the kind of complications that disable systematic models but that do not paralyze our passionate life in society allows us in retrospect to see that the dispensation from "any danger of mistake" in forming a "just idea" of the passions predicates not the absence of mistake (Hume makes all kinds of them) but the absence of danger. No idea we form will have any consequences on the passions that affect us; any idea will be just because it will in due

---

22. Joseph Addison, *The Spectator* no. 131, ed. George A. Aitken, 8 vols. (London: John C. Nimmo, 1898), 2:269. I have tried to paint as benign a version of this robinsonade as Hume could desire. But it ought to be noticed that though Hume ostentatiously discounts the significance of real property and family name, their importance can be registered immediately by comparing Hume's fantasy with William Godwin's story of Caleb Williams, a character who has nothing but curiosity, knowledge, and technical capacity—none of which are sufficient to save him from the options of obliteration or mechanization.

course have to be adjusted to respect if not explain those vicissitudes that elude explicit ideation. Mistake is built into the system. In the course of book 2 Hume delineates what Pierre Bourdieu calls a "field of opinion," and the failure of his system prepares for the yielding of the systematic to "doxa," that which goes without saying. Hume's success consists in his ability to render the narrow field of opinion impotent before the immense realm of doxa in which we carry on our everyday practices, according to whatever "cultural habit" or "custom." The misfirings of the system do not suggest the need for a new model but induce a practical evaluation of the irrelevance of any model or opinion on the operation of the passions. "Unlike the estimation of probabilities which science constructs method-ically on the basis of controlled experiments from data established accord-ing to precise rules, practical evaluation of the likelihood of the success of a given action in a given situation brings into play a whole body of wisdom, sayings, commonplaces, ethical precepts ('that's not for the likes of us') and, at a deeper level, the unconscious principles of the *ethos* which, being the product of a learning process dominated by a determi-nate type of objective regularities, determines 'reasonable' and 'un-reasonable' conduct for every agent subjected to those regularities." Bour-dieu caps that Humean statement with an axiom from the *Treatise:* "'We are no sooner acquainted with the impossibility of satisfying any desire . . . than the desire itself vanishes.'"[23] The kind of home truths about the passions that Hume encounters in establishing his rule for the pas-sions expose the limitations of rationalistic discourse and deflect him into a "literary" discourse of sayings and analogies which affirm that the pas-sions go without saying. He practices what all of us practice. Theory or rule or system may have no consequences on practice, but the strategic representation of theory's impotence does systematically inculcate the in-evitability of a return to practice.

Reading the *Treatise* is a course in learned ignorance. That "habitus" or "immanent law, *lex insita,* [which] is laid down in each agent by his earliest upbringing, which is the precondition not only for the co-ordination of practices but also for practices of co-ordination" is laid down again by Hume.[24] The *Treatise* is that text where we can all but see Hume taking the responsibility for saying what goes without saying and doing so as he draws, *in order* to draw the line between the field of opinions and doxa, diminishing the former into a manipulation of irrelevant diagrams, and expanding the latter to include the whole range of human behavior.[25]

---

23. Pierre Bourdieu, *An Outline of a Theory of Practice,* trans. Richard Nice (Cambridge: Cambridge Univ. Press, 1979), p. 77. Bourdieu quotes from *T,* p. xviii.

24. Bourdieu, p. 81

25. Compare the doctrine of one of Hume's more ferocious pupils, Edmund Burke: "It

The difference between Hume and any reader of Hume is that although we share the same habits, dependent on the same doxa, only Hume can be responsible for drawing the line between the arbitrary and the natural and for persuading us of the naturalness of that line. The difference, I would claim, is the best account of the effectiveness of "a theory of justice [or art or economics] which remains fairly close to common sense belief."[26] All of us, including Hume, adjust to circumstances; but only Hume as the composer of this text is capable of the adjustment of the circumstances in which subsequent adjustment will occur.

If there is a danger of mistake for Hume, it would seem to lie in the evident redundancy of his representation of what goes without saying. But like the irony which Horkheimer and Adorno discover in Hume's dialectic of enlightenment, this supplementarity does not simply befall Hume (although it may in time be his undoing); he accepts it as he accepts the burden of persuasiveness, as intrinsic to his project. Indeed, this redundancy is what gives him the possibility of a project, the capacity to identify his scheme with the model, to transform what is perceived as a "retrospective necessity" by everyone else into a "prospective necessity" for himself.[27] The mechanical employment by which Hume acquires fame is a variety of what Bourdieu calls "*officializing strategies*, the object of which is to transmute 'egoistic,' private, particular interests . . . into disinterested, collective, publicly avowable legitimate interests." It enables him to augment the "capital of authority necessary to impose a definition of the situation, especially in the moments of crisis when the collective judgment falters [and] to be able to mobilize the group by solemnizing, officializing, and thus universalizing private incident."[28]

In part, the hazard of explicitness in drawing the line between the field of opinion and doxa is justified as necessary to avoid a greater hazard; danger of mistake is substituted for the greater perils suggested in the various metaphors of conflict that percolate throughout book 2, most having to do with the "combat between reason and passion," and all implicitly preceded by a dismissive "supposed." Hume risks explicitness in order to show not only that passion "wins" the combat with reason (as society wins over nature) but also that the combat is really no conflict at

---

cannot at this time be too often repeated; line upon line; precept upon precept; until it comes into the currency of a proverb, *to innovate is not to reform.*" "Letter to a Noble Lord," *The Selected Writings of Edmund Burke*, ed. W. J. Bate (Random House: New York, 1960), p. 497.

26. David Miller, *Philosophy and Ideology in Hume's Political Thought* (Oxford: Oxford Univ. Press, 1981), p. 96.

27. Bourdieu, *Outline*, p. 9.

28. Ibid., p. 40.

all (nature is a philosophical fiction): reason cannot oppose passion; indeed, what we call reason is, except for a fairly specialized faculty responsible for judging the accuracy of abstract propositions, actually a "calm passion." What was supposed to be in opposition to passion turns out to be a modification of passion—those original existences which cannot be opposed. Reason—that name for a field of opinion where practices are contested, sides are taken, where the arbitrariness of all we know and do might be taken as an issue—is explicitly engaged in order to include it once and for all within the regulative boundaries of a doxa in which there is no danger of mistake.

If "crisis" seems too strong a characterization for anything that happens in the *Treatise* (crisis having been deftly assigned its place in the Conclusion of book 1), it is because of Hume's success in transforming all hazard into mere mistake (an unknown that is a quantity and for which a value can be inserted) and in persuading us that there is no danger of that. Emblematic are the comparisons of the passions of hunting and gaming with the passions of philosophy in the last section of book 2. Hume observes that the "idea of utility" is requisite to the pleasure that one takes in hunting:

> A man of the greatest fortune, and the farthest remov'd from avarice, tho' he takes a pleasure in hunting after partridges and pheasants, feels no satisfaction in shooting crows and magpies; and that because he considers the first as fit for the table, and the other as useless. Here 'tis certain, that the utility or importance of itself causes no real passion, but is only requisite to support the imagination. . . . To make the parallel betwixt hunting and philosophy more compleat, we may observe, that, tho' in both cases the end of our action may in itself be despis'd, yet, in the heat of the action, we acquire such an attention to this end, that we are very uneasy under any disappointments, and are very sorry when we either miss our game, or fall into any error in our reasoning. (*T,* p. 452)

The conceit of the hunter (as of the gambler, which follows) is a revision of and answer to the figure of the miser. At one level, it shows that the very rich, though free of avarice, will always find something to do besides fingering their gold. At another, Hume uses the conceit to figure philosophy as an aristocratic activity which fancies utility as an incentive to pleasure. One hunts for the sport. And part of the sport is missing one's target now and then.

Hume's gambit is even clearer in the gaming conceit:

> The pleasure of gaming arises not from interest alone; since many leave a sure gain for this entertainment: Neither is it deriv'd from

the game alone; since the same persons have no satisfaction, when they play for nothing. . . .

The interest, which we have in any game, engages our attention, without which we can have no enjoyment, either in that or in any other action. Our attention being once engag'd, the difficulty, variety, and sudden reverses of fortune, still farther interests us; and 'tis from that concern our satisfaction arises. . . . And this pleasure is here encreas'd by the nature of the objects, which, being sensible, and of a narrow compass, are enter'd into with facility, and are agreeable to the imagination. (*T*, p. 452)

Gaming is entertaining because it is risky. But the risk is carefully calculated. One knows what one's chances are. Knowing what one's chances are does not, of course, make them any better: there is no insurance that one will win at roulette, hit a partridge, or deliver a pretty truth. But the real calculation of risk pertains not to the compass of the roulette wheel that one employs in gambling but to the boundary that the draftsman of society draws in order to encompass both the gaming as an "entertainment" and the imagination that takes pleasure in it. For Hume the fact that I play is an unequivocal sign that I can afford to lose, that there is no danger in mistake.[29]

The comparisons with hunting and gaming acquaint us with the ab-

---

29. It is this emphasis on security that explains how Hume, who abhorred stockjobbing (see "Of Public Credit" and the discussion in Chapter 5 below) could endorse gambling, a practice that had been conventionally associated with reckless financial speculation in attacks on Walpole and Walpolians. See, for example, Pope's *Epistle to Bathurst*. For remarks on the associations made between Whig policies, gambling, and speculation in eighteenth-century satire, see Vincent Caretta, *The Snarling Muse* (Philadelphia: Univ. of Pennsylvania Press, 1983), p. 74. P.G.M. Dickson explores the connections between the boom in stockjobbing and the prodigious increase in gambling of all kinds in his *The Financial Revolution in England: A Study in the Development of Public Credit, 1688–1756* (New York: St. Martin's, 1967), pp. 491–92 and 497. Hume's gambling conceit identifies a safely middle-class aristocracy. See George Bataille: "In the market economy, the processes of exchange have an acquisitive sense. Fortunes are no longer placed on a gambling table; they have become relatively stable. It is only to the extent that stability is assured and can no longer be compromised by even considerable losses that those losses are submitted to the regime of unproductive expenditure." Bataille, "The Notion of Expenditure," in *Visions of Excess: Selected Writings, 1927–1939*, ed. and trans. Allan Stoekl (Minneapolis: Univ. of Minnesota Press, 1985), p. 123. To attempt to deny the ruinous possibilities inherent in gaming is coincident with Hume's implicit aim of repudiating the savage connotations of the association of philosophy with hunting as glossed by Michel Serres: "For Plato and a tradition which lasted throughout the classical age, knowledge is a hunt. To know is to put to death—to kill the lamb deep in the woods, in order to eat it. Moving from combat with prey outside the species to killing inside the species, knowledge now becomes military, a martial art. It is then more than a game; it is, literally, a strategy. These epistemologies are not innocent: at the critical tribunal they are calling for executions. They are policies promulgated by military

sence of crisis by suggesting that the writing of philosophy presupposes "very great wealth." Wealth, like fame, is created out of metaphor, by virtue of representation; it is a symbolic capital, induced by mimesis, but capital nonetheless. This wealth goes without saying, as the capital presupposed by any saying at all—or at least any saying that is in no danger of mistake. Also left unsaid, however, are alternate possibilities. What do we call a man who shoots birds, any kind of bird, in order to put food on the table? And what do we call a man who shoots birds, all kinds of birds, perhaps never missing, and leaves them to rot where they fall? Or the man who gambles in order to acquire what he can obtain in no other way? Or the man who gambles past ruin, offering up for his stake notes that are the ghosts of a vanished fortune? None of those forms of behavior fit within Hume's versions of gaming and hunting because each involves a crisis that has been definitively excluded from those activities, as crisis has been written out of the official version of philosophy that Hume proposes. Yet crisis, like the real, it goes without saying, is there.[30]

We shall find a suggestion of that crisis by turning from the indirect passions to the direct, which are summarily treated by Hume in the penultimate section of book 2. The sequence of indirect to direct, odd at first glance, makes good sense. The direct passions are themselves not actually direct. They are merely derived in a less complicated fashion than passions like pride and humility or love and hatred. Indeed, the sequence of Hume's discussion encourages the impression that in some way the direct is derived from the indirect. And though there is no principle in the mind that would allow us to convert such an impression into a just idea, it does not seem irresponsible to speculate that the *derivativeness* of a passion like desire is itself derived from the demonstration of the moral philosopher's ability to explain so much by paths of indirection. Hume cannot mean "original existence" at the point in the *Treatise* (p. 415) where he makes the claim, since it is clear by that point that passions are derived.

Yet the discussion is not seamless. Hume first distinguishes joy and sorrow from hope and fear according to the degree any good or evil is probable; then he turns to desire:

---

strategists. To know is to kill." *Hermes*, trans. Josue V. Harari and David F. Bell (Baltimore: Johns Hopkins Univ. Press, 1982), p. 28. It goes without saying that Hume's denial of murderous intent is part of his strategy of knowledge.

30. "If there is a separate field in which no one can keep cards up his sleeve without being resoundingly defeated, it is certainly mathematics. Let no one enter here is he is an illusionist. Inversely, all philosophy, all discourse, all texts which avoid this field keep some elbow room to cheat *ad infinitum* and to seem to everyone never to be mistaken. The criterion of truth is used at the risk of error" (Serres, *Hermes*, p. 111).

DESIRE arises from good consider'd simply, and AVERSION is deriv'd from evil. The WILL exerts itself, when either the good or the
absence of the evil may be attain'd by any action of the mind or
body.

Besides good and evil, or in other words, pain and pleasure,
the direct passions frequently arise from a natural impulse or instinct, which is perfectly unaccountable. Of this kind is the desire
of punishment to our enemies, and of happiness to our friends; hun-
ger, lust, and a few other bodily appetites. These passions, properly
speaking, produce good and evil, and proceed not from them, like
the other affections.

None of the direct affections seem to merit our particular attention, except hope and fear. (*T*, p. 439)

The definition of desire, the basis of all the direct passions, is followed
by an afterthought; Hume mentions another sort of direct passion in another mode "besides" that he is examining. At a loss to derive this passion
besides passion, Hume attributes it to an instinct which, however, is
"perfectly unaccountable." "Of this kind is the desire . . . and a few other
bodily appetites": desire returns as an *example* of the passions besides
passions, but it is hard to credit the generic gesture: could joy or hope or
anything that measures probabilities, anything that is not desire be imagined to have the power that Hume here admits? The passions besides
passions are the desire besides desire—a desire that displaces the direct
passion of desire by instantiating a desire that is irreversible. The direct
passion of desire is reversible because it is derived: consider a good, and
you will desire; consider a good impossible, and you will no longer desire;
replace the good with an evil, and desire becomes aversion. Because the
passion besides passion does not consider good and evil but produces
them, it cannot be acquainted with the impossibility of satisfaction; because it shortcuts the imagination, it can learn nothing. Aversion is not
the opposite of desire but a desire itself. Desire here names the whole
field of passions besides passions, but not as its generic name—rather, as
the name for that which cannot be named because it is not nominal. It is
the term for a dispersed plenitude of particular desires or bodily appetites
that cannot be accounted for, that have no relations to any objects, no
properties. Parsimony yields an indefiniteness for which it cannot account. And for a moment Hume concedes a monstrous heap of desires.
But this phenomenon does not merit our attention because it allows for
no derivation; it cannot be narrated except as what it is not, a lacuna after
which the narrative proper starts up again, our attention turned to what is
of value. To waste time thinking about a productive desire would be a
dangerous mistake.

If our excursus through the passions cannot be said to have made it any easier to imagine an "original existence" which "contains not any representative quality," perhaps it has clarified how equivocation about original existences works to Hume's advantage. He profits in the limits of our imagination by enlisting our sympathy in a project of indirection that advances by a series of remedial adjustments towards a kind of success. Hume's practice here supplants another kind of approach aimed not at remedy but at cure, at closing the "small Distance betwixt me & perfect Health." In a letter to Henry Home a fortnight after the publication of the *Treatise* Hume is explicit about what kind of success this would be: "My principles are also so remote from all the vulgar sentiments on the subject, that were they to take place, they would produce almost a total alteration in philosophy: and you know, revolutions of this kind are not easily brought about" (*HL*, 1:26). After Copernicus, Newton. After Newton, Hume.[31] This revolutionary version of success, which views philosophical writing as neither description nor persuasion but as the instantiation of principles that could *take* place and powerfully "*produce* almost a total alteration in philosophy," seems to eschew indirection for a direct action of the sort only paralleled in the *Treatise* by those orphaned versions of the direct passions that "produce good and evil, and proceed not from them."

Those bold hopes were short-lived. Compare Hume's rueful retrospect on the failure of the *Treatise* to reach or impress an audience:

> That you may see I wou'd no way scruple of owning my Mistakes in Argument, I shall acknowledge (what is infinitely more material) a very great Mistake in Conduct, viz my publishing at all the Treatise of Human Nature, a Book, which pretended to innovate in all the sublimist Part of Philosophy, & which I compos'd before I was five & twenty. Above all, the positive Air, which prevails in that Book, & which may be imputed to the Ardor of Youth, so much displeases me, that I have not Patience to review it. But what Success the same Doctrines, better illustrated & exprest, may meet with, *Ad huc sub judice lis est.* (*HL*, 1:91)

Hume interprets the failure of the *Treatise* as empirical evidence of the empiricist's dictum, "There is no quality in human nature which causes more fatal errors in our conduct, than that which leads us to prefer whatever is present to the distant and the remote, and makes us desire objects more according to their situation than their intrinsic value" (*T*, p. 538).

---

31. "Here, therefore, moral philosophy is in the same condition as natural, with regard to astronomy before the time of *Copernicus*" (*T*, p. 282).

The passion for innovation, for revolution, has been responsible for a fatal error in the conduct of the *Treatise*. It died because of Hume's failure to be appropriately indirect and measure his steps toward success rather than to seek it all at once—an error in conduct that he intends to rectify in the future; retrospect on the *Treatise* forecasts the two enquiries, the *Four Dissertations*, and the various essays that will follow. The failure of the *Treatise* would seem to have realized the fears that Hume avowed in the letter to Dr. Arbuthnot, that he had "no Hopes of delivering my Opinions with such Elegance & Neatness, as to draw to me the Attention of the World"; his failure would seem to be the consequence of delivering them to the world "maim'd & imperfect."

The coroner's report holds no surprises. In light of the argument of the *Treatise*, dedicated to correcting all notions of violent change, it is rather Hume's entertainment of a revolutionary aim that looks odd—it is as if the labeling of the *Treatise* as revolutionary is itself a revisionary tactic in anticipation of failure, designed to prepare what might be called an ideology of revision that will make possible further adjustments. Whether or not the *Treatise* was in fact revolutionary, *characterizing* it as revolutionary explains the failure of the *Treatise* in terms of the *Treatise* itself. Revolutionary aims are invoked in order that they may be definitively cast out in favor of a revisionary strategy which Hume is practicing here, which, indeed, he has been practicing all along.

4

The Example of the Female

For this is above all others the wisdom the eloquent man wants, namely—
to be the regulator of times and persons.

Cicero, "The Orator"

Hence arises the . . . strong and irreconcilable Aversion to all Giants with
his most humble & respectful Submission to all Damsels. These two Affections of his, he unites in all Adventures, which are alwise design'd to rescue
distrest Damsels from the Capitivity & Violence of Giants.

Hume, "Historical Essay on Chivalry and Romance"

The comparison of the *Treatise* to a stillborn child ought to be regarded
skeptically. A dead child is supposed to stop all inquiries—the figure that
appalls. Yet like his natural history of society in the *Treatise*, Hume's autobiographical plot *requires* that a gap, a death of nature or of naive ambition,
fall between the "savage" author and the socialized man of letters. The
Treatise entitles us to ask by what art it was killed.

The postmortem in the autobiography revises this more clinically
circumstantial account sent to Henry Home in 1737:

> I am at present castrating my work, that is, cutting off its nobler
> parts; that is, endeavoring it shall give as little offence as possible,
> before which I could not pretend to put it into the Doctor's hands.
> This is a piece of cowardice, for which I blame myself, though I
> believe none of my friends will blame me. But I was resolved not
> to be an enthusiast in philosophy, while I was blaming other enthu-
> siasms. (*HL*, 1:25)

Prior to publication the *Treatise* was not regarded as a live child but as a
mere body; and it is formed not by parturition but by castration. Whatever
the motives for this "piece of cowardice," the *Treatise* was indisputably
sent to the press "maim'd": it lacked a part, the section "Of Miracles," in
its published form. Deprived of its most flagrant member, which, if

flaunted, would almost certainly have stirred a murmur among the zealots, the abridged *Treatise* was incapacitated of its revolutionary power. Hume does not regard the castration as a deformation, however; on the contrary, Hume made his cut in the service of form—not a violent eruption of desire but a prudential act engineered in the "calm" passion of composition, plastic surgery (*T,* p. 276).[1]

Cutting the *Treatise,* rendering it "incapable of the rougher and more boisterous emotions" ("Of the Delicacy of Taste and Passion," *ST,* 27), not only meant its incapacitation *for* society; it implied a particular version or figure *of* society. Falsely called unprincipled, Hume deliberately altered his text according to the bedrock Humean principle that "the stronger the relation is betwixt ourselves and any object, the more easily does the imagination make the transition, and convey to the related idea the vivacity of conception, with which we always form the idea of our own person" (*T,* p. 318). As the suppression of "Miracles" marks Hume's conversion from the goal of revolution to remediation, so does it forecast a different, nonphilosophical audience. Hume recognizes that a "man of learning and reflection can make allowance for these peculiarities of manner; but a common audience can never divest themselves so far of their usual ideas and sentiments, as to relish pictures which nowise resemble them" ("Of the Standard of Taste," *ST,* p. 21).[2] What then is the public for whom the canny author fashions a resemblance? It is no surprise that Hume is most explicit on this matter in an exchange with his bookseller, when, referring to the rough handling of the first volume of *The History of England,* he patiently observes, "The Public is the most capricious Mistress we can court; and we Authors, who write for Fame, must not be repuls'd by some Rigors, which are always temporary, where they are unjust." (*HL,* 1:222).[3]

---

1. This is not inconsistent with the fact, noted by Gary Shapiro, that the early reviewers of the *Treatise* charged Hume with "making points simply for effect." Shapiro, "The Man of Letters and the Author of Nature: Hume on Philosophical Discourse," *The Eighteenth Century* 26, no. 2 (1985): 125. No doubt much of the *Treatise* remained crude. Hume's "piece of cowardice" could and did destabilize the argument; it was no guarantee of success. Scoring points is, however, a long way from bringing about a Copernican revolution in philosophy.

2. Cf. Voltaire's advice to d'Alembert to try "if you can, to weaken your style, write dully, certainly no one will guess your identity. One can say good things in a heavy way. You will have the pleasure of enlightening the world without compromising yourself; that would be a fine action and you would be an apostle without being a martyr." Quoted in Kingsley Martin, *French Liberal Thought in the Eighteenth Century* (1929; rpt. New York: Harper & Row, 1963), pp. 97–98.

3. Even when he repents of authorship, the connection between public and woman stands: "But I am so sick of all those Disputes and so full of Contempt towards all factious Judgments and indeed towards the Prejudices of what is call'd the Public, that I repent

When conceived of as feminine, the idea of the public requires that objects be devised in such a manner that they give back a feminine image, which does not smite the reader but flatters, and thereby promises to acquire for the author that durable fame which is the end of composition. Hume's revision of the *Treatise before* it had the chance to fail, before he could be compelled to alter his style, remedies the illness under which he suffered by transforming his monstrous heap of desires into an object body upon which calm, surgical acts could be performed, allowing the conversion of the "subordinate movement" of passion into the "predominant" movement of the imagination ("Of Tragedy," *ST,* p. 35). For a philosophical readership he has already begun to substitute a feminine public whose "castrated" figure his writings will ideally mirror. He has begun his embassy from masculine philosophy to polite letters, a domain which, Hume acknowledges, is and ever ought to be ruled by women. ("Of Essay Writing," *ST,* p. 40).

A means of refinement, castration is a fully symbolic act: the break is no more conspicuous to a reader than any other partition of the *Treatise,* nor is the lopped-off member completely lost, a dead letter. "Of Miracles" is not suppressed for long: once detached it is no longer a "noble part" and can appear in another book, recomposed so as not to deform the object. The point of the calm passion of composition is that *nothing* is lost. Hence the irony at hand—that despite Hume's refinement, the *Treatise* failed to produce the fame which Hume designed—has no force.[4] The castration of the *Treatise* is a species of eloquence, which has value relative only to its position within the symbolic discourse of a career that advances by indirection. "Truth will prevail at last," Hume writes to the printer William Strahan, "and if I have been able to embellish her with any De-

---

heartily my ever having committed any thing to Print. Had I a Son I shou'd warn him as carefully against the dangerous Allurements of Literature as James did his Son against those of Women; tho if his Inclination was as strong as mine in my Youth, it is likely, that the warning woud be to as little Purpose in the one Case as it usually is in the other" (*HL,* 1:461). This is a peculiarly fantastic fantasy, since, of course, Hume not only did not father a son, but the enabling condition of his career is to respond to the allure of the feminine public by a castration that makes authorship a necessarily barren romance.

4. The irony is, indeed, keen. In the anonymous *Letter From a Gentleman to his friend in Edinburgh* (1745), ed. Ernest C. Mossner and John V. Price (Edinburgh: University Press, 1967), Hume responds to a stringent attack on the *Treatise* bolstered by ample quotation: "I was perswaded that the Clamour of *Scepticism, Atheism, &c.* had been so often employ'd by the worst of Men against the best, that it had now lost all its Influence; and should never have thought of making any Remarks on these *maim'd Excerpts,* if you had not laid your Commands on me" (p. 3). Having cut insufficiently, Hume had exposed himself to the brutal selection of beauties by reviewers.

gree of Eloquence, it will not be long before she prevail" (*HL*, 1:235). Not long, but some time. Truth is a woman; or at least only a truth that has been castrated can prevail over an effeminate public. And once philosophy is conceived as a manner of composition within a social composition, the philosopher's work does not begin and end in a *Treatise*, or, indeed, in philosophy; the philosopher turns himself on all sides in a "perpetual occupation" that integrates his public and private life.

Refinement is general and purposive. The plot of purpose follows the pattern of induction. "The more these refined arts advance, the more sociable men become. . . . They flock into cities; love to receive and communicate knowledge, to show their wit or their breeding; their taste in conversation or living. . . . Particular clubs and societies are everywhere formed; . . . and the tempers of men, as well as their behavior, refine apace" ("Of Refinement in the Arts," *ST*, pp. 50–51). Aggregated into greater units, individuals find their impulse toward egoistic competition channeled toward social cooperation. Learning, no longer the peculiar right of the learned, becomes conversable—not merely something everyone can talk about but that which is talked, shared by all. Shared by *all*—both men and women. For if refinement works to restrict the narrowness of individual men by gathering them together and converting their necessitous work into luxurious occupation, it also recombines men and women into a formation that, no longer compelled by the exigencies of biology and sustenance, is for the first time fully social. Embedded in the model of refinement is a categorical judgment that equates necessity with biology under the sign of an exigent desire that, whether alimentary or erotic, produces engrossing but transitory, furtive, and fractious combinations. Part of the project of classical economics will be to supplant subsistent sex with sex as fantasy, so that under the sign of general correspondence copulation will be conversation and vice versa. This is ostensibly a feminization of culture because it is supposedly women who induce men to an increased sociability. "What better school for manners," Hume asks, "than the company of virtuous women, where the mutual endeavor to please must insensibly polish the mind, where the example of the female softness and modesty must communicate itself to their admirers, and where the delicacy of that sex puts every one on his guard lest he give offence by any breach of decency?" ("Of the Rise and Progress of the Arts and Sciences," *ST*, p. 93). The "example of the female" is the precedent which schools the learned to soften his learning, the solitary male to dampen his ardor.

When Hume comes to name the notion that should inform men's behavior, he calls it "*gallantry*, the natural product of courts and monarchies."

As nature has given *man* the superiority above *woman*, by endowing him with greater strength both of mind and body, it is his part to alleviate that superiority, as much as possible, by the generosity of his behavior, and by a studied deference and complaisance for all her inclinations and opinions. Barbarous nations display their superiority, by reducing their females to the most abject slavery; by confining them, by beating them, by selling them, by killing them. But the male sex, among a polite people, discover their authority in a more generous, though not a less evident manner; by civility, by respect, by complaisance, and in a word by gallantry. (*ST*, pp. 90–91)

The generous male alleviates his natural superiority by a "complaisance" "studied" in the example of the female whom in his gallantry he seeks to please. Male superiority is not denied, but the *appearance* of superiority is regarded as a "breach of decency," to be avoided like any other "peculiarity of manner." Men abridge their power in order not to make a breach. Gallantry accords an extraordinary privilege to the feminine as example and telos, but while effacing female agency. In alleviating their superiority, men "discover their authority," rooted not only in their generosity but in their *ability* to be generous, an ability that comes, as all indirect power does in Hume, from men's capacity to incapacitate themselves.[5] What merely happens to the savage is deliberately undertaken by the gallant man of letters. Richard Sennett observes that of "authority it may be said in the most general way that it is an attempt to interpret the conditions of power, to give the conditions of control and influence a meaning by defining an image of strength."[6] Sennett's "interpret" is congruent with Hume's "discover." Although it is the example of the female which induces the male to enter society or to compose a particular kind of book, only the male can choose to castrate himself, an interpretation or discovery of authority that defines an image of strength and designs a reading and a reader. Power is either direct and barbarously phallic, or it is polite and a function of self-castration. Under either dispensation the female (reader), who is *assigned* her exemplary status, has no power. She has had done to her what the gallant (author) does to himself. The woman's inability to cut off any noble part removes her from any authority: even more, it virtually removes her from any embodiment. She is the idea that

5. The original gallant was Adam. On Addison's use of *Paradise Lost* to express approval of "Adam's temperance of his intellectual authority with gentleness," see Jean H. Hagstrum, *Sex and Sensibility: Ideal and Erotic Love from Milton to Mozart* (Chicago: Univ. of Chicago Press, 1980), p. 14.

6. Richard Sennett, *Authority* (New York: Vintage, 1981), p. 19.

induces the male and as idea can make neither choices nor demands; indeed, she can never be anything but a creature of pride or vanity who is pleased to gaze at her image mirrored in the softened figure of the male. She can polish, but she cannot cut.

This imagined incapacity of the female allows Hume's casual adoption of the monarchical court as his model of civility. It is not an obvious choice. Hume himself recognizes that "it is impossible for the arts and sciences to arise, at first, among any people, unless that people enjoy the blessing of a free government" ("Of Refinement," *ST,* p. 75). Moreover, Hume's monarchism ignores d'Alembert's warnings of the potential abasement of the man of letters at court,[7] and it seems inconsistent with his own frequent humanist espousals of the republic of letters. But the inconsistency is mitigated by the substitution for the male monarch of "the fair sex, who are the sovereigns of the empire of conversation. I approach them with reverence," writes Hume; "and were not my countrymen the learned, a stubborn and independent race of mortals, extremely jealous of their liberty, and unaccustomed to subjection, I should resign into their fair hands the sovereign authority over the republic of letters" ("Of Essay Writing," *ST,* p. 40).

The exception that Hume makes for his countrymen the learned actually applies only to the British Isles; he applauds the fact that in "a neighboring nation . . . the ladies are, in a manner, the sovereigns of the *learned* world, as well as of the *conversable*" (*ST,* pp. 40–41). A monarchical government conducive to both learning and conversation does not require an absolute and male sovereign. A more condign surrogate can be devised by resigning superiority to women, who thereby become, in impotent paradox, the sovereigns of the republic of letters. Authority so received is authority only in a manner of speaking: woman neither legislates nor executes; she functions strictly as the *standard* of taste (in the same way that money functions as the standard of value). By putting the woman in the place of the sovereign, Hume ingeniously establishes a republic which has all the blessings of a monarchy with none of its terrors: there can be no pretense to divine right, and a standard cannot enforce its judgments by punitive action on subject bodies.[8] By resigning sover-

7. D'Alembert, "Essai sur la Société des Gens de Lettres et des Grands," *Oeuvres completes de d'Alembert,* 5 vols. (Paris, 1821) 4:357–58.

8. Hume is here, of course, following the conventions of a discourse that the French had themselves been perfecting since the seventeenth century. In *La Paradise des Femmes: Women, Salons, and Social Stratification in Seventeenth-Century France* (Princeton: Princeton Univ. Press, 1976), Carolyn C. Lougee comments: "Three revisions of traditional thought created concepts of feminity upon which female authority could build, transforming traditionally acknowledged femininity attributes from liabilities into assets. A revised epistemol-

eign authority to women, the gallant Hume converts political hierarchy into theater and, not incidentally, lays claim to a special kind of authority on behalf of the essayistic man of letters whose formidable capacity to incapacitate himself distinguishes him alone as generic man.

As for society, so for commerce. In Hume's essay "Of Commerce" the division between the learned and the conversable world is paralleled by that between ancients and moderns; the distinction between republic and monarchy corresponds with that between the private individual and the state; what Hume calls "woman" in the earlier essay he calls "commodity" here. The goals are the same: both to legitimate the process of refinement and encourage the production of luxury in modern society. Hume develops a theory of labor that annexes it to commodity production under the rubric of passion: "Every thing in the world is purchased by labour; and our passions are the only causes of labour" (G&G, p. 293). Demand comes first; supply follows. Though commodities may be luxuries from the perspective of state policy, Hume argues that they perform the crucial role of providing images that stimulate the artisan to work, labor that can be stored up for the state's future use. "The more labor, therefore, is employed beyond mere necessaries, the more powerful is any state." Within this enriched and powerful state the sovereign, the addressee of Hume's essay, is just a different kind of laborer. In order that the mechanism operate smoothly, the monarch must be induced both to renounce the "violent method" of interference in the natural course of commerce and actively to encourage manufacture (p. 294). The essayist designs that inducement as an appeal to the sovereign's passion for power and as a reorientation of that passion toward indirect satisfaction. Once again, induction and inducement are complementary. The history of commerce will advance because it is natural; parts will be organized into greater wholes according to an all but inexorable mechanics. But at every moment in that mechanism there are gaps between causes and effects, between needs and satisfactions, which threaten the breakdown of the system, because of a preference for the immediate over the remote or because of a direct, regal passion of violent character and destructive potential. As in the passage on the causes of art which we examined in Chapter 1, the gap is crossed by an artifice which represents the mechanism and induces the desiring subject, monarch or artisan, along the path of indirect satisfaction, to labor.

---

ogy which emphasized the value of human feelings made non-rational woman the repository of sentiment. Alterations in social values denigrating heroic strength made weak woman into the representative of delicacy. And cosmologies celebrating love as the creative principle of the universe turned lustful woman into the purveyor of beneficent love" (p. 31).

What commodities do for the working man, the essay "Of Commerce" does for the sovereign: infuses passion.[9] And "nothing," Hume writes in the *Treatise* "is more capable of infusing any passion into the mind, than eloquence, by which objects are represented in their strongest and most lively colours. We may of ourselves acknowledge, that such an object is valuable, and such another odious; but 'till an orator excites the imagination, and gives force to these ideas, they may have but a feeble influence either on the will or the affections" (*T*, pp. 426–27). But no more than eighteenth-century Britain is Athens is the Enlightenment man of letters an orator. For worse and for better. For worse because "in ancient times, no work of genius was thought to require so great parts and capacity as the speaking in public"; classical orators aspired to "perfection of their art, which was infinite, and not only exceeded human force to attain, but human imagination to conceive" ("Of Eloquence," *ST*, pp. 60, 61). They dealt with the "jealousy of their audience" by hurrying them away "with such a torrent of sublime and pathetic, that they left their hearers no leisure to perceive the artifice by which they were deceived. Nay, to consider the matter aright, they were not deceived by any artifice. The orator, by the force of his own genius and eloquence, first inflamed himself with anger, indignation, pity, sorrow; and then communicated those impetuous movements to his audience" (*ST*, p. 66). Moreover, what man with an interest in educating sovereigns can fail to be impressed by the account of how Julius Caesar "that haughty conqueror . . . was so subdued by the charms of Cicero's eloquence, that he was, in a manner, constrained to change his settled purpose and resolution, to absolve a criminal, whom, before that orator pleaded, he was determined to condemn" (pp. 66–67). The mediocre level of debates in the public assemblies of modern states is clear testimony of the decline in oratorical aspiration and execution.

Yet in one sense this decline is for the better because it *has* to be for the better. If the change from the ancient to the modern *is* a progress, then the decline of oratory, or at least the adjustment of its method and its aims, must share in the progressive change. The very features of contemporary public deliberations that contribute to, if not account for, the low caliber of oral debate—the "multiplicity and intricacy of laws," a "more chaste taste and superior good temper," and the assumption of the

9. See Diderot: "It is almost useless to enlighten the lower orders, if the blindfold remains on the eyes of those ten or twelve privileged individuals who dispose of the earth's happiness. There you have those whom it is important to convert. . . . To whom, thus, will the philosophe address himself strongly, if not to the sovereign?" *Oeuvres politiques*, pp. 141–42, quoted in Charles Alan Kors, *D'Holbach's Coterie: An Enlightenment in Paris* (Princeton: Princeton Univ. Press, 1976), p. 318.

greater "disorders of the ancient governments"—are those aspects of modern society that Hume everywhere endorses in his moral and political essays.

Nowhere more than in this essay is the strategic moderation of Hume clearer. Though he finally identifies as the major reason for the dearth of memorable oratory the fact that "we are satisfied with our mediocrity, because we have had no experience of any thing better," and displays throughout a nostalgia for that scene where "the true genius arises, [and] draws to him the attention of every one, and immediately appears superior to his rival" (*ST*, p. 69), he does not propose means whereby modern orators can retrieve the experience that would elevate their discourse. The person who had renounced such hopes as the very condition of his career in the letter to Dr. Arbuthnot could hardly affirm such dangerous and wasteful ascendance. On the contrary, the essay concludes with a series of mitigations: the acknowledgment that "an elevated style has much better grace in a speaker than a writer," the admonition to compose arguments beforehand, and the observation "that, even though our modern orators should not elevate their style, or aspire to a rivalship with the ancient; yet there is, in most of their speeches, a material defect which they might correct, without departing from that composed air or argument and reasoning to which they limit their ambition. Their great affectation of extemporary discourses has made them reject all order and method, which seems so requisite to argument, and without which it is scarcely possible to produce an entire conviction on the mind" (*ST*, p. 71). There is an ambiguity between the subjunctive and the imperative in Hume's "should" which indicates his ambivalence toward the estimable example of the ancients. Despite his express admiration for their oratorical style, Hume ends by both severing that mode from modern assemblies as an irrecoverable experience and prescribing a direction for modern mediocrity that takes as its standard not sublime elevation but careful *ordonnance:* the remedy for the "material defect" is derived not from graces especially appropriate to a speaker but from those that belong to a writer.[10] The virtues Hume aims to inculcate in his contemporaries, "order and method," are the virtues of prose compositions—the virtues most acces-

---

10. Hume would not wince at the cynicism evident in Lord Chesterfield's advice to his son "at the time he was about to enter Parliament, . . . to rehearse a speech either about the size of the land forces or about the award of places and pensions." Such "prepared eloquence" was just the sort of inocuously careerist rhetoric Hume had in mind. *Lord Chesterfield's Letters to His Son*, 26 March 1754, cited in Quentin Skinner, "The Principles and Practice of Opposition: The Case of Bolingbroke versus Walpole," in *Historical Perspectives: Studies in English Thought and Society*, ed. Neil McKendrick (London: Europa, 1974), p. 98.

sible to the contemporaries of David Hume in the thoroughly imitable essays of David Hume.

Hume's ambivalence and the option he takes to escape it are fully explicable in terms of those choices he made in revising the *Treatise*. At one time, as the letter to Arbuthnot testifies, Hume did indulge the dream of rhetoric, of an eloquence that would immediately manifest his superiority to all his predecessors and that could not fail to produce a complete alteration in the sentiments and behavior of its readers. But that effect could be attained only by a "vehemence of thought and expression" in alliance with a "vehemence of action" which is "now esteemed too violent, either for the senate, bar, or pulpit and is only admitted into the theatre to accompany the most violent passions which are there represented." The difference between vehemence in the assembly and vehemence in the theater lies in the crucial difference between passions that are represented and therefore indirect and passions that are direct and therefore dangerous. Oratory recklessly transgresses the boundary between the imaginable and the inconceivable, between the representation of the passion and the passion itself: for the assembled ancients the hurrying torrent of the sublime and the pathetic "left no leisure to perceive the artifice by which they were deceived. Nay, to consider the matter aright, they were not deceived by any artifice. The orator . . . first inflamed himself with anger." Not an art that concealed art, ancient oratory cancelled art and hence is antipathetic to the Humean strategy that prudently demystifies its persuasiveness in order to allow a reader the leisure to appreciate the artifice by which he has been deceived. That leisure refreshes the reader of Hume, who can, ideally, make reading Hume a perpetual occupation.

Hume ultimately rejects the ancient style for the same reason that he enjoins the imperious actions of the contemporary sovereign: the means "by which they commanded the resolution of their audience" (*ST*, p. 70) constitute a violent method of strong but limited duration. And the reservations against this display of brute superiority suggest the motives against violence: the lapse of indirection in the sublime moment is a violence against the sovereignty of the orator as well as against his auditors: *both* are subjected to powerfully antinomian passions. Because the theater is the "there" where passions come to be represented, all violence is supposed, ineluctably referred to the convention that is the condition of its recognizability. The assembly, however, is not "there" but "here," determined in the first and last instance by the power of a voice which utterly literalizes the trope of sympathy by turning communication into a matter of moving bodies. To speak as Cicero did to Caesar is to command rather than induce; but to command the sovereign is to empty sovereignty of its legitimacy according to an imperative which can have no authority because it proceeds from no artificer. If the man of letters discovers his authority by a gallant alleviation of his superiority, the sublime orator loses his in his very elevation to the height of command: he is overthrown by the force of his own genius. Oratorical passion serves no interest or economy; the orator's perfection of his art ends in a waste of spirit.

A similar critique, though in much stricter economic terms, is advanced by Adam Smith in his illustration of the category of "unproductive labour":

> The labour of some of the most respectable orders in the society is . . . unproductive of any value, and does not fix or realize itself in any permanent subject, or vendible commodity. . . . The sovereign, for example, with all the officers both of justice and war who serve under him, the whole army and navy, are unproductive labourers. They are the servants of the public, and are maintained by a part of the annual produce of the industry of other people. Their service, how honourable, how useful, or how necessary soever, produces nothing for which an equal quantity of service can afterwards be procured. . . . In the same class must be ranked, some both of the gravest and most important, and some of the most frivolous professions: churchmen, lawyers, physicians, men of letters of all kinds; players, buffoons, musicians, opera-singers, opera-dancers, &c. The labour of the meanest of these has a certain value, regulated by the very same principles which regulate that of every other sort of labour; and that of the noblest and most useful, produces nothing which could afterwards purchase or procure an equal quantity of labour. Like the declamation of the actor, the harangue of the orator, or the tune of the musician, the work of all of them perishes in the very instant of its production.[11]

Orators and rulers are linked and diminished by Smith as they are by Hume. Yet Smith's economics cannot account for whatever it is that makes kings and orators different from other servants or buffoons. Unlike Hume's essays, Smith's economics silently represses the antagonist political order. Hume engages the forcefulness of command not only by censuring its wastefulness but by deliberately assigning it to a past that we can now only read about in essays or books—thus not merely antiquating arbitrary power but announcing its modern successor, the mode of repre-

11. Adam Smith, *The Wealth of Nations* (New York: Random House, 1937), bk. 2, chap. 3, p. 315.

sentation.[12] There are two criteria of modernity for Hume: the ascendancy of woman as sovereign and the emergence of the man of letters as the successor of the classical orator.

The difference between the modern rhetorician and the ancient is a matter of manner. A naked display of passion, the style of ancient eloquence was one "where . . . swelling expressions were not rejected as wholly monstrous and gigantic." It is just those parts that Hume would cut off in the interest of both speaker and audience. Opting for the mediocre over the gigantic, for the modern over the ancient, with whatever lingering regret, reflects a preference for methodical artifice over the imperiously necessitous.[13] It is not a renunciation of power; rather Hume chooses (necessarily, he would have us believe, given the lacunae in our experience) a power that is not openly avowed and flagrantly exercised but that makes only the most general claims in the most regular way, that persuades rather than commands. Though deprived of its imperiousness, sovereignty is preserved and protected from usurpation by its double assignment to the idea of the woman, who has no power except that which is ceded to her, and to the productive activity of the man of letters, whose sovereign control subsists in his manufacture of sovereignty, his artful representation of woman as an idea that will induce him to continued labor.[14]

12. I do not want to suggest that there is no politics in Smith's account; Kurt Heinzelman seems to me right when in his comments on this passage he ironically observes, "Apparently, Smith would have exempted economists from the category 'men of letters of all kinds.'" *The Economics of Imagination* (Amherst: Univ. of Massachusetts Press, 1980), p. 153. Smith's politics is the politics of exemption, as it is for Hume. What I do want to claim (and what I think is implicit in Heinzelman) is that as economist Smith has no basis for such an exemption in the terms of the economic theory he promotes, whereas Hume provides himself with such a basis by taking his stand and making his claims on the more general terrain of representation, an area which, as I shall argue at greater length in the next chapter, is coincident with the discursive formation of the man of letters and which comprises the economist as it does the historian and the philosophical essayist.

13. In his essay "The Principles and Practice of Opposition: The Case of Bolingbroke versus Walpole," pp. 93–128 Quentin Skinner makes an excellent case for the parliamentary career of Bolingbroke as the exemplary instance in the eighteenth century of this necessary and calculated shift in strategy.

14. Hume reflects and adjusts a widespread oppositional stance. As John Cannon observes, "Denunciation of monarchical power had a good popular appeal and place bills were part of the stock in trade of opposition from the time of [Robert] Walpole to the 1780's." He quotes Horace Walpole's remark that it "must be remembered . . . that while any two [parts of government] are checking, the third is naturally aiming at extending and aggrandizing its power. The House of Commons has not seldom made this attempt like the rest. The Lords, as a permanent and as a proud body, more constantly aim at it. The crown always." John Cannon, *The Aristocratic Century: The Peerage of Eighteenth-Century England* (Cambridge: Cambridge Univ. Press, 1984), p. 159.

Hence, though "nothing is more capable of infusing any passion into the mind than eloquence," "eloquence is not always necessary. The bare opinion of another, especially when inforc'd with passion, will cause an idea of good or evil to have an influence upon us. . . . This proceeds from the principle of sympathy or communication; and sympathy . . . is nothing but the conversion of an idea into an impression by the force of imagination" (*T*, p. 427). Superior to eloquence, sympathy is not restricted to face-to-face encounters, not susceptible to monstrous swelling or anarchic confusion, and, crucially, not aimed toward overpowering one resolution by a more powerful resolution—not, that is, launched toward a single, decisive moment of inflamed passion, but composed. Composition, unlike oratory, is a *labor* of conversion—the writer copying down his ideas (themselves copies of his impressions) and thus, whether we have reference to letter, fair copy, or published text, converting ideas into graphic, communicative impressions so that the reader can repeat the process in reverse, performing the same sort of labor. The text is a place of correspondence and conversation, a market in which the exchange of ideas is stimulated by the luxury status of the impressions that an author makes (refining them from the truth that one already has) and that a reader receives (the new impressions are fundamentally a surplus version of that idea of herself that she already has). To embellish the truth is necessarily to prevail because, as Hume knows better than anyone else, the truth is man's passion for embellishment.

To write of impressions and ideas is to supply epistemological terms for Hume's Addisonian characterization of his essays and himself as essayist: "I cannot but consider myself as a kind of resident or ambassador from the dominions of learning to those of conversation, and shall think it my constant duty to promote a good correspondence betwixt these two states, which have so great a dependence on each other" ("Of Essay Writing," *ST*, p. 39). Each movement in Hume's career is glossed and justified by this allegory: the local movement described in the *Treatise* from the solitary and skeptical reasoning in the philosopher's cabinet to the common room where he can be released from skeptical darkness by conversation, backgammon, and port; the movement from Ninewells, the provincial family estate, where the unbroken company of his books was mitigated only by the presence of his sister and brother, to the intellectual life of Edinburgh, where Hume became embroiled in the hurly-burly fraternities of other thinkers and doers, to London, and, finally and inevitably, to Paris. Finally and inevitably because in each stage of his transit Hume discovers that the dominion at which he has arrived, though promising a release from the provincialism, the factionalism, and the monotony which he associates with the dominion of the learned, simply transposes those defects into a different key: learning had an edge in Edinburgh, and Hume often found that edge turned against him.[15] Cosmopolitan France could be regarded not only as the dominion of conversation but also as the "neighboring nation" where the mutual dependence of learning and conversation was both understood and performed. Only the Parisian salon instantiated the Humean mixed government, a republic of letters ruled by a sovereign woman.

Hume's first success as an ambassador is announced in a letter from Mme Dupre de St. Maur in 1757, who writes: "Little versed as I am in the English language, you have made it easy for me by the clarity and beauty both of your style and of your ideas. I found your history a treatise of philosophy applied to the most interesting facts. Never has any book held my attention so completely, and never have I had so good an opinion of myself as when I was reading you" (Mossner, p. 424). In her characterization of Hume's *History* Mme Dupre de St. Maur echoes Hume's own conviction that history's "records of wars, intrigues, factions, and revolutions, are so many collections of experiments, by which the politician or moral philosopher fixes the principles of his science" (*Natural History of Religion,* quoted in Mossner, p. 301). According to Mme Dupre de St. Maur, the agreeable accommodation of philosophical idea to historical impressions has fixed the principles of Hume's "science" in a reader who recognizes herself in what she reads and is pleased to regard a self better than she had thought she was. Such is the sentimental education contrived by a moral philosophy based on pride.

But if Mme Dupre de St. Maur's letter announces Hume's success, its consummation occurs in the first letter written to Hume by Mme La Comtesse de Boufflers, mistress to a count of the blood, "l'Idole du Temple," and princess of the salons. His history, she exclaims,

> animates a noble emulation, it inspires the love of liberty, and instructs at the same time to be submissive to the government under which one is obliged to live; in a word it is a fecund source of morality and instructions, presented with colors so lively that one believes that one sees them for the first time.
>
> The clarity, the majesty, the touching simplicity of your style, ravishes me. Its beauties are so striking, that despite my ignorance in the English language, they were not able to escape me. You are, Monsieur, an admirable painter. Your tableaux have a natural grace,

15. Mossner's biography is the best source for information on the many attacks, almost all of them religiously motivated, that dogged and defeated Hume's attempts to acquire a secure institutional position, academic or otherwise, in Edinburgh.

an energy which surpasses that which the imagination itself could attain.

But what expressions shall I employ, in order to make you understand the effect your divine impartiality produces on me. I would have need on this occasion of your own eloquence, in order to render my thought. In truth, I believe that I have before my eyes the work of some celestial substance disengaged from passion, who for the utility of men has deigned to write the events of the former times. . . .

All these sublime qualities are so strongly above the understanding of a female, that it little befits me to speak of it: and I already have great need of your indulgence, for the faults that I have committed against discretion and propriety by the excess of my veneration for your merit. I request, Monsieur, that you will keep this letter the most profound secret. My conduct has something of the extraordinary about it; I fear that it will attract blame to me and I would be aggrieved if the sentiment which dictates to me were to be misunderstood. (*HL*, 2:367; my translation)

The Comtesse de Boufflers celebrates the chiasmic crossing of learning into conversation and conversation into learning. By applying his philosophy to facts, Hume has reached the public he sought; by reading Hume's *History*, the countess has become conversant with principles of which she had been ignorant. A statement of his success, the letter of the countess also represents the triumph of Hume's art, what J. C. Hilson has aptly termed his "sentimental historiography," which conjoins rational pleasures with the emotional.[16] "The perusal of a history seems a calm entertainment; but would be no entertainment at all, did not our hearts beat with correspondent movements to those which are described by the historian" (*ECPM*, p. 45). And Hume's description has surely induced such correspondent palpitations. Moreover, the *History*'s power to animate emulation, inspire love, and inculcate submission is attributed to Hume's "impartiality"; he evinces no peculiarity of manner that would be inimitable for the female reader.[17]

The success of Hume's *History* can be gauged by comparing the remarkable testimony of the hyperbolic countess with the failed experi-

---

16. J. C. Hilson, "Hume: The Historian as Man of Feeling," in *Augustan Worlds* ed. J. C. Hilson, M.M.B. Jones, and J. R. Watson (New York: Barnes & Noble, 1978), p. 209.

17. Hume never takes the side of Machiavelli: to the ancient question, Is it better for a prince to be loved or feared? he would always answer love—even to the extent of emasculating the monarch.

ment in reading history that Hume recounts at the beginning of his essay
"On the Study of History":

> I remember I was once desired by a young beauty, for whom I had
> some passion, to send her some novels and romances for her amuse-
> ment to the country; but was not so ungenerous as to take the ad-
> vantage, which such a course of reading might have given me, being
> resolved not to make use of poisoned arms against her. I therefore
> sent her Plutarch's Lives, assuring her, at the same time, that there
> was not a word of truth in them from beginning to end. She perused
> them very attentively, till she came to the lives of Alexander and
> Caesar, whose names she had heard of by accident, and then re-
> turned me the book, with many reproaches for deceiving her. (*ST,*
> p. 95)

Determined not to take advantage, Hume observed a gallantry beyond
the call of desire and generously curtailed the power he had been invited
to exercise by renouncing the use of "poisoned arms." By substituting
Plutarch for a novel, he adopted the course of fiction ("there was not a
word of truth in them from beginning to end") emptied of romance. But,
of course, there was a truth, or, rather, two truths—the names of the
conquerors Alexander and Caesar—which, when recognized, disturbed
the woman's attention and convicted Hume of deceit. Recognized by
even the ignorant female reader who is the unknowing target of Hume's
passion and the butt of his indirect anecdote about passion, the mighty
arms of Alexander and Caesar summon a historical reality (a world where
actions have consequences) which is not the domain of novels and romances and which cannot help but disturb an attention based on the
pleasant illusion that at least one action, reading novels and romances,
has no consequences—an illusion that ideally makes possible the consequences of the passion that romances excite. As armed conquerors, Alexander and Caesar are also a composite sign of the desire for conquest
that Hume has not completely suppressed. Although he has substituted
good history for bad romance, a kind of passion by representation (without touching) is performed (Hume would use the "beautiful representations" of Plutarch to smite as they had smitten him)—but dissipated in
the discovery of the deceit: Hume's subterfuge is overthrown by the ancient conquerors' greatness. The appearance of Alexander and Caesar is
the revelation both of the existence of desire and of *Hume's* desire; it
marks out the path of Hume's deviousness and exposes his impotence.
The lesson of reading Plutarch is that there are or were Alexanders and
Caesars in the world and that Hume is not one of them.

The reply of the countess to Hume's *History* demonstrates that the straight path of indirection is best: to call history (though it may not contain one word of truth) *History* rather than to disguise it as fiction. The difference between the success of Hume's *History* and Plutarch's with the female reader can be attributed to at least two features. First, there is the difference between a modern history and an ancient one. The reputations of Alexander and Caesar are so monstrously swollen that there is no way for the historian to command their fame to his aim. This fact of experience helps to explain the rhetorical strategy of Hume embedded in the compositional sequence of *The History of England;* written backward, the *History* in no way violates or contests the chronological precedence of the ancients to the moderns (Hume does not doctor the dates); but it does practically render the ancients as *effects* of Hume's method, which is derived and developed in encounters with more proximate and less prepossessing historical figures.[18] Second, whatever advantage Hume acquires as the result of his *History* is an advantage he derives rather than one he takes. Impartial historian, Hume is also impersonal author, mediated by manuscript, printing press, title page, and, for the countess, translator. He seems to respond to no invitation; he merely creates the conditions for the indirect satisfaction of female desire. Of course there is a disguise, in that Hume has masked both the crucial abridgment of noble parts and the contrivances of merchandising. The ignorance of the woman, however, to which she confesses and clings, enables her to submit happily to such marginal deception.

Hume's essay "On the Study of History" furnishes another, equally exacting standard by which to adjudge the success of his *History.* In that essay Hume complains of women's attraction to *"secret* history . . . [which contains] some memorable transaction proper to excite their curiosity," and he claims that he does not see "why the same curiosity may not lead them to desire accounts of those who lived in past ages, as well as of their contemporaries" (*ST,* pp. 95–96). The Comtesse de Boufflers' excited approbation of the historian's depiction of the "peace and serenity sparkling with splendor" that distinguished Charles I among his calamities and of the "trouble and remorse, inseparable cortege of crime, following the step of Cromwell and taking their seat on the throne with him" (*HL,* 1:366–67), attests to just such a merger of private fantasy with public theater.

18. The Settlement is that historical moment to which Hume gravitates: once the Settlement is settled by the historian the rest of history holds no perils. Even so, it is significant that Hume's first success occurred in France. In England, even what Hilson describes as his sympathetically "impartial" portrayal of Charles I as "sentimental hero" caused a row. It is notable that the "ideal response" to the *History* quoted by Hilson was penned in Rome by a traveling Scot, Robert Adam. See Hilson, "Historian," pp. 211–12, 219–20.

Yet the countess's letter is, after all, unnecessary to certify Hume's success. It would have been enough if the countess, and a great many like her, had bought *The History of the Stuarts:* the price paid, the reading experience could have been inferred. The reading itself need not have been remarked upon. That it is indicates a different kind of attention from that which Hume's perfect reader is supposed to give. Although the reading is little more than a tissue of the kind of polite epistolary conventions that one would expect in the correspondence of a lady of quality with a famous author (the conventions, that is, make Mme de Boufflers *recognizable* and make her prose *acceptable*), it is exactly the little more, the calculated excess, that accounts for its interest and for the powerful fascination that this woman in particular acquired for Hume. Notice that according to Mme de Boufflers, Hume's excellence is related to a certain style of "clarity," "majesty," and "simplicity." There is an unsettling difference between the style attributed to Hume and that which Hume designed. "Majesty" does not belong in the series; it sticks out (cf. Mme Dupre de St. Maur's "clarity and beauty"). Ideally, of course, Mme de Boufflers would find *her* majesty in Hume's simple and clear style as the reflection of her own idealized image, absent any disturbing peculiarity. But her attribution of majesty to the style marks it as peculiarly powerful, indicates a something about the style in excess of simplicity and clarity, its unalloyed fidelity to the historical referent, that provokes her confessedly excessive response. The difference between Hume's style, as Mme de Boufflers characterizes it, and a simple reflection of her own idealized image *is* her characterization of it.

Oddly, Mme de Boufflers' description of the effect of Hume's style echoes Hume's account to Dr. Arbuthnot of the effects of the ancients on him: as he was "smit" by their "beautiful representations" she cannot escape "striking beauties." But the echo is not perfect. Hume was smit by and with representations. His reader is struck by beauties that cannot be represented, by an "energy which surpasses that which the imagination itself could attain." The representations of the ancients are precisely that which the imagination *can* attain and on which Hume's own fetishistic imagination got stuck. By "majesty," by "natural grace," by "energy," Mme de Boufflers attempts to name something in the style that is different, that gives it its peculiar power, and about which one can form no adequate idea. She is trying to name that which strikes her. Struck by Hume's beauties, she is ravished, but even in the fullness of her ravishment feels something missing: the proper eloquence to render her thoughts. Ravished, the reader does not take on the author's power with his knowledge. What she comes to know is her incapacity, as if being struck, being ravished, is not being penetrated or filled but being castrated. Like Hume, then, as he described himself to Dr. Arbuthnot, she is defending against being struck, but unlike him she devises a style rather than a symptom: she adopts the *topoi* of inexpressibility and incapacity. This too has a skewed symmetry with Hume's reading of the ancients: her claims for the "utility" of his prose are thwarted by her confession of a response that forwards no moral purpose. What is different in Hume's style is that which thwarts its aims. The difference between Hume's response to Cicero, Plutarch, and Seneca and the countess's response to Hume parallels the difference between classical writers and classical orators: the former relied on beautiful representations; the latter sought "the perfection of their art, which was infinite, and not only exceeded human force to attain, but imagination to conceive." Hume, as the countess reads him, is successful in avoiding the pitfalls of the moralist; instead he accomplishes by and in his composition the effects of that higher oratory. What is at stake for her is reading how that effect—a striking that cannot be identified with any idea or representation—is achieved in prose; she attempts to imagine the inconceivable, to discover Hume's secret. Hence Mme de Boufflers does not waste her spirits but identifies the perfection of Hume's art in a confession of incapacity that empowers her to represent that which is beyond her imagination and her eloquence—to represent that which strikes her as "a celestial substance *disengaged* from passion." By identifying that disengagement from passion, she represents the cut that *produces* the phallus as a pure signifier, a "celestial substance," and that is the striking power of Hume's style.

    This is the perfect reading of Hume by someone who is not the perfect reader. The perfect reader would be someone like Mme Dupre de St. Maur, a sympathetic reader whose attention is held completely and who finds what she should find, an opinion of herself higher than she had ever held before. The response of such a reader is merely the token she exchanges in grateful payment for that access of vanity. The perfect reader of Hume is capable of being influenced—animated, inspired, instructed—but not of influencing; she can be represented to herself but is herself incapable of representing. She performs the play of her own passion on a stage designed by Hume's eloquence. The perfect reading of Hume remarks on a failure of sympathy, and is represented in a writing that reenacts the disequilibrium of the experience by stressing the incommensurability of experience with any vehicle of communication. Despite its simplicity and clarity, Hume's composition has found a reader on whom it produces a violent impression and who, in turn, designs a violent impression on him, aims to engross him by the volatility with which she affects the conventions. The countess's retrieval of the experience of an oratory, the last echo of which, Hume tells us, is long gone, is like a woman experiencing the severance of that which she never had, experiencing it as the fiction of experience, the invention of difference between author and reader, man and woman. She reads the cutting off as an imposition executed by a technique of disengagement that may incite metaphysical raptures but is nothing more (or less) than the empowering of style—an *occupatio* that she can virtuosically reproduce and counter by her own eloquent denial of eloquence. The transference of power which Hume admired and feared in classical oratory is effected by a reading that strikes home. Although the Comtesse de Boufflers is ready to subject herself to the course of history that Hume represents, she impetuously uses her subjection as the means forcefully to engage Hume in a "secret" history of her own devising.

The countess insists on mistaking Hume. And those mistakes are dangerous because they are the right mistakes to make. If she compliments his "impartiality," she undoes her praise with the epithet "divine." "*Divine* impartiality" and "*celestial* substance" invoke a religiosity wholly at odds with any intent that might be ascribed to the author of *The History of the Stuarts*, who also wrote an essay in which he described the mind as

> subject to an unaccountable elevation and presumption, arising from prosperous success, from luxuriant health, from strong spirits, or from a bold and confident disposition. In such a state of mind, the imagination swells with great, but confused conceptions, to which no sublunary beauties or enjoyments can correspond. . . . Hence arise raptures, transports, and surprising flights of fancy; and, confidence and presumption still increasing, these raptures, being altogether unaccountable, and seeming quite beyond the reach of our ordinary faculties, are attributed to the immediate inspiration of that Divine Being who is the object of devotion. ("Of Superstition and Enthusiasm," *ST,* pp. 146–47)

The "elevation and presumption," the unaccountable "raptures" attributed to the inspiration of a deity, aptly describe the enthusiasm of the countess's response. But if her elevation is enthusiastic, the sense of fault that accompanies its expression and produces the demand for secrecy seems to attest to "certain unaccountable terrors and apprehensions, proceeding either from the unhappy situation of private or public affairs, from ill health, from a gloomy and melancholy disposition, or from the concurrence of all these circumstances. In such a state of mind, infinite unknown evils are dreaded from unknown agents; and where real objects of terror are wanting, the soul, active to its own prejudice, and fostering its predominant inclination, finds imaginary ones, to whose power and malevolence it sets no limits" (*ST,* p. 146).

If this characterization of the psychology of superstition, with its reference to dread and unlimited malevolence, seems too strong to suit the Comtesse de Boufflers, it is nonetheless true that her letter closes with testimony of her fear of attracting blame and her anticipation of grief at being misunderstood—evidence of an "unhappy situation," or of a gloomy disposition, either of which would impell her to insist on secrecy. Even the circumstances of the transmission of the letter to Hume, via the intercession of the conspiratorial Alexander Murray, reflect the kind of priestly mediation which is the preferred vehicle of the superstitious.[19] It is not surprising that the countess should feel either elevated or secretive, but it *is* peculiar that the enthusiasm and the superstition, which Hume takes pains to distinguish and divide, should both appear in the same "moment" and indeed be tied together as part of the same economy of excess and fault (this peculiarity, as we shall see in Chapter 7, is shared with Jean-Jacques Rousseau). What is even more peculiar is that enthusiasm and superstition should emerge as a response to Hume's simplicity and clarity. Hume may not have caused this response; but he has been unable to prevent its *éclat* in that reader for whom his prose is expressly designed.

The style of moderation, like the genre of history, is a path between two extremes: the excess of simplicity and the excess of refinement.[20] And though Hume warns against each extreme, he insists that we "ought to be more on our guard against the excess of refinement than that of simplicity; and that because the former excess is both less *beautiful* and more *dangerous* than the latter" ("Of Simplicity and Refinement in Writing," *ST,* p. 46). Beyond laying down this general principle, Hume distinguishes styles according to genre, urging that "a greater degree of simplicity is required in all compositions where men and actions, and passions are painted [i.e., histories], than in such as consist of reflections and observations. And as the former species of writing is the more engaging and beautiful, one may safely, upon this account, give the preference to the extreme of simplicity above that of refinement" (p. 46). It is hard

19. Hume later had a falling out with Murray, who presumed on his connection to demand Hume's patronage. The breach was healed by Mme de Boufflers, who, like the Cicero described in "Of Eloquence," persuaded her Caesar to pardon the transgressor.

20. "When a man of business enters into life and action, he is more apt to consider the characters of men, as they have relation to his interest, than as they stand in themselves; and has his judgment warped on every occasion by the violence of his passion. When a philosopher contemplates characters and manners in his closet, the general abstract view of the objects leaves the mind so cold and unmoved, that the sentiments of nature have no room to play, and he scarcely feels the difference between vice and virtue. History keeps a just medium between these extremes, and places the objects in their true point of view" ("Of the Study of History," *ST,* pp. 98–99).

to locate a standard of "mere simplicity" in this account of the demands of historiography. Plain reflections and observations require refinement, which Hume identifies with ornament. Because the actions it narrates are more engaging and beautiful, historiography demands less refinement; but that does not translate into simplicity as such, only "a greater degree of simplicity," which, though hypothetically capable of being assigned to that prized "latitude" of moderation, here leads, in Hume's passage, to a "preference [for] the extreme of simplicity above that of refinement." That a medial "latitude" is nothing other than a hypothetical or theoretical "point" articulating two unstable extremes becomes evident when Hume observes that "it is with books as with women, where a certain plainness of manner and of dress is more engaging than that glare of paint, and airs, and apparel, which may dazzle the eye, but reaches not the affections. Terence [or Hume] is a modest beauty, to whom we grant every thing because [s]he assumes nothing, and whose purity and nature make a durable, though not a violent impression on us" (pp. 46–47). If it is with books as with women, then there is no option betwixt extreme simplicity and extreme refinement, no midpoint between plainness and glare; "woman" is here the sign of extremity, the kind of extremity to which females must have recourse in order to make an impression on men. If it is with books as with women, it is because "the good fortune of a book, and that of a man, are not the same" (p. 43)—and there is no latitude between the disaffiliation of the book from the man and the figuration of the book as a woman: book and woman, each stands in an essentially figurative relation to man, as nothing simple in itself.

The woman, like the book, is a luxury, and the fluctuations between extremes of simplicity and refinement can take place only under the general sign of luxury, which, Hume reminds us from the beginning, is a "word of uncertain signification" (*ST,* p. 48). Luxury has no simple; because it has not, Hume, following Mandeville and others, can persuasively argue that the abuse of luxury that is the legacy of the humanist and Christian traditions ought to be converted into an appreciation of the productive and progressively liberating effects of refinement.[21] So much to the good. But because luxury *is* an equivoque, it "may be taken in a good as well as a bad sense"; the "bounds between the virtue and the

21. For a survey of this tradition see John Sekora, *Luxury: The Concept in Western Thought, Eden to Smollett* (Baltimore: Johns Hopkins Univ. Press, 1977), pp. 23–131. See also Quentin Skinner, *The Foundations of Modern Political Thought,* 2 vols. (Cambridge: Cambridge Univ. Press, 1978), p. 43, on Renaissance humanists and luxury. This endorsement of luxury is intimately connected with the fall away from teleology in Hume's moral philosophy commented on by Alasdair McIntyre in *After Virtue* (Notre Dame: Univ. of Notre Dame Press, 1981) pp. 213–17.

vice cannot . . . be exactly fixed" (p. 48). Refinement lacks that neat, remedial principle of self-restraint that "belongs" to avidity; if luxury is itself excess, defining what is too much excess, that excess which takes us beyond the economic toward individual and social ruin, becomes extremely difficult. What Hume settles on is a version of the vicious as engrossment: "A gratification is only vicious when it engrosses all of a man's expense [both of money and of labor—that is, his energy], and leaves no ability for such acts of duty and generosity as are required by his situation and fortune" (p. 57).[22] The civic returns as a good which is ascribed to us by our position: for example, the duty of the rich to feed the poor. But this civic notion of good masks a more fundamental problematic which hangs on the margin of Hume's concern; for it is not just widows and orphans who might lack "bread for six months" because of the rich man's gratifying "dish of peas at Christmas"; there is no reason to restrict the sacrifice of good to the remote, no reason that vicious luxury could not lead to the starvation of one's own family or even of one's own self; or, to put it in macroeconomic terms, no reason why if luxury is that which stimulates the labor of all, vicious luxury should be restricted to the rich, no reason why the pursuit of arcane or fantastic luxuries should not engross the whole populace, the whole state—no reason, for example, why people would not rather read than eat.[23] If refinement is what makes the economy go, vicious luxury is what erases the bounds between a restricted economy and one generalized beyond any measure. Refinement's globalism is theoretically unchecked, its processive aggrandizement potentially and radically diseconomic.

Hume offers two solutions; one, the (providential) principle of balance, is explicit, and the other, the intervention of the sovereign, is only adumbrated (there are good reasons for Hume's taciturnity on this point; I shall take them up in Chapters 5 and 6). Balance emerges as a self-regulating economy of vices during Hume's consideration of the utopian possibility of extirpating vicious luxury: "Remove the vices, and the ills

22. A trait that distinguishes the self-indulgent, wasted aristocrat from the prudent and ascendant merchant: "The habits of luxury dissipated the immense fortunes of the ancient barons; and as the new methods of expense give subsistance to mechanics and merchants, who lived in an independant manner on the fruits of their own industry, a nobleman . . . retained only that moderate influence, which customers have over tradesmen." Hume, *The History of England*, 6 vols. (1778; rpt. Indianapolis: Liberty Classics, 1983), 4:384.

23. See the writer for the *Grub Street Journal* who "expressed dismay at what he called this 'national *Insania*' and deplored the fact that so many 'persons in the lowest stations of Life' were 'more intent upon cultivating their Minds than upon feeding and cloathing their Bodies.'" R. M. Wiles, "Middle-Class Literacy in Eighteenth-Century England: Fresh Evidence," in *Studies in the Eighteenth Century*, ed. R. F. Brissenden (Toronto: Univ. of Toronto Press, 1968), p. 51.

follow. You must only take care to remove all the vices. If you remove part, you may render the matter worse. By banishing *vicious* luxury, without curing sloth and an indifference to others, you only diminish industry in the state, and add nothing to men's charity or their generosity. Let us, therefore, rest contented with asserting, that two opposite vices in a state may be more advantageous than either of them alone; but let us never pronounce vice in itself advantageous" (*ST,* p. 58). A curious condensation has occurred. Hume still claims to be talking about something called "vicious luxury," but by setting that which is in excess of boundaries within boundaries, within a balance, by speaking of that which is vicious as though it were a virtue, he has actually shifted back to luxury, which is by definition that which can be balanced, an economical excess that stimulates labor. There seems to be no way to talk about virtuous luxury without stepping across the line of healthy excess into the vicious. There seems to be no way to talk about vicious refinement without drifting into fantasies of the inconceivable. And no way to talk about the fantastic without its excessiveness to all conception tripping us into the notional security of virtuous excess. And so on. How long could such refinement engross us?

We will never know. Hume begins to close his analysis and his essay by inviting us to "rest contented." Is this foreclosure of further refinement to be attributed to Hume's sloth, or is it a performance of that imperious banishment of vicious luxury which we have just been told is futile? Is it a balance or imbalance? As the letter from the Comtesse de Boufflers demonstrates, once the path of luxury, of gallantry, of historiography, or of essay writing is adopted, there is no way to assure that a reader, taught to refine, will rest contented in sympathy with the author's design. In that letter the equivocalness of luxury asserts itself according to a figurative dynamics that disorders the antithetical code (virtuous vs. vicious, the vice of luxury vs. some other countervailing vice) with which Hume would discipline refinement to the kind of economy in which men could have their cake and eat it too. The figure of luxury, of woman, disarranges the antithesis as a fluctuation between "extremes": between submission and sovereignty, superstition and enthusiasm, simplicity and refinement, excess and secret fault. "Extremes" here belongs in scare quotes because it suggests some measurable distance between limits beyond which nothing lies. But it is the equivocalness embedded in the word "luxury"— installed in the figure of woman and displayed in the letter of the Comtesse de Boufflers—that it both opens space for indirection and permits indirection to escape calculation and control. Neither progressive nor moral, refinement looks like nothing more than the play or ploy of a striking mistress.

The letter of the Comtesse de Boufflers, then, at once fulfills Hume's success and takes it too far or, to put a finer point on it, displays success as a luxury that is equivocal, both fruitful and vicious. It does so by dramatizing the incapacity of a masterfully simple and clear style preemptively to subdue a violent response by the woman. The letter is a reflection of Hume's writings, to be sure, but it reflects more than Hume in his pride would like; it displays in excess the technique and ideology of Hume's composition, and in representing the theater of Humean representation, marks out that place which is secluded from representation, where the man and the woman can conduct a secret history—a place out of society, where polite conversation surrenders to the engrossment of direct passion. By "removing part," that "noblest part," which is transformed, like Belinda's lock, into a "celestial substance," Hume "may [have] render[ed] the matter worse."

The unsettling equivocation in Hume's style lies in the crucial and most vulnerable articulation of Hume's composition: the gap between the partiality of the individual and the harmonious cooperation of the whole, a gap across which the force of induction/inducement must operate: induction on individuals regarded as material quantities, inducement on individuals whose labor is subject to the power of representation. Hume regards labor not as production but as performance: society may be envisioned as a marketplace by the liberal economist, but the marketplace is nothing other than a theater. The question will be whether that theatricality need and can be repressed. Is it, for example, a "material defect" if the laboring class recognizes the theatricality of its labor, understands it as a performance, and thereby perceives a sovereignty apart from this labor as represented and representing?[24] Can the sovereign subject

24. The problem, perceived by many commentators on eighteenth-century mores, was usually associated with the "present rage of imitating the manners of high life [which] hath spread itself so far among the gentlefolks of lower life, that in a few years we shall probably have no common folk at all." British Magazine 4 (1763): 417, quoted by Neil McKendrick, "Commercialization and the Economy," in The Birth of a Consumer Society, ed. Neil McKendrick, J. H. Plumb, and John Brewer (Bloomington: Indiana Univ. Press, 1982), p. 25. McKendrick's essay has an excellent discussion of this rage of imitating in the context of incipient consumerism in the eighteenth century. Joyce Oldham Appleby explicates the strength of the reaction to this consumerism. "A consumption-oriented model of economic growth," she writes, "threatened major interests of the ruling class that had coalesced in Restoration England. Dangerous leveling tendencies lurked behind the idea of personal improvement through imitative buying. The notion that the wealth of nations began with stimulating wants rather than organizing production robbed intrusive social legislation of a supporting rationale." Appleby, Economic Thought and Ideology in Seventeenth-Century England (Princeton: Princeton Univ. Press, 1978), p. 511.

choose not to be attracted by commodities? Can it be imagined that the sovereign subject could be so cut off from inducements that he would not labor but would retreat (or advance) into a solitude (or a solidarity) that is either a solipsistic darkness or a violent method?[25]

25. One hedge against the universal recognition of theatricality is the class distinction that is built into Hume's conception of his own performance: he does not write essays for the multitude; he writes *polite letters* directed to sovereigns, who are addressed in terms of the conventions to which they are accustomed. The example of the Comtesse de Boufflers' response to Hume's *History* shows, however, that that privileged audience is not predictable in its response to inducement, perhaps because of women's peculiar status: they are like workers (or slaves) in their forced submission; but unlike them because they are part of the best society. Similarly, the difference between Hume's sovereigns (the king, the woman) and the putative subjects of the state (the common laborers) is itself a delicately factitious one, endangered by both the necessary postulate of some direct passion that must be redirected in everyone (not simply in the monarch or the female reader of history) and by the Humean model of progressive refinement, which envisages the rise to politeness of all members of the state—a refinement that would eventually dissolve the distinction between the refined and the crude. Cf. Gibbon: "In the present imperfect condition of society, luxury, though it may proceed from vice or folly, seems to be the only means that can correct the unequal distribution of property." *The Decline and Fall of the Roman Empire*, ed. J. B. Bury, 7 vols. (1909; rpt. New York: AMS Press, 1974), 1:59.

5
The Commerce of Letters

Philosophers never ballance betwixt profit and honesty, because their decisions are general, and neither their passions nor imaginations are interested in the objects.

Treatise

. . . a creature, who traces causes and effects to a great length and intimacy; extracts general principles from particular appearances; improves upon his discoveries; corrects his mistakes; and makes his very errors profitable.

Essays

I

If a philosopher is not a creature like other men, it is because he is occupied at a level of generality removed from partiality or interest. This is not the defense of the incapable. "One knows," writes d'Alembert, "the story of the philosopher, whom his enemies had reproached for despising riches only out of a lack of talent for acquiring them; he entered into commerce, enriched himself there in a year, distributed his gain to his friends, and subsequently restored himself to philosophy."[1] The anecdote represents the philosopher as demonstrating his business sense while bracketing his illustrious career as a mere deviation from the contemplative life. But it does not unequivocally corroborate the purity of philosophical retreat. The philosopher evidently feels impelled to prove his disinterestedness by indulging his interest. To put a slightly finer point on it, the philosopher has an interest in his disinterest—otherwise, how would it be that his mockers could coax him from his study? It may be, however, that the acquisitive diversion is actually philosophy in practice: "Prejudices of every kind are given up without noise and without violence, because the property of the true philosophy is not that of forcing

1. D'Alembert, "Essai sur la Société des Gens de Lettres et des Grands," *Oeuvres completes de d'Alembert*, 5 vols. (Paris, 1821), 4:368.

any barrier, but of waiting for the barriers to open themselves before it, or of detouring when they do not open of themselves."[2] Truth and, because *it* is true, philosophy will prevail. So much at least is the implicit lesson of the "master narrative" that d'Alembert expresses for the philosopher of the Enlightenment.[3]

Like Hume, d'Alembert dissociates true philosophy from a violent method. Its detour is as much a part of philosophy as is its static truth. If it is true that there "is no quality in human nature which causes more fatal errors in our conduct, than that which leads us to prefer whatever is present to the distant and the remote," the philosopher can do no better philosophy than to put off present philosophizing. Once, or, as Hume indicates, often: "I have frequently, in the course of my life, met with interruptions, from business and dissipation; yet always returned to my closet with pleasure" (*HL*, 1:451). Hence a philosopher will be a man like any other when he chooses to acquiesce in the sport of commerce; but though like any other man, the philosopher is also better, for his success in the world is not only assured by his philosophy, which presumes in its general principles the particular capacities necessary to commercial success, but that philosophy from which he sets out is also that haven to which he can return. The plot of philosophy's commerce in the world will be the subject of this chapter.[4]

To address the commercial aspects of Hume's career requires situat-

2. Ibid., p. 339.

3. I borrow the term "master narrative" from Fredric Jameson, who argues that "individual period formulations always secretly imply or project narratives or 'stories'—narrative representations—of the historical sequence in which such individual periods take their place and from which they derive their significance." He redefines Louis Althusser's concept of "expressive causality" as "a vast interpretive allegory in which a sequence of historical events or texts is rewritten in terms of some deeper, underlying, and more 'fundamental' narrative, of a hidden master narrative which is the allegorical key or figural content of the first sequence of empirical materials." Jameson, *The Political Unconscious: Narrative as a Socially Symbolic Act* (Ithaca: Cornell Univ. Press, 1981), p. 29. Such a model applies to d'Alembert's anecdote, excepting the insistent criterion of secrecy. D'Alembert's story is available to everyone as the authorized master key to interpret the often wayward, ostensibly unphilosophical practices of the philosophes.

4. For another version, which accepts self-division as the philosopher's lot, cf. Diderot: "Our philosopher does not count himself an exile in the world; he does not suppose himself in the enemy's country, he would fain find pleasure with others, and to find it he must give it; he is a worthy man who wishes to please and to make himself useful. The ordinary philosophers, who meditate too much, or rather who meditate to wrong purpose, are as surly and arrogant to all the world as great people are to those whom they do not think their equals; they flee men and avoid them. But our philosopher who knows how to divide himself between retreat and the commerce of men is full of humanity." Quoted by Kingsley Martin, *French Liberal Thought in the Eighteenth Century* (1929; rpt. New York: Harper Row, 1963), p. 92.

ing the symbolic scheme which we have been examining in a more general context. Here is another of the postmortems that the young Hume composed in response to the disappointing sale of the *Treatise:*

> I am now out of Humour with myself; but doubt not in a little time to be out of Humour with the World, like most unsuccessful Authors. After all, I am sensible of my Folly in entertaining any Discontent, much more Despair upon this Account; since I cou'd not expect any better from such abstract Reasoning, nor indeed did I promise myself much better. My Fondness for what I imagin'd new Discoveries made me overlook all common rules of Prudence; & having enjoy'd the usual Satisfaction of Projectors, 'tis but just I should meet with their Dissapointments. However, as 'tis observ'd that with such sort of People one Project generally succeeds another, I doubt not but in a day or two I shall be as easy as ever, in Hopes that Truth will prevail at last over the Indifference & Opposition of the World. (*NHL,* p. 5)

Hume's renewed hopefulness is owed to his increased experience with the perils of authorship, which tells him that no reversal is necessarily a final breakdown and thus cause for despair—on the contrary, each reversal is itself "generally" reversed. Success is described as the triumph of truth over indifference, but it is not to truth that the credit is given. Instead, Hume, however sardonically, seems to be relying on some mechanism that will produce work after work and supply the occasion necessary for the triumph of truth.

Hume's confidence is soundly based, founded in part on the very failure of the *Treatise.* Hume may have exaggerated the catastrophe, but the exaggeration served a purpose: it justified his acting as though the book had never been published. Anonymous and unread, the *Treatise* could be revised and republished in different formats, at different times, and with different publishers. Although the first edition was published in 1739 and 1740 (and remained unsold in 1756), sections of the *Treatise* appeared in *An Enquiry Concerning Human Understanding* (1748), *An Enquiry Concerning the Principles of Morals* (1751), and the essay "Of Passions" (1752); another portion was intended for the "Fourth Dissertation," which was never set up in print. The *Treatise* appeared under the imprint of three publishers: books 1 and 2 were printed by John Noon; book 3 was originally published by Thomas Longmans; and Andrew Millar published all the later reworkings of the *Treatise* during Hume's lifetime. Hume displayed no detectable paternal reverence for the remains of the first child of his brain, which he vended through different agents in different packages to different markets at different times, adapting to the fluctuation of public taste.

This canniness was not something in which Hume was instructed, perhaps by a veteran bookman, subsequent to the failure of the *Treatise*. In his dealings with the publishers during the first negotiations over publication he not only restricted the contract to the first two books of the *Treatise*, retaining the right (of which he took shrewd advantage) to negotiate with another publisher for the third; he sold only the rights to the first edition, "reserving for himself the rights to any future edition" (Mossner, p. 112). Although inexperienced in the trade, Hume pursued his interests with considerable acumen. And from the very first those interests were understood in terms of future, successive, and altered editions of the *Treatise*. Hume's transactions prepared him for success and for failure.

Hume managed the *Treatise* not as a child, attached to him by bonds of nature, but as his property, which, as we have seen, subsists not in simple possession but in a *mode* of possession. Property remedies the easy change of objects by establishing a relation of articulated transfer which allows for the circulation of objects. It remedies the problem of ineradicable scarcity, some people having more and some less than they need, by exploiting the promise. Promises are "certain *symbols* or *signs* instituted, by which we might give each other security of our conduct in any particular incident" (*T*, p. 524). The promise stabilizes the potentially volatile relations between constancy and transference by configuring a triangle that reroutes the avidity of the individual in an oblique path of possessions without satisfaction and of lack without despair. Promise incorporates deferral as a conventional attribute of the relation of the object to the individual—a deferral that is executed by those symbols with which we guarantee our conduct in any given instance and which, of course, can be transferred from instance to instance without losing their instrumental value. Because of the promise, one can never fully catch up to what one does not have, and by the same token one always has what one does not have; hence deferral involves no sacrifice. Like society itself, property brings people together in a convention that is also a separation: men join in a community in order to "separate themselves from the community, and to distinguish betwixt their own goods and those of others" (*T*, p. 495). The promise, then, simply makes explicit a symbolic mediation that belongs to each aspect of property—stability and transference—and belongs to property in general.[5]

---

5. It is no accident that this definition of property reads like a prospectus for a postal

Hume's management of the *Treatise*—his use of different publishers for different parts, his reworking of it into different forms—reflects his efforts to resist easy change and to overcome the scarcity both of the object itself and of the satisfaction that it can bring. If the castration of the *Treatise* undermines the biological metaphor for authorship by instituting a symbolic understanding and use of the text, it also marks the entrance of Hume into commerce as a proprietor. There is no place where one can point to a completed body and work, to the *Treatise* whole and entire. Early on, as we have seen, Hume projected such a result in his explanation to Michael Ramsey of his refusal to send him draft pages from the manuscript because such "loose bits of Paper" were "none of them worth to any Body & I believe scarce to myself" (*HL*, 1:9). The complete book never materialized. Intentionally. What Hume learned in the composition of the *Treatise* was not only the truth of Callimachus' (and Addison's) dictum that "a great book is a great evil"; he also discovered that disconnected parts are worth something to somebody and to himself most of all.[6] The "whole" is a theoretical moment of immediate possession, a philosophical fiction like the state of nature. It is not the immediate possession of the whole that defines the value of the *Treatise* for Hume or its interest for anyone else; rather, it is the relation in which those parts stand to one another and to the individual. The scattering of parts, as long as they are held together as property by copyright, is a means of turning scarcity into plenty.

If Hume's proprietorial emendation of the *Treatise* can be regarded as a renunciation of the goal of revolutionizing philosophy, it is also an acceptance of limited success and a precaution aimed at insuring it. Deleting "Of Miracles" from the text produced two commodities where there has been only one. The cut increased Hume's stock and initiated the scattering of pieces that might possibly produce a successful yield. Both the revision of the *Treatise* and the *seriatim* publication of the books on understanding, passions, and morals represent a partition of employments which refines Hume's industry and works to the increased advantage of the whole.

Hume's partition of his employments is one of the chief characteristics of his career. Witness his explanation of his decision to accept the

---

service. As we shall have occasion to observe later in this chapter and in the next, there was an intimate relation between the eighteenth century's theories of property and its epistolary culture.

6. Callimachus, *Athenaeus* 3.1, quoted in H. L. Pinner, *The World of Books in Classical Antiquity* (Leiden: Sijthoff, 1958), p. 14. Addison quotes the Greek phrase without attribution at the beginning of *Spectator* no. 124.

invitation "from General St Clair to attend him in his new employment at the Court of Turin":

> I shall have an opportunity of seeing Courts & Camps, & if I can afterwards, be so happy as to attain leizure and other opportunities, this knowledge may even turn to account to me, as a man of letters, which I confess has always been the sole object of my ambition. I have long had an intention, in my riper years, of composing some History; & I question not but some greater experience of the Operations of the Field, & the Intrigues of the Cabinet, will be requisite, in order to enable me to speak with judgement upon these subjects. (*HL*, 1:109)

Hume confesses that he leaves his study with "infinite regret" but recognizes that "in certain situations, a man dares not follow his own judgment or refuse such offers as these." Unlike the earlier stint in Bristol, which was justified as therapy, the decision to join St. Clair is explained as a choice that will advance a career already undertaken. Hume does not foresee becoming a general and hardly plans to remain a secretary. His detour is part of a career understood as a calculus which can transform all necessities into opportunities. The life in camp and courts is a diversion but also a diversification.

The name that Hume uses for a career of such plasticity is not author but "man of letters." Malesherbes gave a historical rendering of the strategy by which scattering is troped into diversification when he observed that in "a century in which every citizen can speak to the entire nation by means of print, those who have the talent for instructing men or the gift of moving them—in a word, men of letters—are, in the midst of dispersed people, what the orators of Rome and Athens were in the midst of a people assembled."[7] The superiority of the modern man of letters to the "orators of Rome and Athens" is a consequence of his different strategic position. For although the extraordinary power of the orator was owed to his presence among the people whom he could address as one man by speaking to and in the moment, hurrying them to decision and action by a sublime style, his weakness was, as we have seen, the direct complement of that power. Considered from an economic perspective, the power of the orator was an immediate possession alive only in the *éclat* of his eloquence; it may have satisfied all his avidity, but only for a time (it had no stability), and it was possible only for a few (it could not be efficiently transferred)—it was presence without promise. The power of

7. Quoted in Arthur M. Wilson, *Diderot: The Testing Years, 1713–1759* (New York: Oxford Univ. Press, 1957), p. 162.

oratory forged a sensible object which absorbed orator and auditors into a single, impassioned whole; but the sensible object of oratorical power had no relation to the orator or to the audience, since its very sublimity was the dissolution of all object relations. By writing to a dispersed people, the man of letters loses direct power, but the dispersal of his words, always contained and regulated by the social convention of property, insures that scarce texts become multiplied a thousandfold, that despite the distribution of his words his claim to them remains stable, and that any transference of his words to another will not diminish his gain. Gramsci's observation has held true for the man of letters since the consolidation of print culture: "The mode of existence of the new intellectual can no longer consist of eloquence, the external and momentary arousing of sentiments and passions, but must consist of being actively involved in practical life, as a builder, an organizer, 'permanently persuasive' because he is not purely an orator."[8] Both the orator and the man of letters are "in the midst" of the societies in which they speak and write. But the orator's centrality must be a literal fact; he must be in the center of the state because his power extends only so far as his voice carries. The modern man of letters is, on the contrary, situated in the midst of a people whose very dispersion makes the actual fact of a center only a metaphor. If he is central, it is not because he resides in a territorial, institutional, or political center but because of his symbolic role and symbolizing practice.[9] The man of letters is not only one, like everyone, whose property is symbolic, but singularly that one whose symbols are his only property: he is at the farthest remove from any mystified, fetishized attachment to any sensible object.

8. Antonio Gramsci, "The Formation of Intellectuals," in *The Modern Prince and Other Writings*, trans. Louis Marks (1957; rpt. New York: International, 1980), p. 122.

9. There were other forms of institutional centrality than the forum and more immediate examples of forceful oratory than Cicero with which Hume as man of letters had to contend. Alexander Carlyle writes of Hume's near and influential predecessor Francis Hutcheson that in his lectures at the University of Glasgow Hutcheson's "elocution was good, and his voice and manner pleasing, [and] he raised the attention of his hearers at all times; and when the subject led him to explain and enforce the moral virtues and duties, he displayed a fervent and persuasive eloquence which was irresistible." Even his "learned and ingenious" lectures on Grotius were "adapted to every capacity" and attended "not only by students but by many of the people of the city." *The Autobiography of Dr. Alexander Carlyle of Inveresk, 1722–1805*, ed. John Hill Burton (London and Edinburgh: T. N. Foulis, 1910), p. 78. That Hutcheson is a particular instance of the restrictive oratorical posture with which Hume generally contends reinforces Gary Shapiro's insight (applied to *The Dialogues of Natural Religion*) that the man of letters seeks "to subvert the pedagogical relation"; see "The Man of Letters and the Author of Nature: Hume on Philosophical Discourse," *The Eighteenth Century* 26, no. 2 (1985): 120.

Malesherbes' static contrast between the places of the orator and the man of letters in their respective societies implied that the man of letters somehow *finds* himself in the midst of a dispersed people and conducts his career accordingly. But in her study *The Printing Press as an Agent of Change* Elizabeth Eisenstein has argued that the dispersal of the community was not something which the man of letters came upon and to which he prudently adapted; the printing press that made the career of the man of letters possible was fundamentally responsible for the cleavage between centered ancient and dispersed modern. The invention of the printing press excited the humanist dream of a diffusion of books across the world and made possible the rise of a class of men who would pursue that dream by supplying Aldus and his descendants with the raw material to be transformed into printed books and distributed through multiplying channels of trade to the remote corners of the civilized world. At the center of this dispersion would be the man of letters, the author of those books whose revolutionary effectiveness consisted in a dispersion regulated both by the uniform replication that the printing press allowed and by the fact that the dispersed, reproduced properties would always have a determinate, copyrighted relation to their author. The disinterested propagation of ideas, which was the aim of the republic of letters, was never separate from the individual's ambition for the success of his own writings.[10]

According to Voltaire's definition of the term in the *Encyclopédie*, the man of letters

10. On the antimony between citizenship and vanity, see Shapiro, "The Man of Letters," p. 124. Regulation of dispersion did not happen all at once. The syncopation that threatened to unhinge the man of letters' assurance of centrality can be adduced in the layered revision of Erasmus' *Adagium* "Festina Lente." Erasmus' enthusiastic praise of the dissemination of humanist texts across the world is revised according to the perception that at the center of that dispersion is not merely the humanist author but also Aldus' printing press. Both the "Herculean task" of restoring classical texts and the ambition of Aldus to build up "a library which has no other limits than the world itself" are threatened by the unsavory practices of ignoble printers, who print too many texts too cheaply. Erasmus attempts to reterritorialize the globalizing dispersion of texts by appealing to the intervention of the prince, who would suppress the "unbridled license" of profiteering printers, and who would sponsor the activity that occurs under the trademarks of Aldus and Froben. *Erasmus on His Times: A Shortened Version of the "Adages" of Erasmus*, trans. Margaret Mann Phillips (Cambridge: Cambridge Univ. Press, 1967), pp. 3–17. Copyright, printing, and humanism compose a historical nexus: "Scribal culture," according to Elizabeth Eisenstein, "could not sustain the patenting of inventions or the copyrighting of literary compositions. It worked against the concept of intellectual property rights." *The Printing Press as an Agent of Change* (1979; rpt., 2 vols. in 1, Cambridge: Cambridge Univ. Press, 1982), p. 299.

has even greater dimensions in our time than the word 'grammarian' had among the Greeks and the Romans. . . . Today the *man of letters* often adds to the study of Greek and Latin that of Italian, Spanish, and especially English. The profession of the historian is a hundred times vaster than what it was for the ancients; and natural history has grown in proportion to that of the nations. One does not require a *man of letters* to study thoroughly all this material; universal knowledge is no longer within the grasp of one man, but true *men of letters* place themselves in a position to proceed into these different fields even if they cannot cultivate all of them.[11]

Not only do true men of letters strategically place themselves in a position to proceed into different fields; men of letters are those who are prepared, like Hume, to take tactical advantage of whatever position they are placed in, to make it a new center. There is, for example, no documentary evidence that Hume planned to write a history before being given the offer by General St. Clair. He might have remained an author by staying at home; and it is difficult to see how the attachment to the army could be anything but a disruption of the vocation of authorship; but the ambition of being a man of letters supervenes on possible disruption and renders it an opportunity for the advancement of a career in which a circumstance becomes a position and a diversion becomes a refinement.

11. *Denis Diderot's "The Encyclopedia": Selections,* ed. and trans. Stephen J. Gendzier (New York: Harper Torchbooks, 1967), pp. 166–67. Cf. Cicero's observation in *De Oratore* 1:5.20 that "no man can be an orator complete in all points of merit, who has not attained a knowledge of all important subjects and arts" (trans. E. W. Sutton and H. Rackham [1942; rpt. Cambridge: Harvard Univ. Press, 1979], p. 17). Cf. also Professor Shaw's exclamation over Johnson during his visit to St. Andrews that "this is a wonderful man; he is master of every subject he handles"—which is unintentionally ambiguous praise for someone who presents all the hallmarks of a man of letters but who would want to represent himself as a man of learning. *Boswell's Journal of "A Tour to the Hebrides,"* ed. Frederick A. Pottle and Charles H. Bennett (New York: Literary Guild, 1936), p. 47. The tension between Johnson as conversationalist and disputant is intricate with the same ambiguity. In the eighteenth century the versatility manifest in the man of letters is paradigmatic as well as exemplary. Cf. Voltaire: "What then is luxury? It is a word without any precise idea, much such another expression as when we say the eastern and western hemispheres: in fact, there is no such thing as east and west; *there is no fixed point* where the earth rises and sets; or, if you will, every point on it is the same time east and west. It is the same with regard to luxury; for either there is no such thing, or else it is in all places alike." *The Works of Voltaire,* trans. William F. Fleming, 22 vols. (New York: Dingwell-Rock, 1927), *Essays* (n.v.), p. 216. And Fernand Braudel: "The essential characteristic of capitalism was its capacity to ship at a moment's notice from one form or sector to another, in times of crisis or of pronounced decline in profit rates." *The Wheels of Commerce,* vol. 2 of *Civilization and Capitalism: Fifteenth–Eighteenth Century,* trans. Sian Reynolds (New York: Harper & Row, 1982), p. 423.

The scholar becomes an attaché; the moral philosopher becomes a historian: Hume remains a man of letters.

For Hume the relation between individual and state is synechdochal: the whole state is like the individual man in that it is avid of gain and in that it must acknowledge and accept the conventions that inhibit the violent expression of that avidity and mitigate its satisfaction. If the whole state can stand for the individual man, and the part for the whole, the man of letters (a man of many parts) is the idealization of the state as individual and individual as state. The career of the man of letters was a mechanism adapted to the "historical contradiction" that J.G.A. Pocock argues arose from the need for increased specialization in eighteenth-century culture:

> Specialization was a prime cause of corruption; only the citizen as amateur, propertied, independent, and willing to perform in his own person all functions essential to the polis, could be said to practice virtue or live in a city where justice was truly distributed. There was no *arte* that he must not be willing to make his own. But if the arts proved to have been built up through a process of specialization, then culture itself was in contradiction with the ethos of the *zoon politikon* and if it were argued . . . that only specialization, commerce, and culture set men free enough to attend to the goods of others as well as their own, then it would follow that the polis was built up by the very forces that must destroy it.[12]

Typically, the man of letters exhibited the amateurism that historically characterized the humanist but in a context that was less civic than social and that turned the ready virtue of the citizen into a lability or virtuosity that was its *refinement*—making versatility a specialization in its own right, accessible to only a few and with claims to an executive privilege over the other specializations that compose modern society.

The managerial aspect of the man of letters' virtuosity—his ability to mobilize in his own interest the "conjunction of forces," the "partition of employments," and the "mutual succour" that make society advantageous[13]—is most clearly exemplified in a 1756 letter from Hume to his publisher of longest duration, Andrew Millar:

12. J.G.A. Pocock, *The Machiavellian Moment* (Princeton: Princeton Univ. Press, 1975), p. 499.
13. The man of letters was a more advanced and sophisticated representative of the general consequences of what Pocock calls "the proposition that property was the basis of social personality [which] was to make personality itself explicable in terms of a material and historical process of diversification, refinement and perhaps ultimate decay and renewal."

I had a Conversation yesterday with Messrs Kincaid & Donaldson, where I made them a Proposal, which I hope will be for both your Advantage. They told me, that you had only about 400 compleat Sets of my philosophical Writings. I am extremely desirous to have these four Volumes, with that which you will publish this Winter, brought into a Quarto Volume. They said, that the small Size was rather more proper for their Sale; and therefore, they woud gladly take at present 200 Sets of the four Volumes, to be pay'd for by so many of their Shares in the Quarto Edition as woud be Equivalent. . . . If the History meet with Success, it will certainly quicken the Sale of the philosophical Writings; & the taking two hundred Sets from you leaves you so small a Number on hand, as gives you a certain Prospect of coming soon to a new Edition. . . . If you agree to this Proposal, they empower'd me to desire you to put the 200 Copies on board a Ship with the first Occasion, and to write them a Letter by which they may be sure, that there is no Mistake in the Conditions. The bringing these scatterd Pieces into one Volume will of itself quicken the Sale; & every new Edition has naturally that Effect. (*HL*, 1:236)

Hume refers to three different books or editions and articulates the flux and reflux of their dispersion and gathering. The *Essays and Treatises*, published in 1753–56, collected all of Hume's previously published writings, dispersed under various titles, into four octavo volumes. But that collection itself is segmented and, therefore, itself somewhat dispersed—allowing the gathering of "these scattered Pieces into one volume," which, as a new edition, will have the natural effect of quickening the sale, even though Hume expects that the price of the quarto will be the same as, or even slightly higher than, the octavos. Novelty will quicken the sale: novelty not as a stimulus to curiosity (there will be nothing new in the "new" edition) but novelty as luxury—the simple refinement of a preexistent object which does not alter its substance at all but merely changes its properties.

By gathering the four volumes into a single book, Hume probably hoped to take advantage of the traditional valuation that estimated a quarto more highly than an octavo volume. Isaac Watts had endorsed the valuation, while lamenting its passing, in 1729: "Now we deal much in Essays, and most unreasonably despise systematic learning, whereas our Fathers had a just Value for Regularity and Systems; then Folio's and Quarto's were the Fashionable Sizes, as Volumes in Octavo are now"

J.G.A. Pocock, *Virtue, Commerce, and Society* (Cambridge: Cambridge Univ. Press, 1985), p. 119.

(Mossner, p. 139).[14] In retrospect, after the triumph of the octavo, the natural relation between systems and quartos can be seen to have been merely fashionable. Hume takes advantage of that fashion by including his essays and his treatises (a melange of which Watts would almost certainly have disapproved) in a quarto, which can no longer be regarded as intrinsically suited to any particular contents (there is no longer any systematic support for a "just value"), and he thereby produces a luxury. The size itself cannot be said to establish its luxuriousness: the sale will quicken not because the new edition is a quarto but because the quarto is a new edition. Newness is luxury and luxury is mere innovation—another edition. There is no essential reason why the quarto could not have come first and the octavo followed: novelty would have been achieved, the sale quickened, either way. It would be a mistake to neglect the *cachet* still associated with the quarto, yet what logic there is to the sequence of Hume's editions seems to derive most concretely from a progressive movement of condensation: scattered essays and treaties are collected in four volumes; the set of four is then packed between two covers.

But to express that logic in terms of a progressive sequence is wrongly to pose diachronically what is at all times conceived synchronically and mistakenly to characterize as condensation a process that is always dispersive. The error can be seen as soon as one asks, "Of *what* does a new edition quicken the sale?" A new quarto cannot quicken the sale of a quarto edition which did not previously exist. It is hard to see how the addition of the quarto would accelerate the sale of the octavo editions. What it quickens, of course, is the sale of Hume's essays and treatises, which are never identified with any particular edition, at the same time that they exist nowhere else but in those editions: essays are not sold; the *Essays* are sold. Hume's works are his property, objects that stand in a relation to him that is always stable (they are always Hume's essays) and is always transferable (Hume's *Essays* are constantly being sold, sometimes slowly, sometimes quickly). Moreover, because of the capacity of property to be promised, it is accurate to say that the new edition of the quarto quickens the sale of the octavos (not in itself, only because there is no such a thing as an edition or an object in itself). The new quarto

---

14. Compare Johnson's reported judgment of the different formats: "No man, Johnson used to say, reads long together with a folio on his table. Books, said he, that you may carry to the fire, and hold readily in your hand, are the most useful after all. Such books form the great mass of general and easy reading. He was a great friend to books like the *French Esprits d'un Tel;* for example, *Beauties of Watts,* etc., at which, said he, a man will often look and be tempted to go on, when he would have been frightened at books of a larger size, and of a more erudite appearance." *Johnsonian Miscellanies,* ed. G. B. Hill, II, 2, quoted by A. S. Collins, *The Profession of Letters, 1780–1832* (London: Routledge, 1928), p. 65.

edition will sell more rapidly than the octavo, but the possibility of there being a new edition depends on the promise of Messrs Kincaid and Donaldson to yield shares in the new quarto (an as yet absent object) for delivery of the octavo. Thus the condensation of the *Essays and Treatises* is part of a new scattering of texts contrived by *increasing* the number of the editions, which permits their wider distribution to different vendors and their broader dispersion to a greater number of readers.

A new edition is, then, merely *another* edition in the important sense that it does not replace or supersede the previous edition: it displaces it to another bookseller and another market (Millar is in London, and Kincaid and Donaldson are in Edinburgh), but that displacement is actually a dispersion within a single and comprehensive territory tied together by well-understood property relations. The two editions do not compete with each other; the subdivision of one into two is an augmentation of forces. The edition of the *History* functions in the same way ("If the History meet with Success, it will certainly quicken the Sale of the philosophical Writings"). The partition of employments into history and philosophy enhances the prospects of each and of Hume's work as a whole.[15] The mutual succor among parts assures that the failure of one will not damage another; on the contrary, the success of one should buoy up the other.[16]

In "Of the Jealousy of Trade" (included in both the octavo and the quarto editions), Hume argues that the "emulation among rival nations serves rather to keep industry alive in all of them: And any people is happier who possess a variety of manufactures, than if they enjoyed one single great manufacture, in which they are all employed. Their situation is less precarious; and they will feel less sensibly those revolutions and uncertainties, to which every particular branch of commerce will always be exposed" (G&G, p. 347; see *ST*, pp. 78–79 and *HL*, 1:272). In the nation of "Hume" the one great manufacture is parceled out to different

15. Johnson indirectly endorsed the principle of "mutual succour" in his response to Boswell's question whether the simultaneous advertisement of both Sir John Hawkins's and Dr. Burney's *History of Music* would not hurt each. "'No sir,'" Johnson answered. "'They will do good to one another. Some will buy the one, some the other, and compare them; and so a talk is made about a thing, and the books are sold'" (Boswell, *Tour*, p. 50).

16. In the event, the projected cooperation between the two Scottish publishers was not prolonged. In 1763 Millar sought and obtained in Chancery an injunction against Donaldson for piratical publication of Thomson's *The Seasons*. That action bcame the basis for *Millar v. Taylor* (who sold some of Donaldson's editions) in 1765, the only success that the London booksellers could claim in prosecuting their claim to a common law right to perpetual copyright. The issue was finally decided against the London booksellers, and perpetual copyright in Edinburgh and Westminster, in the case *Donaldson v. Hinton* (Millar by this time being dead) in 1773–74.

manufacturers in order to afford the greatest prosperity consistent with the greatest security.

Like states, like men, like books: each level is related to every other according to a scale of generality and constitutes a terrain that is definite and composed—by commerce for states, by social exchange for men, by the man of letters for books. What contains all the levels, promotes their multiplication, establishes their specificity, and regulates their affiliative groupings is the supervisory concept of the greatest generalization, the social composition. All groups—whether of states, individuals, or books—are societies, even and especially men of letters: "Our connection with each other, as men of letters, is greater than our difference as adhering to different sects or systems. Let us revive the happy times when Atticus and Cassius the Epicureans, Cicero the Academic, and Brutus the Stoic, could all of them, live in unreserved friendship together, and were insensible to all those distinctions, except so far as they furnished agreeable matter to discourse and conversation" (*HL*, 1:172–73). Whether or not such amity, where all differences have become refinements of discourse, is realizable, the conditions of its possibility do not depend on the pious revival of a classical harmony but on the actual capacity of Humean, liberal society to transform all individual desires into symbolic differences and to recuperate all differences as stimuli to commerce.

When considered within the context of this commerce, the *History of the Stuarts* loses its generic specificity. It is not a different kind of discipline or of writing but just another edition (albeit a more popular one) to be contracted and sold. If, however, history is just another edition, all editions are history—that is, all editions stand in relation to the *Treatise* as history stands to philosophy, as its experimental application. The various editions of Hume's writings discover in the world the principles of society and the relations of property that the *Treatise* proposes, and *fix* those principles by an appropriately indirect practice. Commercial history—negotiations, contracts, competition, and profit—is the detour of Humean moral philosophy into the world, the route by which its truth struggles to prevail.

The publication of books vitally concerns the man of letters: the ability to publish and to continue to publish gives him his singular, historical existence; it is that mechanical employment which frees him from ascriptive ties, immunizes him from accident, and, in sum, distinguishes him from the mere biological entity, the savage body that lives and dies. Publication grants an existence to the man of letters by giving him a living; and publication will ideally enable him to extend that living beyond the deathbed into a posthumous future where his existence as man of letters will continue as long as publication ensues and contracts hold. To say there is always something posthumous about the career of the man of letters is only to express the difference between publication and production. We can imagine for Hume a point where productivity, the toil of setting pen to a blank piece of paper and coming up with a new invention in epistemology, politics, morals, or economics, any writing at all that is not correspondence or correction, becomes not only unnecessary but otiose. The capacity to manipulate the symbols that compose books, which are the property of books, is always on the verge of being transformed into the practice of manipulating books as symbols. In fact, the idea of this imagined point is linked to a distinct impression, the moment in Hume's career when he extends his refusal to write the ecclesiastical history, which he had half-heartedly projected and to which he had been urged by publishers and philosophes, to a determination (made roughly around 1762) to write no more books at all but to devote the rest of his life to the correction of the editions of his work that continued to pass through the press. That resolution was to be violated only by the letters he continued to write to friends and associates, the autobiographical essay in which he denied a life that was anything but posthumous, an essay "Of the Origin of Government," a will by which he distributed his property and endeavored to guarantee the posthumous publication of his long-suppressed *Dialogue Concerning Natural Religion*, and a hybrid production, the *Exposé Succinct*.

The transformation of production into correction represents a transition to a stage of almost pure profit—a living apparently maintained with minimal labor. Hume at that point would seem to have achieved what he claims: that independence which is the true measure of the success of a man of letters, an autonomy which elevates him even above the monarch.[17] It verges on that "sphere of play" which Jean Baudrillard defines as "the fulfillment of human rationality, the dialectical culmination of man's activity of incessant objectification of nature and control of his exchanges with it. . . . Wishing itself beyond labor but *in its continuation*, the sphere is always merely the esthetic sublimation of labor's constraints."[18] Yet a minimum of labor is still labor. And the fact that labor continues after financial independence has been achieved suggests that

---

17. "I wonder how Kings dare to be so free: They ought to leave that to their Betters; to Men who have no Dependance on the Mob, or the Leaders of the Mob. As to poor Kings they are obligd sometimes to retract and to deny their Writings" (*HL*, 1:336; see also *HL*, 1:327).

18. Jean Baudrillard, *The Mirror of Production*, trans. Mark Poster (St. Louis: Telos, 1975), p. 40.

"independence" is not a term without equivocal significations. For the man of letters there is no *otium* after *negotium*.[19]

II

The acumen that the young Hume displayed in the conduct of his career is no more extraordinary than the precocity of his philosophical statement. Published in January of 1739, when Hume was still twenty-seven years old, the *Treatise* had been sketched out in the main during the period of intense activity, interrupted only by the disease of the learned, when Hume was between the ages of eighteen and twenty-three. The sagacity of the philosopher and the canniness of the man of letters are mutually implicated. Once the importance of remedying direct passion, of adjusting it to the exigencies of social life, is philosophically understood, it can be practiced. Or take the converse: once the adjustment of desire is practiced by the writer, it presupposes an understanding. Wherever we begin, the understanding of the process of labor is an act of labor within that process. We can never discover by observation (only imagine as fiction) any moment prior to a labor that has always already begun. Because of the prevenience of the social composition, it is not necessary to regard Hume as *planning* a career and therefore somehow deducing, without any experience of the world, the moves he should make *vis-à-vis* printers in Edinburgh and London or readers in Paris. Instead, Hume practices a career, as he composes the *Treatise*, by making one adjustment after another in a continual labor of perpetual refinement.

We do not have to worry the question of precocity in Hume because there is no maturation. The body is dis-organized in order to be re-organized, dis-composed in order to be re-composed. The technique remains constant. March 16, 1740:

> I wait with some Impatience for a second Edition principally on account of Alterations I intend to make in my Performance. This is an Advantage, that we Authors possess since the Invention of Printing & renders the *Nonum prematur in annum* not so necessary to us as the Antients. Without it I shoud have been guilty of a very great

19. See the testimony of one of Hume's heirs, William Hazlitt: "The kind of conversation that I affect most is what sort of a day it is, and whether it is likely to rain or hold up fine for to-morrow. This I consider as enjoying the *otium cum dignitate*, as the end and privilege of a life of study. I would resign myself to this state of easy indifference, but I find I cannot. I must maintain a certain pretension, which is far enough from my wish. I must be put on my defence, I must take up the gauntlet continually, or I find I lose ground." "On the Disadvantages of Intellectual Superiority," *Selected Writings* (Harmondsworth: Penguin, 1970), p. 191.

Temerity to publish at my Years so many Noveltys in so delicate a Part of Philosophy. (*HL*, 1:35)

March 25, 1771:

This is the last time I shall probably take the pains of correcting that work, which is now brought to as great a degree of accuracy as I can attain; and is probably much more labour'd . . . than any other production in our language. This power, which Printing gives us, of continually improving and correcting our Works in successive Editions, appears to me the Chief Advantage of that art. (*HL*, 2:239)

Different "works," but the same statement. The same statement because the same technique. The invention of the art of printing, which separates us from the ancients as decisively as does the loss of oratorical power (a loss which is certainly connected with that technological advance), is the condition for this technique; printing promises permanence and a standard of uniformity which make correction desirable and a machinery of reproduction that makes correction possible.

It would be difficult to exaggerate the significance of the printing press to Hume's philosophical project. The printing press makes possible the metaphor of the impression and the associated "copy theory of knowledge."[20] The generalizable properties of the printing press serve, as much

20. The ancient antecedent for the copy theory of knowledge (famously reinvoked by both Descartes and Locke), which relied on available technology, is Plato's metaphor of the wax tablet in *The Theaetetus*. Socrates instructs Theaetetus, "When a man has in his mind a good thick slab of wax, smooth and kneaded to the right consistency, and the impressions that come through the senses are stamped on these tables of the 'heart' . . . then the imprints are clear and deep enough to last a long time." Though similar in its operation to the printing press, which is the implicit model that underwrites all associationist psychology, Socrates' illustration serves a purpose that is nearly opposite to Hume's. Socrates is interested in describing *differences* in men's facility of accurate judgment: hence the emphasis on a "good thick slab of wax" and the subsequent differentiation between a person who has a "shaggy heart," and those whose "block is muddy or made of impure wax, or over soft or hard." *Plato's Theory of Knowledge: The "Theaetetus" and the "Sophist" of Plato*, trans. with commentary by Francis MacDonald Cornford (1935; rpt. London: Routledge & Kegan Paul, 1951), 194. C–E, p. 126). The printing press is invoked by Hume as a standard of uniformity, not a register of differences: one imprint is the same as the next—neither stamp nor paper varies. Moreover, the printing press is qualitatively different in another way: it provides not only for standard replication but also for an indefinite reproduction and dispersion, which was the case with neither the wax tablet nor, even more notoriously, with the mintage of coins carrying the imprint of the royal visage. On the minting of coins, a preferred metaphor in explicitly political contexts, see Marc Shell, *The Economy of Literature* (Baltimore: Johns Hopkins Univ. Press, 1978), esp. chap. 1. For a reading of *Hamlet* that focuses on the question of the royal seal, its replicability, and the consequences for concepts of sovereignty

as the elastic security of custom, to mitigate the pyrrhonistic tendency of Hume's critique of causation:

> When we infer effects from causes, we must establish the existence of these causes; which we have only two ways of doing, either by an immediate perception of our memory or senses, or by an inference from other causes; which causes again we must ascertain in the same manner, either by a present impression, or by an inference from *their* causes, and so on, till we arrive at some object, which we see or remember. It is impossible for us to carry on our inferences *in infinitum;* and the only thing, that can stop them, is an impression of the memory or senses, beyond which there is no room for doubt or enquiry.

"An impression of the memory or the senses": in the conjunction of the two endpoints of ideational inference Hume equates an appeal to the testimony of sense data with historical knowledge. And it is from history that he takes his example:

> Thus we believe that CAESAR was kill'd in the senate-house on the *ides* of *March;* and that because this fact is establish'd on the unanimous testimony of historians, who agree to assign this precise time and place to that event. Here are certain characters and letters present either to our memory or senses; which characters we likewise remember to have been us'd as the signs of certain ideas; and these ideas were either in the minds of such as were immediately present at that action, and receiv'd the ideas directly from its existence; or they were deriv'd from the testimony of others, and that again from another testimony, by a visible gradation, 'till we arrive at those who were eye-witnesses and spectators of the event. 'Tis obvious all this chain of argument or connexion of causes and effects, is at first founded on those characters or letters, which are seen or remember'd, and that without the authority either of the memory or senses, our whole reasoning wou'd be chimerical and without foundation. Every link of the chain wou'd in that case hang upon another; but there wou'd not be anything fix'd to one end of it, capable of sustaining the whole; and consequently there wou'd be no belief nor evidence. (*T,* pp. 82–83)

---

in the state and the mind, see Coleridge's *The Friend* (1818), ed. Barbara Rooke, vol. 4 of *The Collected Works of Samuel Taylor Coleridge,* ed. Kathleen Coburn (Princeton: Princeton Univ. Press, 1969), 2:451–55, and Jerome Christensen, *Coleridge's Blessed Machine of Language* (Ithaca: Cornell Univ. Press, 1981), pp. 249–53.

In explaining historical belief we return, either in memory or in fact (say, by pulling a book from the shelf), to the impression, the character or letter, which was its cause. What makes the justification of historical belief a more complicated proposition than the retrieval of other sorts of impressions which ground our "conclusions or principles" is that the impression to which we return is itself a sign of another derivation: the chain of testimonies that reach back to the original, indubitable testimony of an eyewitness to the historical event.

The problem emerges clearly in Hume's discussion "Of Unphilosophical Probability," where his aim is to weaken the case for rationalistic claims of certainty by identifying "degrees of belief and assurance" and by illustrating how reasoning from proofs "degenerates insensibly" into probabilities. "'Tis certain," he writes, "that when an inference is drawn immediately from an object, without any intermediate cause or effect, the conviction is much stronger, and the persuasion more lively, than when the imagination is carry'd thro' a long chain of connected arguments, however infallible the connection of each link may be esteem'd" (*T,* pp. 143–44). We should probably append a ghostly "in some measure" to that "long," since it is not clear what, if anything, makes the difference between an immediate inference and a long chain. Hume's silence on this point is not owed to an inability to specify but to an interest in encouraging the reader to imagine degeneration to probability occurring almost at once, thus narrowing as much as possible the scope for rational proofs.[21] But if degeneration occurs, it does not proceed *past* probability into pure ignorance or doubt. As warrant for that security Hume appeals once again to a historical example, choosing, in effect, the longest possible chain to enforce the probability of certainty. Though he admits that his preceding reasoning may suggest the conclusion "that the evidence of all ancient history must now be lost, or at least will be lost in time, as the chain of causes encreases, and runs on to a greater length. . . . [It nonetheless] seems contrary to common sense to think, that if the republic of letters, and the art of printing continue on the same footing as at present, our posterity, even after a thousand ages, can ever doubt if there has been such a man as JULIUS CAESAR" (*T,* p. 145).

The reason for this assurance is that "tho' the links are innumerable, that connect any original fact with the present impression, which is the foundation of belief; yet they are all of the same kind, and depend on the fidelity of Printers and Copists [*sic*]. One edition passes into another, and

---

21. On Hume's skepticism and views of probability, see Robert J. Fogelin, "The Tendency of Hume's Skepticism," in *The Skeptical Tradition*, ed. Myles Burnyeat (Berkeley and Los Angeles: Univ. of California Press, 1983), pp. 401–2.

that into a third, and so on, till we come to that volume we peruse at present. *There is no variation in the steps.* After we know one, we know all of them" (*T,* p. 146; emphasis added). Historical certainty (or probability) is confirmed because of the uniformity of the impressions transmitted down to us by posterity, and that uniformity is assured by the consistency of the process for transmitting those impressions. But what is peculiar about this explanation is Hume's attribution of uniformity to the fidelity of printers *and* copyists. Both the making of impressions and the mechanical uniformity of replication are specific features of the technology of the letter press. How can the very distinction between copyists and printers be explained except by imagining a printing press that constitutes the difference as significant by eliminating for all time all the stray differences introduced by copyists? Hume at once exploits and elides the technology of the press, as indeed he must if he is going to make the continuous connection with the ancients at which he aims (at least where the question of oratorical eloquence does not come into consideration). It is as if, like the republic of letters, which is a general, transhistorical corporate body, the *art* of printing antedates the invention of the press. Hume reads back the features of the press onto history in general in order to characterize a history in which nothing changes, in which no discontinuity has occurred or can happen—as long as there are *cognoscenti* to practice their art of preservation. Hume's redemption of the ancient past from decay involves a denial of any alterity in the past—a denial which can be read as a suppression because of the substitution of the contingent fidelity of copyists and printers for the automatic reliability of the press—and a suppression made necessary because the invention of the printing press is itself a variation in the steps of a history for which it supplies the model.

An apposite analogue to this maneuver occurs in "On the Rise and Progress of the Arts and Sciences," where Hume, in the course of discriminating between the relative virtues of republics and monarchies, runs through a thumbnail history of the West:

> Greece was a cluster of little principalities, which soon became republics. . . . Each city produced its several artists and philosophers, who refused to yield the preference to those of the neighboring republics; their contention and debates sharpened the wits of men . . . ; and the sciences, not being dwarfed by the restraint of authority, were enabled to make such considerable shoots as are even at this time the objects of our admiration. After the Roman *Christian* or *Catholic* church had spread itself over the civilized world, and had engrossed all the learning of the times, being really one large state within itself, and united under one head, this variety of

sects immediately disappeared, and the Peripatetic philosophy was alone admitted into all the schools, to the utter depravation of every kind of learning. But mankind having *at length* thrown off this yoke, affairs are now returned nearly to the same situation as before, and Europe is at present a copy, at large, of what Greece was formerly a pattern in miniature. (*ST,* pp. 80–81; third emphasis added)

The analogue here to the distinction between copyists and printers is the inexplicable moment in which the all but inexplicable yoke ("engrossed," as we shall have occasion to see later, is a key word in this context) of the Catholic church is thrown off. Characteristically, that moment of historical change is blurred by the "in some measure" locution, here "at length." Of course, this historical sketch is more than analogous to Hume's discussion of historical certainty, since the crux is identical in both accounts: the Renaissance begins in the moment of the transition from monastic copying to printing, when hegemony is dissolved by introducing a new and improved type of copying free from absolutist arbitrariness—hence returning us to the same situation as before and rendering modern Europe as a copy at large of republican Greece.[22] The advent of the printing press contributes to the casting off of the yoke, but the existence of the printing press as a mechanical means of reproduction encourages us to disregard any deviations from uniformity that might have preceded it, indeed, to disregard the existence of the machine itself as a factor in historical

22. Another equally exaggerated version of this indefinitely elastic "in some measure," which allows Hume to reduce epochal divergences into momentary articulations, occurs in "Of the Balance of Power," where Hume attempts to develop the fundamentally economic notion of balance as a maxim for contemporary politics by showing its natural occurrence, however unremarked, in political history. Although he admits that the Romans, unlike the Greeks, were almost completely ignorant of this maxim "founded so much on common sense and obvious reasoning," Hume fails to engage the implications of the millenial continuity of an efficient but "unbalanced" empire on his notions of natural balance and common sense. Indeed, despite the powerful historical precedent of the Roman empire, Hume can suavely claim, "Enormous monarchies are, probably, destructive to human nature; in their progress, in their continuance, and even in their downfall, which never can be very distant from their establishment" (G&G, pp. 352, 355). In the case of the Roman "monarchy," that "not very distant" covers a thousand years. The gap is closed by the historian's generalization, which, nature negligent, imposes a limit on the engrossment of empire. This claim of return without difference helps to make sense of the question why, given the three centuries that have intervened between the invention of printing and Hume's career, that moment should have such power over Hume's imagination. An answer that situates the general problematic is the crucial place that the Revolution of 1688 has in Hume's historiography: it raises most immediately the problem of return without difference, in this case constitutional resistance, and it is the historical event that Hume in his *History* is most concerned to resolve. See Duncan Forbes's persuasive reading of Hume's treatment of resistance and the Revolution in *Hume's Philosophical Politics* (Cambridge Univ. Press, 1975), pp. 96–101.

change, which is not, rightly considered, change at all ("history informs
us of nothing new or strange" [*ECHU*, p. 83])—merely a return to an
original state or impression by a copying that revises eras of depravity into
the sign of an interruption that makes copying both necessary and possible.

Hume, then, invokes a mechanism without a machine. But not, crucially, without mechanics. At one point in the section "Necessary Connection" Hume asks, "Before we are reconcil'd to this doctrine, how
often must we repeat to ourselves, *that* the simple view of any two objects
or actions, however related, can never give us any idea of power, or of a
connection betwixt them: *that* this idea arises from the repetition of their
union: *that* the repetition neither discovers nor causes anything in the
objects, but has an influence only on the mind, by that customary transition it produces: *that* this customary transition is, therefore, the same with
the power and necessity?" The immediate answer to the question "How
often must we repeat to ourselves?" is "As often as necessary." The more
considered reply is "As often as possible," since the necessity to repeat is
not only accounted for by the clear insufficiency of a "simple view"; the
desirability of repeating is presupposed by the representation of repetition as the advent of an "idea of power" or "necessity." Even Hume's
ostensibly glum prediction that "with the generality of readers, the biass
[*sic*] of the mind will prevail, and give them a prejudice against the present doctrine" is the pretext for him to give an *account* of that "contrary
biass" and thereby repeat his doctrine (*T,* pp. 166–67). As the corruption
of texts makes the corrective labor of printers necessary, so does the reflexive bias of readers make necessary the repetition of proofs.[23]

The *Treatise* is little more than a skein of repetitions. What else could
such a long book be and still make sense, still make a consistent impression?

> If all the long chain of causes and effects, which connect any past
> event with any volume of history, were compos'd of parts different
> from each other, and which 'twere necessary for the mind distinctly
> to conceive, 'tis impossible we shou'd preserve to the end any belief
> or evidence. But as most of these proofs are perfectly resembling,

---

23. Hume is not the only Scotsman to perceive the benefits of correction. The anecdote
is told of one solution to the question among the clergy of the relative depravity of the old
evil, whisky, and the new one, tea. "One minister in a Stirlingshire village had the problem
settled for him nicely by his parishioners: their last cup of tea was always 'qualified by a
little whisky, which is supposed to correct all the bad effects of the tea.'" (Marjorie Plant,
The Domestic Life of Scotland in the Eighteenth Century, p. 115, quoted in T. C. Smout, *A History
of the Scottish People: 1560–1830* (1969; rpt. London: Fontana press, 1985), p. 268.

the mind runs easily along them, jumps from one part to another
with facility, and forms but a confus'd and general notion of each
link. By this means a long chain of argument, has as little effect in
diminshing the original vivacity, as a much shorter wou'd have, if
compos'd of parts, which were different from each other, and of
which each requir'd a distinct consideration. (*T*, p. 146)[24]

As we learn from the letter to Dr. Arbuthnot, the single discovery
that enabled the *Treatise* was Hume's finding that "the moral Philosophy
transmitted to us by Antiquity, labor'd under the same Inconvenience
that has been found in their natural Philosophy, of being entirely Hypothetical, & depending more upon invention than Experience" (*HL*,
1:16). That first observation came to Hume like a "new Scene of
Thought," an aboriginally impressive experience; henceforth he takes responsibility only for the mechanical repetition of that impression in "perfectly resembling" proofs, invention after invention. Hume's writing is in
some measure nothing more than repetition and his career, his historical
identity, a strategy for putting himself in a position where he can repeat
himself over and over again.[25] The idea of progress in Hume's career is
indissolubly bound up with a relentless repetition, a paradox that Eisen-

24. Cf. Johnson on the composition of the *Dictionary:* "A large work is difficult because it
is large, even though all its parts might singly be performed with facility; where there are
many things to be done, each must be allowed its share of time and labour, in the proportion
only which it bears to the whole; nor can it be expected, that the stones which form the
dome of a temple, should be squared and polished like the diamond of a ring." (*Samuel
Johnson: Rasselas, Poems, and Selected Prose*, ed. Bertrand H. Bronson (New York: Rinehart,
1952), p. 233. The other side of Johnson's distaste for the project of monumental architec-
tural construction is his fondness for the easy anecdotal style: "I love anecdotes. I fancy
mankind may come in time to write all aphoristically, except in narrative; grow weary of
preparation and connexion and illustration and all those arts by which a big book is made. If
a man is to wait till he weaves anecdotes into a system, we may be long in getting them,
and get but few in comparison of what we might get" (Boswell, *Tour*, p. 22). Johnson and
Hume evidently have in mind two entirely different things, and perhaps only for Johnson is
it accurate to speak of a "book," since the architectonic metaphor is wholly alien to Hume,
who thinks not of books as works (nor of anecdotes as morsels) but of composition as labor,
which may run from one book to another, through essay after essay. For Hume, once you
get the hang of the technique of repetition (avoiding, for example, the too frequent recur-
rence of "uncommon expressions, strong flashes of wit, pointed similes, and epigrammatic
turns" ["Of Simplicity in Writing," *ST*, p. 44]), a long book is as easy to write as a short one;
the telling difference is in the receptivity of the reader.
    25. A fulfillment of a Ciceronian aspiration: "For I am not looking for an eloquent man,
or for any other mortal or transitory thing; but for that particular quality which whoever is
master of is an eloquent man; and that is nothing but abstract eloquence, which we are not
able to discern with any eyes except those of the mind." "The Orator," *Cicero's Orations*,
trans. C. D. Yonge (London: Bohn, 1852), 4:410.

stein regards as a fundamental aspect of the technology of printing, which was a "duplicating process that made possible not only a sequence of improved editions but also a continuous accumulation of fixed records. For it seems to have been permanence that introduced progressive change."[26] Hume's argument for the reliability of historical knowledge opens up a space for him to take that strategic position by the substitution of copyists and printers for the printing press and by ascribing to their art the securing of the continuity requisite for knowledge not only of history but of anything that comes to us in books—and by implication all impressions and the very idea of progress.[27]

The importance of correction can be illustrated by reference to Hume's approving and repeated quotation of "a saying of Rousseau's that one half of a man's life is too little to write a Book and the other half to correct it" (*HL*, 2:243; see also *HL*, 2:304). This wish might, on the face of it, be taken as a rough description of Hume's "life": "half" of it was devoted to writing the *Treatise*, "half" to correcting it.[28] In fact, the pub-

26. Eisenstein, *The Printing Press as an Agent of Change*, p. 124. In its paradoxical endowment of a historical identity to the man of letters through the repetition of letters or characters, the printing press functions as a kind of theater, for, as Stephen Greenblatt observes, "at the deepest level of the [theatrical] medium itself the motivation is the . . . renewal of existence through repetition of the self-constituting act. The character repeats himself in order to continue to be the same character on the stage. Identity is a theatrical invention that must be reiterated if it is to endure." *Renaissance Self-Fashioning* (Chicago: Univ. of Chicago Press, 1980), p. 201.

27. This schematic version of Hume's project does not diverge fundamentally from the view of Hume's philosophical writings expressed by L. A. Selby-Bigge in his introduction to the *Enquiry*. "Hume's philosophic writings," Selby-Bigge warns, "are to be read with great caution. His pages, especially those of the *Treatise*, are so full of matter, he says so many different things in so many different ways and different connexions, and with so much indifference to what he has said before, that it is very hard to say positively that he taught, or did not teach, this or that particular doctrine. He applies the same principles to such a great variety of subjects that it is not surprising that many verbal, and some real inconsistencies can be found in his statements. He is ambitious rather than shy of saying the same thing in different ways, and at the same time he is often slovenly indifferent about his words and formulae" (*ECHU*, p. vii). What Selby-Bigge identifies as the application of the same principles, I would call the principle of repeatedly applying the same principle. The relation between this principle of repetition and "the indifference to what he has said before" is a productive one.

28. I would include within this correction the *History* as well as the essays and dialogues. Even if one identifies, as James Noxon does, a shift in Hume from psychological to historical explanations (*Hume's Philosophical Development* [Oxford: Clarendon, 1973], p. 25), that shift can still be read not only loosely as a correction of the *Treatise* but as a correction in terms that the *Treatise* supplies and "anticipates": there is nothing in the *History* that does not fit the sense of the historical as proposed by the *Treatise*. Moreover, the possibility of the shift lies in some of the contradictions between psychological and epistemological, empirical, and rational modes of explanation that Noxon investigates. That it has such inconsistencies

lication date of the *Treatise* of 1738 does all but halve a life begun in 1711 and ended (somewhat later than anticipated) in 1776. Such arithmetic is, however, not only crude but erroneous: for, as we have seen, the autobiography induces by virtue of its shift to a posthumous perspective, which presupposes two versons of life: the biological, whose termination is a vicissitude not to be reckoned, and the career of the man of letters, which is formed in the face of that contingency, as an anticipation and overcoming of the merely biological. Given the contingency of death and the importance of correction, such anticipation is imperative. In order to assure that there will be time for correction, correction must begin as early as possible. Hence the publication date of the *Treatise* is not a suitable index for the halving of Hume's life because the *Treatise* was already being corrected in manuscript. Death is the possibility of a disproportion between writing and correction; the defense against that potential disproportion is the incorporation of a balance into every moment of writing, a writing that is already half a correction, a production that is already a reproduction. In order to insure that there will be half a life available (this is Hume's version of Zeno's paradox) for correction, correction must begin before the writing is completed, which is to say that not only is every error or inconsistency in the *Treatise* something that might be corrected, but also that the errors, inconsistencies, and, above all, the sense of writing to the moment are functions of the correction that is a dynamis and

---

makes the *Treatise* not a less but a *more* complete work—or if the inconsistencies make it a less finished work, they make it a more powerful work because more corrigible. My aim here is to invoke a tyranny of works: part of Hume's desire to characterize the *Treatise* as juvenile is to distinguish himself as *author*, one who has a life apart from the publication which he has produced and which appears to entail him. The difficulties and stakes in such a project are admirably addressed by Ilay Campbell in his superb, albeit intensely partisan *Information for Alexander Donaldson and J. Wood Booksellers in Edinburgh Against John Hinton, Bookseller in London, and Alexander McConoghie, Writer in Edinburgh, January 2, 1773.* Arguing against claims for perpetual copyright, Ilay Campbell distinguishes between the author's doctrine and a proprietor's publication and gives an ingenious twist to the pure empiricism of his analysis: if the author is distinct from the inventor as an ideal figure, it does not follow that he deserves material fruits; rather his award ought to be appropriately ideal: fame. *The Literary Property Debate: Six Tracts, 1764-1774*, ed. Stephen Parks (New York: Garland, 1975), pp. 6-7. Campbell's argument, dependent on various contributors to the debate through the century, is both earlier and more sophisticated than the idealist mystifications promulgated by German philosphers (who were, after all, competing in a much more primitive market system), which are related and uncritically endorsed by Martha Woodmansee in her article "The Genius and the Copyright: Economic and Legal Conditions of the Emergence of the 'Author,'" *Eighteenth-Century Studies*, Summer 1984, pp. 425-48. Woodmansee's title does not indicate her restriction of her study to the German setting, which has the predictable and unfortunate result of yielding metaphysical answers to legal, economic, and political problems.

mode of production.[29] The need to correct becomes the empirical excuse for an ideal of almost pure repetition, one which is not simply a reproduction by the printer in response to the whims of the reading public. Disinterestedness and independence are intimately bound up with the practice of correction, as Hume boasts to his printer William Strahan: "I am perhaps the only author you ever knew, who gratuitously employ'd great Industry in correcting a Work, of which he has fully alienated the Property; and it were hard to deny me the Opportunity of Exercising my Talents" (*HL*, 2:239).[30]

Among the concatenation of terms, such as "adjustment," "remedy," and "refinement," that Hume deploys, "correction" has claims to some privilege. For one thing, the correction of texts is a way of dealing with corruption that is made available by the technology of the very culture that, as Pocock argues, was responsible for the corruption of classical values. Figurative extension of the correction made possible by the printing press allowed one to imagine that cultural advance, although ostensibly disruptive, contained within it its own principle of self-restraint. More: if composition could be imagined to be correction from the very first, as in Hume's notion of turning "rude Materials" into "Words," corruption as a danger or even as a concept could be imagined to be squeezed out of any consequence.[31] The other reason for the privilege of correction among its synonyms of adjustment and remedy is that correction *gives* synonymity to those other terms. That is, if adjustment, or remedy, or refinement seems at one time or another more appropriate in terms of a specific context, it is correction which supervenes over the shift from one context to another. Correction most closely coincides with the privileged metaphor

29. And of thinking: "In every judgment, which we can form concerning probability, as well as concerning knowledge, we ought always to correct the first judgment, deriv'd from the nature of the object, by another judgment, deriv'd from the nature of the understanding" (*T*, p. 182).

30. The service Hume provided was a real one. In his *History of the Art of Printing* William Walsh, who maintains that the "Correctness of a Book is that which makes it valuable, and delightful to the Reader, yea, registrates Honour to the Memory of the Printer," attributes the reasons for the decay of printing in Scotland to the general failure of printers to keep a correcter. Walsh chides his brethren for the false economy of failing to employ a laborer who "adds both to our Credit and Interest," especially when "there are Abundance of young Men fit for this Work among us, who want Bread." *The History of the Art of Printing . . . and a Preface by the Publisher to the Printers in Scotland* (Edinburgh, 1713), pp. 20–21. By claiming disinterest (which is only the interest of registrating honor to his memory) Hume hopes to perform the Erasmian labor of correcting texts (albeit his own, rather than Plato's or Plutarch's) and yet distinguish himself from the hungry clerk, basely serving the printer, which is what in the eighteenth century such labor has come to imply.

31. The price for sustaining such a notion is continual vigilance, perpetual occupation: "But there is no End of correcting" (*HL*, 1:379).

of composition: it is the dynamis of composition, a substitution for writing, an adjustment of production into refinement. Only continual correction, of texts and society, offered Hume a plausible defense against that "self-generating" corruption that was the bane of virtue in a commercial society and promised to solve the "problem of existing as a universal value in particular and contingent time."[32]

III

Hume never reneged on his promise to Francis Hutcheson "to make a new Tryal, if it be possible to make the Moralist & Metaphysician agree a little better" (*HL*, 1:33). That trial entailed a technique for inducing if not unity then balance—a balance of power, a balance of trade. The relations between morals and metaphysics are part of an economy. What makes this particular version of the economy synechdochic of the liberal economics that Hume, the philosophes, and Adam Smith variously espoused is the extraordinary, if inevitably equivocal, privilege ascribed to the middleman.[33]

To embrace the role of the middleman was a specifically antimercantilist and implicitly cosmopolitan posture. Mercantilism, which evolved by "finding ways of diminishing risks," tended toward parochialism, since "any trade involving more than an exchange between neighbours demanded a knowledge of market opportunities and involved risks." Ideally, trade was conducted in a town with a centralized marketplace "between men known to one another who would allow credit for short periods with little risk of loss, where knowledge of market opportunities was increased and supervision of trade was easier." The middleman, who was often a foreigner and characteristically neither a producer nor a consumer of goods, was distrusted.[34] Although the prejudicial restrictions against middlemen gradually diminished with the expansion of national trade, this represented no fundamental shift in economic thinking. It reflected the choice of the lesser evil: the risk in dealing with middlemen had become less than the risk of doing without them. That this change was

32. Pocock, *The Machiavellian Moment*, p. 501.

33. For comments on the ambiguity of the various uses and constituencies of the terms "middling rank" and "middle power" in Hume, see Forbes, *Philosophical Politics*, pp. 176–78.

34. L. A. Clarkson, *The Pre-Industrial Economy in England, 1500–1750* (London: B. T. Batsford, 1971), p. 136. Clarkson quotes the Rev. Thomas Lever, who, preaching at St. Paul's Cross in 1550, inveighed against middlemen as "Marchantes of Myscheyfe that goe betwixt the barke and the tree: Betwixt the Husband man that getteth the corne, and the householder and occupyeth Corne" (p. 136).

less than fundamental is attested to by the development of the great international trading companies such as the Company of Merchant Adventurers in the sixteenth century. Toleration of them suggests a more enlightened form of self-interest; that they were granted privileges, intended to diminish their risk by suppressing competition, argues that toleration had been extended within a concept of economic interest that was continuous with the market-town psychology.[35] Hume disdainfully comments on this regressiveness in the *History of England:*

> The company of merchant-adventurers, by their patents, possessed the sole commerce of woolen-goods, though the staple of the kingdom. An attempt made during the reign of Elizabeth to lay open this important trade had been attended with bad consequences for a time, by a conspiracy of the merchant-adventurers, not to make any purchases of cloth: and the queen immediately restored them their cloth.
>
> It was the groundless fear of a like accident that enslaved the nation to those exclusive companies, which confined so much every branch of commerce and industry. (*History of England*, 5:143–44)

The "transitional phase" toward industrial capitalism that occurred in the eighteenth century coincided with a substantial change in attitude toward the middleman, or what Charles Wilson calls "the merchant-entrepreneur," whose ability to integrate the various components of the economy and whose "opportunistic sense" made him the beneficiary of increasing social acclaim and financial rewards.[36] In Humean economics the employments of the middleman in the mercantilist system—such as reducing "the risks and inconveniences of distant trade" for producers, smoothing out "price fluctuations over time and distance" for consumers, and "sorting raw materials into different qualities and types suitable for different purposes"[37]—are abstracted into a principle of dynamic balance.

---

35. The relations among these huge joint stock companies and between them and the state which enfranchised them were not always harmonious. See Michael McKeon's fascinating account of the complicity between the court of Charles I and the Royal Company in fomenting war against the Dutch in 1664 and 1665, over the vocal protests of merchants large and small, even those who had suffered from Dutch expertise or violence. McKeon's research teaches the very Humean lessons of the connection between an institutional restraint of trade and an eventual military interdiction of trade, and of the dangerous consequences when monarchical intervention supplants the market's self-regulation. McKeon, *Politics and Poetry in Restoration England: The Case of Dryden's "Annus Mirabilis"* (Cambridge: Harvard Univ. Press, 1975), pp. 99–131.

36. Charles Wilson, *England's Apprenticeship: 1603–1763* (New York: St. Martin's, 1965), p. 312.

37. Clarkson, *Pre-Industrial Economy in England*, pp. 136–37.

Indeed, it is not only the function of the middleman, but his inexorable, entrepreneurial emergence into strategic prominence within a resistant mercantilist system, that makes him an epitome of the mechanism of the Humean self-regulating economy.

Rather than reverse mercantilism Humean economics corrects it according to a dynamics which it unconsciously obeyed. Put in another way, if mercantilism is a way of diminishing risks, it does not follow that free market economics seeks to increase risks (although it does try to increase the willingness to take risks). Optimally, there is in economic practice no "danger of mistake." Humean economics works on psychology, not on the market, which supposedly operates itself. If the difference between mercantilist and Humean attitudes toward trade is the difference between a psychology which regards trade as a transaction in which one of the participants must lose and a psychology which appreciates trade as an exchange in which both participants win,[38] the difference does not result from a modification of the objects that are exchanged; insofar as one has an objective or use value greater than the other, the loss remains the same. But, of course, there is no value in objects, only in property, which derives that value from the passion invested in it.[39] Hence a change in psychology is a transformation of the exchange itself—a transformation marked not by the elimination of risk and the idea of loss but by a contextualizing of risk, so that loss in one narrow individual, geographical

38. Axiom put by Louis Dumont, *From Mandeville to Marx: The Genesis and Triumph of Economic Ideology* (Chicago: Univ. of Chicago Press, 1977), p. 35. See Braudel's *Wheels of Commerce*, pp. 219 and 544, for versions of the mercantilist formula by Montchrestien, Montaigne, and Voltaire. The ability of both participants in an exchange to "win" seems to be owed to the operation of a Humean pride: though we may feel inferior to a great man and feel a loss to ourselves in our comparison with him, an attachment to the great man (by some relation of contiguity, resemblance, or cause and effect), while it does nothing to change what one might call the objective basis of the comparison (I am still less wealthy, handsome, etc., than he) does change the context of the comparison by making his attachment to me a source of pride—*vis-à-vis* another. Comparisons cannot be odious because whatever risk is involved to one member's self-esteem is mitigated an inclusion of the compared within an augmented, aggrandized self, which becomes the basis for a new comparison.

39. For Hume, labor does not necessarily give value or right. Miller observes "that 'labour' is not regarded by Hume as creating a distinct title to property, but merely as one of the ways in which we may possess an object. . . . He does not see it as morally superior to the other modes of possession, nor as the source of a stronger title to property, except in so far as the alteration *produced* by labour forms a relation which the imagination finds especially striking." David Miller, *Philosophy and Ideology in Hume's Political Thought* (Oxford: Oxford Univ. Press, 1981), pp. 69–70. Although "produced" blurs the discriminations that Hume carefully made in the *Treatise*, I would basically agree. Surely Miller's central insight is that "strikingness" of one kind or another is the basis of entitlement and of value—a basis for what I shall describe below as a communication theory of value.

region, social class, or economic index (such as money supply) will be regarded as gain for the whole. That gain may not be immediately perceptible to both members in the exchange (indeed, it is entirely possible to conceive that each member thinks he is getting the better or the worse of the transaction); but because we share the conviction that immediate loss is gain for the whole and that each individual is part of that whole, we believe that there must be eventual gain (albeit invariably postponed, like all the gratifications of our avidity as individual men) for me/us/everyone—even the ostensible loser in a particular trade. This deferment may look like sacrifice of one's own interests for the interest of the greater public, but the loss is mitigated by the speculative relationship that has, under a Humean notion of property, been introduced into every exchange: that is, since we never possess anything immediately, *even our gain* (which partakes of the nature of a promise), deferment of that gain is only another sort of mediation, correspondent to all the other differences that articulate man's social being.[40] Man's ability to generalize himself, to understand (liberal) economics as intimately as he understands himself, makes the issue of sacrifice of the personal to the public irrelevant; there is no essential difference between the personal and the public, no locus where the machinery of sacrifice can be set up and the rite performed—no priests, no kings. The feeling that one has lost in a transaction is just that, a *feeling*, which for the mercantilist has unrivalled vividness and immediacy. The belief engendered is not so much false as insufficiently true: the error lies in a narrowness or partiality that distorts perception and thereby thwarts the smooth operations of the greater economy.

The belief in eventual or general gain should always override the perception of loss—so much so that the belief need not be attached to any particular perception of its own: it is fundamentally a belief in economics as a mechanism independent of our thoughts and immune from our petty triumphs and defeats. "A self-regulating market demands nothing less than the institutional separation of society into an economic and

40. Joyce Oldham Appleby finds this psychology implicit in sophisticated mercantilist doctrine of the seventeenth century. "The dilemma created by accepting the rightness of pursuing one's interest in situations where mutual dependence was essential could be resolved only by uniting self-interest to the faithful performance of promises. This required that those who engaged in market transactions identify with the whole commercial system. Concern for the immediate bargain had to give way to an appreciation of the future course of trade." *Economic Thought and Ideology in Seventeenth-Century England* (Princeton: Princeton Univ. Press, 1978), pp. 189–90. It is that "giving way," which unbalances the claimed identification, as much as the implicitness of this perception that distinguishes mercantilist theory from Hume's theory and practice.

political sphere," with the consequence that "the economic point of view
. . . be emancipated from the political."[41] Hence it is the role of Hume
to anatomize the property relations among men and determine an economy independent of the narrow and partial perceptions, inclinations, and
practices of individual men, social groups, and nation-states (while arguing that given certain adjustments that narrowness and partiality can be
useful). The doctrine of emancipation will be that this economy is a self-
regulating mechanism which seeks its own balance and in seeking it progressively improves the lot of all parts within the whole—a mechanism
that is thwarted in its benign operations only by the hodgepodge of mercantilist devices invented to manipulate the market. Yet mercantilism paradoxically commands the ground of the aboriginal, even the instinctual.[42]
Within economic history it exactly corresponds to the state of savagery in
Hume's natural history of society or to the direct passions in Hume's study
of the passions. However natural, liberalism must be indoctrinated, its
foreignness mitigated by an inducement more vivid than the impression
of narrow self-interest. The claim may be that the market, in its various
indirections, is self-regulating, that liberal economics is natural, but the
truth of that claim will be approved by individual agents within the econ-

41. Karl Polanyi, *The Great Transformation* (New York: Rinehart, 1944), p. 71; Dumont,
From Mandeville to Marx, p. 36. Appleby has forcefully argued a revisionist reading of mercantilism that disputes such conventional characterizations as those of Wilson's and Clarkson's. She claims that it is "the differentiation of things economic from their social context
that truly distinguishes the writings of the so-called mercantilist period, not their infusion of
social and political goals into economic policy" (*Economic Thought*, p. 236). This is not a point
I care to argue—certainly Hume teaches that such revisionism is always possible, that the
differentiation of economics (what Dumont describes as "emancipation") is always already
occurring; what is crucial for me is the "so-called" because it is the calling of such by the
North Britons of the eighteenth century which represented their theoretical entrepreneur-
ship, their capitalizing on the insights as well as the mistakes of their predecessors, and
which made revisionism possible. For an un-Humean version of this eighteenth-century
emancipation of economics, see R. L. Meek, who states that the "Physiocrats assumed that
the system of market exchange which it was their main purpose to analyse was subject to
certain objective economic laws, which operated independently of the will of man and which
were discoverable by the light of reason. These laws governed the shape and movement of
the economic order, and therefore . . . the shape and movement of the social order as a
whole." Meek, *The Economics of Physiocracy* (London, 1962), p. 19, quoted in Maurice
Dobb, *Theories of Value and Distribution since Adam Smith* (Cambridge: Cambridge Univ.
Press, 1973), p. 40.
42. For another example of this trope, more specifically directed to the articulation of
politics and economics, see Addison's characterization, in *Spectator* no. 119, of the "people
of mode in the country" as exhibiting the "manners of the last age. They have no sooner
fetched themselves up to the fashion of the polite world, but the town has dropped them,
and are nearer to the first state of nature than to those refinements which formerly reigned
in the court, and still prevail in the country."

omy only if the beliefs that accompany the perception of loss can be modified, if men's feelings about their transactions can be changed, if the middleman also possesses the initiative, foresight, and ingenuity of the emergent capitalist entrepreneur.

One way to regard Hume's literary life is to observe that his early astuteness about the handling of his own career demonstrates that he had quickly developed for himself an understanding of his career as that of a versatile middleman: the eighteenth-century man of letters as gentleman gone to trade. Defoe's characterization of the complete English tradesman neatly jibes with Voltaire's delineation of the man of letters' special virtuosity: "That he has a general knowledge of not his own particular trade and business only; that part indeed well denominates a handicraftsman to be a *complete artist;* but our complete tradesman ought to understand all the inland trade of England; so as to be able to turn his hand to any thing, or deal in any thing, or every thing, of the growth and product of his own country, or the manufacture of the people, as his circumstances in trade or other occasions may require; and may, if he sees occasion, lay down one trade, and take up another, when he pleases, without serving a new apprenticeship to learn it." [43] More circumstantial evidence includes Hume's complaisance about the failure of the first edition of the *Treatise*, his exploitation of that bulk to derive and vend essays and dissertations, his mediation between Scottish and English publishers to assist in the unloading of inventory and the regulation of price, the sorting of works into such qualities as "moral" and "metaphysical," his amassing of parts into larger units, his encouragement of the translators Jean-Baptiste-Antoine Suard and the Abbé le Blanc, and his services to French authors such as Madame Riccoboni and Rousseau, for whom he procured English translators, publishers, and patrons. In fact, his self-definition as "ambassador" in "Of Essay Writing" is followed by this promise: "I shall give intelligence to the learned of whatever passes in company, and shall endeavor to import into company whatever commodities I find in my native country proper for their use and entertainment. The balance of trade we need not be jealous of" (*ST,* p. 39). [44]

43. Daniel Defoe, *The Complete English Tradesman*, 2 vols. (1727; rpt. New York: Augustus M. Kelley, 1969), p. 4.

44. Hume was anticipated in this connection by Addison, who, in *Spectator* no. 69, indicated that "factors in the trading world are what ambassadors are in the polite world." It was Hume's project to generalize the distinction between trading and polite world into a virtual identity. Note, however, that in the exchange of commodities for intelligence, knowledge has lost any claim to disinterestedness. It is on this concept of learning as commodity as much as any other that Hume differs from Johnson, whose position, assigned to him and retained for him by Boswell, was monarchic rather than ambassadorial. This is the primary

There is no need to attribute anything like an innate idea of trade to Hume to account for this expertise. We have biographical evidence of an apprenticeship in commerce, however brief, in Bristol, where as part of his self-prescribed remedy for the disease of the learned he clerked for Mr. Michael Miller, who, Mossner informs us, was a "sugar-merchant importing from the West Indies," and who was "in all likelihood . . . also involved in the slave-trade" (Mossner, p. 88). A descendant of the merchant-adventurers of the fifteenth and sixteenth centuries, Miller was an excellent example of the middleman in the grand manner, and it can scarcely be doubted that the shrewd and attentive young clerk picked up some of the mysteries of the trade during his short tenure. His first extant letter from Reims after the Bristol episode is seasoned by the commercial vocabulary that will characterize Hume's commentary on his life and work until his death. "I am now arriv'd at Rheims," he writes, "which is to be the place of my Abode for some considerable time, & where I hope both to spend my Time happily for the present, & lay up a Stock for the future" (*HL*, 1:19). "Spend" in order to "lay up Stock"—an expenditure that is not a loss but an investment: this is the language of commerce, the psychology of the middleman. Nonetheless, if Hume's conduct of his career makes "middleman" more than metaphor and if his experience in Bristol anchors that conduct in biographical fact, it is not clear how that profits us, since to characterize Hume as merely a merchant does not engage his historical self-conception: middlemen, after all, did exist and were recognized within the mercantilist system with which Hume broke. To come to terms with Hume's practice, like coming to terms with economics itself, will mean *not* reducing the metaphor to its literal referent;

---

symbolic significance of Johnson's "patriarchal" procession to the "feudal" north in 1773, which was designed to *display* a learning that would intimidate the weak, provoke the surly, and stimulate the eager. Hume, like Smollett, MacKenzie, and so many others, traveled the north-to-south (and east to Paris) route that was the path of ambition for North Britons who, like Roderick Random, had only their learning to rely on. That learning, an antique remnant of a glamourous but savage past, was recognized as valuable only as it was marketable in polite society. For the Scottish middleman, the preferred trope was the chiasmic exchange of opposites (learning in conversation and conversation in learning). For Johnson, English learning advanced in ceremonial reversal not only of the disastrous southward march of the Pretender in 1745 but of his careerist progeny as well. In part Johnson's tour sought to demonstrate that the Scots merely pretended to learning and had nothing of value to export least of all a "Hobbist" in Tory dress (*Tour*, p. 239). Johnson went north in order that he could refuse to converse. It was no disappointment for Johnson and Boswell to wander safely and futilely "through the glens in search of a vanishing patriarchical society" (Smout, *History of the Scottish People*, p. 208), for the safety and futility were connected to each other and implicated in Johnson's claims (advanced by the lowland Boswell) to eminence. The trope of the tour, feudal in its own right, was not the chiasmus but the Augustan trope of power, the antithesis.

instead of regarding the man of letters as a version of the merchant, we need to understand the merchant as a progenitor of the emergent and newly dominant man of letters.

In part the man of letters' advantage over the merchant is a matter of scale. If the merchant goes between producer and consumer regulating supply and demand, the man of letters negotiates between individuals and the larger formation which comprises them. Writing against faction, Hume avers, "For my part, I shall always be more fond of promoting moderation than zeal; though perhaps the surest way of producing moderation in every party is to increase our zeal for the public" (G&G, p. 107). Like the merchant, Hume mediates between two factions, each intent on pursuing its interest at the expense of the other. Like but different from the merchant, the man of letters executes his mediation doubly, by mediating not only particular factions but *factionalism* in general with the idea of the public. Hume adopts the Mandevillian strategy of exploiting rather than repressing zeal: moderation is attained by inducing zeal towards an idea of the public emancipated from partisan interests. The public, like the economy, is an idea within a plot of indirection, constantly being regulated, adjusted, and corrected by the man of letters, who makes possible the local negotiations between Tories and Whigs.

Another advantage derives from the kind of perspective that allows the man of letters to write: "If we consult history we shall find, that, in most nations, foreign trade has preceded any refinement in home manufactures, and given birth to domestic luxury." History teaches that foreign trade acquaints men

> with the *pleasures* of luxury and the *profits* of commerce; and their *delicacy* and *industry*, being once awakened, carry them on to further improvements, in every branch of domestic as well as foreign trade. . . . And at the same time, the few merchants, who possessed the secret of this importation and exportation, make great profits; and becoming rivals in wealth to the ancient nobility, tempt other adventurers to become their rivals in commerce. Imitation soon diffuses all those arts; while domestic manufacturers emulate the foreign in their improvements and work up every home commodity to the utmost perfection of which it is susceptible. ("Of Commerce," G&G, pp. 296–97)

Consulting history is the foreign trade of the man of letters, who gives the past a form that allows him to import its lessons into the present. The historian can place the merchant within the past, whereas the merchant not only cannot place the historian; he cannot know the historian, who comes after him, who as refinement is made possible by the merchant's "commerce with strangers." The historian can, of course, know the merchant: know how he once possessed secrets, know how he acquired great profits, know how he excited imitation—he knows the process which the merchant made possible and by which he is determined. The secrets of the merchant are consigned to the *past* by the historian: they are secrets he "possessed," now become the property of the man of letters through an act of historical sympathy.

What the man of letters knows it is possible for anyone to know.[45] His historical consultation—to acquaint men with what they would become acquainted with in the course of time—is intended to *correct* the course of time, to reinforce and accelerate imitation and diffusion by offering himself as an example open to the emulation of all. More than knowing that merchants possessed secrets, more than knowing *what* secrets the merchants possessed, the man of letters' advantage inheres in a technique of dissipating secrecy—the last remnant of narrowness and partiality clung to by the historical merchant. It is also the last vestige of the conspiratorial that tainted the merchant's success and inhibited the enlightenment of which he was the carrier.[46] There is nothing conspiratorial in the practice of the man of letters, who does not speak, let alone whisper—who writes plain English so that all who run may read. Of course, the magistrates' concern for the conspiracies of merchants was never more than superstition; there is, it turns out, no secret to the merchant's secret, which is a technique that can be mastered by everyone and to the profit of each and all: "As the multitude of mechanical arts is advantageous, so is the great number of persons to whose share the productions of these arts fall. . . . Every person, if possible, ought to enjoy the fruits of his labour, in a full possession of all the necessaries, and many of the conveniences of life. No one can doubt, but that such equality is most suitable to human nature, and diminishes much less from the *happiness* of the rich than it adds to that of the poor" ("Of Commerce," G&G, p. 296).

The equality that Hume foresees implies a coincidence of the techniques of the merchant with the labor of each member of the commonwealth. Ultimately, the merchant will be eliminated by a diffusion of his function across the whole social landscape.[47] The middleman as such van-

45. See Hume's patient and scrupulous labor of "adding the Authorities to the Volumes of the Stuarts" in order to make his foreign trade with the past transpicuous and unimpeachable (*HL*, 1:316).

46. Braudel notes that as "early as 1385 in Evreux in Normandy, the defenders of public order were protesting about producers and retailers who agreed among themselves 'by whispering in each other's ear, by speaking low or by signs, and in strange or hidden words'" (*Wheels of Commerce*, p. 49).

47. Istvan Hont and Michael Ignatieff make the observation (linking Adam Smith and Hume under the rubric of "civic discourse") that for Smith "because modern economies

ishes because ideally each man becomes his own middleman, or, as Adam Smith would later put it, "Every man thus lives by exchanging, or becomes in some measure a merchant."[48] The commercial system imagined by Hume promises gain for everyone because it avoids assigning loss to anyone.[49] Labor is nothing other than the technique for matching indirect passions with satisfaction indirectly acquired.[50] The career of the man of letters is the most abstract labor of all. Its virtuosity and its (post)historical privilege consist precisely in the fluidity of its transfers among diverse labors, its capacity to imitate any employment. When Hume offers himself as an example for emulation, he is proposing that one emulate nothing in particular but emulate his imitation in general.[51] This can be imagined to create wealth if it can be seriously believed (and there is nothing about which Hume is more serious) that "a noble emulation [not gold, not goods] is the source of every excellence" (*ST*, p. 93).

Hume identifies the chief advantage of the man of letters over the everyday merchant at the beginning of "Commerce":

> The greater part of mankind may be divided into two classes; that of *shallow* thinkers, who fall short of the truth; and that of *abstruse* thinkers, who go beyond it. The latter class are by far the most rare: and I may add, by far the most useful and valuable. . . . All people

were the first capable of sustained 'improvement,' because they were the first to draw themselves beyond the cycle of luxury, corruption and decline, the share of the labourer could continue to grow in absolute terms, even though the oppression of the superior orders might prevent it from increasing in relative terms." "Needs and Justice in the *Wealth of Nations*," in *Wealth and Virtue: The Shaping of Political Economy in the Scottish Enlightenment*, ed. Hont and Ignatieff (Cambridge: Cambridge Univ. Press, 1983), p. 6.

48. Smith, *The Wealth of Nations* (New York: Modern Library, 1937), p. 22.

49. The most artfully contrived version of such an economy is the fluid translatability of Yorick in Sterne's *A Sentimental Journey through France and Italy*. See Eve Kosofsky Sedgwick's acute interpretation of the fluidity in *Between Men: English Literature and Male Homosocial Desire* (New York: Columbia Univ. Press, 1984), pp. 67–82.

50. Cf. Marx's comment that "this abstraction of labour as such is not merely the mental product of a concrete totality of labours. Indifference towards specific labours corresponds to a form of society in which individuals can with ease transfer from one labour to another, and where the specific kind is a matter of chance for them hence of indifference. Not only the category, labour, but labour in reality has here become the means of creating wealth in general." Marx, *Grundrisse*, trans. Martin Nicolaus (New York: Vintage, 1973), p. 104. On the development and diffusion of new techniques in eighteenth-century Britain, see Peter Mathias, *The Transformation of England* (New York: Columbia Univ. Press, 1979), pp. 27, 30–31, 34, and 39, for defenses against outsiders' acquisition of "secret processes."

51. In his discussion of the dissemination of information aimed at encouraging agricultural improvement in eighteenth-century Scotland, R. H. Campbell uses 1770 as the benchmark to separate two kinds of emulative discourse: an earlier one when "most writers were encouraging Scots to follow the ways of others," from a later one relying on "examples of improved practice in Scotland." *Scotland since 1707: The Rise of an Industrial Society* (New York: Barnes & Noble, 1965), p. 35.

of *shallow* thought are apt to decry even those of *solid* understanding, as *abstruse* thinkers and metaphysicians, and refiners; and never will allow any thing to be just which is beyond their own weak conceptions. There are some cases, I own, where an extraordinary refinement affords a strong presumption of falsehood. . . . But when we reason on *general* subjects, one may justly affirm, that our speculations can scarcely ever be too fine. . . . General reasonings seem intricate, merely because they are general. . . . But however intricate they may seem, it is certain, that general principles, if just and sound, must always prevail in the general course of things, though they may fail in particular cases; and it is the chief business of philosophers to regard the general course of things. (G&G, pp. 226–27)[52]

Advantages of scale and perspective are made possible by an abstruseness that elevates the man of letters above contingencies. The general is that order of discourse which determines itself as free of risk. Similarly, the transformation of each laborer into a middleman is a generalization of exchange which eliminates the risks that fret merchants, not by minimizing them, as under a mercantilist system, but by dispersing them through a system so intricate that it is capable of adjusting to any contingency. At the level of the general the contingent is only the name for the space between something and something else that permits exchange, the circulation of property, the transactions of sympathy.

A question that might arise from this web of analogies and imitations is this: if under the sign of the general everyone comes to be a middleman, what specific advantage belongs to the man of letters as economic agent? My rationale for applying the metaphor of middleman to Hume is not only to frame the ideal but to show its crucial limitations as a description of the man of letters' practice. The man of letters constantly supersedes whatever mediation he makes or whatever type he emulates. For example, his dissipation of secrecy is presented as a way of generalizing exchange by making everyone a middleman and thereby avoiding the assignment of loss. But a corollary of that diffusion is an avoidance of the assignment of capital. Power, Hume wants to think, does not lodge with capital. Given the general composition of Hume's career, one would naturally expect to find power identified with knowledge in his economics,

---

52. This is a version of what might be called the Ciceronian imperative. The orator, Cicero generalizes, "always, if he can, diverts the controversy from any individual person or occasion. For it is in his power to argue on wider grounds concerning a genus than concerning a part; as, whatever is proved in the universal, must inevitably be proved with respect to a part" ("The Orator," *Cicero's Orations*, 4:395).

but if it were, power would suffer the diffusion that is the general fate of knowledge. *All* the merchant's secrets are diffused. All knowledge is diffused except the particular *technique* for dissipating secrecy, which remains secret: in every format of discourse and in every arena of practice, the man of letters' technique, whether it be for correction, induction, diffusion, diversification, or emulation, remains the basis of his distinction, his symbolic capital.[53] It is because of the inimitable power of his technique that Hume can persuade himself that an account of commerce can be concluded without mention of capital—and that the force of representation can replace more material factors like land, machinery, and bank accounts. Hume's carefully duplicitous practice will be to argue for the generalization of the function of the middleman (turning the literal fact into a generally available metaphor) from the position of the triumphant capitalist undertaker, who is *not*, however, except in a metaphorical sense a true capitalist. The man of letters metaphorically takes the position of the capitalist in relation to the middleman in part to convince himself and us that capital is merely metaphorical and that literary relations can satisfactorily take over from economic ones. And it is because capital is metaphorical in and for the man of letters (a capital of metaphors or correspondences) that he is vulnerable to the brute, material thing, capital itself. Duplicity, however, may seem like a hard charge; I shall try to justify it in several readings of Hume's essays on economics.

In the general course of things the function of the middleman is assumed by money, which, as Hume defines it, "is not, properly speaking, one of the subjects of commerce; but only the instrument which men have agreed upon to facilitate the exchange of one commodity for another" (G&G, p. 309). No subject, money is the medium and marker of commerce. Medium because marker, for "money is nothing but the representation of labour and commodities, and serves only as a method of rating or estimating them" (p. 312).[54] What stimulates manufacture is nei-

---

53. This paradoxical notion of a secret that not only remains secret despite openness but that, in fact, depends for its peculiar force on publicity is not restricted either to Hume or to the eighteenth-century man of letters. Eisenstein remarks of the "new 'underground' which was inhabited by men of letters" in the sixteenth century, that those "'secret' societies presented an especially dramatic contrast with the older guilds and lodges in their paradoxical exploitation of publicity. Far from being restricted to small closed circles of adherents, they extended invitations to unknown readers and by hinting at mysteries revealed only to the initiated, appeared to use secrecy as a recruiting device" (*The Printing Press as an Agent of Change*, pp. 274–75). The notion of the open secret—something that is put to practical and public use and offered for emulation but which remains mystified and is constantly recuperated as the symbolic capital of an elite—is probably most fully elaborated in the wonderful complications of Hume's great essay "Of Taste."

54. "Money is not riches, as it is a metal endow'd with certain qualities of solidity, weight

ther the glitter of gold nor the availability of labor as such but the representation of labor's cheapness—a rating assigned by the disposition of money within the commercial network. As for labor, so for commodities. "It seems a maxim almost self-evident," Hume observes, "that the prices of every thing depend on the proportion between commodities and money, and that any considerable alteration on either has the same effect, either of heightening or lowering the price. Encrease the commodities, they become cheaper; encrease the money, they rise in their value" (p. 316). Money "oils" the economy of things.

It is when Hume says what "almost" goes without saying, defines the doxa, that his prose thickens, temporarily marring the transparency of what he writes to the subject it represents. The same thing happens in the world of commerce:

> Where coin is in greater plenty; as a greater quantity of it is required to represent the same quantity of goods; it can have no effect, either good or bad, taking a nation within itself; any more than it would make an alteration on a merchant's books, if, instead of the ARABIAN method of notation, which requires few characters, he should make use of the ROMAN, which requires a great many. Nay, the greater quantity of money, like the ROMAN characters, is rather inconvenient, and requires greater trouble both to keep and transport it. But notwithstanding this conclusion, which must be allowed just, it is certain, that, since the discovery of the mines in AMERICA, industry has encreased in all the nations of EUROPE . . . ; and this may be justly ascribed, amongst other reasons, to the encrease of gold and silver. Accordingly we find, that, in every kingdom, into which money begins to flow in greater abundance than formerly, every thing takes a new face: labour and industry gain life; the merchant becomes more enterprising, the manufacturer more diligent and skilful, and even the farmer follows his plough with greater alacrity and attention. This is not easily to be accounted for. (G&G, pp. 312–13)

A correction of the particular, the general cannot escape its origin. In order to be truly general, the argument about money must be able to take account of exceptions to the general course of things. The test is most conspicuous in the case of the enlivenment of economic activity by the influx of gold from America. But it is no less urgent in the example of the merchant who is imagined by Hume as somehow opting for the use of

---

and fusibility; but only as it has a relation to the pleasures and conveniences of life" (T, p. 311).

Roman characters rather than for Arabian in spite of their inconvenience. It does not matter whether any merchant would actually make such a decision; that Hume imagines he could so choose brings into existence a possibility that ineluctably disfigures the very type of the commercial agent.[55] How can we account for this possibility generally? And is this particular example to be accounted for by the same argument that explains the peculiarity of American gold? Is there a general account for violations of the general course of things?

The problem of the merchant is complicated if we imagine the selection of these Roman characters as not simply some wild aberration that marks him out as an eccentric en route to failure, but rather as made by someone whose industry is somehow increased by his ostensibly diseconomic embrace of the inconvenient—for then we would have the paradox of the diseconomic serving the economic. Such a paradox emerges because Hume has trouble rating a novelty or excess. As we have seen in Chapter 4, he wants to slice luxury into the virtuous and the vicious: the luxury which is essential to the improvement of commerce and that which

55. Defoe had taken the possibility seriously. When, in *The Complete English Tradesman*, he avows his intention to assist the tradesman in understanding "perfectly well all the methods of correspondence, returning money or goods for goods, to and from every county in *England*; in what manner to be done, and in what manner most to advantage," he adopts "correspondence" to indicate an extension of exchange from the simple question of matter to the problem of "manner"—a manner which includes the appropriate "trading stile," discussed in letters 2 and 3. In letter 2, "Of the Tradesman's writing Letters," Defoe instructs the young tradesman how "to correspond . . . like a man of business" and furnishes examples of the inconvenient styles—whether "rumbling and bombast" or modishly pointed—that tradesmen are apt to adopt. In letter 3, "Of the Trading Stile," Defoe defines the "perfect stile or language" as that "in which a man speaking to five hundred people, of all common and various capacities, Ideots and Lunaticks excepted, should be understood by them all, in the same manner with one another, and in the same sense which the speaker intended to be understood." But, as the *OED* indicates, although *correspondence* connotes "the action or fact of . . . answering to each other in fitness or mutual adaptation; congruity, harmony, agreement," it also implies "intercourse or communications of a secret or illicit nature." And although Defoe endorses the standard of universal perspicuity, denouncing "all Exotic sayings, dark and ambiguous speakings, affected words," he makes an exception for "a kind of a cant in trade, which a Tradesman ought to know . . . which none can speak but themselves" and affirms that "this in letters of business is allowable, and indeed they cannot understand one another without it." Perspicuity and universality can only extend so far; at a certain point, that point where merchants define themselves as a fraternity with its own particular advantages, everyone else must be put in the position of "Ideots and Lunaticks," reading or listening to an incomprehensible cant, the secret language of the "trade" (*The Complete English Tradesman*, pp. 17–27). The Scots were less likely to make such exceptions: even the merchants in Glasgow, Alexander Carlyle informs us, were induced to form clubs in order to profit from enlightenment. *The Autobiography of Dr. Alexander Carlyle of Inveresk, 1722–1805*, ed. John Hill Burton (London and Edinburgh: T. N. Foulis, 1910), pp. 81–82.

is truly excessive and therefore dangerous. The gain in life by labor and industry, in enterprise by the merchant, in diligence and skill by the manufacturer, and in alacrity and attention by the farmer are of uncertain signification. Hume welcomes the surplus industry; but insofar as that animation is unaccountable it also appears vicious.

But the argument is only momentarily suspended. The gears of the corrective mechanism engage. An account *must* follow or the general course of things and the discourse of the man of letters must fail:

> To account, then, for this phenomenon, we must consider, that though the high price of commodities be a necessary consequence of the encrease of gold and silver, yet *it follows not immediately* upon that encrease; but *some* time is required before the money circulates through the whole state, and makes its effect be felt on all ranks of people. At first, no alteration is perceived; *by degrees the price rises*, first of one commodity, then of another; till the whole at last reaches a just proportion with the new quantity of specie which is in the kingdom. In my opinion, it is only in this interval or intermediate situation, between the acquisition of money and rise of prices, that the encreasing quantity of gold and silver is favourable to industry. (G&G, p. 313; emphasis added)

For some time more gold is available to a few people, making it possible for them to buy goods at the old prices—thus stimulating the industry of all to acquire the gold and thereby the goods. Hence although the high price of commodities is generally the necessary consequence of an increase of money, in this case there is a sequence of more gold, more labor, more goods, which makes it seem as if gold produces goods and labor rather than merely rating them—as if, that is, the representation precedes and causes the labor and commodities which it represents. This is a moment where the peculiar "weight" of gold has a force out of all relation to its symbolic function. The interval that follows marks out a kind of imperialist wish-fulfillment in which the possibility of infinite enrichment seems a reality for everyone—a wish wholly without reference to society. It is a romantic moment in which for a time effects are wildly out of proportion to their causes—*must be* so because the very surplus that gives gold a magical vivacity and force disables it as a reliable instrument of measurement.[56]

The general reasserts itself in the familiar claim that "some time is

---

56. It goes without saying that this reading is not in accord with the way an economist might read Hume's account. I do not mean to commit myself to the absurd thesis that the wrinkles that mar Hume's exposition could never be ironed out. Of course they could; such is the task of economic historians and other reasonable men. Literary criticism is a different sort of practice.

required" for the circulation to restore an inevitable equilibrium. But the appeal to "some time" introduces an authentic temporality into an economy designed to render time as nothing more than one variable of a mathematically derived proportion. That phrase which Hume normally employs as a convention for the necessary adjustments that occur in the general course of things coincides here with an immeasurable break which has no natural check. For "some time," more satisfaction can be achieved by the laborer under the dispensation of gold than can be attained within the economy. For "some time," superstitious regard for gold is astonishingly efficacious: as if by magic, the fetish produces the goods that the vulgar wishes it would. The thaumaturgy of gold is the capacitation of desire.

There is a mimesis here between the discovery of gold in America and the appearance of the uncertain signification of money in Hume's essay, each of which is followed by an unaccountable suspension of the regularities of nature. Hume has defined money as a representation, something so completely and immediately known that it is not even an object of knowledge—only an instrument to the knowledge of other subjects. Its explosion from the mines of the Americas, however, makes money unknowable because it is neither an instrument of measure nor a measurable commodity. Technically, there is no way of knowing when this interval will end or, indeed, if it will end (there is no standard of subsistence from which to measure gain). What if gold were to keep erupting out of the earth and spilling into England in ever greater quantities, eliminating scarcity? How could the economy ever adjust? How could there be an economy?[57]

Eventually, of course, things do settle down. Like water, gold reaches its level. Balance prevails. In Hume's discourse (as opposed to

---

57. Compare Eugene Rotwein's note to his discussion of this passage: "There is in fact no basis for arguing that the expansion of employment from a single increase in the money supply will necessarily prove ephemeral." Rotwein, "David Hume, Philosopher-Economist," in *David Hume: Many-Sided Genius*, ed. Kenneth R. Merrill and Robert W. Shahan (Norman: Univ. of Oklahoma Press, 1976), p. 127n. The natural bounty that could stimulate labor has its converse in the natural disaster that could interrupt commerce: "You'll scarcely believe what I am going to tell you; but it is literally true. Millar had printed off some Months ago a new Edition of certain philosophical Essays; but he tells me very gravely, that he has delay'd publishing because of the Earthquakes. I wish you may not also be a loser by the same common Calamity" (*HL*, 1:141). Now it is not quite clear whether "literally true" is meant to extend to the substance of Millar's account or only to apply to the fact of his account, whether, that is, the story of earthquakes was—and was recognized by Hume as—Millar's way of fabulating some secret of the trade, which dictated delay, to the uninitiated. Compare Defoe: "Trade is a Mystery, which will never be completely discover'd or understood; it has its Critical Junctures and Seasons, when acted by no visible Causes, it suffers Convulsion Fitts, hysterical Disorders, and most unaccountable Emotions" (quoted in Pocock, *Machiavellian Moment*, p. 454).

the world, which it so curiously mimics) that balance is attained by the invention of an imperceptible alteration. "No alteration is perceived," although an alteration must be occurring for the degrees of rising prices to follow. If the cause is known by inference from its effects, the effectiveness of the imperceptible alteration in reestablishing the equilibrium of Hume's discourse makes perceptible the causal intervention of the author, whose representation causes the argument—let us say the *economy* of the argument—to work. Hume stakes his invention against gold, one representation against another, in order to enforce a general course of things that cannot be trusted to proceed on its own. His intervention suppresses as much as possible all traces of its action; indeed, it can only be traced as the representation of the imperceptible, a display of the invisible hand.

The emancipation of economics from politics cannot be total because the general course of things is never emancipated from the eruption of the contingent. Another way of putting this would be to say simply that the economy can never be emancipated from representation; and not only is *money* a word of uncertain signification but signification itself is uncertain, perhaps unmasterable. It is in this respect that the possibility of the merchant's choosing Roman numerals over Arabian parallels the aftermath of the discovery of American gold. The possibility of the choice seems to violate the rationality of the economic type. Yet there is also a moral for the duplicitous: insofar as the possibility testifies to a susceptibility to signs apart from their strictly indexical function, it also attests to the strategic privilege and power of the man of letters. This latter moral can be anchored in biographical detail.

I have already referred to the episode in Bristol when, as diversion from the arduous labor on the *Treatise*, Hume clerked for a merchant, Michael Miller. Of significance here is the quarrel that led to Hume's departure. Here is Mossner: "The quarrel was over matters literary: David's corrections of grammar and style in Miller's letters. Exasperated at the repeated criticisms of his young clerk, Miller is said to have told him that he made £20,000 with his English and would not have it improved." Mossner accepts the account and concludes that as "a result of this quarrel, David left Bristol harbouring deep resentment" (Mossner, p. 90). It may be, as Mossner conjectures, that some of the sarcasms Hume later directed at merchants arose from his bitterness at not having his learning suitably appreciated by Miller. It may also be because Miller, like Mossner, insisted on a sharp distinction between literary and commercial matters. But more important for Hume's theory and practice is the nature of the difference between the young man of letters and his employer, which subsists in divergent attitudes toward representation: Miller's rough pragmatism versus Hume's elegance. That difference, however, manifests itself only on the basis of an apparent mutuality of interests: Hume could find employment with the middleman because his learning did equip him as a clerk who could efficiently adjust Miller's books. But difficulty appears when Hume's adjustments within the mechanism become Hume's corrections of the mechanism. What to the clerk looks like a simple extension of his labor, to the merchant, who "looks for fidelity and skill in his factor or super-cargo" (*T*, p. 405), identifies a laborer who is not merely the clerk that he ought to be. Hume's correction is an adjustment of adjustment, an excessive refinement, which marks out a technique that, according to the merchant's reckoning, is of no value and therefore diseconomic. Instead of doing what he is supposed to do, Hume is doing what he wants to do: serving not his own economic interest but deploying a power apart from the economy. Correction of grammar and style is not a representation that estimates or rates; it is a technique that acts on representation as such and treats it as a *cause* rather than as the gauge of the concurrence of causes that constitute the market.

Hence it is both undecidable and immaterial who in this little allegory of economics and power stands for Arabian notation and who for Roman. Could we interrogate Hume, he would almost certainly argue that his corrections were aimed at eliminating inconveniences in the merchant's records and correspondence; Miller would surely counter that the stylistic corrections made by his clerk were both insolent and inefficient. What is important is that a real difference emerges, or at least a difference that raises the thorny question of what "real" differences might be.

That question is the explicit topic of Hume's essay "Of Parties in General," which divides factions "into PERSONAL and REAL; that is, into factions founded on personal friendship or animosity among such as compose the contending parties, and into those founded on some real difference of sentiment or interest" (G&G, p. 128). Real differences are sensible; that is, no matter how trivial they might be, such as "the difference between one colour of livery and another in horse-races," they are based on some actual appearance, about which men can agree to disagree. In that sense the division between personal and real is not antithetical, since as Hume shows, personal differences can spring from real; the real division is between real and unreal differences—the latter a category that Hume does not name but which he does introduce in passing in his discussion of the "civil wars which arose some few years ago in MOROCCO between the *blacks* and *whites*, merely on account of their complexion":

We laugh at them, but I believe, were things rightly examined, we afford much more occasion of ridicule to the MOORS. For, what are all the wars of religion, which have prevailed in this polite and knowing part of the world? They are certainly more absurd than the MOORISH civil wars. The difference of complexion is a sensible and a real difference: But the controversy about an article of faith, which is utterly absurd and unintelligible, is not a difference in sentiment, but in a few phrases and expressions, which one party accepts of, without understanding them; and the other refuses in the same manner. (G&G, p. 130).

The notion of a difference in polar opposition to the real surfaces as a matter of "a few phrases and expressions," which somehow are not sensible. Those unreal differences function like that Humean marvel the imperceptible alteration—though here not to adjust an interval but, rather, to concoct one as the sufficient space for violence to erupt. The provocative incomprehensibility of those phrases describes a style that has been purified to a point where correspondence cannot occur—the kind of pure style indicated by the difference between Arabian and Roman notation, and the kind of mutual incomprehensibility that precipitates the violent method of Miller's dismissal of his clerk. The practice of the middleman and the practice of the man of letters cannot be harmonized; their discord arises over problems of power and of representation. Hume fails: he does not persuade the merchant of the convenience of an elegant style, and he is fired from his job. The merchant triumphs because he is able to dismiss the insubordinate clerk. Yet Hume succeeds because the merchant's exercise of his prerogative proceeds from a recognition of the power of representation and is an acknowledgment that that power belongs to a clerk whom he cannot accommodate within his commerce. We have then a contest which can be described in several ways—but every way it is described, someone loses; it is impossible to consider the contest as economic exchange, since it emerges from and is sustained by differences that are unreal, that cannot be measured or rated. The contest cannot be conceptualized without taking account (in Roman or Arabic notation?) of what may be an exercise of an unaccountable power. Insofar as the man of letters wants to distinguish himself from the merchant, he must disable the analogy between them by exploiting the unreal difference made possible by the detachment of the signifier from any conventional signified, which is then used as slogan and weapon in a conflict that is theological or quintessentially ideological, that turns on nothing other than articles, phrases rather, of faith.[58]

58. Perhaps the most conspicuous literary example of this kind of debate is the controversy between Thwackum and Square in Fielding's *Tom Jones*. But an example closer to Hume may be found in chapter 2 of Goldsmith's *Vicar of Wakefield*, where the vicar reports

Hume's subsequent practice as man of letters both relies on the affinities between his practice and the middleman's and capitalizes on the difference; it both effaces the uncertainty of representation and exploits it. Hume works out the implication of his quarrel with Miller by correcting it, that is, by representing in all his writings the reason why, if things are considered in a general way, such a quarrel, with its antagonism, its display of power, and its perception of loss should never have occurred; yet his very capacity to correct depends, as the general on the particular, on the possibility of such a quarrel—which specifies the peculiar power of the man of letters, his particular generality, as the figure who corrects. Hume's experience with Miller encapsulates the history of the man of letters since the medieval age—the progress of the clerk from merchant's instrument to his collaborator and then to a man of letters emancipated from the merchant's employ. This emancipation can only be achieved— as long as it is to remain in the real world, the world of commerce between men and nations—in terms derived from the merchant, but it demands a practice of representation that the merchant cannot rightly appreciate—a practice which, however, will impose on him as a power that induces him into the larger composition.[59]

The affiliations between the career of the man of letters and the market economy form an ideological knot. Because he represents, both rates and causes, the man of letters can inculcate the belief in the self-regulating economy by which he thrives. The fundamental problem that Hume faces in the elaboration of his economics is how to describe a system that is based on balance but that requires excess or novelty for its dynamism. It is a problem that he returns to again and again in these essays, but paradigmatically in "Of Interest," where he tells the story of the origin of economics:

---

that during the preparations for his son's wedding he engaged in a theological dispute on the virtues of monogamy with the father of the bride: "It was managed with proper spirit on both sides: he asserted that I was heterodox, I retorted the charge: he replied, and I rejoined." A relation advised him "to give up the dispute . . . at least until my son's wedding was over. 'How,' cried I, 'relinquish the cause of truth. . . . You might as well advise me to give up my fortune as my argument.'" Informed that he *has* lost his fortune, the vicar clings to his argument with all the more fervor. What makes it a theological argument and ridiculous is that it has no relation to anyone's fortune, can be carried on with the same vigor in the face of the wreck of family circumstances or, indeed, in the wake of the ruin of empires. What makes this a particularly Humean episode is the intimate relation—coincidental verging on causal—between the argument, what Hume would call factionalism, and financial ruin.

59. See Braudel's discussion of the technical education of merchants in quattrocento Italy and the importance of this educated class to the flowering of culture in the Florentine Renaissance (*The Wheels of Commerce*, p. 408).

> Every thing useful to the life of man arises from the ground; but few things arise in that condition which is requisite to render them useful. There must, therefore, beside the peasants and the proprietors of land, be another rank of men, who receiving from the former the rude materials, work them into their proper form, and retain part for their own use and subsistence. In the infancy of society, these contracts between the artisans and the peasants, and between one species of artisans and another are commonly entered into immediately by the persons themselves, who, being neighbours, are easily acquainted with each other's necessities, and can lend their mutual assistance to supply them. (G&G, p. 324)

The infancy of society looks different from the way it does in the *Treatise:* here it is a state of happy artisanry, characterized by personal contracts entered into "immediately" by cooperative neighbors. All the conventions of society are in place except the promise, unimaginable without distance. And then "industry encreases" and "views enlarge when it is found that the most remote parts of the state can assist each other as well as the more contiguous, and that this intercourse of good offices may be carried on to the greatest extent and intricacy." The same question arises here that applies to the origin of society: how do "views enlarge"? How do men see an advantage in what is distant when they are immediately satisfied? "Hence the origin of *merchants,* one of the most useful races of men, who serve as agents between those parts of the state, that are wholly unacquainted, and are ignorant of each other's necessities." The merchant brings the light necessary to enlarge the view; he makes men aware of parts of the state with which they have been "wholly unacquainted" and becomes, by virtue of that knowledge, the agent between them.

> Here are in a city fifty workmen in silk and linen, and a thousand customers; and these two ranks of men, so necessary to each other, can never rightly meet, till one man erects a shop, to which all the workmen and all the customers repair. In this province grass rises in abundance: The inhabitants abound in cheese, and butter, and cattle; but want bread and corn, which in a neighbouring province, are in too great abundance for the use of the inhabitants. *One man discovers this.* He brings corn from the one province, and returns with cattle; and, *supplying the wants of both,* he is, so far, a common benefactor. (G&G, pp. 324–25; emphasis added)

"One man discovers this"—Humeanism distilled. The whole of economics depends on the original experience of one man. And what does that one man discover? He sees double. Instead of a single society of benign immediacy, he sees two parts of an as yet unrealized whole. Instead of subsistence he sees abundance and necessity. Instead of a simple reciprocity between a producer and a consumer, he sees two producers and two consumers—"two things possessed, two things desired."[60] At the origin of economics is a moment homologous to that in book 2 of the *Treatise*, when the investigator (abstracting the dual relations of ideas and impressions) has "true system break in upon [him] with an irresistible evidence" (*T*, p. 286; see Chap. 3 above). The discovery of system is the merchant's only advantage. His considerable disadvantage would seem to be his lack of anything to sell or trade—but only "seem to be" because the system providentially makes it possible for lacks to be converted into assets. At the initial stage, when he has no goods on hand, the merchant, taking advantage of his solitary discovery, "supplies wants"—"supplies" in the double and Derridean sense of *acquainting* each part with its partiality, of the existence of necessities that until that point had never been known, and of acting as the agent who will fill those wants for both parties.

There is, of course, the simple but crucial matter of setting up shop. The Humean merchant's only capital is his discovery: his knowledge must be employed to infuse passion, stimulate labor, and extract abundance; but knowledge is also stock that must be carefully reserved. The merchant succeeds without expending his knowledge by *representing* the goods of one group to another as desirable, in order that he might procure goods to trade. Before people know themselves as producers they are acted on as consumers. What has been produced has its value only insofar as it can be reproduced in the language of the merchant. Technically, demand precedes supply as consumer precedes producer; demand "produces" production as its reproduction.[61] W. W. Rostow has defined economic "take-off" as that "decisive interval in the history of a society when growth becomes its normal condition";[62] for Hume such growth begins at the beginning—with the merchant's first appearance and with the imita-

---

60. Turgot's formulation, quoted in Braudel, *The Wheels of Commerce*, p. 173. It ought to be mentioned that for the sake of brevity I am swerving from the full-scale de Manian reading that moment and formulation invite. Such a reading would explain the recognizability of a "quadruple schema" (Braudel, p. 175) according to the virtual identity of merchant and rhetorician in men of letters' legends of commerce. The merchant recognizes an economic schema in human activity because he imposes on strangers the familiar rhetorical schema of the chiasmus, which is a way of getting two polar things to turn into a balanced exchange among four.

61. On the priority of demand to supply, see Neil McKendrick's fascinating essay "Commercialization and the Economy," in *The Birth of a Consumer Society* (Bloomington: Indiana Univ. Press, 1983), esp. pp. 9–33. On the parasitism of production on reproduction in political economy, see Jean Baudrillard, *The Mirror of Production*.

62. W. W. Rostow, *The Stages of Economic Growth: A Non-Communist Manifesto* (Cambridge: Cambridge Univ. Press, 1960), p. 33.

tion he induces. The decisive interval is always now. By persuasively converting goods into commodities the merchant acquires credit. Credit, the first, energizing surplus, is wholly the "product" of a mercantile rhetoric that persuades producers to believe in a system which they are not able fully to see, let alone understand—ever. "As the people encrease in numbers and industry, the difficulty of their intercourse encreases: The business of the agency or merchandize becomes more intricate; and divides, subdivides, compounds, and mixes to a greater variety. In all these transactions, it is necessary and reasonable, that a considerable part of the commodities and labour should belong to the merchant, to whom, in a great measure, they are owing. And these commodities he will sometimes preserve in kind, or more commonly convert into money, which is their common representation." Although the merchant is a middleman who brings remote parts into correspondence by stimulating supplementary production and consumption, the effect, curiously, is not to facilitate immediacy on a larger scale but to make things more intricate, so that only a specialist in the system of the general can see it steadily and see it whole—a specialist who takes the profit due him for the aboriginal risk of staking everything on a hypothetical credit that fathered commerce: "Merchants . . . beget industry, by serving as canals to convey it through every corner of the state: And at the same time, by their frugality, they acquire great power over that industry, and collect a large property in the labour and commodities, which they are the chief instruments in producing" (G&G, pp. 325–26).

I will not dispute the traditional characterization of Adam Smith as the exponent of a labor theory of value; but if true for Smith it is not true for Hume, who connects value to interest, derives interest from labor, and finds labor produced by the persuasiveness of merchants. Hume essays a *communication* theory of value in an economics almost completely deontologized, which puts what Smith called "unproductive labor"[63] at the very base of a system that is nothing but superstructure, an intricate array of representations. Unproductive labor produces only its own advantage, communicates as an exercise of power.

Economics is not completely deontologized because it is not completely enlightened. There remains that dark recess in the machine, responsible for its operation but also culpable for the intricacy that mystifies its workings; there remains that canal that produces, the conduit that baffles, that place-saver, measure-maker, and profit-taker, the merchant, who is duplicitous by his very nature and who tries to make his nature essential to the continued operation of the machine he has set in motion.

63. See Chapter 4 above.

"One man discovers this"—the essential advantage of the merchant, which gives him power over that which he finds and in finding makes. And Hume discovers this: the metaphysics of humanism, which is a metaphysics of power, produces its dialectic of enlightenment by exposing government as subject to no state secret but ordered by a general commerce and then by exposing the secret of the merchant's trade; it projects its telos as the man of letters, who uses his credit to increase his capital, who goes between merchant and prince, learned and conversable, England and France, man and woman, who discloses everything but that secret which allows him to dominate by virtue of a technique of correspondence and correction—exchanging, rating, measuring, representing—that will allow him to endure, to preserve his advantage even in the potential perfection of a self-regulating system which abstracts all other labor into a mode of exchange.

Preserve by defending. The peril affecting the position of the go-between is most succinctly evoked in the essay "Of the Jealousy of Trade" in which Hume regards the exception to the generally benign dissolution of all barriers to free commerce:

> The only commercial state, that ought to dread the improvements and industry of their neighbours, is such a one as the DUTCH, who, enjoying no extent of land, nor possessing any number of native commodities, flourish only by their being brokers, and factors, and carriers of others. Such a people may naturally apprehend, that, as soon as the neighbouring states come to know and pursue their interest, they will take into their own hands the management of their affairs, and deprive their brokers of that profit, which they formerly reaped from it. But though this consequence may be actually dreaded, it is very long before it takes place; and by art and industry it may be warded off for many generations, if not wholly eluded. (G&G, pp. 347–48)[64]

Holland, that state which has historically contributed most to the refinement of the market, has the most to dread from continued improvements in commerce, since the perfection of the mechanism will extinguish the need for their services. The market casts out the historical as it casts out the particular, casts out the historical *as* the particular. The perfection of

64. Hume's interpretation of the plight of the Dutch, though more optimistic about the prowess of their "art and industry," is in essential agreement with Rostow's retrospective judgment: "The Dutch became too committed to finance and trade, without an adequate manufacturing base—partly because they lacked raw materials at home, partly because the financial and trading groups predominated rather than the manufacturers" (Rostow, *The Stages of Economic Growth*, p. 33).

the mathematical equilibrium of the market will have a history (that narrative of refinements which led up to it, its natural history) but will not be *in* history. Therefore it is possible to conceive of a state of things wholly severed from tradition, and truly evolutionary insofar as all previous, merely instrumental social forms can be imagined to be wholly annihilated. Annihilation does not seem to be too strong a word here.[65] If one of the glaring omissions in Hume's essays on politics and economics is an explanation of how war can arise within the market economy he describes, that lack is overcompensated for by the relentlessness of the engine he invents, which is able to abolish the inconvenient by expropriating the profit by which it has thrived: the Dutch have nothing but their expertise; once that is shared they become nothing at all. No blood will be shed, and there may still be a place called Holland on the map of Europe, but the Dutch will have no function and, therefore, no existence in the general course of things. The perfection of the mechanism is ruthless but impartial. History is the progressive annihilation of the merely particular.

Though beyond change, the perfected mechanism does require adjustments and that allows for its potential modification by those in the know. Such knowledge is either a matter of occupation (the canniness that has accounted for the profit of Dutch brokers in the past) or of education (the Dutch could read Hume's essay).[66] Foreknowledge could enable the

65. "Any object may be imagin'd to become entirely inactive, or to be annihilated in a moment; and 'tis an evident principle, *that whatever we can imagine, is possible*" (*T*, p. 250).

66. The Dutch brokers are, of course, one of the audiences that the man of letters could count on to read everything he wrote and to have a command of both English and French, having no native tongue except the language of commerce. Moreover, most manuscripts of the philosophes were translated into print in Holland, as Hume observes when he writes that "there is a general Tranquillity established in Europe; so that we have nothing to do but cultivate Letters: There appears here a much greater Zeal of that kind than in England; but the best and most taking works of the French are generally published in Geneva or Holland, and are in London before they are in Paris" (*HL*, 1:492). There was a good reason for this: the tight censorship of Enlightenment texts made possible by the stranglehold over the production and distribution of books under the privilege system of the *ancien régime* made it necessary to publish those texts abroad. Pierre Bayle's "Notes from the Republic of Letters" was published in Rotterdam. The Dutch had an interest in the republic of letters, since most of the French books and newspapers before the French Revolution were published in Holland; and the French citizens of the republic of letters had an interest (an interest not synchronous with that of the individual states where they lived and owned real property) in the preservation of Dutch independence—since Holland was just about the only place where they could get their writings printed and sold (Eisenstein, *The Printing Press as an Agent of Change*, pp. 137–38). As far as the enterprise of publishing went, then, the Dutch could hope to ward off extinction as long as the French monarchy could ward off its destruction. The irony lies in the mutual dependence between the Protestant, republican

Dutch to "ward off" inevitable extinction. Hume does not say just exactly what means they might use, but it is clear that they cannot just go on as they have, improving a mechanism which, when perfected, would eliminate them. Subsistence becomes most urgent for those whose function has been most abstracted into pure gain because the most efficient are most vulnerable to extinction.[67] Although he will continue to open up lines of trade, passing along commodities and information, the prudent broker will secretly introduce complexities in order to shore up his expertise and insure his survival. Because he cannot appeal to the state, whose interests he does not share, the broker can defend himself only by mystifying his practice.[68] Like the critic and the philosopher he will have an interest in invoking a *"je ne scai quoi,* of which 'tis impossible to give any definition or description, but which every one sufficiently understands" (*T,* p. 106).[69]

It is to this necessity of saving place that Hume's attack on paper money ultimately has reference. For if money has chiefly "a fictitious value" and precious "metals are considered chiefly as representations" (G&G, p. 322), it is not clear why paper money is not its logical refinement. If the movements of trade are best characterized by a hydraulic metaphor—the famed "quantity-specie flow mechanism"—why should not paper, the most fluid specie of all, be the currency of choice? Hume's various answers have in common an understanding of gold as somehow reinforcing the "natural proportion" between labor and commodities that is distorted by those who "endeavour artificially to encrease" paper credit (p. 311). Whatever one thinks of the argument, its terms, which deploy the bankrupt opposition between a natural good and an artificial evil, are tendentious. Hume comes closest to saying what he means by the natural

---

printers and the Catholic absolutists who ruled France, a mutual dependence reproduced in the relations between the philosophes, who could be interpreted as attacking the basis for arbitrary authority, and the monarch who honored them with places and privileges for doing so. See Chapter 6 below.

67. A principle noted with glee by Johnson, who instructed Boswell: "Depend upon it, this rage of trade will destroy itself. . . . Trade is like gaming. If a whole company are gamesters, it must cease, for there is nothing to be gained by trade. And it will stop the soonest where it is brought to the greatest perfection" (*Tour,* p. 193).

68. See Braudel's discussion of the international financiers, mostly Dutch, who advanced credit to Continental governments, both at home and abroad, in the seventeenth and eighteenth centuries. Braudel notes that "public credit did not completely wipe out the financial powers. . . . [For] behind this apparently open market, there was in fact a small group of merchants and financiers, all seasoned speculators, who dominated the state loan activities— taking their revenge as it were" (*The Wheels of Commerce,* p. 537).

69. "'Tis not solely in poetry and music, we must follow our taste and sentiment, but likewise in philosophy" (*T,* p. 103).

value of gold when, after describing the "inconvenience" attendant on "the encrease of trade and money," he adds that it "is compensated by the advantages, which we reap from the possession of these precious metals, and the weight, which they give the nation in foreign wars and negociations" (p. 311). Foreign policy is less the issue here than the notion of weight. Gold slows things down; it may make commerce efficient by insuring that no one "must take payment in commodities" (p. 319), but gold also benignly retards transactions because it has a mass that requires transit, and therefore intermediaries. The weightiness of gold marks out a space between the poles of the exchange for him who represents advantage and disadvantage to the producer/consumer and the consumer/producer. Hume clings to gold, despite the ostensible logic of his argument, because the logic of his argument would drive *him* out; although he attains his place only by displacing the merchant, he nonetheless requires the concept of the middleman, as opposed to the wholly speculative stockjobber, in order to imagine having a place at all.[70] Land to goods, goods to commodities, commodities to gold—and no further. Gold's weightiness is the last sense of a locus of value on which one can take a stand.

The peculiar status of gold in Hume's economic essays invites a reconsideration of the figure of the miser in the *Treatise*. In Chapter 3, I concluded that the miser was a figure of the imagination, whose wealth gave him all that Hume meant by power. Miserliness reappears in the economic essays under the sign of government hoarding of precious metals. In "The Balance of Trade" he argues that there is

a practice which we should all exclaim against as destructive, namely, the gathering of large sums into a public treasure, locking them up, and absolutely preventing their circulation. . . . There seems, indeed, in the nature of man, an invincible obstacle to that immense growth of riches. A weak state, with an enormous treasure, will soon become a prey to some of its poorer, but more powerful neighbours. A great state would dissipate its wealth in dangerous and ill-concerted projects; and probably destroy, with it, what is much more valuable, the industry, morals, and numbers of its people. The fluid, in this case, raised to too great a height, bursts and destroys the vessel that contains it; and mixing itself with the

70. "The ideological thrust was constantly toward the absorption of stockjobber into merchant: the rentier, who frightened social theorists, into the entrepreneur who did not. Virtue was now the cognition of social, moral and commercial reality, and everything possible had been done to eliminate the element of fantasy and fiction which had seemed so subversive of property and personality" (Pocock, *Machiavellian Moment*, p. 456).

surrounding element, soon falls to its proper level. (G&G, pp. 340–41)

Hume's scenario here fits with the hypothesis I advanced regarding the miser: the duration of his imaginary kingdom is limited either by the threat of robbers or by the advent of illness. Holding in too much gold makes both states and individuals fall sick.[71]

But when the issue is the circulation of paper money rather than gold, Hume alters the argument. In this view, he claims

> it must be allowed, that no bank could be more advantageous, than such a one as locked up all the money it received, and never augmented the circulating coin, as is usual, by returning part of its treasure into commerce. A public bank, by this expedient, might cut off much of the dealings of private bankers and money-jobbers; and though the state bore the charges of salaries to the directors and tellers of this bank . . . , the national advantage, resulting from the low price of labour and the destruction of paper-credit, would be a sufficient compensation. (G&G, p. 312)

Hume added an apt note in a later edition, that "this is the case with the bank of AMSTERDAM." Gold versus paper, the bad miser versus the good. Hoarding is equivocal; its relative merit, as either an aggressive accumulation or a defensive withdrawal, is dependent on the context. That equivocalness, which we found in the figure of the miser, derives from the concept of gold as a "fiction." "Fiction," like "luxury," is "a word of uncertain signification." Hume has always valued that uncertainty because, like the "conjunction of infirmity, and of necessity" which he found in its "greatest perfection" in natural unnatural man (*T*, p. 485), it allows for a manageable dynamism. Paper money is not a fiction but a delusion, "a counterfeit money, which foreigners will not accept of in any payment, and which any great disorder in the state will reduce to nothing" (G&G, p. 311)—or if not exactly to nothing, then to what Hume, in describing the uncomposed *Treatise* to Michael Ramsay, called "loose bits of Paper; here a hint of a passion, there a Phenomenon in the mind. . . . And none of them worth to any Body" (*HL*, 1:9; see Chap. 2 above).

Hume adheres to the gold standard because though it has no value in and of itself, gold facilitates the belief in value without which economic

---

71. Rostow remarks, "What can we say, in general, then, about the supply of finance during the take-off period? First, as a precondition, it appears necessary that the community's surplus above the mass-consumption level does not flow into hands of those who will sterilize it by hoarding, luxury consumption or low-productivity investment outlays" (*The Stages of Economic Growth*, p. 49).

174   The Commerce of Letters

activity cannot be rationalized. The gold standard produces the feeling of a correspondence between the token of exchange and wealth, just as a luxury commodity elicits the sense of something worth consuming, something that could satisfy an appetite. In Chapter 3, I described the way that in the *Treatise* the philosopher acquires symbolic capital for the practice of philosophy by comparing it to hunting and gambling. The same sort of mimesis privileges precious metals: gold and silver are uniquely valuable because they persuasively imitate wealth, though wealth they are not. Paper credit can never be anything more than the simulacrum of wealth—the excess of excess, a wholly imponderable convenience. Hume's writings on money reify that "naturalism" with which he has been tagged since the powerful commentary of Norman Kemp Smith: Hume can countenance the geyser of gold from the Americas because it must be transitory. As an element of nature gold must be scarce. The geyser will run dry.[72]

Like a fiction, gold has an impressiveness that, though it makes no final claims on a hypothetical real, can be imagined to distinguish it as the credibly symbolic from the merely imaginary. Hoarding is bad insofar as it occurs within a system regulated by gold and silver, within an *economy* proper. Hoarding becomes good, even vital, when it becomes the defensive gesture of (re)establishing an economy within a speculative empire that threatens to outrun all possible regulation, all correspondence, all measure—where effects no longer seem proportionate to any causes. Hoarding becomes a virtue when credit is to an airy thinness beat, when representation, apparently self-propagated and uncontrolled, threatens to engross the globe and more. Hoarding is a reterritorialization, a retardation and inhibition, that sets anew the borders within which balance can occur, where refinement can be regarded as a progressive virtue, and where civilized states and men of letters can confidently take and safely enjoy their profits—a space within which symbolic correspondence must

72. On this type of economic Lisbon Philo's comment in the *Dialogues Concerning Natural Religion* is authoritative: "And what argument have you against such convulsions? . . . Strong and almost incontestable proofs may be traced over the whole earth that every part of this globe has continued for many ages entirely covered with water. And though order were supposed inseparable from matter, and inherent in it, yet may matter be susceptible of many and great revolutions, through the endless periods of eternal duration. The incessant changes to which every part of it is subject seem to intimate some such general transformations; though, at the same time, it is observable that all the changes and corruptions of which we have ever had experience are but passages from one state of order to another; nor can matter ever rest in total deformity and confusion. What we see in the parts, we may infer in the whole" (*Dialogues*, p. 174).

be intensely equivocal, enfolded like a double entendre that separates the knowing from the unknowing and the unknown.[73]

IV

Hoarding and reterritorialization are both ways of "warding off"—of correcting automatic adjustments and inhibiting mechanical efficiency. Each is a technique for keeping a technique secret and profitable. Even the simplest operation participates in this duplicity. Consider abridgment, fundamental to Hume's ethics and his style. Because everything in nature "is carried on in the easiest and most simple manner," Hume infers that "'tis necessary, therefore, to abridge these primary impulses, and find some more general principles, upon which all our notions of morals are founded" (*T*, p. 181). On his revisions of the *Treatise* he comments, "I believe the philosophical Essays contain everything of Consequence relating to the Understanding, which you woud meet with in the Treatise; & I give you my Advice against reading the latter. By shortening & simplifying the Questions, I really render them much more complete. *Addo dum minuo*" (*HL*, 1:158).[74] Ideally, abridgment and simplification produce a more general and therefore more complete statement. The same technique can, however, further a strategy of suppression, when the general principle is abridged in the service of some more primary impulse, such as the acquisition of gold or the preservation of one's standing.

That double action appears in various defensive maneuvers by Hume. One principle on which he repeatedly took his stand was a philosophical indifference to controversy. To Henry Home in 1748: "The other work is the *Philosophical Essays*, which you dissuaded me from printing. I won't justify the prudence of this step, any other way than by expressing my indifference about all the consequences that may follow" (*HL*, 1:111). To Gilbert Elliot of Minto in 1751: "To tell the Truth, I was always so indifferent about Fortune, & especially now, that I am more advanc'd in Life, & am a little more at my Ease, suited to my extreme

73. Defoe, obsessively aware of this problem of overextension, "solves" it for *The Complete English Tradesman* at the outset (pp. 1–4) by arbitrarily distinguishing between his subject, the tradesman, who only conducts inland exchanges, and the merchant, who trades internationally—a literal example of the reterritorialization of a term that otherwise tended to escape any referent and the only way Defoe could pretend to appeal to a substantive and shared virtue in his readers.

74. Cf. Hume's preface to his Abstract of the *Treatise:* "My expectations in this small performance may seem somewhat extraordinary, when I declare that my intentions are to render a larger work more intelligible to ordinary capacities by abridging it" (*T*, p. 363).

Frugality, that I neither fear nor hope any thing from any man and am very indifferent about Offence or Favour. Not only, I would not sacrifice Truth & Reason to political Views, but scarce even a Jest" (p. 156). And to John Clephane in 1753 (referring to the *History*): "When I say that I dare come no nearer the present time than the Accession, you are not to imagine that I am afraid either of danger or offence; I hope, in many instances, that I have shown myself to be above all laws of prudence and discretion" (p. 171). Indifference to attacks is possible because of an indifference to one's own particular opinions: "As to my opinions, you know I defend none of them positively: I only propose my Doubts where I am so unhappy as not to receive the same Conviction with the rest of Mankind. It surprizes me much to see anybody who pretends to be a man of Letters, discover Anger on that Account; since it is certainly by the Experience of all Ages, that nothing contributes more to the Progress of Learning than such Disputes & Novelties" (p. 265). Toleration of dispute is not the same as fighting oneself: "I hope your Lordship, as my Friend, will congratulate me on the Resolution I took in the beginning of my Life, that is, my Literary Life, never to reply to any body" (p. 320).[75] Hume's resolution never to reply anchored the distinction between a public and private life. The literary life is a course of published texts that might provoke attack by the vulgar; but no answer would follow; no answer *could* follow without sacrificing that independence essential to the man of letters' prestige and power.

There are two kinds of disputes. The lower order of dispute, which may be labelled the Warburtonian, after its most dogged and inventive practitioner, occurs in public and through publications. Victory is the goal, and argument is waged in terms of the zero-sum calculus which Hume associated especially with religious enthusiasts. It has a style: the florid, abusively *ad hominem* sort of polemic with which William Warburton and his confederates felt most comfortable.[76] And it allows for considerable

75. Cf. "My Own Life" (*HL*, 1:3).

76. Although Warburton did have allies, he was nonetheless something of a *rara avis*. The exceptional nature of this spiky controversialist is explicated by Johnson as an effect of his almost unique success in obtaining preferment through his learning in an age where learning had declined just because it no longer obtained notice or conferred advantage (Boswell, *Tour,* p. 56). Warburton is the period's best example of a man of learning who gloried in his rejection of the Addisonian model of ambassadorship. As a polemicist Warburton neither restricted himself to religious topics nor to one side of the issue. As A. S. Collins notes, in 1747 Warburton wrote an anonymous pamphlet, *A Letter from an Author to a Member of Parliament,* in support of perpetual copyright, and in 1762 he wrote *An Enquiry into the Nature and Origin of Literary Property* (also anonymous), in contravention of his own arguments. Collins, *Authorship in the Days of Johnson* (1927: rpt. Clifton, N.J.: Augustus M. Kelley, 1973), p. 85. Warburton's tracts are reprinted in *Horace Walpole's Political Tracts, 1747–1748, with Two by*

tactical ingenuity: Warburton was not only active on a variety of fronts, scouting out blasphemy wherever it might lurk; he was also capable of such ruses as enlisting Richard Hurd to collate and edit his marginalia on a copy of Hume's *Essay on the Natural History of Religion*, and to publish them as an anonymous attack on the infidel (Mossner, p. 326). The Warburtonian disputant metaphorizes publications as moral acts which are intrinsically either virtuous or vicious according to a prescriptive Christian ethics; every printed text is a volley in the unceasing war between good and evil.

If Warburton's savage rejection of polite discourse follows from his custom of writing "letters just as he speaks, without thinking any more of what he throws out," [77] Hume's progressiveness implies an ambition to speak just as one would write. Every particular dispute ought to be guided by the principle of correspondence and commerce. Winning or losing is unimportant: refinement is all. Published arguments have merit only insofar as they promote and sharpen further discussion. This view of argument is the truth that Hume argues for, the truth that he would have prevail. In practice, publication is the ticket of admission into a group with whom one can exchange letters. "Republic of letters" may have never been anything more than a figure of speech, but the society of letters, a cosmopolitan group which was formed by and lived through correspondence, was, in the eighteenth century, a literal fact. In his letters Hume *does* reply: he answers criticisms and states objections. One exchange, between Hume and Robert Wallace on Hume's essay "Of the Populousness of Ancient Nations," was a celebrated example of cogent and civil debate.[78] If Warburton had written a letter to Hume, Hume could have replied. But, of course, Warburton would never correspond with Hume. Therefore, by refusing to answer Warburton in print, Hume merely reinforces a symmetry between the worlds of publication and correspondence. Principle is a way of excluding from discourse those with whom you would prefer not to correspond.

The consistency of Hume's principles—not to amend out of fear, to countenance dispute, never to reply—makes it possible to gauge his deviations. The abridgment of the *Treatise* is the foremost example; but there are also the withholding of the *Dialogues Concerning Natural Religion* from publication and the suppression of the essays "On Suicide" and "On the Immortality of the Soul." These suppressions were neither perma-

---

William Warburton on Literary Property, 1747 and 1762, ed. Stephen Parks (New York: Garland, 1974).

77. Johnson to Boswell, *Tour*, p. 66.

78. Montesquieu was so impressed that he sought a translator for these letters (Mossner, p. 267).

nent nor secret (Hume sought the advice of friends). Nonetheless, in each case material was withheld in order to avoid a controversy that the man of letters had professed himself bound to suffer for the sake of the progress of learning. Such suppressions can be defended as prudential steps taken to avoid retaliation by the religious (see Mossner, p. 326). They can also be written off as Hume's temporizing for the sake of sales.[79] From the latter perspective we could feel justified in indicting the whole notion of the man and of the republic of letters as an ideological formation transparently serving the interests of a few well-placed individuals able and willing to manipulate public opinion to obtain and preserve a privileged status.

Yet a Namierite thesis feels too crude. Neither Hume nor his colleagues betray any cynicism about their conduct. The evidence of Hume's suppression describes something more, I think, than a banal contradiction between behavior and professions—as if principles could be merely wrong or irrelevant.[80] Hume and his colleagues did not abandon principle in favor of expediency but collaboratively defined the limits of the general application of principle. Such collaborative policy, far from being a violation of the general, *institutes* the general as a coherent and bounded set of conventions. At some point processes of refinement and diffusion must be circumscribed for there to be an economy, a *course* of things.[81] The man of letters strategically adopts the ultimate position of generality, the circumscriptive position of the generalizer himself— which, if not irreducible, because it finally is named as something particular, is at least the last position to be reduced. The payoff for the man of letters is to make the possibility of that reduction seem of extraordinary gravity, and his defense equivalent to a defense of the economy, the state, or the self, thus naturalizing all his tactics of warding off as what anyone would do under the circumstances. Moreover, authorial suppression presupposes control over the course of his writings: some things he can keep out of print; others he chooses to publish. The difference between manuscript and print seems to pivot on the author's will.

79. For the mercenary hypothesis, see John Herman Randall, Jr., *The Career of Philosophy from the Middle Ages to the Enlightenment*, 3 vols. (New York: Columbia Univ. Press, 1962), 1:631.

80. Along these lines, see the excellent critique of the Namierite thesis in Quentin Skinner's "The Principles and Practice of Opposition: The Case of Bolingbroke versus Walpole," in *Historical Perspectives: Studies in English Thought and Society*, ed. Neil McKendrick (London: Europa Publications, 1974), pp. 93–128.

81. Hume is well known for his espousal of a free press; yet his advocacy discovers its limit in the prospect of an irremediable "unbounded liberty," which he regarded as "one of the evils" attending a mixed government (G&G, p. 98).

Suppression was part of the business of publishing in eighteenth-century Britain. Hume learned that lesson, slowly, through experience with Andrew Millar, the bookseller whom Hume selected to replace Noon for the second edition of the *Treatise*. Their association, extended by Millar's publication of *The Philosophical Essays* in 1742, was tightened in 1748, when Millar became the sole publisher of the *Essays* and assumed the role of Hume's publisher of choice. Given the evident satisfactoriness of this connection to both parties, it is somewhat puzzling that in 1754 Hume chose as publisher for *The History of the Stuarts*, his most ambitious enterprise, the Edinburgh bookseller Baillie Hamilton. Certainly the terms were very good, and Hume was no doubt pleased by Hamilton's open enthusiasm for the work. But there also seems to have been a good measure of nationalism involved in Hume's choice. Confident of success, Hume believed he could afford to patronize a Scottish publisher in much the same manner as he patronized the Scottish writers John Home, the author of *Douglas;* Thomas Blacklock, author of *Poems of Mr. Blacklock;* and William Wilkie, author of the *Epigoniad*—and for the same reasons: to demonstrate that the English did not possess any cultural trade secrets, that, given the proper attitude and the appropriate organization, Scots, or rather, North Britons, could write better British drama, better British poetry, better British history, and publish more successful books than the English.[82] Hume's nationalism was neither regressive nor naive; it furthered the greater strategy of breaking down the barriers of parochialism and secrecy from which Scotland had suffered and of promoting a wider commerce of culture and commodities.[83]

82. "A North Briton . . . was a Scotsman committed to a restatement of English culture in such terms that it would become British and then Scotsmen would make their way in it." J.G.A. Pocock, "Hume and the American Revolution," in *Virtue, Commerce, and History* (Cambridge: Cambridge Univ. Press, 1985), p. 128. On Hume's anglophobia, see Forbes, *Hume's Philosophical Politics*, pp. 188–89.

83. In this respect Hume was part of a Scottish front that had long been casting about for the proper formula for prosperity in the face of English commercial power. T. C. Smout describes both the hopes for prosperity that pro-Union sentiment involved and the disappointingly slow realization of those hopes in *A History of the Scottish People*, pp. 225–26. R. H. Campbell summarizes the difficulties: "The mercantilist policy of the seventeenth century, with its attempts to encourage foreign enterprise to Scotland, and its provision of privileges for advanced forms of industrial organisation, showed that Scots were fully aware of the need to tackle the deficiencies of the country's economic structure. The lack of success attending their efforts demonstrated the difficulties of doing so. The commercial integration which followed the parliamentary union offered the economic carrot of access to markets in England and her colonies, but required the speedy elimination of the hazards in the way of improvement if Scottish industry was to survive its exposure to unprotected competition from England. Fear of competition was a potent influence in the opposition to the proposed union and in the disillusionment and resentment which was often its immediate conse-

Hume's confidence did not last long. The first volume of the *History* was published in November of 1754. It very soon became clear that the book was the victim of a triple catastrophe: abused by the Whigs for its supposed Jacobitism, slandered by the religious for its atheism, the book, despite the rousing controversy, was an all but complete failure in the crucial English market, even though Hamilton had opened a bookshop in London in order to facilitate its vending. By April Hume was admitting defeat to Millar, who had offered to buy out the remaining copies and the copyright from the cowed Hamilton:

> I am entirely of your Opinion: Your offer to Baillie Hamilton was very reasonable, & ought to have been receiv'd with thankfulness, not Peevishness. He is a very honest Man, & far from being interested: But he is passionate & even wrong headed to a Degree. He has made it sufficiently appear in his Conduct of this whole Affair. I think the London Booksellers have had a sufficient Triumph over him; when a Book, which was much expected & was calculated to be popular, has had so small a sale [in] his hands. To make the Triumph more compleat, I wish you wou'd take what remains into your hands, & dispose of it in a few Months. (*HL*, 1:217).

Hume's calculations of popularity have gone awry; he capitulates and cedes the spoils to the victorious Millar. Hume vented his suspicions of why the *History* had failed in a letter one month later to the printer William Strahan, who was an informal partner of Millar: "Every body writes me & tells me, that the Conspiracy of the Booksellers contributed very much to retard the Sale. I hope, that Mr. Millar's Industry will redress this Inconvenience; tho' it is not so easy to put right what has once been set wrong. . . . You are better acquainted with these Matters than me: But if the Booksellers had not a great Influence, whence could proceed the great Difference of the Sale in Scotland & England? The Freedoms with Religion ought here to have given more Displeasure; & the Cry of Jacobitism as much, notwithstanding what may be imagined" (p. 222).

As we shall see, Hume's suspicion of a conspiracy of booksellers was not merely Scottish paranoia. Regardless of conspiracies, however, the incident with *The History of the Stuarts* taught the lesson that Hume's chosen maxim from Bayle—"A man of letters should always live in a capital" (*HL*, 1:205)—was practically ambiguous: it did not simply refer to one's street address. Hume's concession to Millar involves an acknowledge-

---

quence in Scotland." Campbell, *The Rise and Fall of Scottish Industry: 1707–1939* (Edinburgh: John Donald, 1980), pp. 6–7.

ment of capital and of London as the capital of capital.[84] The ability of Hume to take residence in Millar's capital may demonstrate once again the man of letters' ease of self-centering: Hume did not have to travel to London in order to take his place within the capital; he only had to write a few letters—and sign them, of course, since they were contracts. Yet the motive belongs to the booksellers, not Hume, who merely seizes the opportunity given to him. Moreover, Hume's easy adaptation to the monopolistic practices of the Conger—the semilegal cartel of London booksellers—jars with his claims for independence as man of letters.[85] That tension is neatly exemplified by Hume's attempt to eradicate it, when, after agreeing to shift from Hamilton to Millar, he sells all rights to the *History* for a lump sum, thus divesting himself of any future profits (*HL*, 1:244). Mossner plausibly interprets this agreement as Hume's device to extricate himself from the obligation to attend to the minutiae of "mere publication" (Mossner, p. 315)—as if, having positioned himself within the London publishing machine, the man of letters' wish that publication would be "mere" were thereby fulfilled and henceforth publication would take care of itself; as if the Millar who had been a hindrance to the dispersion of Hume's texts would by the magic of a contract be transformed into a transparent medium for their regular, businesslike dissemination. By such a transaction Hume could hope to turn an ostensible defeat into a real victory: he would pay the devil his due, and his profit would be a position of disinterested independence, the restoration of the partition between the publications and manuscript, between a mechanical instrumentality and a project of generalization. Hume's voluntary submission to Millar would successfully reproduce the principle of all socialization in Hume's schema: an abridgment of primary impulses to accomplish a greater gain through indirection. By this one adjustment, then, Hume

84. For a consideration of the evidence of the domination by London of the British book trade in the eighteenth century, see John Feather, "The Commerce of Letters: The Study of the Eighteenth-Century Book Trade," *Eighteenth-Century Studies*, Summer 1984, pp. 420–22.

85. See, as one example among many, his comment about the *History* to the Abbé le Blanc: "The great Distance, which I have always kept from all Party & Dependance, from all Satyre and Panegyric, has made the Public entertain Expectations from this Work" (*HL*, 1:193). Writing from a Pocockian perspective of civic humanism, Nicolas Phillipson considers the progress of enlightenment in eighteenth-century Scotland in terms of a fundamental tension between independence and adjustment to commercialization in his lucid and useful essay "The Scottish Enlightenment," in *The Enlightenment in National Context*, ed. Roy Porter and Milkuláš Teich (Cambridge: Cambridge Univ. Press, 1981), pp. 19–40. Following Peter Gay, Charles Camic employs independence as one of the key terms in his analysis of the Scottish Enlightenment in *Experience and Enlightenment: Socialization for Cultural Change in Eighteenth-Century Scotland* (Chicago: Univ. of Chicago Press, 1983), pp. 46–47 and passim.

could hope, once the *History* was completed, to have prepared for himself a future practice of nothing but repetition and refinement in the amusing correction of his works.[86] Millar's practice was not the same as Hume's. Nowhere is that clearer than in his inveterate disregard for the supposed distinction between manuscript and publication.[87] And nowhere is that disregard more strikingly evident than in his employment of the letter by which Hume signed over to him all future rights to the *History*. In describing to Millar the just completed second volume of the *History*, Hume mentions that its politics would balance and cancel whatever evidence of partiality could be gleaned from the first, and goes on to promise: "I shall give no farther Umbrage to the Godly: Tho' I am far from thinking, that my Liberties on that head have been the real Cause of checking the Sale of the first Volume. They might afford a Pretext for decrying it to those who were resolv'd on other Accounts to lay hold of Pretexts" (*HL*, 1:218). That promise to provide no pretexts itself became a pretext through the agency of Millar, who passed the letter along to John Brown, who in turn referred to Hume's reservation in his own *Estimate of the Manners and Principles of the Times:*

> When this Gentleman found that his History, though larded with irreligion, did not sell among the *licentious;* and that the *serious* were shocked at his Treatment of Religion, and on that Account were not

86. "One reason of my remaining in London is the correcting a new Edition of my History, which I oversee as anxiously, as if any body were concern'd about it, or ever woud perceive the Pains I take in polishing it and rendering it as accurate as possible. I can only say, that I do it for myself and that it amuses me" (*HL*, 2:188). One of the most telling paradoxes of Hume's career was his insistence on remaining a staunch supporter of the London booksellers in their dispute over literary property with Scottish booksellers even when the story of the suppression by the London booksellers of the first edition of his *History* had become a featured example of oppression in the Scotsmen's legal brief. In theory Hume would seem to be the ally of the plaintiffs' antimonopolistic empiricism. In practice his decision to transfer his future hopes to the spread of authorial fame rather than to the increase of proprietorial profits exactly exemplifies both the distinction and the priorities developed by the Scottish booksellers. See Ilay Campbell, *Information for Alexander Donaldson and J. Wood, Booksellers in Edinburgh* (1773), in *The Literary Property Debate: Six Tracts, 1764–1774*, ed. Stephen Parks (New York: Garland, 1975), pp. 17, 6, and 10. The difference would seem to lie both in Hume's compulsion to submit and in his desire to represent that compulsion both to himself and to others as a free and deliberate act of self-mitigation. Hume's interest is in disinterest, as his labor is nothing more than an amusement. Committed to an integrative practice, he careers between two views, willing neither to argue that "composition" is a sort of "incorporeal essence" nor to accept that it can be reduced to a "*corpus*" (Campbell, *Information*, pp. 12 and 52).

87. Even Campbell, arguing against the principle of perpetual authorial copyright, because he bases his argument on the literal meaning of *publication*, insists on the "essential difference" made by the act of publication (*Information*, pp. 11–12).

Purchasers; he ordered his Agent (but too late) to expunge the exceptionable Passages; assigning for the Reason for his avoiding every Thing of this Kind in his second Volume, "that he would not *offend the Godly*." Now this very Man, in Defiance of all Decency, hath for several Years carried on a Trade of Essaywriting; in the Course of which he hath not only misrepresented, abused, and insulted the most essential Principles of *Christianity*, but, to the utmost of his Power, shaken the Foundations of all Religion. In these sorry Essays, he had no fear of offending the *Godly*, because he knew the *Godly* were not to be his *Buyers:* But when he finds that his History must *sell* among the *Godly*, or *not sell* at all; *then* comes the Panic upon him; *then*, forsooth, he will not *offend the Godly*. Here, therefore, a *Character* is clearly developed. With St. Paul, *Godliness* was Gain; But with *this* Man, *Gain* produceth *Godliness*.[88]

Hume responded indignantly to the attack and to Millar's hand in it: "I am told, that one Dr Brown has published a Book in London, where there is a Note containing personal Reflections on me, for which he quotes a Letter I wrote to you. What Sort of Behaviour this is to make use of a private Letter, without the Permission of the Person to whom it was addressed, is easily conceivd; but how he came to see any of my Letters I cannot imagine; nor what I wrote that coud give him any handle for this Calumny" (*HL*, 1:249). The extent of Hume's anger can be measured by his response to Millar's self-justification:

> I got [your letter,] where you had inserted the Passage which probably gave Dr Brown Occasion for his fine Reflexion; which surely I shall never take the least Notice of. I must however beg the Favor of you, in order to prevent all such Misrepresentations for the future, that you woud burn all my Letters, which do not treat of Business; that is, I may say all of them. For as all Business is clos'd between us, there can be no use of keeping the Letters. I own to you, that it would be very disagreeable to me, if by any Accident these Letters shoud fall into idle People's hands, and be honord with a Publication. As to what you say, about your Frankness & Openness in mentioning things, which malevolent People sometimes make a bad Use of, I can readily excuse you: For I find it is an Infirmity of my own. (*HL*, 1:256–57)

Injunction and resolution came to nought: obviously, Millar did not burn Hume's letter; nor did Hume at this time break off his business relationship with Millar: he was to continue as publisher of the *History* until his

<hr />

88. John Brown, *An Estimate of the Manners and Principles of the Times*, 2 vols. (London: L. Davis and C. Reymers, 1757), 2:86–87, quoted in Mossner, p. 308.

death. Nevertheless, Hume's sarcasm about Millar's "infirmity" is surely well justified. It would stretch credulity to imagine that the canny printer, who had marshalled the forces of London booksellers against all outside competition, would be so naive as to pass a letter along to a controversialist like Brown without expecting it to fuel his polemical engine.

The episode displays not only Hume's suppression, which contradicts his principle of never revising to avoid controversy, but also the precariousness of the control that he could thereby acquire. Millar acted as if there were no such things as private communications, as if everything were available to be published, regardless of the intentions of the author. Intention belongs not to Millar—we cannot know whether he *intended* that Brown should reply so flagrantly—but to a system which does not distinguish between private and public, between the religious and the infidel, or between motives and acts, a system which, insofar as it is identified with the organization of the Third Conger, is nevertheless identical with the interests of Andrew Millar.

A wider historical context will clarify the instability of the relations between correspondence and publication in the eighteenth century. Earlier, I argued that the printing press was a privileged metaphor for the eighteenth-century man of letters. The signal weakness of that claim was the absence of any historically specific criterion that would distinguish between the experience of an eighteenth-century man of letters and that of any post-Gutenberg humanist, who, like Erasmus, for example, was sensitive to the revolutionary difference that printing makes. If, however, there are three discrete features of text production that the invention of the printing press highlighted—uniform replication, infinite reproduction, and indefinite dispersion—the last remained *in potentia* until the eighteenth century, when, in England at least, a distribution that could rapidly saturate a market became for the first time a real possibility.

Five dates are crucial to that development: 1688, when the Settlement brought relative tranquility to English political and economic life after a half century of turbulence; 1695, when the Licensing Act expired; 1707, when the Act of Union consolidated England and Scotland into a single political entity and, by eradicating the imposts that inhibited commerce across the territorial boundaries, transformed Great Britain into a single inland market; 1710, when the Act of Anne, however ambiguously, established a standard copyright; and 1711, when parliamentary statute created a unified post office for the British Isles.[89] The expiration of the

---

89. Ian Watt calls attention to two other dates, not representing the enactment or expiration of statutes, which deserve mention: 1686, when the White Paper Makers incorporated, evidence of a reduction of the extreme dependence of English printers on foreign sources

Licensing Act released London booksellers from most governmental restrictions and was to a considerable degree responsible for a rapid expansion of the "number of printers and presses both in London and the provinces."[90] The Act of Union opened up the Scottish market to the organized London booksellers. By assigning a fourteen-year term of copyright to books not yet published (capable of being extended another fourteen years if the author remained alive) and twenty-one years to books *already* published,[91] the Act of Anne gave the London publishers a weapon for moving against the provincial booksellers, primarily the Scots, who had, since 1695, invested most of their enterprise and capital in the lucrative business of producing cheap reprints for local markets. Gwyn Walters quotes the Glasgow bookseller Robert Foulis's testimony that "to the Act of Anne [the London booksellers] owe all their power in Scotland; for previous to that Act, they had no more connection with Scotland than with China. . . for [until 1710] they never complained of the Scots although [the Scots] reprinted whatever they pleased."[92] The London booksellers' malignancy was not motiveless: they ruthlessly deployed the weapon with which they were provided not only because they wanted to sell more books but also because by normalizing copyright the act made copyrights commodities in their own right, which could be speculated upon and traded in the same fashion as bills of exchange.[93] Scottish reprints undermined the value of their stock.

One year after the Scots were forced to acknowledge that British books were legally English books (even if they had been written by Scottish authors), they began to receive them by the post. The establishment of a national post office gave the London booksellers both relatively open access to all retail vendors and the means to apply the weapon of the Act of Anne.[94] With the extension of the postal system came a prodigious rise in the number of newspapers; conspicuous among the many advertise-

---

for good-quality paper; and 1720, when Caslon set up his type foundry, initiating the growth of a home industry that was eventually to turn "England into an exporter of type and a leader in typographical design." "Publishers and Sinners: The Augustan View," *Studies in Bibliography* 12 (1959): 4.

90. Terry Belanger, "Publishers and Writers in Eighteenth-Century England," in *Books and Their Readers in Eighteenth-Century England*, ed. Isabel Rivers (New York: St. Martin's, 1982), p. 8.

91. Gwyn Walters, "The Booksellers in 1759 and 1774: The Battle for Literary Property," *The Library*, 5th ser., 29 (September 1974): 290, n. 13.

92. Ibid., p. 246.

93. Belanger, "Publishers and Writers," p. 15; on bills of exchange, see John Brewer, "Commercialization and Politics," in *The Birth of a Consumer Society*, p. 205.

94. See Howard Robinson, *The British Post Office: A History* (Princeton: Princeton Univ. Press, 1948), pp. 90–98.

ments for fashionable London commodities scattered throughout the newspapers were notices of new books and new editions produced by the London printers and wholesaled by the London booksellers—books which wealthy individuals often ordered and had delivered by the postmen who brought the weekly paper.[95] The case was not much different for the retailers themselves. Terry Belanger describes the custom:

> Provincial dealers in books generally employed London firms as their agents—indeed, the provincial booksellers absolutely required such representatives. Since most of the books sold in the provinces were published in London, and since the country men needed an uninterrupted supply of these books to be able to continue in business, they had no choice but to accept the regulation of the trade by the booksellers in the capital. The best that the provincial dealer could do was to establish a strong link between himself and one of the large copyright owners in London, in order to assure himself of a supply of the London-owned and London-produced books that he needed for his customers.[96]

The provincial dealer linked himself by a line of credit to a London agent, who in turn shared the resources of his brethren in the trade.

The conduits for that linkage were the roads that conveyed the horse post. Although they were generally ill-maintained and hazardous in the early eighteenth century, the post roads were steadily improved in order to expedite the transactions—personal, political, and commercial—between distant parts of the kingdom which the unified postal system first made possible and then virtually necessary.[97] To state the case most point-

95. R. M. Wiles, "Middle-Class Literacy in Eighteenth-Century England: Fresh Evidence," in *Studies in the Eighteenth Century*, ed. R. F. Brissenden (Toronto: Univ. of Toronto Press, 1968), p. 55.

96. Belanger, "Publishers and Writers," p. 11. Watt describes a similar dependence of London printers on the dominant booksellers, which he attributes to the requirement for printing of "both a large initial capital outlay . . . and a considerable regular volume of business to meet costs and wages" ("Publishers and Sinners," p. 7). The second seems the more weighty reason: though perhaps greater than the booksellers', the capital outlay for the printers was hardly prohibitive—their mushrooming numbers during the century attests to that—but access to markets was controlled by the booksellers, and with it the ability to turn fixed into surplus capital. Even the difference in the required capital outlay was probably not so great later in the century, when the payments for the copyrights that would make a bookseller estimable in the trade had escalated far beyond the kind of prices that were being paid in the late seventeenth century, which is the source of Watt's evidence for his claim.

97. A good indicator is the increase in the number of statutes dealing with the roads. "In the first half of the eighteenth century an annual average of about eight road Acts, generally authorizing turnpikes, went through Parliament. The flow increased fivefold during the two

edly, the London booksellers could control, as James Ralph maintained, "all Avenues to the market," [98] because first of all, there *were* avenues, the post roads, which made extensive trade regular and rapid and, second, because all those avenues led to London—the center from which they radiated. Although it was possible to send mail and newspapers on the byroads that intersected the London routes, such traffic was regulated by the supervision of Ralph Allen, who was himself a contractor of the central post office—roughly equivalent in function to the retailers who received their shipments from the London agents and distributed them to their customers. [99]

Fernand Braudel identifies three types of commercial transport in the eighteenth century: that supplied by a peasant or agricultural "labour force that offered its services whenever the 'farming calendar' permitted"; that provided by "a specialized transport trade, with a degree of organization"; and that furnished by "the regular system of mails and deliveries with fixed timetables." [100] In the conduct of overland trade everywhere in Europe (except in Holland), it was the second which predominated, with all the competitive uncertainty and irregularity that went with it. [101] Apart from the newspaper business, the only major enterprise that took full advantage of the third, serially articulated, geometrically elaborated, and governmentally insured means of transport was the book trade—which represented an unprecedented rationalization of merchandising and shipping opportunities. The booksellers' commerce rode piggyback on the newsman and the postman: they sent one sort of communication, advertisements, in order to excite demand for another, books, which were transported along routes expressly designed as lines of communication.

The elegant symmetry of the British book trade is unique in the eighteenth century. It might be contrasted with the French trade, which, as Robert Darnton has demonstrated with stunning exactitude, was extremely fragmentary and intricate. In part this was because of the schizophrenic division imposed on the trade by the French system of royal

---

decades ending in 1770." Though the turnpikes were by no means all good roads, the profit incentive seems to have raised their quality above that of the parish roads, which relied on statute labor. Phyllis Deane, *The First Industrial Revolution* (Cambridge: Cambridge Univ. Press, 1965), p. 71.

98. James Ralph. *The Case of Authors by Profession* (London: 1762), p. 60, quoted in Mossner, p. 314.

99. See Robinson, *The British Post Office*, pp. 100–109. For a thorough but idealized version of Ralph Allen's career, see Benjamin Boyce's biography, *The Benevolent Man: A Life of Ralph Allen of Bath* (Cambridge: Harvard Univ. Press, 1967).

100. Braudel, *The Wheels of Commerce*, p. 353.

101. See Braudel's discussion of French transport, p. 354.

privileges, which forced publication of unlicensed books beyond the borders of France and required unlicensed publishers to develop clandestine routes in order to deliver their fugitive wares to outlaw booksellers and readers. In part it was because of the desultory connections that the enfranchised and unenterprising Parisian *libraires* maintained with provincial booksellers.[102] Nowhere in Europe was the fit between scheme and model so neat as in Great Britain; and no business in the mideighteenth century exemplified so fully the integration of the product with the means of production and distribution as did the publishing industry.[103]

Increasing efficiency of transport, tending toward the goal of abstracting distance into pure exchange, becomes a mode of domination according to where one positions oneself within the system devised. So much seems uncontroversial and, perhaps, unobjectionable. But a complaint like James Ralph's, that the "Booksellers were Masters of the Avenues to every Market and by the Practice of one Night's Postage could make any Work resemble Jonah's gourd after the worm had smote it," applies not to the rationalization of transport but to the way the mail system was used to *inhibit* trade.[104] At the cost of a postage stamp (paid for by the receiver) letters such as this one could be circulated to every retail bookseller in Great Britain:

St. Paul's Church-yard, London Nov. 2, 1759

Sir,

The authors of books, as well as the persons to whom, for valuable considerations, they have transferred their copy-right, having

102. On the contest in France between "a strategy of smuggling and a strategy of protection and privilege," see Robert Darnton, *The Business of Enlightenment: A Publishing History of the "Encyclopédie," 1775–1800* (Cambridge: Harvard Univ. Press, 1979), pp. 154–65. See also John Lough's discussion of smuggling in *Writer and Public in France: From the Middle Ages to the Present Day* (Oxford: Clarendon Press, 1978), pp. 178–79. In respect to the book trade even the Dutch were no exception to the singularity of British rationalization. Since a substantial portion of what they published consisted of outlawed French books for the French market, they were compelled to adopt the furtive and oblique channels appropriate to their marginal status.

103. The newspaper business notwithstanding: the proliferation of provincial papers of wide circulation showed the failure of the London newspapers to dominate completely the network they used. See Wiles, "Middle-Class Literacy," pp. 60–62. Roy Porter attributes the mid-century improvement of British roads (well in advance of the dredging of the canals) to turnpike building by private contractors. Porter, *English Society in the Eighteenth Century* (London: Penguin, 1982), pp. 207–8. For a discussion of the patchy improvement of Scottish roads and of the importance of the turnpike trusts, see Campbell, *Scotland since 1707*, pp. 51–53.

104. Ralph, *Case of Authors*, p. 60, quoted in Mossner, p. 314.

for some years past been greatly injured in their property, by sundry persons fraudulently and clandestinely in *England*, and openly in *Scotland* and *Ireland*, reprinting and vending the same, to the particular loss and injury of the said authors and proprietors, and to the detriment of the fair trader in general; the booksellers of *London*, in their own defence, have been forced to take proper measures to stop this growing evil: and, upon mature consideration, with the advice of persons *eminent in the law*, have come to a general agreement to prosecute, by due course of law, all such persons as shall be detected in either printing or vending piratical editions of the books which are their property. . . .

But the booksellers of *London* being desirous to stop these illicit practices *by the most gentle methods*, and not to harrass persons by a law-suit, who may through ignorance or inadvertency be liable thereto, have directed me to give you this notice; that, if you have any *Scotch*, or other pirated editions of *English* books, they will take them off your hands, at the real price they cost you, and give you in return to the same value in the genuine editions of the said books, at the lowest market-price; *upon condition*, that you will engage not to purchase or vend any such pirated editions for the future. And they doubt not but this fair proposal will induce the country booksellers in general (as many have already done) to deliver up their piratical editions directly, and no more encourage this illicit trade.

If, after this notice, any person shall be detected in selling any pirated book, and is prosecuted for so doing, he must not blame anyone but himself, as it will not be in the power of any of his correspondents to compromise the suit for him, for no favour will be shewn to one person more than to another. . . .

By order of the Committee,
John Wilkie[105]

After the lapse of the twenty-one year grace period bestowed by the Act of Anne, the London booksellers were once again faced with the competition of provincial printers—who dared reprint the "copyrighted" works of Shakespeare, Milton, and Prior—and formed a "united front" to resist the incursion.[106] Combatting this shameless competition, John Wilkie signed his name but wrote for a committee, which derived part of its power from its ability efficiently to represent itself—through a mem-

---

105. Quoted by Alexander Donaldson in *Some Thoughts on the State of Literary Property* (London: Donaldson, 1764), pp. 15–17, reprinted in Parks, *The Literary Property Debate*.
106. Walters, "Booksellers," p. 290. See p. 293 for a sample list of pirated editions.

ber and through a member's letter, which circulated along the same routes the committee shipped its goods. The efficiency of representation, the ease of circulation, and the offer of a "fair proposal" combined to constitute those "*gentle methods*" by which the London booksellers hoped to "induce" the retailers to reject Scottish reprints. The committee trusted to the Humean mechanics outlined in Chapter 1: the circulation of what Alexander Donaldson called "this artful, sly, and insinuating letter" would itself serve as an induction of the individuals into a network commanded by a central committee with immense capital reserves, and the message of the letter would induce individuals by applying information about rights and interests to persuade the merchants not to withdraw from the confederacy.[107]

Even this brief sketch disables the hypothetical distinction between correspondence and publication, insofar as the former supposedly expressed the eighteenth-century ideal of an "informed, entertaining exchange carried on between persons belonging to a circle of familiar acquaintances, who shared a common knowledge of literature, history, and . . . social institutions,"[108] and the latter involved both mercenary calculations and an invitation to anyone who could afford the price either of a book or (after about 1740) of membership in a circulating library. The same postal system which Howard Anderson and Irvin Ehrenpreis have argued was the precondition for the extraordinary flowering of an epistolary subculture in the eighteenth century was systematically subsidized and manipulated by publishers to achieve their ends.[109] My point is not merely that some letters were personal and some commercial but that the very rationalization of the system which contributed to the stylistic experimentation in the familiar manner of the Augustans was designed so that it could produce profit for the government directly through the stamp tax and indirectly by facilitating commercial transactions.[110] The national postal system furnished a new, reliable source of income for the government and for any organization which, like the booksellers' Conger, could, by means of its position in the system, replicate the ratio of center to periphery managed by the state and therefore acquire a measure of the

107. Donaldson, *Some Thoughts on the State of Literary Property*, p. 20.

108. Howard Anderson and Irvin Ehrenpreis, "The Familiar Letter in the Eighteenth Century: Some Generalizations," in *The Familiar Letter in the Eighteenth Century*, ed. Howard Anderson, Philip B. Daghlian, and Irvin Ehrenpreis (Lawrence: Univ. of Kansas Press, 1966), p. 274.

109. Ibid., pp. 269–70.

110. Some of the money was reinvested. Boyce gives an interesting account of the wealthy postmaster Ralph Allen's eagerness to subsidize a "correct" (authentic and moralized) edition of Pope's letters (*The Benevolent Man*, pp. 67–68 and 74–75).

state's dominance over every aspect of private correspondence. Indeed, before the state's commitment of its resources to the railroad—one of the best indicators of Great Britain's near approach to economic "take-off"[111]—the rationalization of the postal system, along with the dredging of canals, is perhaps the best example of nonmilitary capital investment—an investment of which the publishing industry, both by chronological propinquity and functional compatibility, could reasonably regard itself as an intended beneficiary. No text that changes hands in the postal system is without interest to the government or to the Conger.

That interest is emblematized in the affiliations between the stamp, which was willingly purchased by all correspondents, giving the government a kind of property in the letters it transmitted, and copyright, which left the author's name in place on the title page but which drastically altered the property relations between him and "his" text. And, of course, it was the claim of the booksellers that all the rights that they asserted were backed up by the law—or, in Wilkie's barely veiled terms, should "gentle methods" fail, more violent ones, legal remedies, would be pursued. The difference beween personal and public wavers perceptibly in a circular letter which is signed by a man who represents a committee, directed to individuals who are willy nilly parts of a ratio, and which offers inducements while threatening imposition. The same ambiguity appears in the letters of a Pope or a Walpole, which are familiar but intended for the eyes of a group of like-minded men and women, spontaneously candid but artfully contrived, written as epistles but copied by the writer, who has an eye on future publication. But ambiguity evaporates when the exigencies of state or commerce override pacific customs.

Moreover, for neither booksellers nor postal agents is the law the court of last resort. If it is the generic distinction of the familiar letter of the eighteenth century to handle deftly that "*tertium quid*—not self, not subject, but reader,"[112] the autonomy of the genre and of the social realm as a sanctuary of conversation and private correspondence is radically compromised when we add a *quaternium quid* to every letter—not *the* reader but *another* reader. Here is the postscript to a letter, quoted by Howard Robinson, from *The Correspondence of Jonathan Swift:* "To the gentleman of the Post Office, who intercepted my last letter addressed to Mrs. Whiteway at her house in Abbey Street, together with a letter enclosed and addressed to the Dean of St. Patrick's [Swift]. When you have sufficiently perused this letter, I beg the favour of you to send it to the

---

111. Rostow, *Stages of Growth*, p. 55.
112. Anderson and Ehrenpreis, "The Familiar Letter," p. 278.

lady to whom it is directed. I shall not take it ill though you should not give yourself the trouble to seal it." Robinson also quotes from two different letters from John Gay to Swift: "The letter you wrote was not received till eleven or twelve days after date, and the Post Office, we suppose, have very diligent officers, for they had taken care to charge for a double letter"; "If I do not write intelligibly to you, it is because I would not have the clerks of the post office know everything that I am doing." [113] Eighteenth-century letter writers were keenly aware of a practice which Robinson details at some length: the interception, opening, and copying of letters by warranted officials of the post office. The intrusion with warrant was completely legal—it was approved by the statute that enfranchised the Post Office in 1711—and though it was apparently practiced with intermittent zeal throughout the century, it had the effect of supplying a third ear, an official and public ear, to every "conversation" through the mails. [114]

I say "apparently" because although the records show some fluctuation, the records are useless: the legalizing of interception, opening, and copying with warrant was generally regarded as implicit approval of the legitimacy if not the legality of the practice without warrant. [115] Although all such intervention would fall under the general rubric of "reason of state," the variety of the offices involved at every level of the government and the postal system and the latitude of discretion allowed both by the pretext of legality and the cloak of secrecy bring reason into kissing distance with caprice: anyone's letter could be opened by almost any official at any time, for any reason or no reason at all: opened and *copied*—to be circulated or filed, awaiting the moment that it could be put to use by the state *in propria persona* or the state's officials in their less than uniformly proper persons. Hence it is not surprising that the correspondence of the resolutely apolitical and ordinarily lucid Horace Walpole "frequently repeats the belief that letters were opened." And hence it seems apt to supplement the generic imperative supposed operative in the familiar letter, "When you write always remember you are corresponding with another person," with Bolingbroke's admonition to Swift, "If you answer by the post, remember while you are writing that you are writing by the post." [116]

Like the government, the Conger did not defend by paper alone.

113. Robinson, *The British Post Office*, p. 123.
114. Ibid., pp. 113–25.
115. See Kenneth Ellis's summary of those quasi-legal methods in *The Post Office in the Eighteenth Century: A Study in Administrative History* (London: Oxford Univ. Press, 1958), pp. 63–65.
116. Walpole and Bolingbroke quoted by Robinson, *The British Post Office*, p. 123.

Walters quotes a 1759 letter of John Whiston announcing that "riders shall be appointed, the first of May, to inspect all the booksellers shops in England, and give intelligence of what they can find out." Such intelligence squads had a long pedigree; Walters finds something of a precedent in the 1637 Star Chamber Codifying Decree, which "had empowered the stationers to organize search parties for unlicensed premises and unlicensed books." [117] Of course, the Conger was not the Stationers' Company, and in the lapse of the Licensing Act no such precedent had any legal authority. The actions of the booksellers were technically illegal: not only were the booksellers applying to matters of copyright privileges tied to licensing; but in addition, as the eventual success of the case brought against them by the Scottish bookseller Alexander Donaldson was to certify in 1774, they did not in actuality hold copyright to the works they sought to impose in their own editions on the provinces. But in its technical violations of the law the Conger was doing neither more nor less than what the government itself did: the potent execution of the law required the prudent commission of technical illegalities, of tactical violations of the legal fiction that distinguishes between what is allowed and what is forbidden, what is public and what is private. Both exploited the rich and potentially dangerous ambiguity in that privileged eighteenth-century term *intelligence*. It had become possible to announce in celebratory terms that "one of the improvements of life in which the present age has excelled all that have gone before, is the quick circulation of intelligence, the faithful and easy communication of events past and future by the multitudes of newspapers which have been contrived to amuse or inform us." [118] But as the practice of the booksellers shows, *intelligence* was in fact ambiguous: the improvement of communication *to* the periphery depended on the continual appropriation of any and all secrets *from* the periphery. For the booksellers, as for the government, the circulation of intelligence was a technique of "hegemony-maintenance"; [119] when push came to shove, the desirability of circulating gave way to the exigency of accumulating intelligence. And in the eighteenth

117. Walters, "Booksellers," p. 292.
118. *The Adventurer* no. 35 (1753), quoted in Collins, *The Profession of Letters*, p. 20.
119. The term is employed by Walter Adamson in his commentary on Gramsci, *Hegemony and Revolution: A Study of Antonio Gramsci's Political and Cultural Theory* (Berkeley and Los Angeles: Univ. of California Press, 1980), p. 174. A similar critique is implicit in Wordsworth's contemptuous reference in the 1800 Preface to *Lyrical Ballads* to urbanized man's "craving for extraordinary incident, which the rapid communication of intelligence hourly gratifies." *Literary Criticism of William Wordsworth*, ed. Paul M. Zall (Lincoln: Univ. of Nebraska Press, 1966), p. 21. Any reader of Wordsworth's Preface who would require scare quotes around *intelligence* to clarify the irony is beyond Wordsworth's cure.

century push very quickly came to shove. If Jean Baudrillard is correct when he asserts that the "monopolistic stage signifies less the monopoly of the means of production (which is never total) than the *monopoly of the code*,"[120] then it follows that effective mastery of a code like the system of correspondence in eighteenth-century Britain, the success of legal and illegal acts, lay in the technique, and no combination in the eighteenth century displayed such mastery as did the government and the booksellers' Conger.

If we scratch only slightly Wilkie's claim to be disseminating information, we expose the threat of the law; but if we push the threat of legal action, we discover a pretext for extralegal pressure. The Conger behaved as if it were backed up by the law, but did not actually depend on the positive force of statute; rather the cartel defended itself or exerted its "rights" by imitating the model that the government offered and using the same system that the government employed. Its ability to discover, not to make—a trait shared with the government—made the combination of London publishers powerful. No one else—not the provincial printer or dealer or the man of letters—could discover as much as the publishing cartel, funded by subscription and enabled by the postal system. The booksellers' imitation of the practices of the government instantiated the illicit mating of the commercial and the political that Hume, like Smith after him, most feared.[121] If, however, the *Treatise* renewed for its age the Lockean eclipse of crimes against persons by crimes against property, it is difficult to fault a combination that pursued its property rights irrespective of the persons, authors and others, on which it imposed—and difficult to sympathize fully with Hume's exasperated reaction to Millar's transmission of his letter to Brown, when the bookseller was just passing along intelligence according to the standard practice of his trade.

In summary, we can isolate four features that account for the success of the Conger. First, it was an organization of parts into an extralegal monopoly. Second, that corporate mass was systematic in its elaboration: it transformed the preexistent avenues for trade into efficient conduits for a communication that extended the organization over a territory that it

120. Baudrillard, *The Mirror of Production*, p. 127.

121. The imitation was hardly one-sided. Especially when secret, the government's intervention was not strictly confiscatory: the letter was eventually passed along, although the government obtained the material profit of a copy which always held the potential for political profit (and, one assumes, blackmail). It makes sense that the government, restricted to warrant by the act that established a unified postal system and which followed by one year the act that established a uniform copyright, would interpret its right to copy as loosely as the London booksellers interpreted theirs.

defined and controlled. Third, the systematic organization was centered in (a) capital. I force the pun because the strength of the Conger depended both on its having a considerable stock of fixed and rolling capital (presses and shops, authors under contract, copyrights, and financial resources) to produce the commodities that would be distributed within the system and on its location within the capital, London, so that it could take advantage of the radiating avenues and the instruments for circulating word of books and books of words. Fourth, it was underwritten by the political power of the state, the methods of which it could safely and profitably imitate. Of the four features the last was probably determinant; the Conger expired when in 1774 political support was withdrawn by the House of Lords, in the Lords' refusal to certify the common law rights claimed by the London booksellers.

Here is one place where the suspension of the priority between the metaphorical and the literal in the man of letters' career as middleman collapses. The "Infirmity" to which Hume sarcastically confesses in his letter to Millar is real, as real as the reserves of money, warehouses, and equipment that the capitalist has at his disposal. Like the savage who is incapacitated for society, Hume is incapable of commerce without Millar and incapacitated for commerce by Millar. Hume's entrance into commerce began with a self-imposed, symbolic incapacitation. The infirmity that Hume discovers in his relations with Millar is the literalization of that symbolic act, an abridgment of Hume's impulse that is imposed rather than chosen and that impoverishes whatever notion of intention or privacy the man of letters would cling to and protect from the system of commercial exchanges. Every representation becomes subject to that exchange and profit-taking, a subjugation made possible and enforced by the materialization of the metaphor of the social composition into the fact of capital which inducts and disposes not only all representations but all those who labor to represent. To grasp for distinctions between the real and the apparent, the letter and the publication, the godly and the ungodly, is a futile attempt to protect a subject that is always subject to capital.

The infirmities of authors compose the strength of the publisher. Millar's interest in promoting controversy about a book which had had lethargic sales can hardly be doubted. Millar offered Hume's letter as an enticement to Brown's frenzied indignation, and Brown leapt to the bait, advertising a book he professed to despise. This was evidently a tactic on which Millar relied: in his dealings with Hume there is at least one other instance when he transmitted an unpublished manuscript, the "Five Dissertations," to the indefatigably contentious Warburton; and even after publication had been suppressed he passed along copies of the provocative "Of Suicide" and "Of the Immortality of the Soul" to various eminent persons, including the not exceptionally discreet John Wilkes (Mossner, pp. 321–24). But more to the point in this case, Brown was published by one of those booksellers, L. Davis, with whom Millar had allied in forming the Third Conger.[122] Although the *Estimate* attacked Hume for writing for gain, it should be kept in mind that, as James Ralph emphasized in *The Case of Authors*, Brown's diatribe was largely directed against the whole class of Grub Street authors, and that Hume was only an incidental target. Ralph sarcastically accuses Brown of being the venal spokesman for the "Company" which controls the book market and suggests not only that Brown and Hume are affiliated in a trade of mutual advantage but also that the real profit accrues neither to Hume nor to Brown, ideologist and counterideologist of the market, but to the company of capitalists whose authors they are.[123] It makes little difference what each of them writes, history or tract, or in what form they write it, informal letter or heated polemic, so long as it is written under contract to a member of the cartel and can be sorted into "qualities" for merchandising according to the "mysteries of the Trade."[124] The writer shares with the public a constitutional infirmity; the bookseller is the bad physician: "The sagacious Bookseller feels the Pulse of the Times, and according to the Stroke prescribes; not to cure, but flatter the Disease: As long as the Patient continues to swallow, he continues to administer; and on the first Symptom of a Nausea, he changes the Dose."[125]

122. Brown's *Estimate* bears the imprint "L. Davis and C. Reymers in Holborn; printers to the Royal Society." L. Davis is listed in a letter by John Whiston as one of the signatories to the agreement among the London booksellers on a scheme to repel the Scottish threat. Walters reproduces the list in "The Booksellers," p. 301.

123. Ralph, *The Case of Authors*, p. 17.

124. The supercession of partisanship is nicely illustrated by the link between Warburton and Hume forged by virtue of their similar victimization at the hands of printers and booksellers. Boswell recounts Johnson's condemnation of the way in which William Strahan, printer for both Hume and Warburton as well as Johnson himself, attempted to increase his prestige by showing around a private letter of Warburton's abusing the Church of Scotland. Strahan proved his intimacy with the writer by breaching his trust and with the incidental result of "raising him a body of enemies" (*Tour*, p. 66).

125. Ralph, *The Case of Authors*, p. 21. Among the instances of Millar's doctoring, particularly infuriating to Hume was the bookseller's premature reprinting of the uncorrected octavo *History* in quarto, his original overprinting of the octavo, and his juggling of sales figures (see *HL*, 1:443–44; 2:212, n. 3, 219, and 225). The full measure of Hume's bitterness over Millar's manipulation appears in this letter to Strahan after the bookseller's death: "There has been a strange Fatality to depress the reputation of that book [*The History of England*]: First the Extravagance of Baillie Hamilton, then the rapaciousness of Mr. Millar: But this last is most incurable. I suppose you will not find one book in the English Language of that Size and Price so ill printed, and now since the publication of the Quarto, however

V

When Hume comes to talk about monopolism, whether it be Roman, Catholic, or English, he usually tropes the massive aborption of material, power, and profit as "engrossment," as when he warns that were it not for intrinsic limits to growth, "commerce . . . would go on perpetually increasing, and one spot of the globe would engross the art and industry of the whole" (*HL*, 1:271).[126] A graphically active version of absorption, engrossment renders the monopoly as voracious and repellently swollen; but because its referent is fundamentally biological, it also evokes a limit beyond which the engorged body cannot grow. We have had occasion to examine several examples of the salient usage of the body metaphor in Hume.[127] The image of bodily engrossment that is most suggestive in the

---

small the sale of the Quarto may be, it shows, by its corrections and additions, the Imperfection of the 8vo so visibly, that it must be totally discredited. Had it been thought proper to let me know the real State of the 8vo Edition, I shoud never have consented to the printing of the Quarto. I suppose the Proprietors will at last be oblig'd to destroy all that remains of the 8vo; I mean, if there appear any hopes of the Sale's ever reviving. If Mr Millar had been alive, his own Interest, as well as the Shame for his Miscarriage, woud have brought him to that Resolution" (*HL*, 2:228).

126. For the Roman and the Catholic examples, see section II of this chapter, above. "Engrossment" was a favored metaphor for monopolistic activity in the eighteenth century. See, for example, Josiah Tucker's Humean maxim, "Give no Assistance to the ingrossing Schemes of Monopolists; but raise a general Emulation among all Ranks and Professions in Things relating to the public Good." Josiah Tucker, *The Elements of Commerce and the Theory of Taxes* (rpt. East Ardsley: S. R. Publishers, n.d.), p. 7. "Engrossed" was used frequently in the disputes about copyright. Ilay Campbell, for example, uses it twice to describe the conspiratorial practices of the booksellers, of which Hume is the named victim (*Information*, p. 17); and Lord Camden, in the most forceful of the speeches delivered in the judgment on *Donaldson v. Hinton*, contemptuously remarks that, "instead of Salesmen, the Booksellers of late Years have forestalled the Market, and become Engrossers" (*The Cases of the Appellants and Respondents in the Cause of Literary Property before the House of Lords, 26 February 1774*, in Parks, *The Literary Property Debate*, p. 54). See also the appearance of "engrossment" in the conversation guides to describe the breakdown of free exchange; in at least one instance it attracts financial metaphors: "Conversation is a Sort of Bank in which all who compose it have their respective Shares. The Man therefore who attempts to engross it, trespasses upon the Rights of his Companions." *The Polite Philosopher* (Dublin, 1734), p. 33, quoted in Leland E. Warren, "Turning Reality Round Together: Guides to Conversation in Eighteenth-Century England," *Eighteenth-Century Life* 8 (May 1983): 68.

127. Besides the imagery of mutilation and references to various texts as children, there is the more explicitly economic frame of reference that emerges in this jocular comment to Mrs. Dysart of Eccles in which Hume congratulates himself on the fact that Edinburgh is unlike "some cities of ancient Gaul" where "there was a fixt legal standard establish'd for corpulency, . . . beyond which, if any Belly presum'd to encrease, the Proprietor of that Belly was oblig'd to pay a fine to the Public, proportionable to its rotundity. Ill wou'd it fare with his Worship & I, if such a law shou'd pass our Parliament." Hume goes on ironically to confess that a "portly Belly is [not] of any use or Necessity. Tis a mere superfluous ornament

context of Hume's fears of monopolism occurs in this reflection on his career in a 1762 letter to David Mallet: "The Truth is, I am entirely idle at present so far as regards writing; and I am very happy in that indolent State. My Friends tell me, that I will not continue long so, and that I will tire of having nothing to do but read and converse; but I am resolvd to resist, as a Temptation of the Devil, any Impulse towards writing, and I am really so much ashamed of myself when I see my Bulk on a Shelf, as well as when I see it in a Glass, that I would fain prevent my growing more corpulent either way" (*HL,* 1:369). Looking at his books on the shelf is like looking at his own body in the mirror—they are the same body and the same likeness. Publication leads to an increasing bulk. But engrossment is resolved into an image by the framing mirror and checked by the sense of shame that the image produces.[128] The metaphor of the body gives flesh to the idea of a self-regulating mechanism; and the reference to the mirror here enacts what is so elusive in the *Treatise:* the *installation* of a reflecting apparatus that will induce self-restraint.[129]

The economic machine is self-regulating, then, because it is a body which lives and dies, and which must watch what it eats. Crossing over from the idea of a mechanism to the idea of an organism enables one to figure to oneself how the mechanism *ought* to work. Organicism is tied to mechanicism by means of the common denominator of metaphor—and in that sense this metaphor of the body figures the metaphoricity of every term that Hume uses to characterize the dynamic equilibrium that obtains in all transactions between men or between "I" and image. Regulation may be defined as a function of law, but what makes law functional is the metaphor of system, which *embodies* an array of forces so that they can be written up in a book, put on the shelf, and observed by a spectator, who is in but not of the body/book/system. The spectator watches as in a theater the operations of this system and detects its unnatural engrossment (as Millar's plans outran Hume's permission, as publication always threatens to escape authorial power).[130] He alone is capable of feeling

---

and is a proof too, that its Proprietor enjoys a greater plenty than he puts to a good use: and therefore, 'tis fit to reduce him to a level with his fellow-subjects by Taxes & impositions" (*HL,* 1:159–60).

128. Shame has its place in economic history. Rostow notes: "As a matter of historical fact a reactive nationalism—reacting against intrusion from more advanced nations—has been a most important and powerful motive force in the transition from traditional to modern societies, at least as important as the profit motive. Men holding effective authority or influence have been willing to uproot traditional societies not, primarily, to make more money but because the traditional society failed—or threatened to fail—to protect them from humiliation by foreigners" (*Stages of Economic Growth,* pp. 26–27).

129. See Chapters 1 and 3 above.

130. Ilay Campbell argues that "it is plain, that whatever an author may be entitled to

shame and of exercising a will to correct that which has failed to correct itself.[131] The man of letters' defenses against Millar and the Third Conger, against monopolism and against his own writing—all partake of a fear of an absorptive growth like that we first encountered in the early letter to Dr. Arbuthnot. The metaphor of the body both explains how mechanisms could behave in such a manner and offers the fantasy of containment.[132] This metaphorization of commercial expansion is, as it were, the economy beyond economy, the identity theory behind Hume's classical economics.

What is left unaccounted for is how a body can become so monstrous, commercial expansion so prodigiously efficient. I have suggested that what empowered the Third Conger was its systematic ability to communicate, to disperse its representations (whether the information or the commodities themselves) at wide range, with great speed and with little cost: its stock is a technique of symbolic labor that it shares with the man of letters, whose self-castration, as we have seen, brings him into line with a dominant system of reproduction. Once effected symbolically, castration can be endlessly repeated, as a correction of desire—but once it has been executed, the surgery cannot easily be reversed. The engrossment of Hume's body is the image of a technique that has mastered the artist.[133] Despite Hume's wish, there is no natural check to a growth that occurs only in the symbolic order. The bulk of books will grow larger and larger despite his shame, despite his will, despite his metaphors. The true Hume, the solitary lover of liberty and philosophical retreat may

---

upon the first publication, he has no foundation in reason, or in the nature of the thing, to expect that this should be repeated, after the book is no longer under his power" (*Information*, p. 10).

131. Or perhaps—and this is an alternative Hume is not prepared to consider—*does* correct itself by producing the supervisory "I" whose sense of shame is little more than a pressure-sensitive shutdown switch.

132. Apart from the letter to Mallet, the most graphic image of this fantasy in Hume is Cleanthe's supposedly reassuring evocation of the self-propagating library in the *Dialogues*, p. 153.

133. If, despite Hume's testimony to Mallet, this connection between writing and the shape of the body seems farfetched, look again at Hume's letter to Dr. Arbuthnot, where the connection between becoming an author, recovering from the disease of the learned, and getting fat is made explicit (*HL,* 1:14–15). There is no space to develop it here, but the argument might plausibly be made that the fear of semi-automatic bodily increase occurs at about the time when concerns with authorial production are supplanted by concerns for the stability of reputation. This is certainly the case with Hume, whose fear of himself as a monopoly is part and parcel of his sense that now that he has stopped writing his fame has become someone else's (a cartel's) property. Whatever else such a hypothesis might turn up, it would certainly anchor itself in Addison's brilliant figuration of the hyperbolic fluctuation of public credit in *Spectator* no. 3.

remain a constant, slender observer; who knows? But the picture of him that is presented to the world, his bulk of writings, grows ever more corpulent.

Hume's attempt to detach himself from a publication that can nonetheless be controlled coincides with his attempts to achieve a "detachment from a life" (Mossner, p. 591) that can nonetheless be lived. The scandal to Hume's pretensions of detachment and control, his wish not to weigh so heavily, is the *Exposé Succinct*, which will be considered in Chapter 7. But for now recall Hume's last-minute engineering of his will and his autobiography: the former would be a document that gives him the privilege of writing with the force of law; the latter would be a composition that gives him the ability to write with the authority of the dead. As we have seen, Hume stipulated that the autobiography be prefixed, as epigraph and epitaph, to the first edition of his collected works. That injunction was directed to the trusted printer and publisher William Strahan. Strahan, Hume supposed, would obey the order that would order Hume's texts. But the prescription miscarried. Because of printing difficulties that delayed a new edition, the autobiography was published separately from the collected works by Strahan and Smith, who thereby added one more book to the bulk on the shelf—an engrossment that would have shamed Hume had he any longer the "I" to see it.

The posthistorical territory which Hume foresees as the most general level of the economy and which is identical with the secure literary fame he labors to reach in his romantic autobiography is a beautiful idealism—not, God save the mark, because the historical is infinite but because the historical is indefinite—not, that is, unimaginable but one particular imagining after another. In the following two chapters we will examine various episodes from late in Hume's career in order better to estimate how imaginations correspond with one another generally and what happens when they do not.

6

A Sentimental Journey to Paris
and L'Isle d'Adam

Who is he, and who does he belong to?
HL, 1:384

I

There were good reasons for Hume to return to Paris. In the late fifties, word of Hume's celebrity in France (mostly enthusiasm for the recently published *History of the Stuarts*), far in excess of his reputation in Britain, was trickling back to him through a variety of sources: his translator, the Abbé Le Blanc; John Stewart, the Scottish wine-merchant; and, later, the Comtesse de Boufflers, whose lively correspondence with Hume began in 1761. It was natural for Hume to want to take advantage of this wave of popularity: "*Vanitas vanitatum, atque omnia vanitas*, says the Preacher: The great Object of us Authors . . . is to gain public Applause. . . . I fancy there is a future State, to give Poets, Historians, & Philosophers their due Reward, and to distribute to them those Recompenses which are so strangely shar'd out in Life. It is of little Consequence that Posterity does them Justice, if they are for ever to be ignorant of it, & are to remain in perpetual Slumber in their literary Paradise" (*HL*, 1:278). Paris beckoned as a foretaste of the full justice that posterity would yet lavish on his work—nay, better than a foretaste because no slumber would dull the mind and eclipse the pleasure. Naturally, Paris would have the appeal of a waking dream.

Hume first mentioned his "Intention of making a journey to Paris" in a letter to the Abbé Le Blanc in 1757. But he postponed the actual trip. Although the war between France and England was Hume's excuse, he did not take immediate advantage of the cessation of hostilities in 1762 to book passage across the Channel. The countess did. She arrived in England in April of 1763, apparently with the chief purpose of meeting

Hume, who, however, inexplicably absented himself to a remote corner of the kingdom, making a rendezvous impossible. Why Hume put off the Paris visit is not entirely clear. Mossner's interpretation, that he "remained apprehensive of Paris because of its very perfection," is plausible (Mossner, p. 390). As we have seen, Paris represented for Hume the quintessentially social realm of conversation in which free intellectual exchange thrived as a corollary of an artfully sublimated commerce between the sexes.[1] Paris instantiated the ideal equilibrium between what Pierre Bourdieu has called "the model of reality" and "the reality of the model"; it was both the symbolic capital of the polite world, and the polite capital of symbols.[2] But in some sense its symbolic function and rhetorical integrity depended on the irrelevance of empirical residence—presupposed, that is, its sameness over whatever distance. This comment in a letter to Le Blanc is focal for the idea and practice of the man of letters: "The Distance betwixt us need be no Impediment to this Correspondence. [If you favor me frequently with your Letters, I shall be able to render you the same Service as if I had the Happiness of living next door to you, and was able to inspect the whole Translation]" (*HL*, 1:199; Greig's brackets). Why should a symbolic ambassador visit a symbolic capital? Why spoil a good thing?

But perhaps Hume did not tarry out of such nice considerations. Perhaps he simply had to wait until he had enough credit. If his determination to go suggested a sense that it was the time to make use of his amassed intellectual credit, his procrastination indicates that intellectual credit was not sufficient security. It was not, however, a question of cash. Hume was comfortably well off.[3] Possession of a plush bank account could not overcome Hume's "*vis inertiae*" (*HL*, 1:194) and induce him to visit France. Indeed, Hume did not exactly "visit"; he occupied a post, as unofficial secretary to the embassy for Lord Hertford, the British am-

---

1. On France as "the model of a truly polite society," see James Moore, "The Social Background of Hume's Science of Human Nature," in *McGill Hume Studies*, ed. David Fate Norton, Nicholas Capaldi, and Wade Robison (San Diego: Austin Hill Press, 1976), pp. 32–35.
2. Pierre Bourdieu, *An Outline of a Theory of Practice*, trans. Richard Nice (Cambridge: Cambridge Univ. Press, 1977), p. 28.
3. Thomas Edward Ritchie notes that Hume's success with the *History* had made him wealthy. "In fact, his temporal circumstances were now in such a thriving condition, that while he was in London, to which place he had gone to superintend the press during the printing of these two volumes [the last two volumes of *The History*], he invested a thousand pounds in the public funds. This exposed him to innumerable jokes from his friends, because he had been in the habit of declaiming loudly against dealing in the Stocks; but he repelled their railleries by arguing that he had bought real stock, and was not a jobber" (Ritchie, p. 143).

bassador.[4] Hume's glad proclamation—"I am now possess'd of an Office of Credit" (*HL,* 1:510)—announces that he has what he needs to sustain him in France, the kind of political credit that talks in the capital of conversation.

Hume's chief duty was to handle the embassy correspondence. As I have argued, the privilege of the man of letters *is* the privilege of correspondence, which is the metaphor and method for linking the realm of learning with that of conversation, reams of manuscript with face-to-face social exchange. Correspondence is the principle of the general and of generalization in general: things correspond; people correspond; men of letters correspond about those correspondences. We have seen Hume's indignation at Millar's crass transgression of that privilege. Yet what of the embassy secretary? Not only does Hume put his pen to hire, but all of Hume's correspondence serves an ulterior motive: the empiricist's discovery of facts is simultaneously their translation into intelligence subject to transmission to the ministry in London. Hume's task was light and easy; whatever it amused the man of letters to do was in the interest of Hertford for him to do:

> Nothing can be more easy & agreeable than my Situation with Lord Hertford, who is a man of strict Honour, an amiable Temper, a good Understanding, and an elegant Person & Behaviour. . . . He has got an Opinion, very well founded, that the more Acquaintance I make, & the greater Intimacies I form with the French, the more I am enabled to be of Service to him: So he exacts no Attendance from me; and is well pleased to find me carry'd into all kinds of Company. (*HL,* 1:420)

It would be unfair to single out Hume as a double dealer, to stamp him as the snake in an imaginary Parisian garden, for most of the luminaries who graced the salons in prerevolutionary France had such double affiliations, whether they possessed government or academic sinecures in France, as did Morellet, Marmontel, and, later, Suard, or connections with foreign governments, for whom they acted as agents, as did Franklin and Grimm. The free correspondence of the social and intellectual coteries of the Enlightenment was penetrated, fissured, and diverted by secret correspondences and hidden affiliations elsewhere.[5] J. H. Plumb's

---

4. Unofficial because the position had already been given, to Hertford's offense, to Charles Bunbury, a "well known rake." Hertford named Hume as his personal assistant until Bunbury could be forced out (Mossner, p. 435).

5. Scandal could ensue. The most notorious instance involved Franklin, who "was accused before the Privy Council on 29 Jan. 1774 of having by underhand means obtained possession of certain letters relating to public affairs, which he transmitted to Boston, and

aphoristic characterization of the mechanics of the eighteenth-century oli-
garchy seems in order here: "The rage of party gave way to the pursuit of
place."[6] Hume, who had always written against factionalism and who has
been accused of identifying "the standpoint of universal human nature
[with] . . . the prejudices of the Hanoverian ruling elite," would seem to
be a likely leader in the chase.[7] Yet the hypothesis of omni-
acquisitiveness fudges more than it clarifies. It does not explain Hume's
earlier rejections of patronage and of political and religious accommodation. Evidently, Hume felt that he could tap Hertford's credit and remain
independent. At least he said as much to Adam Smith:

> I hesitated much on the Acceptance of this Offer, tho' in Appear-
> ance very inviting; and I thought it ridiculous, at my Years, to be
> entering on a new Scene, and to put myself in the Lists as a Can-
> didate of Fortune. But I reflected, that I had in a manner abjur'd all
> literary Occupations, that I resolvd to give up my future Life en-
> tirely to Amusements, that there could not be a better Pastime than
> such a Journey, especially with a man of Lord Hertford's Character,
> and that it wou'd be easy to prevent my Acceptance from having
> the least Appearance of Dependance. (*HL*, 1:391–92)

That Hume soon came to "repine at [his] Loss of Ease & Leizure &
Retirement & Independance" (*HL*, 1:395) is less surprising than his original belief that he could hold office without compromising independence.
Such a belief makes sense only if it presupposes a kind of independence
with a transcedent referent that supposedly immunizes it from the corrup-
tive effects of official transactions.[8] Such is the superior independence of

---

on the strength of which the Massachusetts Assembly petitioned the King to remove the
Governor and Lieutenant-Governor. [Hume's friend] Alexander Wedderburn, as Solicitor-
General attacked [Franklin] with scurrilous vigour, and he was deprived of his office of
Deputy Postmaster-General of the Colonies. From that moment war with the American
Colonies became inevitable" (*HL*, 2:286n). Hume later anticipated a similar predicament,
resulting not from an specific act of treachery but from the conditions of his "credit": "But
here, another office has been conferred upon me, which, though I did not desire it, I could
not avoid; and if I should return to settle in France, after being twice employed by the
English ministry in places of trust and confidence, could I hope that, in case of a war, I
should be allowed to remain unmolested; when even considered in the light of a man of
letters, I could scarcely flatter myself with enjoying that privilege?" (*HL*, 2:172).

    6. Quoted by Roy Porter, *English Society in the Eighteenth Century* (London: Penguin, 1982),
p. 125.

    7. Alasdair MacIntyre, *After Virtue: A Study in Moral Theory* (Notre Dame: Univ. of Notre
Dame Press, 1981), p. 215.

    8. For an interesting account of the importance of independence to Hume in particular
and to Scottish intellectual life in general, see Nicholas Phillipson, "The Scottish Enlightenment," in *The Enlightenment in National Context*, ed. Roy Porter and Mikuláš Teich (Cam-

philosophy, that place whence Hume launched his career and that refuge to which he could hope to retreat come success or failure.

Hume always travelled with this conviction of a refuge, even in Paris: "Yet I am sensible that I set out too late, and that I am misplaced; and I wish, twice or thrice a day, for my easy chair and my retreat in James's Court. Never think, dear Ferguson, that as long as you are master of your own fireside, and your own time, you can be unhappy, or that any other circumstance can make an addition to your enjoyment" (*HL*, 1:412). Regret can be indulged because mastery is occluded, not lost. The unhappy sense of being misplaced carries with it the hidden compensation of the conviction of a secure place to which one can return and exercise a perfect mastery. Hume was susceptible to Hertford's invitation to live the double life of polite conversationalist and government agent because he had been practicing a double life all along: the supposedly open commerce in the republic of letters had always been subsidized by the reserve of philosophy. By making that secret dream of perfect mastery work for him, Hertford demonstrated the vulnerability of philosophy to a politics of fact and penetration.

Hume's vulnerability stems from the uneasy status of philosophical autonomy as an epiphenomenon of credit, itself a simulacrum. Charles Davenant admonishes that

> of all beings that have existence only in the minds of men, nothing is more fantastical and nice than Credit; it is never to be forced; it hangs upon opinion, it depends upon our passions of hope and fear; it comes many times unsought for, and often goes away without reason, and when once lost, is hardly to be quite recovered.
>
> It very much resembles, and, in many instances, is near akin to that fame and reputation which men obtain by wisdom in governing state affairs, or by valour and conduct in the field.[9]

Credit resembles fame; credit resembles honor; credit resembles independence—indeed, in the eighteenth century, as J.G.A. Pocock has demonstrated, credit begins to resemble every virtue. The reification of virtue as credit is the hallmark both of the subjectivization of experience and of the commercialization of morality which were the ideological ben-

---

bridge: Cambridge Univ. Press, 1981) pp. 19–40, esp. 30–31 and 34–35. The vocabulary that Phillipson uses—oriented toward issues of civic humanism, provincialism, and propriety—is different from my own, and his tone is understated, but his admirable survey unfolds a history of extraordinary stresses and compensations that is not, I think, alien to the story I am telling here.

9. Quoted in Pocock, *The Machiavellian Moment* (Princeton: Princeton Univ. Press, 1975), pp. 439–40.

efits bestowed by British empiricism; credit is the solvent that deidealizes the pieties of civic humanism. Two features of that process are pertinent here. First, there is the promise of a rationality which manifests itself as the reflex of economics on everyday social relations. "It seems probable," writes John Brewer, "that a concern for the credit-worthiness of oneself and others affected the personal characteristics and qualities that one valued highly. . . . Whereas the language of personal trust had originally provided the metaphors for borrowing and lending, now, in a curious transposition, the language of finance was employed metaphorically to depict moral and social worth."[10] Second, there is the permeation of this supposed rationality with the element of what Davenant called the "fantastical"—the sense that what every one depended on had no existence except in the opinion that it did exist, that that which made one strongest, on which one could and had to rely, was extremely vulnerable to sudden and finally unpredictable vicissitudes that might completely annihilate it.

Fame is credit with others. Especially when considered as a kind of celebrity, it increases one's value in the eyes of the world, but it also obliges one to perform certain actions in return for the credit extended: Hume writes the *History of the Stuarts;* his increase of fame is attested to by letters from Parisian women; but those letters, which credit him with wisdom or simplicity or majesty, oblige him to correspond—exchange one letter for another. Philosophical reflection would, however, seem to be the antithesis of that commercial nexus, "the material foundation, the equivalent of Aristotle's *oikos,*" requisite "for . . . independence, leisure, and virtue"—"an autonomy [Hume] could not alienate without becoming corrupt." Philosophical reflection instantiates that condition in which the "freeman must desire nothing more than freedom, nothing more than the public good to which he dedicated himself; [for] once he could exchange his freedom for some other commodity, the act became no less corrupting if that other commodity were knowledge itself."[11] But regarded from the outside, from the world of commercial practice, philosophical independence looks like credit with oneself, an imaginary substance on which one relies to persuade oneself that there is no danger of mistake in the departure from philosophy. In practice, the claim for philosophical independence works as a strategy for capitalizing oneself and one's place within the barter system of correspondence as the merchant capitalizes

10. John Brewer, "Commercialization and Politics," in Neil McKendrick, John Brewer, and J. H. Plumb, *The Birth of a Consumer Society: The Commercialization of Eighteenth-Century England* (Bloomington: Indiana Univ. Press, 1982), p. 214.

11. Pocock, *Machiavellian Moment,* p. 431.

himself in the primitive economy described in "Of Interest." The independent philosopher is a fanciful version of himself in which the man of letters believes and which allows him complacently to engage in the commerce of the world.

And it is *always* from the outside that Hume imagines philosophical independence. As we have seen, the primal scene of that independence is recounted in the letter to Dr. Arbuthnot as the solitary reading or devouring of classical moral philosophy. Such is freedom. But Hume *owes* that freedom to Cicero, Seneca, and Plutarch, by whom he was "smit." As Brewer notes, "To be in a man's debt was to be in his power, for it was he, in effect, who determined when the credit that he had extended transmuted itself into a debt for which one had legal liability."[12] The credit that the classical moralists extended to Hume, that sustained his freedom, was transmuted into a debt by the appearance of those symptoms that expressed the failure of the free reader, suspended in autotelic reflection, to dedicate himself to public virtue: the disease of the learned was the liability incurred for philosophical reflection, which could only be worked off by moral action—which, in turn, had to be something *added* to that reading, and therefore alienated from its "material foundation." In Hume's reading, classical moral philosophy dictated a moral action, composition, which involved the curtailment of freedom in a writing that to appear in the world and do its work had to be fashioned as a marketable commodity—the result justified by the commercial morality that receives its theoretical and practical expression in the *Treatise*. Hertford taps in to the open secret, the debt-ridden reserve of philosophical independence, at just the point where it needs the supplement of action to pay off its debts. Fame may be the last infirmity of the noble mind, but credit is the constitutive infirmity (and paradoxical source of power) of the bourgeois mind.

Hume's experience in Paris was everything he expected and more. As expected, he found the company cultivated and stimulating. He was granted entree to all the most important social and intellectual salons: the circles of Mme Geoffrin, Mme du Deffand, Mme d'Epinay, Mlle Lespinasse, Helvetius, and d'Holbach. Everywhere Hume went he found people who knew and respected his work and who vied with one another for the opportunity to honor its author. Yet the celebrity seemed excessive. To receive the "most extraordinary Honours which the most exorbitant Vanity cou'd wish or desire" (*HL*, 1:407) stretches philosophical indifference to extraordinary lengths. Whether one does or does not have such exorbitant vanity, the constant appeal to it feels like an infliction: "I

12. Brewer, "Commercialization and Politics," p. 211.

have now passed four days at Paris, and about a fortnight in the Court at Fontainebleau, amidst a people who, from the Royal Family downwards, seem to have it much at heart to persuade me, by every expression of esteem, that they consider me as one of the greatest geniuses in the world. I am convinced that Louis XIV never, in any three weeks of his life, suffered so much flattery: I say suffered, for it really confounds and embarrasses me, and makes me look sheepish" (p. 410). Hume's sheepish look, the effect of exorbitant flattery, expresses his embarrassment at being put in a position where a comparison with Louis XIV is inevitable but a position that has no basis in the court except on flattery alone.

Although such éclat agrees with the "Plan of life sketcht out" for him by Hertford, Hume resists such embarrassment; he is not comfortable in a society where he can be given away by a look. The life of the court, he writes, "is unsuitable to my Age & Temper; and I am determin'd to retrench, and to abandon the fine Folks before they abandon me" (*HL*, 1:420). Hume's retrenchment follows a path worn by others before him: from the circle of the court to the salons ruled by Mme Geoffrion and Mlle de Lespinasse to the coterie of Baron d'Holbach, whose home, according to Marmontel, "was the rendezvous of those who were called philosophes." [13] It is primarily the group of men associated with this latter salon whom Hume had in mind when he wrote to the Reverend Hugh Blair, "The Men of Letters here are really very agreeable; all of them Men of the World, living in entire or almost entire Harmony among themselves, and quite irreproachable in their Morals" (*HL*, 1:419). Hume practices a retrenchment and a substitution: for flattery, agreeability; for hierarchy, harmony. And, not least of the substitutions: for women, men. Not least for the French men of letters because it was part of the informing motive of the *coterie d'Holbach* to offer a rump congress where, with the exception of the silent presence of the Baronne d'Holbach, the company would be exclusively male, and the men of letters would thereby be freed from the obligation, often vigorously enforced in the salons presided over by ladies, of curtailing their speculative impulses and argumentative spirit. Not least for Hume because although the king was the titular head of the hierarchy of flattery, the chorus of voices that he actually heard was of a decidedly feminine timbre: "All the Courtiers, who stood around when I was introduc'd to Me Pompadour, assur'd me that she was never heard to say so much to any Man. . . . However, even Me Pompadour's Civilities were, if possible, exceeded by those of the Dutchess de Choiseul. . . . There is not a Courtier in France, who wou'd not

---

13. Jean François Marmontel, *Memoires*, 2:9–10, quoted in Alan Charles Kors, *D'Holbach's Coterie: An Enlightenment in Paris* (Princeton: Princeton Univ. Press, 1976), p. 119.

have been transported with Joy, to have had half of these obliging things said to him, by either of these great Ladies" (*HL*, 1:407–8). That Hume is not yet a courtier explains a response somewhat short of transport. That he would not wish to become a courtier, suffering the fate that d'Alembert sourly described as the eventual end of the man of letters under the monarchy, accounts for his subsequent decision to retrench.[14]

Retrenchment meant leaving the court but primarily abandoning the ladies—or at least some of them—as Hume makes clear in this letter to Baron Mure of Caldwell, where he describes his attempts to establish a kind of equilibrium amid the whirl of Parisian life:

> My chief Grievance is, that I allowd myself at first to be hurry'd into too great a Variety of Company, and find a Difficulty to withdraw and confine myself to one Society, without which there is no real Enjoyment. My Connexions with the Ambassador led me to be connected also with Ministers of State and foreign Ministers: I naturally sought and obtain Connexions with the learned: And I was violently carry'd both by their Civilities and my own Inclination to form Connexions with the Fair, without whose Society I never coud in any place pass my time agreeably and who are the Life and Spring of every thing at Paris. I have cut off however all Visits with the Young and Brilliant, and require at least that a Lady be past thirty, before I enter into Correspondence with her. Society is certainly on a very agreeable Footing in this part of the World; and there are particularly more Women of Sense and Taste and Knowledge than any where else. You woud take them all for Vestals by the Decency of their Behaviour in Company. Scarce a double Entendre ever to be heard; scarce a free Joke: What lies below this Veil is not commonly supposed to be so pure. But behold! I have exceeded my Resolution, and have fallen into a Discourse of Gallantry before I was aware. (*HL*, 1:431)

Hume's worldly commentary to Mure composes, both as retrospect and as performance, almost the entire plot of Hume's social relations in Paris. He suffered an almost prodigious multiplication of connections: his relation with Hertford led to connections with governmental officials, and his own natural preference led him to seek out connections with the learned. "Almost" need not qualify "prodigious" to describe accurately the effect of the "Civilities" of the fair, who, acting in alliance with Hume's inclinations but not necessarily in accord with his will, "violently

---

14. D'Alembert, "Essai sur la Société des Gens de Lettres et des Grands," *Oeuvres completes de d'Alembert*, 5 vols. (Paris, 1821), 5:356–57.

carry'd" him into connections with them. Such violence heeds not the
mediations by which agreeable society must be composed; the attraction
was too peremptory for the man of letters, who as remedy performed a
restitution of control by a familiar Humean technique: he "cut off Visits
with the Young and the Brilliant." The hint of sexual danger in the violent
civilities of the Parisian women is corroborated by the interruption and
retrenchment typical of the Humean castration, through which he recov-
ers control by at once retarding prodigious hurry, suppressing inclination,
and instituting a symbolic distance between the man of letters and the
Parisian women. He also reorients a threateningly direct, incipiently
physical passion by restricting his connections to older women: Hume
requires that a woman be safely "past thirty, before I enter a Correspondence with her."[15]

"Correspondence" here is evidently meant with the full freight of
privilege with which Hume has loaded it throughout his career. Hume
has, however, executed a slight but significant reversal of priority. "Correspondence," as we have seen in Hume's writing before Paris, had almost
invariably meant letter writing, a literal usage which was often employed
to project a promised occasion of face-to-face encounter when such a distant means of connection would no longer be necessary. But the letter to
Mure from Paris shows Hume executing an odd reversal between vehicle
and tenor in the word "correspondence." Here "correspondence" directly
signifies conversation, which has become the figure for a kind of episto-
larity; that is, people are to talk as if they were writing letters. Social
relations with these older, tamer women are to be conducted in their
presence but as if they were not physically present (as if their bodies were
historical details to which one could refer in a narrative, but which would
have no particular bearing on the generalized conduct of present relations), as if the physical could never be desired, only promised—the sort
of unredeemable promise that attaches to all property relations. Against
prodigious growth and indecorous hurry Hume opposes, by means of a
cutting off, a process of controlled derivation: from the broad to the narrow, from the loose to the restricted, from the young to the aged. What
has been derived, Hume attests, is a society on an "agreeable [and safe]
footing."

15. Roughly the age that marks what Sterne would call the second of the "three epochs
in the empire of a French woman. She is coquette—then deist . . . : the empire during
these is never lost—she only changes her subjects: when thirty-five years and more have
unpeopled her dominions of the slaves of love, she re-peoples it with slaves of infidelity."
Laurence Sterne, *A Sentimental Journey to France and Italy* (Harmondsworth: Penguin, 1967),
p. 135.

Hume supplies as the single characterization of the behavior of these women of "Sense and Taste and Knowledge," their conversation, in which there is "scarce a double Entendre ever to be heard; scarce a free Joke." [16] Yet if such is the virtue of the correspondence of these women, it seems a peculiar vice of Hume's correspondence about them that he yields to an inclination to crack a joke of his own: "What lies below this Veil is not commonly supposed to be so pure." The metaphor of the veil is unusual in Hume; and it is particularly surprising that Hume employs the veil here as the device to concoct a double entendre: he puns on the equivocal relationship between above and below, appearance and reality, female innocence and female corruption. Despite his retrenchment, away from the glitter of the court and the brilliance of youth, Hume finds a woman whose very decency and agreeableness is nothing but a veil. Woman has been refined to Parisian, and Parisian refined once more; the end result of this refinement is a luxurious equivoque. It does not matter what she says or how she behaves: the refinement that she is is a double sense, a pun that can swing a man instantly from the most respectable, even reverent tone to the coarse banter of the Poker Club. From an "agreeable footing" Hume has, reflecting on this luxury—"past" the age of generation, beyond the need to labor, emblematically unproductive, even sterile—"fallen into a Discourse of Gallantry before," as he says, "I was aware."

Hume's fall drags his reader after him. By reflex the pun equivocates the discriminations that Hume had carefully contrived. Is there not, for example, the possibility of a Sternian double entendre in those characteristics, hallowed in the jargon of empiricism, "Sense" and "Taste" and "Knowledge"? Does Hume mean to hint that all the fine talk about intellectual exchange composed a veil that hid a quite different kind of sensing, tasting, and knowing, as is "commonly supposd"? The thought is intriguing, but being induced to think it is somewhat disquieting. With Sterne (or Yorick) at least one would know where one is or is not—we are warned by Yorick's lighthearted confession that he walks down the streets of Paris "translating all the way"—but with Hume, as with the Parisian vestals, it is not easy to know when he is punning; it is not easy to tell whether the double senses (the same as joking freely?) that we suspect

16. Feminine wit and feminine virtue were not commonly thought to mix. "Wit in women is apt to have bad consequences," commented Elizabeth Montague in 1750. "Like a sword without a scabbard, it wounds the wearer and provokes assailants. I am sorry to say the generality of women who have excelled in wit have failed in chastity" (quoted in Porter, *English Society in the Eighteenth Century*, p. 36).

are the effect of a hasty writing or the contrivance of a careful composition, whether he is enacting or merely citing. It is not as easy with Hume as it is with Sterne because with Hume as with the vestal all is hidden by the sense, taste, and knowledge of his manner.

When in the Conclusion to *An Enquiry Concerning the Principles of Morals* Hume defends the value of his moral philosophy, he asks:

> What philosophical truths can be more advantageous to society, than those here delivered, which represent virtue in all her genuine and most engaging charms, and make us approach her with ease, familiarity, and affection? The dismal dress falls off, with which many divines, and some philosophers have covered her; and nothing appears but gentleness, humanity, beneficence, affability; nay even, at proper intervals, play, frolic, and gaiety. She talks not of useless austerities and rigours, suffering and self-denial. She declares, that her sole purpose is, to make her votaries and all mankind, during every instant of their existence, if possible, cheerful and happy; nor does she ever willingly part with any pleasure but in hopes of ample compensation in some other period of their lives. (P. 302)

Characteristically, Hume's defense of his representations of virtue appeals to the touchstone of the beneficent, affable, properly playful woman, relieved of the oppressive garments by which the religious concealed her charms. Who would not be a votary of this beauty? Who would not follow virtue?

In the salons, however, where Hume actually confronts the refined woman who stands behind his figure of virtue, from whom the "dismal dress" of the divines has been removed, he discovers not a naked but a veiled truth. The so-called "proper interval" between affability and frolicsomeness produces not an easy and familiar approach but a "discourse of gallantry." It is as if the properly playful erogenous zone, securely situated on the naked body, has begun to drift, veiling the nakedness of virtue with an ambient eroticism. Hume's "experiment" would seem to have corroborated the shrill moralism of his quondam assailant John Brown:

> The untractable Spirit of Lewdness is sunk into gentle Gallantry, and *Obscenity* itself is grown *effeminate.*
>
> But what *Vice* hath lost in *Coarseness* of Expressions, she hath gained in a more easy and general *Admittance:* In ancient Days, *bare* and *impudent Obscenity,* like a common woman of the Town, was confined to *Brothels:* Whereas the *Double-Entendre,* like a modern fine Lady, is now admitted into the *best Company;* while her *transparent*

Covering of Words, like a *thin* fashionable *Gawze* delicately thrown across, *discloses*, while it seems to *veil*, her *Nakedness* of Thought.[17]

The good old days of plainspoken obscenity are no more, those days when bad language was uttered in bad company and bad company was to be found in bad neighborhoods. Like Hume, Brown is fascinated by refinement as a means of mobility, a progress that does not quite transgress or violate boundaries, but worse (for Brown, not Hume), commingles them: virtue and vice, ladies and whores, male and female.[18] And, like Hume, Brown, in associating that refinement with a change in language, accepts the complete and necessary transferability of the properties of language and the character of women—each adrift on the eddies of man's opinion. Notice how, in the above quotation, a double entendre, which is verbal, is like a lady, but then when the words are described as having a "transparent Covering of Words" it is as if the idea of double entendre has effected a crossing, become a woman whose nakedness is covered by words, which are like a gauze, as a gauze covering a woman is like words: it is impossible to imagine a double entendre without thinking of a thinly clad woman and impossible to think of a thinly clad woman without imagining a double entendre. This is because the woman as such has dropped out of the reckoning: the veiled woman has no body. Words and gauze cover a nakedness of thought, which the moralist seems to want to attribute to the lascivious intentions of the woman, but which is after all only the *inference* made by the man—by Hume, by Brown—from the veil, from the double entendre, from the veil as the double entendre. The double entendre hides and reveals the thought of the man from himself; he plays with language as if playing with a woman, folding drive and object over on each other, an eroticism that touches no body but that is always touching on the thinking man himself. Double entendre is a way of making sex the mental preoccupation of the male, who effeminizes himself as he toys, fantastically, with the elastic hymen of his own words, a way of almost coming in touch with his naked thought, of almost showing that naked thought—call it desire, call it ambition—to others.

It is useful to know, as Lawrence Stone has informed us,[19] that since

17. John Brown, *An Estimate of the Manners and Principles of the Times*, 2 vols. (London: L. Davis and C. Reymers, 1757), 1:44–45.

18. The difference between Brown and Hume closely aligns with the difference between the projector and the Spectator on reading urban signs in *Spectator* no. 28. Hysteria over hybrid, monstrous signs disables the effortless and profitable combinations that the man of letters executes and that Addison wonderfully demonstrates in the Spectator's visit to the Royal Exchange (*Spectator* no. 69), which is the template for Hume's version of Paris.

19. Lawrence Stone, *The Family, Sex, and Marriage in England, 1500–1800* (New York: Harper & Row, 1977), p. 530.

roughly 1675, gallantry was itself a double entendre that connoted adultery: the idealized veiling the illicit. But for Hume and Brown, empiricist and anti-empiricist, it is not actions but language—or, more precisely, the capacity of language to substitute for actions—that is at stake. Propriety cannot, unfortunately, be sustained—a man will fall; but fortunately he falls not into any opprobrious action but into a discourse of gallantry, which is not a prelude to a seduction but its surrogate: sex in the head not in the bed. They may have different opinions about it, but what disturbs Brown and what comforts Hume come to the same thing: the possibility that falling and sinking are not real but fantastic or linguistic—and for both the context in which that possibility registers is the social. Brown's vice is Hume's virtue: the difference lies in the sentiment of approbation or disapprobation felt by the spectator (*ECPM*, p. 312). For Brown this kind of language practice generates the deep fear that no social differences, however real they are in truth, can be preserved from a discursive solvent that renders them artificial in fact. Whoremongering may have been vicious in the old days, but at least when one went to a brothel one had a vicious *purpose:* to indulge in obscene language and fornication. For Hume this language practice answers the anxiety of the arriviste, who, having climbed above his rank or left his estate, discovers that no rank is above him, that no state is foreign to him because all order is in some measure conventional, a function of the appropriate discourse, and who learns that if one should slip, one could fall no farther than into a net of wit, the double entendre that conventionalizes the very anxiety of getting caught in another man's place. The discourse of gallantry induces the belief that ideology serves all purposes. The woman is a double entendre, a commodified discourse that both instances and reflects on man's capacity to consume without being satisfied and to desire without being engrossed. If virtue parts with pleasure in hopes of "ample compensation," gallant discourse is virtuous because it substitutes wit for act. The company of ladies over thirty is safer than that of the young because, if exceeding one's resolution is inevitable, in the former company it does not hurry one into a situation about which one can form no idea but fortunately causes one to fall into a discourse which is an agreeable footing, where it is the silent virtue of the mature woman to enable the ample compensation of the male jest.

The convergence of the two figures of virtue and vice suggests that both may be versions of another single female figure. There is one which is conspicuous in eighteenth-century moral and economic writings and which is deliberately constituted in antithetical terms that reflect the dependence of her value on the opinion of the male observer. Here is Addison's description of Credit, seated in a Bank, from *Spectator* no 3:

She appeared indeed infinitely timorous in all her Behaviour; And, whether it was from the Delicacy of her Constitution, or that she was troubled with Vapours, . . . she changed Colour, and startled at everything she heard. She was likewise . . . a greater Valetudinarian than any I had ever met with, even in her own Sex, and subject to such Momentary Consumptions, that in the twinkling of an Eye, she would fall away from the most florid Complexion, and the most healthful State of Body, and wither into a Skeleton. Her Recoveries were often as sudden as her Decays, insomuch that she would revive in a Moment out of a wasting Distemper, into a Habit of the highest Health and Vigour.

Addison figures something, that, as J.G.A. Pocock argues (in commenting on this passage), was "irredeemably Subjective," which had a "rationality [which was] only that of opinion and experience."[20] By figuring Credit as a woman Addison attempts to objectify that opinion which is all that makes credit exist, and projects onto the figure the oscillations of strength and weakness that are the function of opinion alone. Woman is chosen according to the convenience of misogynist conventions; but what is interesting is that the masculinist self-consciousness about the fantastic, subjective aspect of credit tends to reflect back on the misogyny: the "woman" that supposedly grounds this figure can be seen to vanish as anything other than a convention useful to men in figuring to themselves their fears about the fantastic qualities of social and economic realities. If there is such a thing as woman, misogyny has nothing to do with her. Alternatively, of course, one could read the equation of woman with credit as an embrace of subjectivity: in this interpretation, the emancipation of economics from politics, which I described in Chapter 5, would be completely congruent with the male bourgeoisie's attempt to emancipate itself from women—not only in the sense of an emancipation from biology or subsistence, but as a freedom from the entailment of inheritance, which inhibits the circulation of property and cannot be thought without thinking of the aristocracy and the whole problematic of ascriptive ties— thus bringing to the surface a political cleavage, which like the gender cleavage, cannot yet be the explicit subject of discourse. It is doubtless the shift from a familially defined notion of property to one based on representation alone that makes possible Hume's amused tolerance of the absence of chastity on the part of Parisian women—who (he wishes) no longer matter.[21] Hierarchical societies require a chaste woman to transmit

20. Pocock, *The Machiavellian Moment*, pp. 456–57.
21. This tolerance has its cost. Just as the tradesman conventionally wants to end his career by investing his money in land, so does he and so does even the speculator want to

property; fraternal societies, as we shall see, require a loose woman to stimulate discourse. In sum, the claim of a purposive negation of the woman in the figure of credit as in the figure of virtue/vice comes to "I would rather play with, speculate upon, my own groundless subjectivity than have to deal with real women." The double entendre defends against the potential giddiness that might follow on such a statement by its indirect enactment, which veils the naked thought from the thinker.

The elusive but insistent equivocations between careful composition and unaware writing, between narration and performance, between writer and reader, as well as those between appearance and reality, above and below, decency and corruption, suggest, then, that the metaphor of the veil is only one instance of a more pervasive double sense. And the sign of that double sense which supervenes over all instances and reticulates their various connections is "correspondence." Because the man of letters corresponds with and about women who are themselves the site of a correspondence, the luxuries of sensing, tasting, and knowing will always be of uncertain equivocation. Whatever illicit pleasure "correspondence" hints at, it is for Hume only pleasure of the mind, a correspondence promised and achieved by a play of words—which is how desire is *supposed* to work. Correspondence, as the letter to Mure shows, is both the aptitude for falling into a discourse of gallantry and the discourse of gallantry itself, a social intercourse that is the resilient veil of a sexual intercourse, which insures that what is below is always partly in mind—and only in mind.

What, when spoken by a man, would be a joke can, when uttered by a woman, only be a mistake. "In order to refute all Calumnies, hear a

---

pass that land along to the next generation. This is the point where double entendres stop working, where representations tend to lose their force. What one does and the contingency of one's doings, in the face of the negation of the woman, is dramatized in the problems of Hume's enforcing his will through his will, which I discussed in Chapter 5. Someone must accept the fiction of a filiation. In Hume's case it was his nephew, that man who fictively became Hume's son by filiatively following Hume's affiliation and likewise changing his name from Home to Hume. But, of course, it could have been anybody or no one. The logic of Hume's enterprise is to make all filiation a fiction. As Burke saw with extraordinary clarity, you cannot embrace that fiction and secure property as well. It would take more space than a note provides to show how Burke's misogyny works as a means of blaming women for becoming disconnected from virtue and biological necessity in order that he can forge the greater, professedly ideological fiction of the Ancient Constitution as a mystical generative principle that penetrates from father to son, without the mediation of women and with the full security that, in its hermeneutical transcendence, the law provides. For an analysis of Burke's genealogy, see my essay "Like a Guilty Thing Surprised: Deconstruction, Coleridge, and the Apostasy of Criticism," *Critical Inquiry*, Summer 1986. On the corrupt substitution for real women of "equivocal beings," see Mary Wollstonecraft, *A Vindication of the Rights of Women* (London: J. M. Dent, 1929), p. 152.

short Story. Not long ago, as I came into a Company, I heard D'Alembert exclaim, *Et verbum caro factum est*. And the Word was made Flesh. This was thought a very good Jest on my past & present Life; and was much repeated. A Lady in telling the Story, said, *Et verbum carum factum est* [And the word was made dear]. When told of her Mistake, she wou'd not allow it to be one" (*HL*, 1:496). D'Alembert's jest plays on several aspects of Hume "past & present." First of all, there is the mildly malicious sport taken with Hume's notorious infidelism by introducing him with the incarnationalist rhapsody of John's Gospel;[22] second, there is probably some play on the fulfillment of the long awaited promise of Hume to substitute for his symbolic presence in Paris his real, physical presence; third, there may be a pointed reference to Hume's pronounced corpulence; fourth, there may be some intended reference to Hume's decision, known and regretted by his French colleagues, to do no more writing, not to compose the projected ecclesiastical history, with d'Alembert mildly rebuking Hume for his shift from a life of laborious writing to a life of Parisian amusement; more generally, d'Alembert could be wittily summing up many of the themes that we have seen circulating in Hume's writings: using the biblical myth of a messiah passing from heaven to earth, word to flesh, by virtue of a divine condescension, as a witty analogue for Hume's self-proclaimed mission to be an ambassador from the realm of learning to the realm of conversation. Whether d'Alembert meant and Hume took him to mean one or all of these senses (or perhaps more) is impossible to ascertain with certainty—the contexts of the salon and Hume's writings authorize them all—but it is certain that d'Alembert's exclamation is a double entendre, a discourse of gallantry into which he falls on the occasion of seeing Hume in the flesh. Moreover, it is also clear that all of the senses of that free joke depend on the auditor's knowing both Latin and Scripture. On this level of paraphrase the mistake of the lady in retelling the jest (if it indeed remains a jest in her retelling) is a typically feminine mistake, a sentimental error of substituting her emotions toward Hume for the fact of his flesh—Hume is dear, therefore his flesh becomes dear—and her refusal to allow that she has made a mistake after having been informed of her error is an instance of that forceful civility that Hume found both so attractive and so threatening. At least it is this sentimentality and civility that Hume seems to want to call attention to in his retelling of the retold jest.

---

22. D'Alembert was not the only one to exploit the comedy inherent in the reverence shown to Hume. Mossner notes that Chastellux commented that the name of David Hume is "as respectable in the republic of letters as that of Jehovah among the Hebrews" (Mossner, p. 480).

Hume's generous interpretation of the lady's generous error pre-sumes she *did* make an error. He simultaneously takes her at her word—she was making no double entendre in retelling d'Alembert's jest, only citing one—and refuses to take her at her word when she denies that she has made a mistake. Such an interpretation not only denies the possibility of advertency by the woman (that she is telling the truth when she denies having made a mistake); it also fails to account for the fact of the mistake itself: how could she commit such an error? The most faithful interpre-tation of the mistake would be that the woman was just parroting d'Alembert. She could know neither Latin nor Scripture; her mistake was therefore a happy accident produced by her ignorance and complaisance: to be agreeable she retold a jest she did not understand; in telling it she brought *caro* into agreement with *verbum* by Frenchifying it—noun into adjective, according to the conventions of French syntax, making its end-ing agree with the nearest nominative, thereby transforming substantive "flesh" into the modifying affect "dear." The peculiar agreeability of the mistake is that a slip of the tongue results in a remark in perfectly good taste. Adherence to her mistake in the face of correction represents a contentment in her ignorance and an implicit elevation of the claims of affection and agreeability over the authoritative precedents of both Latin and Scripture.

But suppose we take her at her word: suppose she did not make a mistake?[23] In that case, we would have to regard the woman's retelling as itself a jest, a deliberate violation of d'Alembert's double entendre, and

23. Whether she did or did not is undeterminable. It is certain that not many eighteenth-century women knew Greek or Latin. It is also certain that men of letters had a considerable investment in women's ignorance. When Addison remarks that "what encourages me in the use of quotations in an unknown tongue is, that I hear the ladies, whose approbation I value more than that of the whole learned world, declare themselves in a more particular manner pleased with my Greek mottoes," he is not ironically encouraging women to study. On the contrary, he is at once indulging in misogynistic irony and being perfectly serious: it is in the interest of *The Spectator* that women prefer light essays with a gloss of classical learning to the real thing. Alexander Carlyle is equally direct when he recalls that in mid-century Glas-gow the "few [women] who were distinguished drew all the young men of sense and taste about them; for, being void of frivolous accomplishments, which in some respects make all women equal, they trusted only to superior understanding and wit, to natural elegance and unaffected manners" *The Autobiography of Dr. Alexander Carlyle of Inveresk, 1722–1805*, ed. John Hill Burton (Edinburgh: T. N. Foulis, 1910), p. 83. Carlyle is not Jane Austen. Al-though he approves of "natural elegance" (who wouldn't?), he more strongly endorses prog-ress, which does not mean educating women into understanding but in spreading the articles of fashion that, though "frivolous," will refine Scottish social life. For an astute contempo-rary analysis of men's investment in victimizing women in these kinds of scenarios, see Mary Jacobus's response to Stanley Fish's entitling parable from *Is There a Text in This Class?* in her essay "Is There a Woman in This Text?" *New Literary History* 14 (Autumn 1982): 117–19.

one that Hume would not (want to) recognize because it was a joke on d'Alembert as well. As deliberate, the lady's jest would be a heightening and subversion of the religious "sense" with which the philosophe plays, but on which he depends for the sensible idea of a mission on which he can play. The lady's retooling of the sentence rejects the analogy between Hume and messiah, ambassador between the realm of the deity and the world of men and women; it dismisses the notion of divine condescension, discards it as an illegitimate logocentrism implicit in the idea of *verbum* as used by d'Alembert for his pun and as imbedded in Hume's conception of his mission and of the privilege of philosophy. "The word was made flesh" is logocentric not merely because it places the word first, but because the mitigation of its absoluteness, which is identical with the absolute sovereignty of the concealed philosophical subject, is somehow engineered by that word, that sovereign, that logos itself. "The word is made dear" not by the condescension of a godhead stuffed to surfeit with learning but by the interpretive response of the woman who receives the word. And here word is nothing other than words: the words the woman has read are made dear by the figure of the author; no ontological distinction is drawn between the figure and the words such as d'Alembert implicitly relies on in his distinction between words and flesh. The joke on d'Alembert, if we take the lady at her word, is that the version of the woman, supposedly more prone to superstition and enthusiasm than the philosophe, is actually more thoroughly secularized.

Whether or not the woman intended to revise d'Alembert, her version is no mistake; the explanations based on deliberateness and inadvertence converge in a failure to acknowledge the priority of a scriptural model and the metaphysics with which it is mutually implicated; they converge in a misreading that exposes the double entendre of d'Alembert, representative philosophe representing another philosophe, as a joke that is not caused by some failing or some mystery or some secret in a woman but springs from the equivocation in the man of letters he is and is representing, correspondent between high and low, the closet and the world, learning and conversation. D'Alembert falls into a discourse of gallantry trying to make an introduction that will adequately correspond with the veil of flesh that is David Hume, equivocating between piety and blasphemy, between the decorum of the host and a flirtatious and barren homoeroticism—thus representing a knot that Hume, that he, that the man of letters cannot escape: the double entendres they tell (and blame on women), the double entendres they are.

II

Alan Charles Kors has ably documented the double sense of the men of letters who frequented the coterie d'Holbach, the most exclusive, most advanced, and most durable salon in Paris. Kors overturns the traditional characterization of the coterie (initiated, perhaps, by Rousseau, who was responsible for the tag "coterie") as a nest of fire-breathing atheists and "indefatigible radicals."[24] Less pervasive among the philosophes than believed, atheism was not especially seditious in a country where heterodox opinions were condoned by a monarchy deeply engaged in jurisdictional disputes with the church. State censors were likely to tolerate occasional blasphemy so long as the writers did not insult the king's person or challenge royal authority. Monarchic policy is finely epitomized in M. Pellison's phrase, "Loi rigoreuse, pouvoir indulgent."[25] Royal tolerance, like royal privilege, was part of a system of credit whereby "every man in authority derives his influence from the commission alone of the sovereign" ("Of Public Credit," G&G, p. 368.).

By and large, the members of d'Holbach's circle played according to the rules and profited from the lenity of power. Speculative they were, but seditious they were not. Morellet, who produced policy memoranda for Choisel, Trudaine, and Turgot, does not seem to stretch the facts when, in his *Memoires*, he remarks of his brethren, "Certainement aucun d'eux n'etait capable d'entrer dans une conspiration, ni dans le moindre projet de troubler le gouvernment et la paix publique."[26] Indeed, the record of their remarkable ascents to positions of wealth and prestige within the ancien régime bespeaks not an adversarial party but a quasi-professional subculture fashioned in the image of the ruling elite.[27] The

24. The term is Peter Gay's from *The Enlightenment: An Interpretation*, 2 vols. (New York: Norton, 1966), 1:398–99, quoted in Kors, *D'Holbach's Coterie*, p. 5.

25. M. Pellison, *Les Hommes de lettres au XVIIIe siecle* (Paris, 1911), p. 35.

26. Morellet, *Memoires*, 1:139, quoted in Pellison, *Les Hommes de lettres*, p. 38.

27. See Rémy G. Saisselin's *The Literary Establishment in Eighteenth-Century France* (Detroit: Wayne State Univ. Press, 1979), for judgments which accord with Kors but which are framed more severely; e.g., "The philosophes may have begun as an antiestablishment party, but by the death of Louis XV they had become the literary establishment" (p. 115). Lev Barba observes: "There is little doubt that French intellectuals in the eighteenth century were aware of the specific nature of their occupational roles and often identified themselves with these roles. . . . And there was social awareness, too, for the manner in which the men of letters perceived and referred to themselves as an occupational group was to a considerable extent accepted by other members of society. Indeed, the most remarkable thing about them was that their emergence as a socially differentiated group was almost a matter of consensus." *French Literature and Its Background: The Eighteenth Century* (London, 1968), p. 80; quoted in Pat Rogers, *Grub Street: Studies in a Subculture* (London: Methuen, 1972), p. 278. On the "emergence" of the philosophes in the French Academy, see Peter Gay, *The*

double sense of the philosophes lay in the correspondence between their claims to a disinterested speculativeness and their advancement to and entrenchment in positions of privilege endowed by the monarchy. As Arthur Wilson remarks, "Not infrequently it seemed that what the *philosophes* wanted was not so much freedom as immunity. What they often demanded was apparently tantamount to the right to say what they pleased when they pleased, plus protection against the counterattacks of their enemies."[28] For the most part the philosophes prudently divided their writings between attacks on orthodoxy and defenses of both the hierarchical system of the ancien régime and their own corporate interests.[29] State and corporation were on the same footing—a footing constantly being adjusted to bring it into accord with the new monied class, whose interests were rapidly becoming the most exigent of all.[30]

Corporate success required the regulation of competing interests. The salon was that place where all differences were treated as mere differences of opinion—all differences, that is, *except* sexual difference.[31]

Enlightenment: An Interpretation, vol. 2, *The Science of Freedom* (New York: Norton, 1977), pp. 79–83.

28. Arthur Wilson, *Diderot: The Testing Years* (New York: Oxford Univ. Press, 1957), p. 163. As Voltaire observed, the institution of privilege politicized all aspects of authorship: "But, supposing you have composed an excellent work, are you aware that you must abandon the repose of your study, in order to make your application to the licenser? If his way of thinking happens to differ from yours, if he chances not to be your friend's friend, if he is in the interest of your rival, or if he is your rival himself, it will be more difficult for you to obtain a privilege, than for a man who has not the protection of the women to get a place at court." "The Profession of Letters," *The Works of Voltaire*, trans. William T. Fleming, 22 vols. (New York: Dingwell-Rock, 1927), 19:70–71.

29. The prudence can be gauged by reading John Lough's account of the use of the *lettre de cachet* and book-burnings of the philosophes' works in *Writer and Public in France: From the Middle Ages to the Present Day* (Oxford: Clarendon, 1978), pp. 183–89.

30. See Saisselin, who observes, "What seems to have happened is that the writers [philosophes] lined up with the new money, but this alignment was disguised by 'philosophy' as universalizing discourse" (*The Literary Establishment in Eighteenth-Century France*, p. 156). The definitive eighteenth-century critique of this connection was Burke's: "Along with the monied interest, a new description of men had grown up, with whom that interest soon formed a close and marked union: I mean the political Men of Letters. Men of Letters, fond of distinguishing themselves, are rarely averse to innovation. Since the decline of the life and greatness of Lewis the XIVth, they were not so much cultivated either by him, or by the regent, or the successors to the crown; nor were they engaged to the court by favours and emoluments so systematically as during the splendid period of that ostentatious and not impolitic reign. What they lost in the old court protection, they endeavoured to make up by joining in a sort of incorporation of their own; to which the two academies of France, and afterwards the vast undertaking of the Encyclopaedia, carried on by a society of these gentlemen, did not a little contribute." Edmund Burke, *Reflections on the Revolution in France* (Harmondsworth: Penguin, 1969), p. 211.

31. I would stress the restriction of my discussion here to the context of the salon. Sexual

The differences among the salons were carefully calibrated. Witness Marmontel, who admits to enjoying the hospitality of the notable Parisian hostesses, but who adds that

> however interesting in *esprit* I found the society of these kind ladies, it did not make me neglect to go and fortify my soul, to elevate, to broaden, to enlarge my thought, and to make it fertile, in the society of men whose spirit penetrated mine with warmth and with light. The home of Baron d'Holbach, and for a while that of Helvetius, were the meeting-places of this society, composed in part of the flower of Mme Geoffrin's guests, and, in part, of some minds that Mme Geoffrin had found too bold and too rash to be admitted to her dinners.[32]

The difference between the salons of Helvetius and Holbach and that of Mme Geoffrin—the former more open, warm, even rash; the latter strictly supervised—reflects the gender of their respective proprietors. It is sexually inflected by the metaphors of feminine receptivity (he becomes "fertile" in order to be "penetrated" and "flower") Marmontel adopts to describe the shift in his relations to his colleagues.

Gender is crucial for Morellet when he discriminates between the salons of Helvetius and Holbach:

> The home of Helvetius drew together about the same people as that of Baron d'Holbach, on different days, but the conversation was less *good* there, and less well-developed. The mistress of the house, attracting to her side the men who pleased her the most, and not choosing the worst, disrupted the society a bit. She did not like philosophy any more than did Mme d'Holbach, but the latter, keep-

---

difference was not the only differential recognized by Hume. There was, of course, class: "The skin, pores, muscles, and nerves of a day-labourer are different from those of a man of quality: So are his sentiments, actions, and manners. The different stations of life influence the whole fabric, external and internal" (*T*, p. 402). But such differences, because they were *class* differences, distinctions between the propertied and the unpropertied, were less troublesome than those between men and women, which affected the status of property and thus the constitution of any society that organized itself in terms of the reproduction of those property relations. Another way to conceive of the distinction is to suggest that class differences did not trouble Hume (at least until the Wilkesite riots) because he did not recognize class as a social phenomenon but a natural fact. Here is the telling opening sentence to "Of Essay Writing": "The elegant part of mankind, who are not immersed in mere animal life, but employ themselves in the operations of the mind, may be divided into the *learned and conversable*" (*ST*, p. 38). Of course, Hume presents us with the analytical tools to regard any so-called natural difference as a naturalized, conventional one and to explode the fictionality of such philosophical facts. See the discussion of refinement in Chapter 4, above.

32. Marmontel, *Memoires*, 1:484–85, quoted in Kors, *D'Holbach's Coterie*, p. 96.

ing herself apart without saying anything, or conversing in a low voice with some of her friends, prevented nothing, whereas Mme Helvetius, beautiful, with an original mind, a lively, natural disposition, greatly disturbed the philosophical discussions.[33]

The preference would seem to go to the "l'effacée" Baronne d'Holbach[34] because of that "plainness of manner and of dress," which, as we have seen, "is more engaging than that glare of paint, of airs, and apparel, which may dazzle the eye, but reaches not the affections" (*ST,* pp. 46–47). All accounts agree that women do not like philosophy: they want neither to talk philosophy nor to hear philosophical talk.[35] Not all of the members of the circles of Helvetius and Holbach would count as philosophers in the sense that they wrote books on philosophical subjects. But all of them counted as men of letters because they *talked* philosophy, the jargon of their trade, the solvent of all differences, including the sexual. The exaggeration of sexual difference in the person of the alluring Mme Helvetius disturbs philosophical discussions.

The movements of the corporation from one venue to another suggest a quest for a purely fraternal, egalitarian society. As Duclos observed, the "moeurs" of the society of the philosophes, which "font a Paris ce que l'esprit du gouvernement fait a Londres, elles conf[o]ndent et egalisent dans la societe les rangs qui sont distingues et subordonnes dans Etat."[36] The egalitarian motive coincided with and colored the desire to escape the inhibition of the woman. Here is Voltaire:

There are in Paris a number of those little societies, in which some woman presides, who, in the decline of her beauty, begins to exhibit the first dawning of her wit. One or two of the men of letters are the first members of this little kingdom. Should you neglect getting yourself admitted in quality of a courtier, you are sure of being held as a declared enemy, and are accordingly allowed no quarter. In the meanwhile, in spite of all your merit, you grow old in the midst of slander and wretchedness; those places which are destined for men of letters, are given to those who can best cabal, and not to those who are only recommended by their talents.[37]

33. Morellet, *Memoires,* 1:386, quoted in Kors, p. 97.
34. Roger Picard, *Les Salons litteraires et la société française* (New York: Brentano's, 1943), p. 311.
35. The single exception to this generalization was Mme d'Epinay, whom Voltaire called "sa belle philosophe" and "la femme qui raison"—and even this rule-proving exception was made from the distance of Ferney, in letters, not talk (ibid., p. 326).
36. Ibid., p. 148.
37. Voltaire, 19:72–73. Cf. the similar connection between loss of beauty and increase of

There is nothing of the language of chivalry in Voltaire: women are royalists, men of letters egalitarian; if not openly seditious against the king, these men can attack the little kingdoms of the females. Yet despite the valorization of male fraternity, there was never a coterie organized for philosophical discussion that met without a woman: despite their professions, the philosophes observed the necessity of woman, if not as ruler, then as rule, on which Hume insisted in "Of the Rise and Progress of the Arts and Sciences." If the presence of a woman on the margins of the salon is the inscription of sexual difference, sexual difference itself is the obligatory sign of the existence of differences which have nothing to do with the shades of opinion that make up philosophical discussion and which, consequently, cannot be composed by philosophical discourse. The presence of women at the coteries is necessary for philosophical discussion to take place: it is the conventionalized sign that establishes a philosophical circle, *bounds* a region of differences that take place within the territory of the same (the male, the abstruse, the general); it is a sign that inscribes within the male salon the excluded hierarchy, which, however much it is professedly detested, is all that gives "talents" value; it is a sign that condenses all possibly subversive, potentially violent, philosophically inconceivable differences within the known and transforms them into a stimulus to talk. A woman is necessary so that a group of men can without absurdity be considered a society, so that the abstruse meets the standards of the general. The sign of woman makes a male circle of discussion possible; it insures that the differences of opinion will always be the same and never lead to violence; and it supplies a conventional discourse into which unaccountable differences may fall.[38] The emergence of suppressed differences are best vented in humor; and women are a familiar joke.

An anecdote will illustrate. Although regarded as a retreat from the oppressive attractions of Mme Helvetius, the coterie d'Holbach, as one would expect, suffered its own turmoil, despite (or perhaps because of) the cipherlike silence, modesty, and plainness of its mistress. Here is Kors's paraphrase of Diderot's account of two incidents that occurred in 1762, the year before Hume's arrival in Paris.

> At almost the same moment of time, it seems, two betrayals occurred: Suard declared his love to the Baronne d'Holbach . . .; and Charles-Pineau Duclos, rival for the affection of Mme d'Epinay, in-

---

wit in Yorick's anecdote of his visit to one of the women's salons in Sterne's *Sentimental Journey*, pp. 134–36.

38. See Eve Kosofsky Sedgwick's general discussion of this employment of women as currency in her introduction to *Between Men: English Literature and Male Homosocial Desire* (New York: Columbia Univ. Press, 1985).

formed the latter, falsely, that Grimm had seduced the Baronne d'Holbach. Mme d'Epinay, infuriated, informed the Baron of both of these events, raising a hornet's nest, to say the least. In the end Suard apologized profusely and, encouraged by his friends, began to seek a wife; Grimm was absolved of the deed and any intention to commit the deed; Duclos was declared *persona non grata* at the coterie; and relations between d'Holbach and Mme d'Epinay were temporarily chilled. The Baronne, however, was so upset by all of this that she became depressed and ill. Her doctor, the famous Gatti (who, if we are to believe Diderot, was also in love with the Baronne), prescribed a milk diet and a regime of horseback riding in the fresh air. Le Roy, who was a great equestrian, was chosen to be her companion on these rides since he had access to the most beautiful woods at Vincennes and so much free time. According to Diderot, however, Le Roy was a "satyr" of no small accomplishment and had a reputation for being carried away by passion and for seduction. In short time, he too declared his love to d'Holbach's wife. The Baronne rejected him, informed her husband, and once agin the coterie was thrown into a turmoil. Le Roy now joined Suard in the cycle of abject apology, depression, and repentance, and he too was forgiven before too long.[39]

This farcical episode, which displays the members of the coterie d'Holbach not only falling into the discourse of gallantry but falling over and out with one another in the process, must qualify Marmontel's and Morellet's claims for the rule of tranquility. The baroness's presence at dinner may not have disturbed talk—she never intruded herself. Nonetheless, her veil of decency seems to have been the occasion for these extracurricular shenanigans—avowals of love, attempted seductions, and betrayals—which forced the exile of two of the coterie's mainstays. The turmoil is not due to the baroness's physical attractiveness but to her status as cipher: not a woman, who is different from a philosopher, she is the sign of a woman, a double entendre by which difference is conveniently symbolized and contained. Although the anecdote shows that there is no more footing in the coterie d'Holbach than in any other society in Paris, the inevitable fall takes predictable forms and just as predictably leads to what Kors accurately describes as a ritual "cycle" of purgation.

If such a farce could be—indeed, *had* to be—acted out with the Baronne d'Holbach, then we must revise our understanding of the hierarchization of the circles of Helvetius and the baron: the disturbance caused by Mme Helvetius could not simply be the effect of her physical

39. Kors, *D'Holbach's Coterie*, pp. 18–19.

attractiveness, since beauty is nothing in itself—it merely elements the sign of woman. Every woman is attractive.[40] Woman is nothing but that which attracts by virtue of the equivocal signification that she is. And if we look again at Morellet's comment, it is not Mme Helvetius's beauty on which he blames her faults as a hostess: it was because she was "beautiful, with an original mind, a lively, natural disposition, [that she] greatly disturbed the philosophical discussions." Beauty and a natural disposition are easy enough to understand and to discount, but the idea of Mme Helvetius's "original mind" is literally inconceivable and profoundly disturbing. What could possibly count as an original mind that is completely and resolutely nonphilosophical? That originality can refer only to something that is both compelling and alien to philosophy, a difference that belongs to woman but that does not belong to her by virtue of the male-imposed sign of woman. The suggestion of that difference is nothing that one can joke about because it escapes the discourse of gallantry. Mme Helvetius is not merely "woman," a sexual being beneath a veil, a correspondence always already known; rather, she has a mind, original and nonphilosophical, which is always already inscribed as a difference inarticulable within philosophical discourse.[41] Mme Helvetius's original mind is a joke on philosophy, which the philosophe defends against by embracing the Holbachian refuge and the familiar, fortunate fall in which he merely follows his "natural" inclination. The difference of Mme Helvetius from Mme Geoffrin and the Baronne d'Holbach is that she prevents philosophy not by an edict or a seduction but by the power of an original mind which compels philosophy beyond its bounds and challenges its privilege. It is a power that the men of letters fear because it is a power about which they can say nothing.

III

Hume's relations with the Comtesse de Boufflers recapitulate, with significant deviations, the general pattern of his Parisian correspondence. As we have seen in Chapter 4, the countess's first letter to Hume both con-

40. As is canonically demonstrated by the weird "love affair" between Horace Walpole and the blind Mme du Deffand.

41. Picard remarks that when Helvetius "avait fait sa provision de sujets et de raisonnements, il lui arrivait de quitter la compagnie, laissant sa femme poursuivre et diriger la discussion, ce qu'elle faisait toujours avec esprit, animation et souvent avec une charmante fantasie" (*Les Salons litteraires*, p. 311). It is the "charmante fantasie" that is the mark of Mme Helvetius's original mind, just as Hume considered Mme de Boufflers' "fairy"-likeness as the mark of her "good genius" (*HL*, 1:361), and just as it is Rousseau's status as an extravagant, "imaginary being" which distinguishes him (see Chap. 7, below).

summated the kind of reading experience that Hume had designed for his prose and, in consummating it, carried that experience beyond the bounds of impartiality into a more direct connection. By confessing to being "ravished" by Hume's prose, the countess transfigured that prose into a discourse of gallantry, turned *The History of the Stuarts* into a pretext for a secret history and a more intimate correspondence between the author and his reader. Her influence was enough to at first frighten Hume, who avoided meeting her during her trip to England in the spring of 1763, and then, apparently, to translate him to France.[42]

Moving the "celestial substance" of Hume, the impartial man of letters, was no small feat. Moved, Hume clearly played the gallant in his letters to the countess. Less perceptible are the movements of their bodies in those irrecoverable lapses of correspondence which occur in the interstices of the discourse. Measles, for example. How interpret the onset of this awkward illness on the flesh of the Comtesse de Boufflers at the moment of Hume's long-anticipated arrival in France, which removes her from the scene of welcome, marks her out as an inflamed, feverish body that must be quarantined lest its contagion spread? Of what are measles symptomatic? Is there a sign in this illness, that the body of the one woman who moved Hume is infected, a zone of peril? Is this contagious illness allegorical, perhaps a dialectical response to the affiliative disease of the learned? Or take death. How decode the untimeliness of the expiration of the Count de Boufflers, who until his death in October of 1764 was only a cipher of no account in the transactions delicately conducted among Hume, the countess, and her official lover, the Prince de Conti? Dead and buried, he matters as never before: as a body that is gone, the absence of a place-saver for certain property relations, the opportunity for new alliances, a proscription of those touches that had passed (or so we conjecture) between the countess and the man of letters before that stroke of fortune. Indeed, is it proper to conjecture that touches *did* take place on the trip (or trips) that Hume made in September and early October of 1764 to the chateau of the countess on L'Isle d'Adam?

If elusive movements of the body seem so important, it is in part because Hume's own studied stoicism, an abridgment of sensibility, exaggerated the least movement into an occasion for exposure or self-loss. Accounts of Hume's demeanor in several Parisian social settings stress an impassiveness bordering on autism. Mossner recounts a story told by Mme d'Epinay of Hume playing at charades:

42. Mossner, pp. 436–37, makes a plausible case that the Comtesse de Boufflers played the key role in persuading Hertford to employ Hume.

He had been cast for the part of a sultan sitting between two slaves, and employing all his eloquence to win their love. Finding them inexorable, he had to try to find out the reason of their resistance. He was placed upon a sofa between the two prettiest women in Paris; he looked at them fixedly, smote the pit of his stomach and his knees several times, and could find nothing to say but, "Well, young ladies; well, there you are, then! Well, there you are? There you are, then?" He kept on saying this for a quarter of an hour, without being able to think of anything else. At last one of the young ladies got up and said impatiently: "Ah! I suspected as much; this man is good for nothing except to eat veal!" Since then he has been banished to the role of spectator, but is none the less feted and flattered.[43]

Mossner also cites the puzzled comments of Lord Charlemont, an English visitor who found Hume's Parisian celebrity "truely ridiculous" and wondered how the French women could possibly delight in his conversation. (Apart from everything else, Hume's pronunciation was notoriously bad.) "And yet no Lady's Toilet was compleat without Hume's Attendance. An Acquaintance with our Philosopher was necessary to the *bel Air.* At the Opera his broad unmeaning Face was usually seen *entre deux jolis Minois,* and his Philosophy, which had formerly been detrimental to his Views of Gallantry, might here have insured his Success. . . . How my Friend Hume was able to indure the Encounter of these french Female Titans, I know not."[44]

The situations are similar: a frozen Hume between two females. "Slaves" or "titans"—it hardly makes a difference, since the submission of the "young and the brilliant" is a kind of aggression, a tactical flattery designed to seduce the reluctant sultan. Yet Charlemont's comment rightly follows Mme d'Epinay's, for in the difference of the situations lies the answer as to how Hume was able to "indure" such encounters. He wards them off. "The broad unmeaning face" may look like stupor but actually signifies a form of stoic self-control: the affectation of affectlessness. Hume's impassivity succeeds by disengaging him from a staged performance. Hume is subject to scorn during the charade; that vulnerability is remedied when he is granted the privilege of not performing but *watching* the entertainment—exactly the same position that Charlemont depicts him in at the opera and identifies as characteristic. In d'Epinay's account, Hume is incapable of performing the charade. Let us say, however, that he *wills* himself to be incapable of performing. Hume's fixed

43. *Memoires et correspondance de Mme d'Epinay* (Paris, 1818), quoted in Mossner, p. 444.
44. Lord Charlemont, "Anecdotes of Hume," quoted in Mossner, p. 446.

look, the same unmeaning face that Charlemont observed (at the same time interpreting that spectatorship as a kind of performance), is a defense against that submissive, "sheepish" look that he saw himself presenting as his unguarded response to the flattery of de Choiseul and *la* Pompadour at court (he'd rather eat than *be* veal). Hume's unmeaning face is combined with and made possible by a smiting of his body, an action that abridges passion, making impassivity more than an accident or an aphasia, but less than an expression. This self-touch/smiting is another version of the Humean castration (Hume's hands smite his stomach and his knees, crossing over, as if cutting off, the genital area, which he does not touch but precisely *omits* touching, symbolically cutting it off).

Whether compulsive or not that castration is a remedial act of violence to forestall a greater violence, the violence of being seduced into seducing, or letting one's body go in a situation where the kind of correspondences that constitute the polite play of a charade lead to social disorder: there is not a single prettiest woman, but the "two prettiest women"—a doubling that is the displaced image of the doublings and inversions that are embedded in the equivocal relations between sultan and slaves, man and woman, in the polymorphousness of desire that is signified for the eighteenth century by the word "Oriental." Surely d'Epinay is right when she denies to Hume's reiterated, "Well, young ladies; well, there you are, then," the designation of eloquence. "There you are" corresponds to an implied "Here I am"—an assertion of a certain, established, determinate distance and a statement, in the most rudimentary form, of a correspondence between the woman outside and the I inside that speaks through and is indicated by this flesh, which is simply the determinate sign of the subject who by this gesture of smiting constitutes himself as already a spectator of the "there," which he can see but not touch. Hume abjures eloquence for representation, a speech that expresses nothing except what his minimal gesture shows, that is, his representation of himself *as* a minimum, as a case of smitten flesh that is not a body but the sign of a spectator within.

Nonetheless, we ought to avoid taking the denials of eloquence of either Mme d'Epinay or David Hume at face value. For if, apart from the more grandiose notions of an antinomian, tempestuous command, we can speak of a more indirect and tactically flexible eloquence, Hume's pathetic performance *is* eloquent because it enables him to get exactly what he wants: he acquires the privilege of being a kind of spectator-in-residence. The titans can be endured because they are made slaves to an Olympian rule: they are allowed to watch Hume watching—but of course not to see the real spectator who, hiding behind the unmeaning figure, remotely corresponds with that blank appearance.

We do not have to depend solely on Mme d'Epinay and Lord Charlemont for testimony about Hume's theatrical privilege; Hume describes it himself in this letter to Hugh Blair:

> I shall indulge myself in a Folly, which I hope you will make a discreet Use of. It is the telling you of an Incident, which may appear silly, but which gave more Pleasure than perhaps any other I had ever met with. I was carry'd about six Weeks ago to a Masquerade by Lord Hertford: We went both unmaskd; and we had scarce enterd the room, when a Lady in mask, came up to me and exclaimd, *Ha, Mons' Hume vous faites bien de venir ici a visage decouvert. Que vous serez comblé cesoir d'honnetetes et des politesses! Vous verrez, pardes preuves peu equivoques, jusqu'a quel point vous etes cheri en France.* This Prologue was not a little encouraging; but as we advanc'd thro' the Hall, it is difficult to imagine the Caresses, Civilities and Panegyrics which pourd on me from all Sides: You wou'd have thought, that every one had taken advantage of his Mask to speak his mind with Impunity. I cou'd observe, that the Ladies were rather the most liberal on this Occasion; but what gave me chief Pleasure was to find, that most of the Elogiums bestowd on me, turnd on my personal Character; my Naivety & Simplicity of Manners, the Candour & Mildness of my Disposition &c. *Non sunt mihi cornea fibra.* I shall not deny, that my Heart felt a sensible Satisfaction from this general Effusion of good will. (*HL*, 1:437)

Hume breaks no rules by attending the masquerade without a mask because the rules do not apply to him; it is his privilege to attend as the only spectator (excepting Hertford, who in this instance relies on the credit of Hume) of a theater in which everyone wears the mask of a performer. Both the privilege and the theatricality are marked the moment Hume crosses the threshold, when a masked Lady presents a "Prologue" to the performance that will follow, a piece of introductory flattery that induces Hume to stay for the remainder of the show—or shower: the cascade of "Caresses, Civilities and Panegyrics which pourd on [him] from all sides." This cascade of compliments is made possible not only by the masks worn by performers but by the absence of a mask on Hume, the naked display of a face which, however, is estimable because it expresses nothing, only those character traits of naivete, simplicity, candor, and mildness which are the conventional inferences made upon a blankness. Hume watches the Parisians watching him watching them, their performance a commentary on his placidity, their unequivocal address a flattery of him that, in the fashion of true sympathy, is a form of self-congratulation. Like Mme Dupre de St Maur, Hume's first female Parisian correspondent, the performers at the masquerade find that Hume has "made it easy for [them] by the clarity and beauty . . . of [his] style. . . . Never has any book held [their] attention so completely, and never have [they] had so good an opinion of [themselves] as when [they were] reading [Hume]" (Mossner, p. 424; cf. Chap. 4, above). The performers are there, and Hume is here; but here and there are linked by a figure that permits a sympathetic cycle of correspondences. If Sterne's Yorick will later discover the perfect story and the secret for social success in Paris to be flattery, Hume, it would seem, has already gone him one better by discovering a secret that does not have to be whispered and will not lead to self-disgust: to flatter by being flattered, by presenting that blank, unmeaning face for the commentary of others, which in no way encroaches on the indifferent I that watches the play.

As the letter of Mme Dupre de St Maur instanced a perfect reading, the masquerade perfects the realm of conversation: it was an incident that gave the man of letters, as he attests, "more Pleasure than perhaps any other I had ever met with." And if the distinction of the Comtesse de Boufflers's letter was to have carried success beyond its bounds, we shall have to search for her originality among the ladies of Paris in evidence of an influence that carried Hume out of the theater. There is no doubt she made him nervous. The last letter he wrote to the countess before his departure for Paris speaks of his pleasure at the prospect of cultivating her friendship and adds the polite "warning . . . that your declarations in my favour have been so frequent and public, both in France and England, that you are bound in honour to maintain them, and that you cannot with a good grace retract upon a personal acquaintance the advantageous terms in which you have so often been pleased to speak of me. There is only one circumstance which can possibly excuse your displeasure against me; if I should be wanting in my regard and attachment towards you" (*HL*, 1:402). Hume's warning, with its anxious explicitness about contracts, seeks to insure that personal presence will make no difference by troping personal relations as the same kind of correspondence that he and the French woman have been engaged in from the first.

Nothing dishonorable followed, if we except only the untoward outbreak of measles. The attachment was maintained and perhaps grew more intimate during the winter and spring of 1763–64, but that it stayed within the format of the contract is evidenced by the arrangement made between the lady and her *maître* upon her departure from Paris to the country retreat of the Prince de Conti in July and August of 1764. The basis of their relations was to be a literary manuscript, John Home's *Douglas*, in which Hume had a proprietary interest and on which he had solicited a critique from the countess. Again, the form of the correspondence was stipulated: it was to be a sequential exchange; Hume was not to write before he received a letter from the countess, to be sent when she had completed her critique of *Douglas*. Hume, however, wrote first on the flimsy pretext of a commission from the Marechale de Mirepoix (which was consigned to a postscript).

The employment of a pretext introduces a double entendre into the correspondence: a contract is not quite broken, but it is not quite kept. Any justification of writing, however reasonable, may betray a desire to write capable of seizing any justification:

> Certain it is, that I have had a great inclination for some days past to pay my addresses to you, but have restrained myself, from reason, as I imagined, but really I believe from pride and humour, surely the most misplaced in the world. But it has happened very luckily, that the Marechale de Mirepoix has given me a commission for you, which saves my countenance, and affords me a plausible pretence for writing; and I believe really, without giving myself too great airs of fortitude, that, were it not for so great a handle, I could have held out two or three days longer at the least. (*HL*, 1:448)

Surely every contract must take into account contingency or luck. And in this case luck is backed up by something more substantial than a fitful providence. The commission has come from a noble woman with royal connections, and, as Hume asserts in the *Enquiry Concerning the Principles of Morals*, "All politicians will allow, and most philosophers, that REASONS OF STATE may, in particular emergencies, dispense with the rules of justice, and invalidate any treaty or alliance, where the strict observance of it would be prejudicial, in a considerable degree, to either of the contracting parties" (*ECPM*, p. 236). "Most philosophers" includes any philosopher who is his nation's acting embassy secretary to a recently hostile power. Because he is "in possession of an Office of Credit," he is *ipso facto* in the debt of the executive power, which could call its counters in at any time, regardless of what other contracts had been made. Now whether or not the commission was *actually* a reason of state is not at all important. There is, after all, no such thing as a reason of state in nature: its existence depends on the degree of emergency one feels when bound by an unfavorable contract and the degree of confidence one has that invoking such a category of excuse will allow one to get away with breaking it. Good conventions—contracts, societies—have conventional ways of breaking them. Reason of state is a particularly powerful one, but like war it is "an incurable Evil, which often springs from the greatest and most unexpected Absurdity, and discourages every project for seeking or improving human society" (*HL*, 2:181). Just because it is not an actual reason of state or a real-life war, Hume's maneuver shows that war is possible at any time and suggests that it may be going on all the time—as the imposition that makes possible every inducement. Unlike the state of nature, war is not a philosophical fiction that underwrites the social composition, but a decomposition of all that makes up the social, a deployment of power which invents its conventions as it goes along in a sequence of nakedly tactical fractures. Once one has invoked "reason of state," the order of custom is suspended, and one cannot anticipate the conduct of one's opponent or easily measure either her force or her will to follow the rules, for "were a civilized nation engaged with barbarians who observed no rules even of war, the former must also suspend their observance of them, where they no longer serve to any purpose; and must render every action or reencounter as bloody and pernicious as possible to the first aggressors" (*ECPM*, p. 220).

If Hume has broken a contract and risked war by acting according to his inclination, has he at least saved countenance? The handle that Hume grasps seems very slippery. In the same gesture of address Hume employs a plausible pretense and exposes the pretense of that employment, destroying, by all rights, its plausibility. Or have we gotten it wrong? That the pretense is exposed may make it implausible as a reason but not necessarily as a pretense. Can one ever do more than pretend to expose and destroy a pretense? We *can* say that this pretense, this handle, made it possible, indeed necessary, that he make his address, and that the exposure of the pretense determines its gallant form: characterized by a correspondence between saying and doing—as this is an apology or justification for an address that is an address, a narrative that is also a performance.

Again: does Hume save his countenance or lose it? Does he breach decency? If Hume, who has rejected any reason for his restraint, embraces this lucky commission as a handle that will allow him to save face, what it is that threatens the face? An inclination? But what do inclinations have to do with faces? There may be a problem of translation here, a failure of perfect correspondence between English and French. Hume is writing in English to a woman who usually replies to him in French. If by saving countenance Hume means saving face, he can mean it only in English, since *countenance* does not have the sense of "face" in French, in which it means "aspect," "air," "figure." If Hume means to save face, to avoid a humiliating disfigurement of that visage he presents to world, why does he not write it? And if he does not mean face but means his whole aspect, air, figure, the entire composition, what is threatening it? It cannot be something on the face. Perhaps something prodigious, a handle: "Were it not for so great a handle, I could have held out two or three days longer." If we read the double entendre that this gallant discourse imposes on us, we can see that the commission saves a countenance threatened by a handle that has grown so extraordinarly great that it would have broken through all Hume's attempts to compose himself.

Perhaps then the pretense of the commission is not only that it is lucky but that *it* is the handle. It is equally possible that the commission is the pretense that allows him to grab a handle and exercise it in an address, thereby saving a countenance that had been defaced by a swollen, unreasonable growth, the proper visage of that "strange uncouth monster" Hume invokes in the Conclusion to book 1 of the *Treatise* (*T,* p. 264). The double entendres of "address," "countenance," and "handle" dramatize the problem of releasing an inclination yet retaining it within some kind of restraint. The double entendres that knot this correspondence collaborate in the gallant enterprise of keeping sexual intercourse politely social. By virtue of double entendre Hume can decorously "address" the countess while exercising his great handle. He does not appear to do what he is doing, even though he must suggest what he is doing in order to do it. The plausible pretense of a gallant's prose knits together passionate release and mannered restraint in a fabric so deceptively woven that it veils the writer from his own performance.

What follows, after Hume has gotten started, is an effort to restore an equilibrium of correspondence in the face of his continued and presumably pleasurable sense that he is erring against contracts, with the countess, with himself:

> We live in a kind of solitude and retirement at Compiegne; at least I do, who . . . have given myself up almost entirely to study and retreat. You cannot imagine, Madam, with what pleasure I return as it were to my natural element, and what satisfaction I enjoy in reading and musing, and sauntering, amid the agreeable scenes that surround me. But yes, you can easily enough imagine it; have yourself formed the same resolution: you are determined this summer to tie the broken thread of your studies and literary amusements.

Hume invokes the privileged topos of solitary "study and retreat" as his "natural element" where he can pursue his "noble resolution" of "forgetting [the countess] entirely before the end of the summer." As we have seen in d'Alembert's parable and in Hume's parabolic practice, it is part of the privilege of philosophy that its special pleasure cannot be imagined by the nonphilosophical who get and spend in the theater of representations that the philosophical spectator observes. And woman is the epitome of the nonphilosophical. So it is a mark of how far gone Hume is that though he repeats, as if by rote, the doctrine of the unimaginableness of *his* natural element, he immediately rescinds that claim. She "can easily enough imagine it." He admits that this woman corresponds with him all the way down, as it were, that she has infiltrated his sanctuary. That concession is the radical justification for his abrogation of a contract (it has already been broken, correspondence has already been going on), for his penetration of her solitude, and his breaking of the threads that she is trying to weave.[45]

Hume continues with his own insistent knitting of increasingly intimate correspondences: "If you have been so happy as to execute your purpose, you are almost in the same state as myself, and are at present wandering along the banks of the same beautiful river, perhaps with the same books in your hand, a Racine, I suppose, or a Virgil, and despise all other pleasure and amusement." The ideality of this correspondence— the same state, the same beautiful river, the same books—is such that only a publisher would think of asking whether the Racine and the Virgil are in quarto or octavo, or under whose imprint they appear. If not precisely *that* wayward conjecture, some contingent idea occasions the exclamation that in marking out a difference overcomes it: "Alas! why am I not so near you, that I could see you for half an hour a day, and confer with you on these subjects?" On what subjects would they confer? Surely not on the particulars of Racine. No, they would converse on sameness in a conference that must be mute and uncritical—the complete presence of each to each in a wordlessness that is, or would be a union, if it were not, finally, the perfection of a correspondence, the imaginable limit of sender and receiver in a proximity so close that it is not necessary to touch for that intercourse to be accomplished. And to have imagined something to exist is to have brought it into existence: "But this ejaculation, methinks, does not lead me directly in my purposed road, of forgetting you. It is a short digression, which is soon over" (*HL*, 1:449).

From a great handle to an ejaculation: but for the size of the equipment this is the same route that Yorick traveled on his sentimental journey; it *is* the sentimental journey, that digression from the purposed road that travels through various representations, translating all the way, exploiting correspondences, folding the sense of words and the sense of a subject into a double entendre which allows one to identify sex and language under the same plausible pretense. It is the telos of a certain kind of phallocentrism that brings us to this absurd but wholly imaginable moment where a man's ejaculation, his direct address, can be transmitted to

---

45. Cf. the contrary "threads of affection" passage in the first section of volume 2 of Sterne's *Sentimental Journey*, where Yorick handily puns on pubic hair, a woman's dress, and the cloth covers of books to weave together a touching consummation.

a female, who as she chooses to read (and can she resist reading that which has broken her threads?), must accept what is offered to her. It is the completely absurd but wholly imaginable consequence of a correspondence model of the mind and of the social world in which it transacts its business that a masturbatory exercise of one's handle is a perfectly adequate correspondent for, is the same as, sexual intercourse. And it is wholly within the character of Hume, of the philosopher, and of the phallus, that once the ejaculation has occurred, disengagement follows. An address that had begun with the gallant overture of an apology for the violation of a contract has shifted its grounds to a point where it is understood that, under the dispensation of the Same which links philosopher and woman in specular intimacy, the only real contract that could be broken is the contract that the philosopher has made with himself to remain on the "right path" and forget the woman. His ejaculation that consummates a desire for indirect climaxes occurs at the moment when he releases himself from that contract but, like the ejaculation of the wakeful Yorick in the last scene of *Sentimental Journey*, occurs only *as* an ejaculation, a meaningless expression, which can be cast as a digession, represented as extrinsic to a purposiveness and control that remains intact and recoverable. As is his practice, Hume immediately corrects himself. The philosopher's contract with himself is exceptionally durable and infinitely elastic: it allows for lucky commissions and sudden emissions.

No doubt this piece of correspondence, though ejaculatory, is a forced address; but it would be preposterous to call it rape because it does not touch a body, nor does it bruise a soul. The Comtesse de Boufflers is no Clarissa. No victim, she cannot be raped or subjected. She writes back. Her reply to Hume consists of two parts: the first is the critique of *Douglas*, which Hume had solicited to reinforce his never very reliable literary judgment by taking the pulse of a lady of sentiment and taste; the second answers Hume's ejaculation.[46] The form of the countess's reply here establishes the pattern for their subsequent correspondence: the acknowledgment of the parallel that Hume describes as existing between them, coupled with an insistence that there is something more to her than can be exhausted or aggrandized by such correspondence.

Her critique of *Douglas* was certainly more than Hume bargained for. She went beyond the assignment of merely rendering judgment by composing a detailed and dismissive analysis (which Hume, unusually academic, insists on calling the result of a "first reading"). As the disappointed Hume recognizes, the discursive character of the response is

46. The countess's critique is extracted in *Letters of Eminent Persons Addressed to David Hume*, ed. J. H. Burton (London, 1849), pp. 223–25.

itself a negative judgment of the play: "I cannot still but flatter myself that the tragedy of *Douglas* is a work of merit, from the sensible pathetic which runs through the whole. The value of a theatrical piece can less be determined by an analysis of its conduct, than by the ascendant it gains over the heart, and by the strokes of nature which are interspersed through it. But I am afraid it has not affected you to the degree I could wish" (*HL*, 1:452–53). Hume is suspended in the dilemma that structures the standard of taste: the countess has regrettably attended to conduct rather than to pathos—yet though he can deplore her procedure in a general fashion, he cannot invalidate it because her chilly response attests to the want of that pathos in the play which is supposed to be its primary virtue. The countess has found this particular place where she can argue with Hume but Hume cannot argue with her. Her analysis is the proof of the failure of *Douglas* to gain the "ascendant" over her heart; the fact that her heart is the test of pathos prevents Hume from acquiring ascendancy by dint of argument or edict. Both the fact of her critique and the fact that she persevered with it despite the intervention of Hume's letter are part of the same "strategy" of demonstrating a discursive competency while resisting its power to prescribe a sympathetic response.

When she does turn to a response to Hume, the countess ignores the ejaculative aspects of his address. She begins instead with a confirmation and extension of the similarities that Hume had imagined: "Sil y a de la ressemblance dans nos occupations actuelles ce n'est pas la seule qui soit entre nous, car il y en a beaucoup aussi dans nos resolutions. Vous voules vous detacher de moy, je ne'en say pas le motif, mais je say bien du moins celuy qui m'oblige aussi a vouloir me detacher de vous." Like Hume she has resolutions; unlike Hume she does not try to imagine the behavior or state of mind of her correspondent. She does know her own motive for detachment; she knows that her esteem for the philosopher's "droiture et . . . bonté de coeur" is an admiration for one who is an "etranger" and who will, sooner or later, depart, having, as she writes, "me degouter de la pluspart des gens avec qui je dois vivre." She goes on to distinguish herself by adding, "Sil n'y avoit encore que cet inconvenient j'y trouverois remede, des livres tiennent lieu de bien des choses, mais le pire est que je ne puis m'en tenir a une simple estime nia une froide admiration. Des qu'on minspire ces sentiments, on touche en même tems ma sensibilité et lon engage mes affections, d'ou il sensuit une veritable peine pour moy, lorsque les circonstances me forcent de me separer de ceux qui ont merité de faire ce progres sur mon coeur." The countess's resolution proceeds from a fundamental difference between her situation and Hume's. He is mobile, she is fixed; his relations with her are a digression, a sentimental journey. She is unable to rely on the remedy of books and cannot adhere to a cold admiration. Her passion cannot travel through, let alone be satisfied by, representations: she is a body that has been touched and would touch. The only double entendre that appears in the letter occurs in a metaphor of exaggerated artfulness, designed to cast out the discourse of gallantry, to dissipate all double senses in the face of the power of nondiscursive sense itself: "Je me regarde comme une foible arbrisseau qui a jetté des *racines* trop loin de soy, et qui par la est exposé a plus dinjures, et de risques" (*HL*, 2:369–70; emphasis added). As the means of corresponding with the countess, Hume had imagined her reading her Racine, an occupation he could imitate in order to confer with her over a distance. But this woman, like the tree by which she metaphorizes herself, like the metaphor itself, has no footing, has thrown her "racines" too far away for them to support her. The metaphor of the sapling unveils an exposure, a place where the body of the woman is, with no above or beneath, simply a body open to injury and risk.

The letters of the Countess de Boufflers are attempts to explain her position without representing herself in a way that will allow Hume the hope that he can satisfy his passion indirectly. They are devised in order to map the relations in which she has been placed with the Prince de Conti and to stake out a region which belongs to her alone and which is dedicated to Hume alone—a place that is nonrelational and that cannot be approached, let alone filled, by any correspondence. Her letters eloquently indicate a body that cannot be communicated. She is capable of invoking the contractual aspects of their relationship when it suits her, as when she indignantly complains that in response to an eight-page letter Hume has sent her only a two-page reply; and she is attentive to correspondences of all kinds—but always with the aim of unsettling Hume's cautious attempts to stabilize their relationship.

Hume responds to these overmatching letters by fluctuating between a defensive reserve based on the conventions of *amitié* ("What amiable, what unaffected, what natural expressions of good-will and friendship!" [*HL*, 1:456]) and an increasingly exaggerated gallantry by which he attempts to defend against the charge that all of his talk about obligation is itself a mark of indifference:

> I could never yet accuse myself, dear Madam, of hypocrisy or dissimulation; and I was surely guilty of these vices in the highest degree, if I wrote you a letter, which carried with it any marks of indifference. What I *said* in particular, I cannot entirely recollect, but I well remember in general what I *felt*, which was a great regard and attachment to you, not increased indeed (for that was scarce possible) but rendered more agreeable to myself, from the marks

you had given me of your friendship and confidence: I adhere to these; I will never, but with my life, be persuaded to part with the hold which you have been pleased to afford me: you may cut me to pieces, limb by limb; but like those pertinacious animals of my country, I shall expire still attached to you, and you will in vain attempt to get free. (*HL*, 1:457)

If not guilty of dissimulation, Hume demonstrates his great capacity for assimilation, embracing the reading that puts him in the wrong as itself a mark of his "general" feeling of "regard and attachment." And he assimilates her correspondence as a similar set of marks, indicating a similar general feeling. Hume is ready to confess to or to relinquish any particular, which may have caused or might yet lead to a misunderstanding. And he seems to go far in self-abasement: he cedes the knife to his mistress and compares himself to a leechlike animal that will adhere despite her best efforts to extricate herself. Later he remarks on "how much am I fallen from the airs which I at first gave myself. . . . Now, I throw myself at your feet and give you nothing but marks of patience and long-suffering and submission." but through it all, though Hume seems to abandon himself, he clings to marks that, whether they be of indifference, friendship, or submission, are nonetheless merely *signs* of a passion and vehicles of its indirection. The knife that Hume offers the countess is the same blade that he has used all along to incapacitate his passion and to protect himself from the engrossment of the body; it makes no difference who wields it, since the purpose is the same, to prove that the flesh can be cut and cut again, with no injury to the general feeling and the feeling of the general which it merely signifies. Every version of passion that Hume represents is, because it is represented, merely conventional, and whether ejaculative or gallant, astonished or masochistic, each version is the mark of indifference.

The only evidence we have of a passage beyond indifference is unmarked. There is no letter that corresponds to the movement of Hume's body that occurred in September of 1764, when he entered that region of touching privacy that the countess held open for him. We have only the letter of Gilbert Elliot of Minto, who, evidently referring to a conversation he had with Hume during his visit to Paris, admonishes, "Before I conclude, allow me in friendship also, to tell you, I think you are on the brink of a precipice"—to which Hume replied, "I cannot imagine what you mean by saying that I am on a Precipice" (*HL*, 1:469 and note). It is surely apposite that Elliot, at this moment of Hume's potentially cataclysmic movement beyond the ties of his friends and his nation, should have recourse to a metaphor of the sublime. The sublime, with its associations of vertigo and the threat of self-loss, comes closest to representing that singular and dangerous point at which Hume stands, poised on a brink that is no sure footing, close to a fall that may end in self-destruction or, worse, not end at all. We could, if we were inclined, read all of the forced jocularity about women in Hume as transformations of the sublime, that trope which suddenly turns a general experience into a moment of intense particularity, the hard crux of self-preservation, which transfigures the flat map of our understanding into a treacherous wilderness of inhuman heights and unknowable depths, which turns all the correspondences by which we orient ourselves into two-headed tokens of blank confusion. We could perform such a reading if it were not that Hume is so precise in rejecting it as unimaginable—rejecting, that is, the sublime as a convention that could apply to wherever he is and wherever his body is to move. And the discourse of the sublime does not apply any more than the discourse of gallantry; indeed, at this "point" in Hume's career, where career begins to take on the sense of an uncontrolled, eccentric movement, the discourse of the sublime and the discourse of gallantry (and, one might add, the discourse of skepticism) resolve into the same thing: a safety net of convention that theatricalizes all risks—the threat to male superiority, to reason, to life itself—that contains the different by making it imaginable to a spectator who is always at some remove from danger: "It is a certain rule, that wit and passion are entirely incompatible. When the affections are moved, there is no place for the imagination" (*ST,* p. 46). We can, however, find no spectator to whatever went on between Hume and countess, no auditor of the Adamic language by which they knew each other on the L'Isle d'Adam. No accounts survive, not even a stray anecdote; the narrative stops. The only evidence we have is that a body has moved, and if we fill the empty space in the narrative of Hume's life and career with the movement of the bodies, touched and touching, of Hume and the countess, it is not because we imagine sexual relations. We do not: the nondiscursive is empty of relations, without properties. It is because the body is our sign for that dense, curiously resistant, absurdly particular historical stuff that cannot be assigned or generalized or composed. And if we do not concede an original mind to the Comtesse de Boufflers, it is not because we want to name her as "mere" body, sentient material of no determinable form or composition, but because her uniqueness has nothing mental about it, at least nothing that we can understand; rather, it is to have been the one to have penetrated the veil of the philosopher and to have dissipated any secret that would need to be veiled, to have exposed that there is nothing in or of the philosopher that cannot be affected. Her uniqueness is to have moved Hume's body without grabbing any handle: the physics are not Newtonian; the power belonged to a body that was neither heavenly nor infernal.

Belonged to a body in two senses, because (1) it is historical in the sense that no more than the influx of silver from the mines in America can its power be recovered from the moment of its action—it is past in a way that nothing else in Hume's career is past; and (2) because what makes the interval of bodily movement an interval is the loss of that power that occurs as the result of the death of the Count de Boufflers. The machinery of discourse starts up again on the intervention of the contingent. A husband dies, a death certificate is issued, funeral obsequies are spoken, a will is read, and a new set of property relations constellate, revising the map of the terrain. This is not the restitution of the balance of the liberal economy but its death, which is the same as the inexorable imposition of the political. The new disposition of property radically alters the distance between the sectors at L'Isle d'Adam which are occupied by the Prince de Conti and his mistress, now a candidate, if not for respectability (the countess never doubted the respectability of any relations she had with a prince of the blood), then for legality, an entitlement to share in rights that belong only to a spouse. Those sectors, hitherto so discrete and inviolate that they might have been two kingdoms ruled by agreeable but distant potentates, have been thrown into a new and embarrassing intimacy; new property relations, enforced by a politics that cannot help but be violent, transform all relations, and in this case retrospectively reconstitute the movement of bodies as sexual relations that are opened to the view of all who regard the prince. In order to save countenance, the countess had to disengage from Hume. The interval is sealed, and it is as if it had never been:

> This late incident, which commonly is of such moment with your sex, seems so little to affect your situation either as to happiness or misery, that I might have spared you the trouble of receiving my compliments upon it: but being glad of taking any opportunity to express my most sincere wishes for your welfare, I would not neglect an occasion which custom has authorised. Receive, then, with your usual, I cannot say, with your constant, goodness, the prayers of one of your most devoted friends and servants. I hope that every change of situation will turn out to your advantage. In vain would I assume somewhat of the dignity of anger, when you neglect me: I find that this wish still returns upon me with equal ardour. (*HL*, 1:476)

Hume has been restored to his independence by a sovereign decree; the composition of property has induced the countess to incapacitate herself and, ironically, to apply Hume's knife on the philosopher himself, who can hardly complain about being returned to the station of spectator and correspondent which is the basis of his privilege—even if that footing is given rather than chosen. There is only the slighting distinction between "usual" and "constant" goodness to register any passion. The countess acts with the credit of a prince who can oblige any man, even a man of letters.[47] The narrative of Hume's career has begun again; the episode of Paris is over. It will be a year before David Hume leaves France, but from the death of the Count de Boufflers it is only a matter of time.

47. Cf. Brewer's comment on the relations between the tradesman and the patrician in the client economy: "Clients in the client economy were not 'free' but tied, no matter how discreetly, to their patrons. Moreover, the client economy compounded one of the greatest problems that faced the eighteenth-century tradesman, namely that of credit and debt. The patricians simply passed on their own indebtedness to the trader by taking credit and failing to pay their bills promptly, or sometimes, not at all. No grievance was felt more strongly than this hidden subsidy to aristocratic wealth" ("Commercialization and Politics," p. 198).

7
"Transactions with Rousseau"

All over the world, as if on a given signal, splendid talents are stirring and
conspiring together to revive the best of learning. For what else is this but
a conspiracy when all these great scholars from different lands share out the
work among themselves?

Erasmus

Les querelles des gens de lettres font le scandale de la philosophie.

Exposé Succinct, "Avertissement des Editeurs"

I

When Hume left Paris, it was for good. But he did not leave empty-
handed: to his mortal regret, he brought Jean Jacques Rousseau back with
him to England. Hume's return with Rousseau completes a transaction
which brackets the whole Parisian episode. In retrospect, Hume's visit to
Paris was as much a mission to meet and befriend Rousseau as it was to
refine a greater intimacy with the Comtesse de Boufflers—not because
befriending Rousseau was Hume's purpose but because it was the countess's. The countess formally introduced the cause of Rousseau, "citizen
of Geneva and author of several writings," in her second letter to Hume,
where she informed him of the *arrêt* executed by the French king against
Rousseau's works and of Rousseau's flight from France, soliciting Hume's
protection (*HL,* 2:367–68).

Hume's reply was speedy and favorable. He assured the countess
that "there is no man in Europe of whom I entertained a higher idea, and
whom I would be prouder to serve." He confessed, "I revere his greatness
of mind, which makes him fly obligations and dependance; and I have
the vanity to think, that through the course of my life I have endeavoured
to resemble him in those maxims." And he offered to use his "connexions
with men of rank in London" to assist Rousseau, adding, "We are happy
at present in a king, who has a taste for literature; and I hope M. Rousseau will find the advantage of it, and that he will not disdain to receive

benefits from a great monarch, who is sensible of his merit" (*HL*, 1:363).
As good as his word, Hume wrote immediately to Rousseau (in London,
where he mistakenly thought him to be), addressing him as the person,
"of all the men of letters in Europe, . . . whom I most revere." He asks
to be permitted "some Liberty of boasting on this Occasion while I pretend, that my Conduct & Character entitle me to a Sympathy with Yours;
at least, in my Love of philosophical Retreat, in my Neglect of vulgar
Prejudices, and in my Disdain of all Dependance: And if these Circumstances had happily prov'd the Foundation of an amicable Connexion
between us; I shou'd have entertain'd the Project of engaging you to
honour this part of the World [Edinburgh] with your Company." Hume
also mentions that he has given leave to some friends in London to "cite
my Name & Authority for paying their respects" (*HL*, 1:365).

One of those friends was Gilbert Elliot of Minto, to whom Hume
praised Rousseau for writings that, despite "a tincture of extravagance in
all of them," have "so much eloquence and force of imagination, such an
energy of expression and such a boldness of conception, as entitles him
to a place among the first writers of the age." The praise prefaced a request that Elliot assist in obtaining a royal pension for Rousseau, who,

> tho he rejects presents from private persons, . . . may not think
> himself degraded by a pension from a great monarch: and it would
> be a singular victory over the French, worth a hundred of our Min-
> dens, to protect and encourage a man of genius whom they had
> persecuted. . . . It would be a favour to the ministers to suggest
> such an action to them. I fancy Rousseau's crime is only some sallies
> of Republicanism, and Protestantism, and satire against French
> manners; for I do not find that, in any of his writings, he has ever
> gone further. (*HL*, 1:366–67)

These preliminaries to a relationship that was to end so disastrously
deserve some attention. Each letter of the correspondence uncertainly
essays a characterization of Rousseau, which hinges on the technical problem of affirming his singularity and yet making that singularity an occasion
for sympathy. The singularity is pronounced: Rousseau's principles on
education, politics, and religion, writes the countess, are "contrary to
ours," and because of this contrariety to the social norm, Rousseau has
been singled out for interdiction by a *parlement* enforcing the laws of the
king. A syndrome emerges: Rousseau is able to bring into play the monarch as literal wielder of power in a specific situation. We can call this a
syndrome because it quickly spreads to Hume, who, faced with an appeal
for help and placed in the awkward position of arranging assistance for
one who refuses all dependence, attempts to exploit the line of credit

that connects him to the throne. Yet even though the king is imagined as the only possible correspondent to Rousseau's singularity, a sense of realism dictates that the king can be expected to sympathize with the plight of Rousseau only if the appeal is couched in terms of the natural antagonism between the king of England and his counterpart, the king of France: the generosity of one will mean the chagrin of the other. Dealing with Rousseau's independence tends to equivocate the supposed autonomy of the king, whose actions are imagined only as reactions; and, of course, if this is so, it is hard to see how in accepting the beneficence of the English monarch Rousseau would escape the influence of the French king to whom the "great monarch" is tied.

Rousseau's posture of singularity also disturbs the discourse of the countess. She doubts Rousseau's claim that his life was in danger but concedes that any prudent person might have done the same in "pareilles circonstances." If Rousseau is as singular as he is said to be, what could the "pareilles" circumstances be? Who would ever find himself or herself in the position of Rousseau, at variance with the principles of education, politics, and religion that all of "us" share? How can we imagine like circumstances if we do not share any principles? And are there such things as circumstances that cannot be like? There is something edging on the unimaginable here in what the countess calls this "delicacy that can appear excessive." The countess presents Hume with something that is not only a problem difficult to solve but difficult to conceive. On the face of it the assignment to help such a character is a task of contradiction.

For Hume evidence of contradiction implies the absence of a real problem. If it is true that we can form "no wish which has not a reference to society" (*T*, p. 363), then Rousseau's professions cannot be taken fully seriously. Hume can reply to the countess with unruffled amiability because for him Rousseau's singularity is merely representative, an exaggerated version of that independence which distinguishes the man of letters and makes him a sympathetic figure. As a man of letters Hume has an interest in sympathizing with Rousseau. If he can sympathize—and there is no imaginable reason to think that he cannot—he will have empirically corroborated the claim that is the central statement of his career: "men of letters" describes a general society or discourse capable of inducing all particulars, even the apparently excessive Rousseau, into its composition. The interest of the man of letters here, as in all instances, is to prove that he has no special interest that does not belong to society in general. If solitude were an authentic possibility, if Rousseau were to be like the man of letters in all circumstances except for some unimaginable difference, it would rupture that discourse of generality which the man of letters deploys to ward off extinction.

Hume could not take Rousseau seriously if he was to take him at all. And he had to take Rousseau, both in the sense that he was bound to honor his promise to the Comtesse de Boufflers and in the sense that, as ideologist and middleman, he was responsible for demonstrating the adaptiveness of the commerce of letters. Hume had been warned that he was making a dangerous mistake—needlessly, as he tells Blair on their arrival in England: "[Rousseau] is a very agreeable, amiable Man; but a great Humorist. The Philosophers of Paris fortold [sic] to me, that I could not conduct him to Calais without a Quarrel; but I think I cou'd live with him all my Life, in mutual Friendship and Esteem. I am very sorry, that the Matter is not likely to be put to a Trial. I believe one great Source of our Concord, is, that neither he nor I are disputatious, which is not the Case with any of them" (*HL*, 2:13). The ironies of Hume's blithe account of their passage from Paris to London are severe, not only in light of their rapid falling-out, which was occasioned in part by something that Rousseau claimed had occurred at Senlis (well before Calais) on the first night of their journey, but also because the characteristics of the two men to which Hume attributes their friendship were actually to contribute to their friction. The lack of disputatiousness, which Hume interpreted so benignly, persisted, but in the event the want of argument bespoke an irreconcilable difference between them. Rousseau expected replies to statements that Hume never recognized as such; and when Hume finally began to perceive the extent of Rousseau's distrust of him, Rousseau had moved to "demonstrations" against which no argument could succeed.

Events moved rapidly. Encouraged by the offer of Hume's protection, in December of 1765 Rousseau traveled from Strasbourg to Paris, where he met Hume and joined him in preparation for the journey to his "asylum" in England. They left by two coaches for Calais in the first week of January 1766, crossed on the ninth, and arrived in London on the thirteenth. Their arrival had been awaited by the worlds of fashion and of letters; Rousseau suffered and Hume rejoiced in the celebrity, which extended to the king and queen, who were eager to catch a glimpse of the famous Swiss recluse. By the time Hume wrote the above letter to Blair boasting of their concord, he and Rousseau had already separated: Rousseau had taken a room at Chiswick, allowing Hume the opportunity discreetly to pursue a royal pension—a mission which Rousseau had approved at Calais. Thérèse Le Vasseur, Rousseau's common-law wife, was delivered, slightly used, to Rousseau by the serviceable Boswell on the thirteenth of February. By March Rousseau's discontent with the frantic sociability of London had increased to the point that Hume finally agreed to his removal to a retreat in Derby, offered by Richard Davenport of

Calveley, friend of Garrick and Sterne. Rousseau departed on the thirteenth of March.

The first indication of discord appeared on the eve of his departure. Each man independently attested to his perception that something had happened, and both agreed that the scene ended in a semblance of harmony with Rousseau in Hume's lap, but the provocations were understood differently by each. Hume thought that Rousseau resented his passive part in Davenport's well-meaning deception of Rousseau: in order to make Rousseau and Thérèse more comfortable on their trip to Wooton, Davenport had attempted to save Rousseau some money and overcome his resistance to largesse by secretly hiring a coach and telling Rousseau "he had found a Retour Chaise for the Place, which he might have for a Trifle." Rousseau suspected a trick, objected to being treated like a beggar, and accused Hume of collaborating in a contrivance about which Hume had certainly been informed but which, he insisted, he had not helped design. When Rousseau later referred to this incident, he did not mention the matter of the coach, but ascribed his suspicions to evidence which, he claimed, showed that Hume had been tampering with his mail. At any rate, Rousseau did finally arrive at his asylum in Wooton, but it was not long to be that refuge which he had professed to seek. A copy of the *St. James's Chronicle* containing Horace Walpole's wicked satire on Rousseau's "hypocrisy," "The Letter from the King of Prussia," which had been circulating in France since December, surfaced in Wooton. Rousseau fired off an outraged reply, imputing authorship to a French enemy (he meant d'Alembert) and hinting darkly at English collaborators (he meant Walpole and Hume). Other mocking attacks, including one by Voltaire, followed, and Rousseau perceived a design, which he imputed to the treacherous hand of Hume. Rousseau began writing to his friends in France of a "conspiracy" in April, when he also broke off correspondence with Hume. He refused the offered pension in May. Finally, on June 23 Rousseau replied to Hume's apprehensive inquiry with a declaration of his conviction that Hume had conveyed him to England in order to "dishonour" him. Indignant, Hume demanded particulars, which, to his surprise, were itemized in the long, amazing letter of July 10—Rousseau's last letter to David Hume. Hume managed an astonished answer, but uncertain and fearful of what Rousseau planned (he had told Hume that he was preparing his memoirs for publication) and unsettled by the rumors that seemed to be circulating everywhere, Hume also put together a more formal reply to Rousseau that included all their correspondence arranged into a narrative sequence, knit by Hume's exposition and underwritten by Hume's annotation. The text was sent to d'Alembert, and publication was left to his discretion. The *Exposé Succinct de la contestation, qui s'est elevée entre M. Hume et M. Rousseau; avec les pieces justificatives*, framed by a preface written jointly by the French editors and by d'Alembert's afterword, was published in Paris in October. An English translation was published by Cadell and Strahan in November. By March of 1767, Rousseau—who had become the recipient of another offer of a royal pension, sought on his own initiative but secretly assisted by Hume—had evacuated Wooton and, penniless, made his way to Dover, where he took ship back to Calais.

II

There can be no description of the contest between Hume and Rousseau without judgment. The claims to be adjudicated are two. There is Rousseau's accusation of treachery, which entailed enormous consequences: "I told you with tears in my eyes, while I embraced you, that if you were not the best of men, you must be the basest. In reflecting on your secret conduct, you must say to yourself, sometimes, you are not the best of men; and I doubt, if, under that impression, you will ever be the happiest" (Ritchie, p. 195). There is Hume's denial: "You say, that I myself know that I have been false to you; but I say it loudly, and will say it to the whole world, that I know the contrary; that I know my friendship towards you has been unbounded and uninterrupted; and that though I have given you instances of it, which have been universally remarked both in France and England, the public as yet are acquainted only with the smallest part of it" (Ritchie, p. 196). There are two primary documents to be considered: Rousseau's bill of particulars in his long letter of July 10, 1766, and Hume's defense, the *Exposé*. Actually, there are not quite two documents. Rousseau's letter first appeared *as* a public document in Hume's publication, nested within Hume's narrative. There is a persistent and weirdly askew symmetry between claim and counterclaim: Rousseau advances a series of charges that have a sort of wild consistency but rests the proof of his accusation on Hume's heart; Hume insists that in his heart he is innocent but rests his defense on Rousseau's letter. It is not the least of the complications of this "affair" that a crossing occurs between the two principals, a consequence, perhaps, of what Rousseau describes as the abysmal quality of the crisis,[1] which produces texts such as this one, which comes from Hume, "after" Rousseau: "Have Compas-

---

1. "Every circumstance of the affair is equally incomprehensible. Such conduct as yours is not in nature: it is contradictory, and yet it is demonstrable. On each side of me there is an abyss, and I am lost in one or the other" (Ritchie, p. 239).

sion, I beseech you," Hume writes to Davenport, "on the most signal Beneficence, exposed to the blackest Ingratitude. You have a heart formd for feeling that cruel Situation" (*HL*, 2:55). At stake in this controversy is the heart of Europe, the manner in which it is formed to feel and the style by which that feeling can be enlisted in an irrevocable judgment.

If we are to adjudge Hume's publication, to which many of his friends were opposed and about which he was at best equivocal, it is necessary to discriminate between defenses. It was not so much the truth of Rousseau's accusation that the *Exposé* defended against—Hume had already answered Rousseau in a brief, pointed letter, remarkable for its composure—as its effect. "I little imagined," he wrote to the Comtesse de Boufflers in August, "that a private story, told to a private gentleman, could run over a whole kingdom in a moment: if the king of England had declared war against the king of France, it could not have been more suddenly the subject of conversation" (*HL*, 2:77). Notions of royal competition have escalated into the metaphor of warfare, which nonetheless remains inadequate to describe the publicity of Rousseau's charges. The lightning-like diffusion of Rousseau's indictment matched and over-matched the amazingly swift dissemination of the Walpole satire, which sparked the feud and on which Hume comments in the *Exposé*. Walpole, he writes, "showed [his satire] to some friends; one took copies, which soon multiplied. This little piece was spread rapidly through the whole of Europe, and it was in the hands of the whole world before I had seen it at London for the first time" (Ritchie, p. 461). Unprotected and unhindered by copyright, winged by the names of Frederick and Rousseau, Walpole's squib described a capacity for unlimited multiplication and dispersion that depended on neither substance nor capital. Going Walpole one better, Rousseau's story seems to have filled every space: "But, dear Madam, I find, that imperceptibly I owe him still a greater grudge than any I have mentioned: he occupies all my thoughts while I am writing to you, and gives me no leisure either to speak to you of myself, or any of our common friends" (*HL*, 2:79). Having robbed Hume of his leisure, Rousseau has disrupted the proper balance among the "three ingredients" of Humean happiness, "action, pleasure, and indolence," and thereby destroyed "the relish of the whole composition" of the self (*ST*, p. 49). Hence, when Hume writes to Strahan in November that it "is necessity, not choice, that forces me on this publication" (*HL*, 2:107), the necessity is not only a defense of his innocence but a defense of his self: Hume must ward off Rousseau's imperial rhetoric in order to end both the Genevan's manipulation of public opinion and his occupation of Hume's own thoughts.

The difficulty of Hume's defense is aggravated by the absence of any real correspondence between him and Rousseau. Rousseau had for a time refused to correspond with Hume at all, and when he does write, it is only to dictate the impossible condition for Hume's reply that it must take place wholly within the strange loop of Rousseau's invention. Rousseau's notorious wariness of any obligation reflects a fundamental suspicion of all exchange as a subterfuge furthering an enterprise of dishonor and domination.[2] Hume's great generosity threatened to overwhelm Rousseau because he had nothing equivalent to return, even as he was positioned in a set of conventions which dictated that as man of letters he had to attempt to give something back—write letters to friends and admirers, extend his thanks, pay his respects—in order to deserve what he had been given. Not only would any return fall short, but the very mediator of the exchanges, the man who carried the letters of the cloistered man of letters to the outside world, was the "negotiator" David Hume: the more Rousseau returned the more he owed.[3] This is to be overwhelmed; this is to fall into the abyss, which is Rousseau's melodramatic version of what I have called the double entendre of the man of letters and the credit economy: "If you are guilty, I am the most unfortunate of mankind; if you are innocent, I am the most culpable (Ritchie, p. 239). Rather than be overwhelmed Rousseau aborted exchange by pressing it to the limit: by recklessly exposing the inevitable dissimulation in every exchange, he deployed the one answer he could make to Hume's generosity and offered a challenge that could not be answered except by a vindicating act of aggression, which would put the lie to that model of self-regulating equilibrium which Hume had sought to impose as natural.[4]

Hume, needless to say, did not quite see it that way. By publishing the *Exposé* he intended, as he wrote to Turgot, to dissipate all secrets that might lie "buryed in Darkness" (*HL*, 2:75) and thereby to quash all suspicion of treachery or conspiracy. He would enlighten what Rousseau had occulted. He would resume the interrupted exchange, reassert his normal occupation, and, by bringing accounts to a final balance, cancel in the customary manner all future exchanges between them. "Thanks to God,"

2. "Every exchange contains a more or less dissimulated challenge, and the logic of challenge and riposte is but the limit towards which every act of communication tends. Generous exchange tends towards overwhelming generosity; the greatest gift is at the same time the gift most likely to throw its recipient into dishonour by prohibiting any counter-gift." Pierre Bourdieu, *An Outline of a Theory of Practice*, trans. Richard Nice (Cambridge: Cambridge Univ. Press, 1977), p. 14.

3. For a discussion of the preferred Rousseauian economy of the parasite see Michael Serres, *The Parasite*, trans. Lawrence R. Schehr (Baltimore: Johns Hopkins Univ. Press, 1982), pp. 103–20.

4. For a survey of the various maneuvers for protracting, interrupting, and destroying the exchange of challenge and riposte see Bourdieu, *Outline of a Theory of Practice*, pp. 10–15.

he writes to the countess after the publication of the French and English versions of the *Exposé*, "my affair with Rousseau is now finally and totally at an end, *at least on my part:* for I never surely shall publish another line on that subject" (*HL*, 2:114).

There were, as Hume and his friends recognized, some risks in publication. Most obviously, Rousseau's letter would persist *in* Hume's book, and despite Hume's precautions to insure the containment of its power, there could be no guarantee of the incapacitation of its rhetoric; after all, he had taken ample precautions with Rousseau before, and to no avail. Hume acknowledged the potential imprudence of prolonging the life of an attack on himself by publishing it, but in a letter to Suard he dismissed its force: "Cou'd I look on Rousseau as one of the Classics of your Language, I shou'd imagine, that this Story, silly as it is, might go to Posterity, and interest them as much as it has done our Contemporaries: But really his Writings are so full of Extravagance, that I cannot believe their Eloquence alone will sustain them" (*HL*, 2:103). That diagnosis is much the same as this later analysis of Rousseau's character: "There is no Need of any Secrecy: [Rousseau's exploits] are most of them pretty public, and are well known to every body that had Curiosity to observe the Actions of that strange, indefineable Existence, whom one woud be apt to imagine an imaginary Being, tho' surely not a *Ens rationis*" (*HL*, 2:164). No longer are Rousseau's writings "tinctured" by extravagance; they are now perceived to be suffused by it. If we are to imagine, it seems necessary to imagine here an imaginary prose that has no center of substance from which it strays, but which is all extravagance. This imaginary prose not only has no agreeable footing; it has no footing at all: it can be sustained only by its eloquence. Such eloquence may induce belief—that is its distinctive quality and socializing tendency—but it is impossible for Hume to believe *about* eloquence that it will survive self-sustained; for, as we have seen, in "Of Eloquence" Hume carefully restricts commanding eloquence to a moment that arises in and is limited to the sound of the orator's voice in an open assembly. No matter what the power of a Demosthenes or a Cicero, it must wane if there is nothing else behind it but his eloquence: people must and will return to their homes, dine, and play backgammon.

It was the historical distinction and mortal threat of Rousseau to meld the commanding power of eloquence and the possibility of self-subsistence into a single problematic. Hume had always claimed that powerful eloquence was lost in the past of antiquity and that subsistence labor was wholly implicated in the fiction of nature: no man could sustain himself on his own outside of the conventions of society. Hume trusts that Rousseau, lacking the various representations of office and privilege,

will perish with the inevitable withering of his hand.[5] Rousseau first
raised this issue when he branded the law of context as a form of obligation, as anything but natural, as an imposition of the *mentalité de le mar-
chand:*

> Il n'est permis de marchander sur le prix des bienfaits que quand
> on nous accuse d'ingratitude, & M. Hume m'en accuse aujourd'hui.
> J'oserai donc faire une observation qu'il rend nécessaire. En appré-
> ciant ses soins par la peine & le temps qu'ils lui coûtoient, ils
> étoient d'un prix inestimable encore plus par sa bonne volonté: pour
> le bien réel qu'ils m'ont fait, ils ont plus d'apparence que de poids.
> Je ne venois point comme un mendiant quêter du pain en Angle-
> terre; j'y apportois le mien. . . . (Ritchie, pp. 478–79)

In the English and Humean translation of this letter "j'y apportois le
mien" is rendered as "I brought the means of subsistence with me"—a
claim that forces Hume's denial. It is not merely what Rousseau charges
against Hume but what he claims for himself that Hume must repudiate:
that Rousseau has a means of subsistence of his own, a rhetorical power
that can in its solitary extravagance, without mediation, turn ink into
bread. Such a power is no doubt unimaginable. But Hume's invention of
a wholly new, desperately redundant category, his imagining of an imaginary being, is empirical evidence of its force. The cause is known by its
effect, which is the tortuous denial of the cause. To imagine an imaginary
being is not to exercise the mind's "authority over all its ideas" as we do
when we figment a centaur (ECHU, p. 48); it is to imagine a being who
is not authorized by our imagination, who is impossible because, all extravagance, there is no idea that corresponds to him.

Hume is forced to such fancies because not only is there no place in
society for Rousseau but there is no place in history. The eloquence of
the ancients is no precedent. The impossibility of Rousseau inheres in an
eloquence that, however unspeakable, is fully printable. The impossibility of Rousseau is the emergence in modern culture of just that violent

---

5. This is the same faith in contextual determination on which Hume had relied in his
warning to Blair, the enthusiastic champion of Macpherson's *Ossian:* "It is in vain to say, that
their beauty will support [Macpherson's verses], independent of their authenticity" (*HL*,
1:399). We verge here on the Romantic claim for the unpropped, unmotivated, wholly prepossessing image, most neatly exemplified in book 4 of Wordsworth's *Prelude:*

A hundred times when, in these wanderings,
I have been busy with the toil of verse,
Great pains and little progress, and at once
Some fair enchanting image in my mind
Rose up, full-form'd, like Venus from the sea.
(1805; 110–14)

method which Hume's story of the irreversible decline of eloquence was designed to cast out: Rousseau's is a modernization of the ancients' power because it depends not at all on the assembly of auditors within earshot of the authoritative voice, but can exert its force over great distances through "a hollow thundering of words" that, by any empirical criterion, makes no sense at all.[6] And it is the capacity of writing to become not a vehicle or a representation of power but the imposition of power itself, a thundering of hollow script, to which Rousseau's attack on Hume's secret project testifies and which it instances by its own brute challenge.

This challenge accepts the schematic mastery of his patron and presses the consequences: "If ever I was fully and clearly convinced of any thing, I am convinced that Mr. Hume furnished the materials for the above paper [the "Letter from the King of Prussia"]. What is still more, I have not only this absolute conviction, but it is very clear to me that Mr. Hume intended I should: for how can it be supposed that a man of his subtlety would expose himself thus, if he had wished to conceal himself?" (Ritchie, p. 231). That Rousseau's indictment may be without substance, that Rousseau himself may be an unintelligible, imaginary being, does not negate but augments his force. As Hume well knew. In Chapter 5 we saw that a "a few phrases and expressions; which one party accepts of, without understanding them, and the other refuses in the same measure" (G&G, p. 130) may be, however insubstantial and unreal, nonetheless sufficient to provoke and sustain theological warfare, a conflict of ideologies anchored in no rational interest. Rousseau's relentlessly unmeaning repetition of his faith in his radical self-subsistence compels Hume, in peril of his own survival, to reply in kind but, if possible, with more force. The inevitable consequence of this riposte is that in exposing the imaginary basis of Rousseau's accusations, he exposes as well the ideological nature of the social composition which the man of letters represents— demonstrates, that is, that the "social and universal" principles which "form, in a manner, the *party* of humankind against vice or disorder, its common enemy" (*ECPM*, p. 298) *are* partisan principles, that "social and universal" are meaningless phrases wielded by one man against another. The limit of social exchange determines its transgression as a state of war, not of nature—the literary kings of France and England smiting each other, with no imaginable interests at stake, in a war of words:

> What achievement so mighty and glorious as that the impulses of the crowd, the consciences of the judges, the austerity of the Senate, should suffer transformation through the eloquence of one man?

6. Cicero, *De Oratore*, trans. E. W. Sutton and H. Rackham (1942; rpt. Cambridge: Harvard Univ. Press, 1979), p. 39.

What function again is so kingly, so worthy of the free, so generous, as to bring help to the suppliant, to raise up those that are cast down, to bestow security, to set free from peril, to maintain men in their civil rights? What too is so indispensable as to have always in your grasp weapons wherewith you can defend yourself, or challenge the wicked man, or when provoked take your revenge?[7]

Rousseau's wickedness is dangerous, then, because he is a man of letters and he is not: he has mastered the fraternal conventions; but with a violent method he turns correspondence into a weapon that threatens to cut through the threads that the men of letters have been trying to tie. And if Rousseau, who simulates so well the man of letters, cannot be composed by that generalization, who can? What is impossible—this particular that engrosses all generalizations or the man of letters himself, who claims nothing in particular but everything in general? That is the question that Hume attempts to ward off by exposing Rousseau in "his" text—or with equal justice it could be said the corporation of the men of letters attempts to ward off, since apart from the *Encyclopédie* the *Exposé* is the chief collaborative production of the Enlightenment. Only the specter of a real and catastrophic impossibility can account for the conundrum of Hume's peculiar yet wholly representative practice. To publish Rousseau is to try to assign to him a defining idea; Hume merely continues the tactics he has practiced all along: he attempts to transform an imaginary being sustained only by his eloquence into an economic being maintained by Hume's connections.

At stake here, as in the allegorical interval of the influx of money from the Americas (see Chap. 5, above), is the reassertion of the general in the face of an unparalleled circumstance. What makes this instance special is that the survival of the generalizer is explicitly implicated in the representation that he makes:: the proof of the impartiality of Hume is in the interest of Hume's survival: "If I be at last obliged to publish my own Vindication in this Affair (which indeed will consist of little more than my Adversary's Accusation) I shall reap this Advantage, that I shall be ever after secure from any Calumny, that he may be tempted to throw out against me. Dead or alive, his Testimony will never have any Authority to defame me" (*HL*, 2:92). Hume's design anticipates the defensive construction of "My Own Life," which we examined in Chapter 2. Here as there survival has nothing to do with the preservation of a merely particular and contingent body from a biological death. Survival is meaningful for the man of letters only as a security of his reputation beyond life and

---

7. Cicero, *De Oratore*, p. 25.

death. Perfect security is pure profit, an advantage that never can be lost. Ideally, Hume will always be out in front of Rousseau because of his indefinitely repeatable capacity to incorporate Rousseau's eloquence into his text by adding the little more requisite to represent Rousseau, whether it be the conventional indicators of historical narrative which cast Rousseau's charges as the merely particular, the eccentrically private, and the already past, or notes which command the authority that Hume has always ascribed to correction. Representation should always triumph over eloquence and the imaginary because it can designate the forum in which eloquence must speak. At least that is the wish. But its fulfillment must overcome the conspicuous problem of gauging exactly how much "little more" is enough: measurement of Hume's advantage will always have to be taken from Rousseau. If it is true that only by publishing his adversary's accusation can Hume secure himself from calumny, it is also true that by that publication he also ties his reputation to Rousseau: if Hume is to become a classic, what are we to say about this writer of whom the man of letters has become the historian and editor, the agent in all senses of the term?

The marriage of advantage to security forecasts a volatile union. Publication will give Hume an advantage over Rousseau that promises security; but that security depends on Hume's persuasiveness that he has *not*, as Rousseau claims, taken advantage of Rousseau. The "little more" that Hume adds, like the "imperceptible alteration" in the "Money" essay, must be cut as close to the bone as possible; it must be the "little more" of necessity, not of choice. Hence the distinction Hume makes in a letter to Jean-Charles Trudaine de Montigny between publication in Paris, where Hume cannot be sure how well his character and conduct are known, and publication in London, which is rejected because it would be "regarded as entirely superfluous" (HL, 2:81). Hence also the concern for the speculative, stockjobbing aspect of the publication: Hume anxiously awaits a future, vindicating (because calumnious) publication by Rousseau. A year after the appearance of the *Exposé* he writes to Adam Smith: "[Rousseau] has retird to a Village in the Mountains of Auvergne as M. Durand tells me; where no body enquires after him. He will probably endeavour to recover his Fame by new Publications; and I expect with some Curiosity the reading of his Memoirs, which will I suppose suffice to justify me in every body's Eyes, and in my own, for the Publication of his Letters and my Narrative of the Case" (*NHL*, pp. 178–79). The shadow of the superfluous hangs over this transaction: from vindicating himself against Rousseau by the *Exposé*. Hume has passed to the need of vindicating the *Exposé* through Rousseau. Publishing has committed him to a machinery of reproduction and profit beyond necessity (publication in London, instigated by Strahan, occurred before Rousseau could have a chance to reply) which can be made historical, justified, quitted, only by the answering publication of Rousseau, his exchange that will balance trade. Rousseau's memoirs, formerly feared as the last recourse of vindictive guile, are now relied on as if they were that reflection that would turn apparent avidity into self-interest or as if they would be that mirror which would give "in every body's Eyes" sensible form to the continued engrossment of Hume's books. Without Rousseau's attack, Hume's preemptive defense actually jeopardizes rather than achieves security, since through his appropriation and publication he has become vulnerable to the charge, made not by Rousseau but by the general public, that his "little more" is tinctured by extravagance. Hume's policy has come perilously close to realizing the secret project of which he had been accused. "The combination formed to ruin" Rousseau has done so by depriving him of his fame.[8] Indeed, Hume's part replays the disreputable behavior of Millar: he has not merely answered Rousseau, but he has appropriated a private letter from another man of letters and transmitted it to another, d'Alembert, for publication at his discretion. The desire for security veils an avidity for profit at all costs, even at the expense of someone else's reputation.

III

It is hardly fair to hang a man on principle. Moreover, Rousseau does not base his indictment on ethical professions but on Hume's behavior. There are, basically, three articles in Rousseau's case against Hume. First, there is coincidence: the coincidence between Rousseau's arrival and isolation in England and the appearance of the letter from "the King of Prussia." There is also the coincidence between Hume's group of friends and Rousseau's circle of enemies: "It is well known," Rousseau writes, "that his friends are all my enemies, —the Fronchins, d'Alemberts, and Voltaires: but it is much worse in London, for here I have no enemies but what are his friends" (Ritchie, p. 229). Second, there is the evidence of Hume's refusal to recognize Rousseau's suspicions; according to Rousseau, Hume's failure to respond to clear indications of his distrust, testified that the distrust was expected. His chief example is the scene that followed

8. "Tho' Rousseau is settled at Cliché, within a League of Paris, no body enquires after him, no body visits him, no body talks of him, every one has agreed to neglect and disregard him: A more sudden Revolution of Fortune than almost ever happened to any man, at least to any man of Letters" (HL, 2:168).

Davenport's manipulation of the coaches and the supposed tampering with Rousseau's mail. Third, there is the evidence of Hume's "confession," his statement in the inn at Senlis on their first night out from Paris, "Je tiens J. J. Rousseau."

There is no impartial narrative which will make all the charges or all of Hume's defenses hang together. But the episode that followed Davenport's ruse with the coaches is a convenient place to begin because, though their versions of the episode wildly diverged, both men at least recognized it as an episode. Here are the two accounts as they appear in the *Exposé*. First, that of Rousseau, who completely ignores the circumstance of the coach, and uses the incident as corroborative evidence of Hume's interference with his correspondence:

> One evening in particular I remember a circumstance of this kind, which greatly struck me. After supper, as we were sitting silent by the fireside, I caught his eyes intently fixed on mine, as indeed happened very often; and that in a manner of which it is very difficult to give an idea. At the time he gave me a steadfast, piercing look, mingled with a sneer, which greatly disturbed me. To get rid of my embarrassment, I endeavoured to look full at him in my turn; but, in fixing my eyes upon him, I felt the most inexpressible terror, and was soon obliged to turn them away. The speech and physiognomy of the good David is that of an honest man; but where, great God! did this honest man borrow those eyes which he fixes on his friend's?
>
> The impression of this look remained with me, and gave me much uneasiness. My trouble increased even to a degree of fainting; and if I had not been relieved by a flood of tears, I must have been suffocated. Presently after this I was seized with the most violent remorse: I even despised myself; till, at length, in a transport, which I still remember with delight, I sprang on his neck, and embraced him eagerly; while almost choked with sobbing, and bathed in tears. I cried out, in broken accents, *No, no, David Hume cannot be treacherous; if he be not the best of men, he must be the basest.* David Hume politely returned my embraces, and gently tapping me on the back, repeated several times, in a placid tone, *Why, what, my dear Sir! Nay, my dear Sir! Oh! my dear Sir!* He said nothing more. I felt my heart yearn within me. We went to bed; and I set out the next day for the country. (Ritchie, pp. 213–15)

Here is Hume's reply, which ascribes the episode wholly to Rousseau's discovery of the ruse with the coaches:

Mr. Davenport had contrived a good natured artifice, to make you believe that a retour chaise was ready to set out for Wooten; and I believe he caused an advertisement be put in the papers, in order the better to deceive you.[9] His purpose only was to save you some expences in the journey, which I thought a laudable project; though I had no hand either in contriving or conducting it. You entertained, however, a suspicion of his design, while we were sitting alone by my fire-side; and you reproached me with concurring in it. I endeavoured to pacify you, and to divert the discourse; but to no purpose. You sat sullen, and was either silent, or made me very peevish answers. At last you rose up, and took a turn or two about the room; when all of a sudden, and to my great surprise, you clapped yourself on my knee, threw your arms about my neck, kissed me with seeming ardour, and bedewed my face with tears. You exclaimed, "My dear friend, can you ever pardon this folly! After all the pains you have taken to serve me, after the numberless instances of friendship you have given me, here I reward you with this ill-humour and sullenness. But your forgiveness of me will be a new instance of your friendship; and I hope you will find at bottom, that my heart is not unworthy of it."

I was very much affected, I own; and I believe a very tender scene passed between us. You added, by way of compliment, no doubt, that though I had many better titles to recommend me to posterity, yet perhaps my uncommon attachment to a poor unhappy and persecuted man would not be altogether overlooked. (Ritchie, pp. 241–42)

Taken together the accounts describe what might be called a case of mismatched physiognomy. As Hume had earlier described his "pupil" to Blair, "M. Rousseau is of small Stature; and wou'd rather be ugly, had he not the finest Physiognomy in the World, I mean the most expressive Countenance" (*HL*, 1:530). In this incident we see not merely Rousseau's face, but his whole body in an unguarded act of expression. If he does nothing to save his countenance, Hume does everything in his power to preserve his own. Part of his explanation to Rousseau of his behavior relies on his tendency to display a constitutional reserve: "What! because sometimes, when absent in thought, (a circumstance common enough with men whose minds are intensely occupied,) I have a fixed look or stare, you suspect me to be a traitor, and you have the assurance to tell me of such black and ridiculous suspicions!" (Ritchie, p. 243). Hume's

9. Compare Walpole's newspaper publication of the deceptive "Letter from the King of Prussia."

abstracted impassiveness contrasts strikingly with Rousseau's abandon: his peevishness, his turns about the room, and his sudden embrace eloquently say *everything* that he is thinking. This ensemble is external, certainly, but not to thought or feeling, of which it is a transparent expression; it is external only to that which is truly, absolutely internal, that pure subjectivity which, according to Rousseau, does not traffic with the outside world. Both philosophes are operating with a dualism, but Rousseau's is absolute, whereas Hume's is strategic, a matter of cutting off and withholding. Hume wants to have it both ways, to be here and there. He wants to socialize amicably and yet retain the epistemologically privileged position of the theatrical spectator who watches the representations he has composed. Rousseau pointedly contests the ingenuous illegibility of the "blank, unmeaning face" which Hume adopts as his defense. For Rousseau Hume's impassiveness is not an endearing social handicap but a deliberate repression in the service of a secret design. Moreover, blankness is never empty; like the *tabula rasa* which once impressed cannot escape a past that is its character, the face is always expressive, always meaningful. Notice how Rousseau tries to penetrate the mask by peering at those eyes that are peering at him. Observe how in revising his version of this incident from a letter to Malesherbes, where he makes a sharp distinction between the "physiognomy and tone of the good David [which] are those of a good man" and his telling, terrifying eyes (Ritchie, p. 187), Rousseau has come to read his insight as impressed on the face itself: what was blank has become a sneer, the perceptible manifestation of what had been there but untraced on the blankness from the first. Under a Rousseauian hermeneutics the face is always an open book. "It is easy," Rousseau declares, "to judge of this man from these slight indications" (Ritchie, p. 217). And Rousseau, empiricist *extraordinaire*, found impressive indications everywhere.

Madame d'Epinay's anecdote echoes here. Not the least of the peculiarities of this episode is that the two men reenact her Oriental charade: one party gesturing, the other mute and transfixed; one wanting to have his barriers broken down, to be seduced from his suspicions, the other incapable of responding in kind. In Rousseau's account, the incident ends with Hume speaking approximately the same lines as he had in the salon: there, "Well, young ladies; well, there you are, then! Well, there you are! There you are, then"; here, "Why, what, my dear Sir! Nay, my dear Sir! Oh! my dear sir" (Ritchie, p. 215). Crucially, however, Rousseau does not recognize the charade, while Hume does—as indicated by his remark, "I believe a very tender scene passed between us." For Hume this is the theater of real life—to which he is a spectator. Simultaneously at the theater and in it, he is, however, vulnerable to a renegade like

Rousseau, who, unlike the Parisian maidens, does not follow the conventions, is not in his own mind performing. Rousseau makes no concessions to the supposed innocence of Hume's spectatorship. Rousseau's virtuosity enables him to work through all the changes of emotion, from peevishness to dark suspicion to an ecstasy of remorse, without any sympathetic response from Hume at all. Because he is not playing a part, he can seduce himself into the state of mind that it was Hume's part to induce.[10] That this is not the same as merely acting out a scene before Hume is sealed by the passionate leap into Hume's lap, which makes a bodily contact for which there is no correspondent in the charade. With Rousseau on his lap Hume is incapable of saying "There you are, Rousseau." Rousseau is forcibly *here*, touching. Hume cannot perform the defensive gesture of touching his stomach and his knee, symbolically severing himself off from the scene before him, because in extending his hand he must touch Rousseau, whose grasp exceeds Hume's reach. Rousseau does everything possible to disable theatricality and Hume's spectatorship. Nonetheless, Hume resists; he still sees a scene *between* them.

There is nothing unusual in Hume's position. If not human nature, it is certainly Humean nature. At the very outset of his personal association with Rousseau he had written regarding the man's celebrity in Paris that "as I am suppos'd to have him in my Custody, all the World, especially the great Ladies teaze me to be introduced to him: I have had Rouleaus thrust into my hand, with earnest Applications, that I would prevail on him to accept of them. I am perswaded, that were I to open here a Subscription with his Consent, I shoud receive 50,000 Pounds in a fortnight" (*HL*, 1:529). Although invited to profit in gold, Hume preferred the profit of pleasure. Had Rousseau been able to intercept Hume's correspondence he could have read this account of a scene that had already passed between them: "I prevaild on him to go to the Playhouse, in order to see Garrick, who placed him in a Box opposite the King and Queen. I observed their Majestys to look at him, more than at the Players. I shoud desire no better Fortune than to have the Privilege of showing him to all I please" (*HL*, 2:8). Hume very carefully chooses the spots in which he will "prevail" on Rousseau. Placed between the two titans of the famous actor whom he sees and the royal couple by

---

10. Rousseau's natural style here is similar to the mode of the monodrama, which was given its modern form by Rousseau's *Pygmalion*. *Pygmalion* was composed as a dramatic piece in 1762; music was added by Horace Coignet in 1770. For a discussion of Rousseau's effort to harmonize music and language in a progressive intensification of passion, see A. Dwight Culler, "Monodrama and the Dramatic Monologue," *PMLA* 90 (May 1975): 369–70. In this scene Hume is the Galatea who would not come to life.

whom he is seen, Rousseau performs in a scene of a sympathetic exchange of glances more interesting than any action on stage. One person, the proud Hume, stands outside of that exchange, watching the drama of celebrity from a position of privilege where he can secretly take his pleasure in the composition he has induced, the affecting scene that passes between the actors he has deftly arranged. Earlier, before his departure from Paris, Hume had written to Blair, "I must however be in London very soon, in order to give an Account of my Commission, to thank the King for his Goodness to me, and to settle the celebrated Rousseau, who has rejected Invitations from half the Kings and Princes of Europe, in order to put himself under my Protection" (*HL*, 1:527). The theater is the scene where Hume's triumph over the king as well as his domination of Rousseau are safely enacted—where, rather than give gratitude, he takes profit, where his truth prevails not by a violent method smiting from above but by means of a sovereign spectatorship exercised from alongside, itself protected by the "blank, unmeaning expression" which he offers to the dimly lit world of impressions and with which no one can sympathize. Hume takes his profit by right, as the one who by his prevenient separation makes the triangulation between Rousseau, Garrick, and the king and queen come to signify.[11] Hume becomes the complete man of letters by detaching himself from the theater and assigning a lack to Rousseau, represented as a relation between the empty playacting of Garrick and the real prerogatives of the monarchs, a lack which enables him who has assigned it to complete the globalizing tendency of his composition.

When challenged by Rousseau's physical sally at Chiswick, Hume engineers a similar detachment by imposing the *idea* of a stage on the uninterrupted contact of bodies, an idea which bounds the embrace of "friends" so they can abut without really touching. Either Hume is completely innocent and good for nothing but eating veal or he is completely guilty and scheming to make Rousseau a playactor who performs for Hume's pleasure and indemnifies Hume's privilege. Not the least lesson

11. The "signifier acts as the formal cause of the triangulation—that is to say, makes possible both the form of the triangle and its reproduction: Oedipus has as its formula 3 + 1, the One of the transcendent phallus without which the terms considered would not take the form of a triangle . . . a crushing operation that extracted a detached object from the chain, a despotic signifier from whose law the entire chain seems consequently to be suspended, each link triangulated. There we have a curious paralogism implying a transcendent use of the syntheses of the unconscious: *we pass from detachable partial objects to the detached complete object, from which global persons derive by an assigning of a lack.*" Gilles Deleuze and Felix Guattari, *Anti-Oedipus*, trans. Robert Hurley, Mark Seem, and Helen R. Lane (New York: Viking, 1977), p. 73.

of this incident for Rousseau is that Hume is impervious to any eloquence except one which occupies his thoughts as well as touching his body— say, a letter that parodies correspondence in order to overpower all the representations by which he composes his world.

IV

Is it necessary to our vindication of Rousseau that we prove malicious intent on the part of Hume? How would intent be recovered from a conspirator so subtle as Hume, whose very malice is to hide his thoughts? Rousseau was aware of the problem. To the Marchioness de Verdelin he admits: "Your objection, drawn from the known character of Mr. Hume, is very strong, and will ever surprise me. Nothing less than what I have seen of an opposite character, was necessary to produce a belief in it. All I can conclude from this contradiction is, that apparently Mr. Hume has never hated any one but me; —but what hatred! what profound art to conceal it, and to satiate it! Can the same heart suffice for two such passions?" (Ritchie, p. 248). What Rousseau calls Hume's "profound art" is that policy of correction which we have found at the basis of a career and a character that has succeeded by acting in canny "opposition" to itself.

This systematic self-opposition becomes evident if we test Rousseau's suspicions that Hume had tampered with his mail. "The letters I wrote," he complains, "did not come to hand; those I received had often been opened; and all went through the hands of Mr. Hume. If at any time a letter escaped him, he could not conceal his eagerness to see it." Hume's answer rehearses Rousseau's pettishness: the complaints about being ruined by postage and his resolution "to receive in England, no letters which came by the post." As a consequence, Hume relates,

> When he went to Chiswick . . . , the postman brought his letters to me. I carried him out a cargo of them: he exclaimed, desired me to return the letters, and recover the price of postage: I told him, that, in that case, the clerks of the post-office were entire masters of his letters. He said he was indifferent; they might do with them what they pleased. I added, that he would by that means be cut off from all correspondence with his friends: he replied, that he would give a particular direction to such as he desired to correspond with. But till his instructions for that purpose could arrive, what could I do more friendly, than to save, at my own expence, his letters from the curiosity and indiscretion of the clerks of the post-office?" (Ritchie, pp. 212–13 and note).

In order to disable the specific charge against him, Hume admits that constitutional abuses systematically taint every clerk within the postal service. Hence, whatever Hume's intention, his roles both as an ambassador who gathers intelligence and as a middleman who transports and stores "cargo" presume his lack of innocence within the system which puts that privilege to work. And because Hume is the sole mediator of Rousseau's commerce with the outside world, particular abuses are difficult to detect and impossible to prove: Rousseau's letters literally go out under Hume's seal (Ritchie, p. 213n).[12]

It is true, however, that what Rousseau has "seen" comes down to very little: letters whose seals show signs of tampering, unsigned satires appearing in the papers, a blank unmeaning face, an "absurd change in the minds of the people who regarded" him, a conversation between Hume and the son of Fronchin. Yet, taken together, these glimpses suggest a composition which retroactively reinforces the enormous importance of something Rousseau had heard on the first night of their passage from Paris at an inn at Senlis:

The critical situation to which he had now reduced me, recalled strongly to my mind the four words which I mentioned above, and which I heard him say and repeat, at a time when I did not comprehend their full force. It was the first night after our departure from Paris. We slept in the same chamber, when, during the night, I heard him several times cry out with great vehemence, in the French language, *I have you, Rousseau* [*Je tiens J. J. Rousseau*]. I know not whether he was awake or asleep.

The expression was remarkable in the mouth of a man, who is too well acquainted with the French language to be mistaken with

12. There is another instance of Hume's tampering with correspondence that tends in a general way to corroborate Rousseau's suspicions about Hume's conduct. Hume had solicited a letter from Walpole stating Hume's innocence in the "King of Prussia" affair. Walpole obliged, but prefaced his remarks with a contemptuous reference to the "exceedingly absurd" set of Hume's French "literary friends" and with the advice that if "Rousseau prints, you must; but I certainly would not, till he does" (Ritchie, p. 245). Hume not only ignored Walpole's advice about publication, but included Walpole's letter in the *Exposé*—with the first paragraph excised. Walpole responded by objecting mildly to the publication and strongly to the abridgment, an objection he repeated even more strenuously in *his* narrative of the quarrel between Hume and Rousseau, to which he added all the correspondence he had had with Hume. "I am sorry to say," writes Walpole, "that on this occasion Mr. Hume did not act quite fairly by me. In the beginning of my letter I laughed at his *learned* friends, who wished him to publish. . . . This commencement of my letter was, therefore, a dissuasive against printing. Could I imagine that Mr. Hume would make use of part of my letter, and suffer it to be printed—and even without asking my consent?" (Ritchie, p. 275).

regard to the force or choice of words. I took these words, however, and I could not then take them otherwise than in a favourable sense, although the tone of voice indicated this less than the expression. It was indeed a tone of which it is impossible for me to give any idea; but it corresponded exactly with those terrible looks I have before mentioned. At every repetition of these words I was seized with a shuddering and horror I could not resist; though a moment's recollection restored me, and made me smile at my terror. The next day, all this was so perfectly obliterated, that I did not even once think of it during my stay in London and its neighbourhood. It was not till my arrival in this place, that so many things have contributed to recal [*sic*] these words to my mind; and indeed recal them every moment. (Ritchie, pp. 236–37)

In the first edition of the *Exposé* Hume appended the following note: "I cannot answer for every thing I may say in my sleep, and much less am I conscious whether or not I dream in French. But as M. Rousseau did not know whether I was asleep or awake, when I pronounced these terrible words with such a terrible voice, how is he certain that he himself was well awake when he heard them?" (Ritchie, p. 236n).

Rousseau bases his claim for malicious intent on an utterance that, he admits, may or may have not been intentional. Hume replies that he is not answerable for what Rousseau says he might have said. Yet Hume does not impugn the veracity of Rousseau; even his suggestion that Rousseau was himself not quite awake acknowledges a plausibility in the attributed utterance. Rousseau says that Hume "was too well acquainted with the French language to be mistaken," and, impelled by his vanity, Hume must agree, for to insist that he was mistaken would convict Hume of the charmingly ineffectual ignorance of the lady who "mistook" d'Alembert's epigram. Whether or not Hume was awake or asleep, or Rousseau awake or asleep, whether or not Hume did or did not in fact say those four words, behind Hume's dodgy reply lies the acknowledgment that he might very well have said "Je tiens J. J. Rousseau."

The implicit becomes explicit in the revised note that Hume prepared for the English edition of the *Exposé:* "If M. Rousseau consult his Plutarch, he will find, that when Themistocles fled into Persia, Xerxes was so pleas'd with this Event, that he was heard to exclaim several times in his sleep, I have Themistocles, I have Themistocles. Why will not M. Rousseau understand my Exclamation in the same Sense?" (*HL*, 2:117). The exclamation seems to have become a settled fact; Hume contests only its interpretation. And the man who earlier had jested about dreaming in French now finds it perfectly reasonable that he may have dreamed in Latin, translating as he went. But suppose it was Plutarch that Hume, waking or slumbering, had in mind: in what sense are we to understand the reference? Does the classical precedent make the utterance any less terrible? Let us consult our Plutarch.

Here is a translation of the relevant episode from Plutarch's life of Themistocles:

> When Themistocles was come to the critical point, he applied himself first to Artabanus, commander of a thousand men, telling him that he was a Greek, and desired to speak with the king about important affairs concerning which the king was extremely solicitous. Artabanus answered him: 'O stranger, the laws of men are different, and one thing is honourable to one man, and to others another; but it is honourable for all to honour and observe their own laws. It is the habit of the Greeks, we are told, to honour, above all things, liberty and equality; but amongst our many excellent laws, we account this the most excellent, to honour the king, and to worship him, as the image of the great preserver of the universe; if, then, you shall consent to our laws, and fall down before the king and worship him, you may both see him and speak to him; but if your mind be otherwise, you must make use of others to intercede for you, for it is not the national custom here for the king to give audience to any one that doth not fall down before him.' Themistocles, hearing this, replied: 'Artabanus, I, that come hither to increase the power and glory of the king, will not only submit myself to his laws, since so it hath pleased the god who exalteth the Persian empire to this greatness, but will also cause many more to be worshippers and adorers of the king.' . . .
>
> The king heard him attentively, and, though he admired his temper and courage, gave him no answer at that time; but, when he was with his intimate friends, rejoiced in his great good fortune, and esteemed himself very happy in this, and prayed to his god Arimanius, that all his enemies might be ever of the same mind with the Greeks, to abuse and expel the bravest men amongst them. Then he sacrificed to the gods, and presently fell to drinking, and was so well pleased, that in the night, in the middle of his sleep, he cried out for joy three times, 'I have Themistocles the Athenian.' [13]

13. Plutarch, *The Lives of the Noble Greeks and Romans*, trans. John Dryden, revised Arthur Hugh Clough (New York: Random House, n.d.), pp. 151–52.

Hume invokes Plutarch to give a sense to his exclamation by putting it in a context.[14] And there could be no context more authoritative for men of letters than republican Athens. This is a citation that is also a site, a place in the past and in books about the past where one can find a territorial precedent for the fraternal relations among enlightened men of letters in the eighteenth century. But what is peculiar about this reference is that it is a little more than classical, since it carries us back, not to Athens pure and simple, but beyond its bounds. In two senses: First, the fraternity of republican Athenians has been transgressed by the expulsion of Themistocles. Second, the narrative which Hume cites takes place not in Greece but in a Persia ruled by an Oriental despot, forerunner of the contemporary sultan.

Like Rousseau the banished Themistocles had to learn a new language. But is not the Plutarch a corroboration of Rousseau's fear that to learn the English tongue would entail learning the language of submission? For Themistocles the choice is easy (Plutarch does not question it); he is a man whose whole career has been governed by an avidity for distinctions, for acquiring the honor of a rank to which, like Rousseau, he was not born. Circumstances were right in Athens for his rise—the profession of liberty and equality, the existence of a foreign threat, a vacuum of authority—and he took advantage of them. It is entirely in character for Themistocles to accept the terms of Artabanus in order to acquire possible distinction and a very real protection.

Themistocles' choice and Hume's approbation equally presuppose an interpretation of the agent's crisis as thoroughly relative: ensnared in circumstances, he perceives the distinctions between Athens and Persia as conventions based on no essential difference. Moreover, Themistocles' easy translation from Greek to Persian reproduces the skillful adaptation to circumstances that had brought him success in Athens. From Themistocles' point of view liberty and equality in Athens were merely code words that guided ambition into customary, socially useful channels; by translating those conventions into the new ones that circumstances have imposed, Themistocles is advancing a career based on tactical ingenuity. No dishonor that. What Aristides said of his plan for burning his allies' ships in harbor, that "no plan could have been more politic, or more dishonourable,"[15] applies to Themistocles' character as a whole: since he is a completely politic man, what might dishonor others could affect him

14. Hume had earlier used the Themistocles story to illustrate the "influence of the imagination on the passions" in the *Treatise* (pp. 425–26).

15. Plutarch, *Lives*, p. 146.

not at all, except insofar as others' perceptions bore on the execution of his policy.

It is as a careerist, then, that Rousseau is allegorized by Hume's citation of Plutarch: the rebuttal to Rousseau's charge that there was a plan to dishonor him entails the denial that "honor" has any substantive meaning when applied to the Genevan *parvenu*. Were this all there was to the allegory it would not stretch conjecture far to anticipate Rousseau's repudiation of a representation which implied that all his professions were merely professional, that his espousal of liberty and equality was an adherence that, given a change in circumstances, he would have been ready to surrender.

Of course there is more to the allegory. It is not entirely up to Themistocles to change his tune or his guise. Circumstances are not stage sets through which a protean player saunters in a succession of graceful self-transformations. What is peculiarly interesting about the Plutarchan context is that far from annulling the conspiratorial pretext, as one would have imagined Hume had intended, it *doubles* conspiracy. Themistocles is banished from Athens because of a conspiracy of his fellow Athenians to "humble his eminence and authority" and to "mitigate and pacify the violence of the envious." [16] This circle, which closes behind the exiled Themistocles, is mirrored by the circle of advisers to which Xerxes retreats after his interview with the Athenian, and where, dropping his mask of disinterest, he rejoices, before drink delivers him to sleep and sleep to the utterance "I have Themistocles." If there is a lesson here it is double, like everything else in this strange parable: Themistocles is no doubt an estimable character because he exhibits that trait of adaptability which is the distinctive characteristic of the man of letters. But it is as if that adjustment to conventions cannot account for shifts of bodies across borders, or for the shiftiness of conventions that respond to unpredictable, overpowering imperatives. It is as if at every crux that requires adaptation, one can find a secret meeting to which the careerist is not privy: the literal convention which imperiously devises, promulgates, and repeals that discourse in and by which Themistocles must practice. Power is produced not by custom but by a breathing together.

In the felt need to respond to Rousseau's charge, to make "sense" of a dramatic moment, Hume appeals to a narrative that motivates those crucial moments of the career when policy no longer seems to work by identifying them as the effects of some sort of meeting of embodied breaths. The idea of a conspiracy appears as a necessary fiction to explain

16. Ibid., p. 148.

the sense of an arbitrary power that sways from some place outside one's discourse. One cries "conspiracy" in default of any idea that more accurately corresponds with one's acute sense that one's career is not one's own practice but the figure of someone else's art. To attribute interruptions in the discursive practice of the careerist or in the community of careerists to a conspiracy is as "natural" as the habits interrupted—an attempt to find an art in the disruptive, even if one must sacrifice to the false gods of secret design. One moral of the Plutarch citation is that a man like Themistocles, immune to dishonor, unencumbered by any essentialist notions of value, can still be had.

It remains to be explained why Hume, attempting to refute the accusation that he supervised a malevolent conspiracy, should invoke a narrative which concedes that there *are* conspiracies, which shows that the republic of letters is a pretense capable of being rescinded at any time, and that, like Mme d'Epinay's charade, overtly installs Hume in the position of the despot, "the master of the life and fortune of any individual" (G&G, p. 116). The answer, I believe, is that Hume is engaged in an act of self-defense beyond justification. He silently accepts Rousseau's charges in order to defend a self that would be destroyed were the charges *wrong*.[17]

In the nocturnal ejaculation at Senlis Rousseau has found a moment when Hume has claimed control in a lapse of control; by asserting his dominance he has let his defenses down. Citing Plutarch looks like a way for Hume to protect himself. The defense, however, reproduces the weakness that was its occasion. The most salient weakness is in the pointed similarity between the careers of Themistocles and *Hume*, and, therefore, of Hume and Rousseau. Hume, like Rousseau, was from the provinces and tried to make his way in the capital of the polite arts; though not illegitimate like Rousseau, he was obliged by an accident of birth—the misfortune of being born the second rather than the first son— to adopt some sort of profession; his concession to Millar and the Conger recapitulates the prudential submission of Themistocles to the Persian king; moreover, if he was not exactly expelled from Paris, he did leave due to political exigencies over which he had no control. The point of characterizing Rousseau as Themistocles is to type him as careerist—a type into which Hume as man of letters must also fit. And by reflex, if Rousseau is, like Themistocles, subject to forces beyond his control, Hume too, as typed by Themistocles, is not free of the same imputation:

---

17. This is not a unique defense in the eighteenth century. In chapter 20 of *The Man of Feeling* Henry Mackenzie depicts Harley's guide to bedlam as betraying his madness by the claim that he is the "Chan of Tartary."

of a vulnerability to the contingent that can be traced in the interruption of discourse and the forced movement of bodies—a power that belongs to a politics apart from and superior to a custodial administration, which in his late essay, "On the Origin of Government," he argues is the umbrella occupation that buffers the arbitrary impulses of monarchs and parliaments.

For Hume to take the position of Xerxes is exactly the same move as turning his conscious or unconscious utterance into a narrative, which in turn is congruent with the strategy of narrativity that he adopts as his general defense against Rousseau. Hume becomes the author of the tale and all its nested stories. Hume takes the position of Xerxes in order to ward off identification with Themistocles; he loses himself in order to save his self—exposes himself as chief conspirator, the breath behind all breathings, because that is the only position which he can seize, at whatever loss of reputation, that will indemnify a self that controls, not suffers, interruption. Beyond castration is the image of the Asiatic monarch. By confessing "I am the conspirator," indeed, "I am the king of conspirators," Hume discloses the dark sultanic secret behind a career of indirection.

Persia is at the end of the line because it concludes a narrative which imposes on the drama of either/or, inside/outside, an irreversible progress terminating in a reply, "I have Themistocles," to which there can be no answer, a riposte which, like Hume's *Exposé*, overpowers the model of exchange. Hume's citation tells the whole story of his career and shows the necessity for the story to be told. If only the proof of "profound art" will restore order in the wake of Rousseau's eloquence, then Hume is ready to confess to artifice and put himself in the place of the sovereign artist. In this note appended as a correction to the second edition of the *Exposé*, Hume sacrifices his reputation in order to triumph over Rousseau, and to continue triumphing over him in an indefinite conflict that will never balance out, in a text that can never be incorporated in the *Collected Works*. Whatever Rousseau might subsequently publish could only be a correction, or something correctible—hence not Rousseauian eloquence but Humean discourse. Narrative and note, Hume's correction engineers a mechanism that is capable of continually reproducing itself.

The perfection of this machine would seem to vindicate Rousseau, however, because Hume's continually resurgent advantage graphically corroborates the asymmetry that Rousseau detected. Hume is struggling to prevail. In this contest of power Humean representation will always succeed but only on the condition that it expose its despotic imposition as serving nothing more than the reproduction of itself—the defense of a self which has been completely mechanized. Rousseau's ability to survive sustained only by his eloquence will never be tested; he will be sustained by the text which depends on him for its very existence. As long as books are printed, Hume will have Rousseau.

Perhaps there has been an excess of delicacy in this interpretation. When pushed, it is true, the enlightened Humean profession "I am a brother"[18] gives way to the dark confession "I am a king," which is an apparently winning move: "There is no place above the king."[19] Yet Hume isn't really a despot, only a reader who tactically identifies with one in order to win a game of representation. No doubt it is something to discover Hume's zeal to trump Rousseau, but it is still only a card that he plays. The game is, moreover, oddly recursive. Hume's adoption of the position of the sovereign reinvolves him in the essential Rousseauian paradox of sympathizing with the singular: he needs to imitate that which is inimitable and which must be inimitable in order for it to be worth imitating. Hence the identification with Xerxes, though ostensibly decisive, really changes nothing for Hume: Hume is able to finesse the problem of unconscious intent by mapping his mind as a classical text, which furnishes the *customary* sign for the inimitably imperious, the Oriental despot. But if Xerxes represents power, that power is itself represented in a classical discourse that has already domesticated it as a condition of its representation. As the unconscious of the man of letters is mapped as a classical narrative, so the political unconscious of Europe is conveniently displaced to Asia, where it can be deliberately imitated in exactly the same fashion as the characters of eloquence, courage, humor, and learning could be appropriated, as we have seen (Chap. 3, above), from bishop, soldier, gownman, and merchant by the wily solitary, estranged from home and all ascriptive ties, and with "pretensions to a better fortune." Where is the difference? Where is the triumph? Xerxes, defeated and retrenched, presented no real threat to the Greeks, let alone to the Romans, let alone to eighteenth-century Europe—as Rousseau, who named his pet dog "Sultan," well knew.

It has been my intent throughout to contest the equation, flattering to the model of sympathetic exchange, between the eighteenth-century man of letters and a "brother." That policy has required taking the sovereign as the sign for a violently imposing politics, which has supposedly been dissipated by the economy of representation that is depicted in the man of letters' works and with which his career wholly corresponds. To force the confession "I am a king" would seem to falsify the enlightening

18. Cf. the letter to Dr. Arbuthnot in Chapter 2, above.
19. Michel Serres, *Hermes: Literature, Science, Philosophy,* trans. Josue V. Harari and David F. Bell (Baltimore: Johns Hopkins Univ. Press, 1982), p. 25.

pretensions of the man of letters' discourse by disclosing the vestigial sovereignty empowering his career. Yet the claim to sovereign power is as vain as the claim to generality which it secretly underwrites. Power is not there. The statement "I am a king" may be the last refuge of the man of letters, but it is nothing more than another identification for a figure, who is nothing in himself but exists only in his supposedly "unbounded and uninterrupted" representations of himself. There are kings in the world. But the man of letters is in truth wholly unlike a king, the name for the real, unimaginable point where power erupts.

"I thought it something very odd," writes Rousseau, unravelling one of the coincidences of his transactions with Hume, "that, exactly after the return of Mr. Hume, who has so much credit in London, so much influence over the booksellers and men of letters, and such great connections with them, his presence should produce an effect so contrary to what might have been expected" (Ritchie, p. 207). It *is* odd; and if we cannot credit Rousseau's paranoid reading of circumstances, we cannot credit Hume's indirect attempt to take responsibility for the conspiracy with which he is charged—a move made to evade the depressing conclusion that consequences contrary to what he or Rousseau or anyone else might expect do happen, and willy-nilly. The career of the Enlightenment man of letters ends with just such a disappointment of expectations: the fall of the Bastille. In that event the influential "combination" that set out "to ruin" Rousseau was shattered by a revolutionary impulse that *en masse* ruined all combinations. Having survived the machinations of the Third Conger, having restored itself after the imperious touch of the Comtesse de Boufflers, the career of David Hume ends here: "A Gentleman told me, that he heard from the French Ambassador, that His Most Christian Majesty had given an Arret prohibiting under the severest Penalties the printing, sending or dispersing any paper of Rousseau or his Partisans against me. . . . It is surely very honourable for me; but yet will occasion that strange Man to complain that he is oppressed with Power all over the World" (*HL*, 2:121–22).[20] The "transactions with Rousseau" that bracket the Parisian episode are themselves enclosed by the *arrêts* of the king, which are transactions with no one but executive actions that, like the calling in of all credit, force without communicating. They unveil the naked thought behind economic exchange—a cruel imperative that does

20. Hume's guess about Rousseau was certainly accurate. Rousseau's parting comment to Davenport—"I am easy to oppress but difficult to humiliate" (quoted by Jean Guehenno, *Jean-Jacques Rousseau*, trans. John and Doreen Weightman, 2 vols. [New York: Columbia Univ. Press, 1966], 2:201)—identifies a constant in his character and definitively distinguishes him from Hume, who, as man of letters, conceived of himself as easy to humiliate but difficult to oppress.

not murmur beneath the minarets of Constantinople but speaks in the capital of polite society itself: "If the prince has become absolute, as may naturally be expected from this situation of affairs, it is so easy for him to encrease his exactions upon the annuitants . . . that this species of property would soon lose all its credit, and the whole income of every individual in the state must lie entirely at the mercy of the sovereign: A degree of despotism which no oriental monarchy has ever yet attained" (G&G, p. 369). The stage character of the Oriental despot explodes in the hint of a political reality that disrupts economics not from the outside as its other but from the "inside" as its necessary limit and inexorable transgression. What honor to Hume in this blind imposition? The repetition of the *arrêt* has nothing to do with the predictable reproduction of the printing press, is not supervised by the "fidelity of copyists and printers." Hume drops out, effaced as middleman or ambassador by a regal *force de main* answering the powerful challenge of Rousseau's antinomian, uncredited eloquence. There is, then, nothing ironical in the fact that Hume's relations with Rousseau begin as succor for one suffering from an *arrêt* and end with the silencing of Rousseau by an *arrêt* that is contrary to any intentions that could be recovered from Hume's text. There is no irony because it is only right. And "right in the West is the King's right."[21] Hume's truth, Hume's career, cannot prevail against it.

We shall leave Hume here, in 1767, having been appointed undersecretary in the Northern Department, nervously facing a reality that is not his representation: "But here [in London], another office has been conferred upon me, which, though I did not desire it, I could not avoid; and if I should return to settle in France, after being twice employed by the English ministry in places of trust and confidence, could I hope that, in case of a war, I should be allowed to remain unmolested; when, even considered in the light of a man of letters, I could scarcely flatter myself with enjoying that privilege? . . . You see then . . . what reason I have to remain in suspense: for even though a permission should be granted me to remain at Paris, in case of a rupture, the most unexceptionable conduct could not free me from suspicion; and I must tremble at every mark of jealousy or ill-will from every clerk in office" (*HL*, 2:172). In case of war. But the case of peace, so vulnerable to rupture that privilege can only be imagined as the pretext for persecution, has come to look a great deal like war. So has the case of Hume come to look a great deal like the case of Rousseau. As in that "singular" case "unexceptionable conduct" is no protection from suspicion. Conversely, the "madman" takes it as a given

21. Michel Foucault, *Power/Knowledge: Selected Interviews and Other Writings, 1972–1977*, ed. Colin Gordon, trans. Colin Gordon et al. (New York: Pantheon, 1980), p. 95.

that the face of every clerk is to be read for those "slight indications" of malevolence that are "easy to judge" (Ritchie, p. 217). Is it that Hume, suffering the imposition of an office he does not desire, an "honorable" *arrêt* which bounds and interrupts his movement, has come to imagine himself as Rousseau or as Rousseau had imagined him? You see then what reason we have to leave Hume hanging, in a suspense of no measure, which will not be restored by natural causes or social convention, and from which no correction will extricate him.

Index

Index

COMPOSED BY GRAPHIC COMPOSITION, INC., ATHENS, GEORGIA
MANUFACTURED BY EDWARDS BROTHERS, INC., ANN ARBOR, MICHIGAN
TEXT AND DISPLAY LINES ARE SET IN CASLON 540

Library of Congress Cataloging-in-Publication Data
Christensen, Jerome, 1948–
Practicing enlightenment.
Includes bibliographical references and index.
1. Hume, David, 1711–1776. I. Title.
B1498.C54   1987   192   86-40048
ISBN 0-299-10750-7
ISBN 0-299-10754-X (pbk.)

17